P9-DBQ-366

LAFAYETTE

A Life

By Andreas Latzko

MEN IN BATTLE
Cassell, 1918

(Published in New York as *Men in War* by Boni &
Liveright, April, 1918; second edition April, 1918;
then confiscated and destroyed by the American
military authorities. Subsequently reprinted in a
cheap edition.)

THE JUDGMENT OF PEACE
Boni & Liveright, New York, December, 1919;
reprinted January, 1920.

SEVEN DAYS
Cassell, 1931
Published in New York by the Viking Press.

LAFAYETTE: *A Life*

First published in a French translation (Paris, Ber-
nard Grasset, 1935), and a Dutch translation
(Amsterdam, Wereld Bibliotheek, 1935). Trans-
lated into English from the German proofs and the
French edition. Published in Switzerland by Rascher
& Cie, A.G., Zürich, Leipzig and Stuttgart; and in
America by Doubleday, Doran & Co., Inc., Garden
City, New York.

THE MARQUIS DE LAFAYETTE

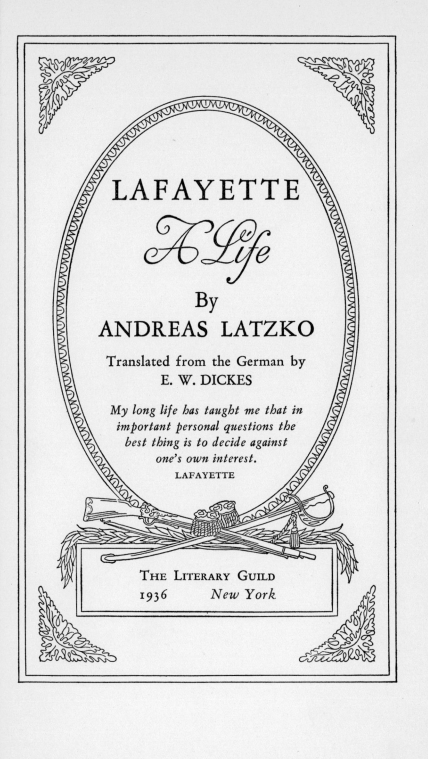

LAFAYETTE

A Life

By
ANDREAS LATZKO

Translated from the German by
E. W. DICKES

My long life has taught me that in important personal questions the best thing is to decide against one's own interest.

LAFAYETTE

THE LITERARY GUILD
1936   *New York*

PRINTED AT THE *Country Life Press,* GARDEN CITY, N. Y., U. S. A.

FRONTISPIECE USED BY COURTESY OF

KENNEDY & COMPANY

COPYRIGHT, 1936
BY ANDREAS LATZKO
ALL RIGHTS RESERVED

FIRST EDITION

6
L369

To the
MARTYRS
of all the
DESPOTISMS

49036

THE text of Lafayette's correspondence with Washington has been given as far as possible in the original, but in some cases, where the original letters have not been available, they have been retranslated from the French version.

Contents

BOOK II: FAME

BOOK III: DOWNFALL

BOOK IV: CAPTIVITY

BOOK V: RETURN TO PUBLIC LIFE

CONTENTS

BOOK I

Youth

I. THE CHÂTEAU DE CHAVANIAC

AUVERGNE TODAY is a rich and populous mining and industrial region, covered with a close network of railways; yet the Château de Chavaniac still lies buried so deeply in the seclusion of its woods that only the traveler who knows the country can detect its tall roof through the treetops. Two hundred years ago the old castle stood in dilapidation, like a sunken wreck. The trackless thickets around it were a meeting place for the wild creatures that wandered freely through the wide forests. They were anxiously avoided by the poverty-stricken country people, and their fauna were spared the battues of the great social gatherings in less inhospitable regions; the occasional solitary huntsmen of the local aristocracy made no effective inroads on the natural increase of the big and small game. Through the winter the thinly scattered seats of the nobility of Auvergne were entirely cut off from all communication; snowstorms and hungry wolves howled around them; these remote châteaux were either left empty or given over to poor relations. The tenant farmers extracted from the sweat and blood of their serfs rather than from the hard soil the sums which the landowners dissipated in Versailles and Paris.

The distinguished company of feudal nobles who assembled for the christening of the baby marquis on the day of his birth, filling several pages of the register in the little castle chapel with their titles and predicates, hurried away after the ceremony from the wilderness of Chavaniac. That evening, September 6, 1757, not one of the noble visitors remained beneath the patched roof of the old fortress.

The baby had been held over the font by his rich grandfather, the Marquis de la Rivière; he had been entered in the register as the very great and very puissant Lord, Monseigneur Maria Joseph Paul Yves Roch Gilbert du Motier, Marquis de Lafayette, Baron de Vissac, Seigneur de St Romain; and there and then he was placed in the charge of two old ladies. His mother remained in the château only as long as her condition necessitated. In duty to her son she must see that the name of Lafayette did not fall into oblivion at Court until he, its only bearer, could himself be there to recall the services of his ancestors.

So the little marquis remained at Chavaniac with his grandmother and aunt. The poor village priest who had received him into the community of Catholic Christendom taught him to pray, to write and to read, and finally introduced him to the elements of Latin grammar. In this company of two pious old ladies and his priestly tutor, this scion of a long line of warriors might easily have fallen into devotionalism but for the wilderness around him, with its dangerous beasts of prey who prowled in hungry packs up to the very doors of the peasants' huts.

There was little that was lordly in the household of the two old dames, but the sight of the lowly hovels and their half-naked and half-starved occupants soon awakened in the growing young lord and master a sense of his high estate. But his consciousness of rank found expression not in the arrogance and lust of dominance of his contemporaries but in a determination to play the protector. All that Lafayette remembered afterwards of the eleven years passed at Chavaniac, which were his whole childhood, was his ambition to defend the peasants from the beasts of prey. The ten-year-old lord of the manor ranged through the woods in search of the legendary werewolf and fed his imagination on the triumphal reception and the gratitude of the peasants that would be his when he returned to them as their liberator from its menace! In his *Mémoires de ma main* Lafayette declares that this childish ambition to free his native place from the fabulous

monster was the first germ of his lifelong passion for taking
the part of the weak against their oppressors.

Apart from this one episode, Lafayette had no significant
memory left of the eleven years of his life that were passed
at Chavaniac. He felt he had cast off his childhood as the snake
sloughs off its skin. If he had heard of psychoanalysis he would
have been able to find in his transplantation from the
neglected ancestral château into the company of his precocious fellow students at college in Paris the explanation of
the "inferiority complexes" that gave his character its particular bent.

What did the eleven-year-old boy know of the world that
lay beyond the impenetrable veil of his forests when he
modestly took his seat alongside his elegant mother in her
coach? That long journey in one another's company might
perhaps be productive of good. His mother's experienced
glance could not fail to notice the shy and awkward bearing
of her big red-haired "savage." She knew well how different
were the manners of other boys of good noble family, all
well drilled by their dancing masters, and it was for her to
prepare the little Crusoe at her side for his first problems
and the wounds to his self-esteem that were in store for him
when he came into the great world.

"Children" in the sense familiar to us did not exist at all
in the noble families of pre-revolutionary France—only
miniature copies of the adults, with little feathered hats,
lilliputian swords, tiny corsets and little neckerchiefs, living
dolls, drilled by their dancing masters until they aped the
manners of Court society like marionettes. The unpolished
Nimrod of the forests around Chavaniac had only the choice
between shame at his awkwardness and replying to his comrades' contempt with his own contempt of their hollow ar-
tificiality.

So the first decade of his childhood raised itself like a
wall round the boy as he stepped for the first time on the
shining parquet floor of his grandfather's hôtel in Paris. He
learned to study his own circle as an outsider, alienated by
the bad habits which had been inculcated imperceptibly day
by day in his relatives and teachers and schoolfellows, and
had become second nature to them.

II. PARIS

THE MARQUISE DE POMPADOUR had been dead four years when in the autumn of 1768 the little Lafayette was assigned his bed in the dormitory of the Collège du Plessis. The Duc de Choiseul was still guiding the destinies of France; the king himself was so hated that he had a road made in a wide circle round Paris to enable him to avoid the city. It bears to this day the name Avenue de la Révolte—the road built in fear of a revolution.

The curses of the exasperated people did not penetrate into the priests' school for young nobles; only the lampoons surreptitiously hawked at the street corners told hair-raising stories of the ageing king's excesses—especially of the so-called "deer park," the Parc-aux-Cerfs; the immature youngsters devoured the sheets with lascivious curiosity. Before long the unspoilt little marquis from the country knew all about the purpose of the many little pavilions in the park, around which a high wall had been set by order of the Pompadour. Instead of jealously imposing on the king her own faded attractions, the marquise herself provided him with "diversification." Her agents collected from every part of France little girls of ten to twelve years, to give the crowned debauchee ample choice and variety and so to protect the Pompadour from the danger of a serious rival.

This efficiently organized service continued to operate after her death. Contemporary authorities with inside knowledge estimated the volume of trade at six to seven thousand little girls. The whetted public appetite for sensationalism and the pamphleteers' greed for money produced a wealth of vivid detail, feeding the shocked fancy of the young Lafayette with a succession of ghastly scenes.

The little Latin scholar was too young to understand the second of the king's unpardonable sins. He was used to the stolid submissiveness and resignation of his Auvergne peasants and saw with horror the brutalized faces, distorted with hate, that popped up outside the windows of his sedan chair when he was taken to see his mother on Sundays. At nights he pulled the coverlet over his ears whenever the hellish sounds of a police raid filled the streets: it was said that hunger was driving the work-shy riffraff of all France to Paris, and at the same time grain was getting dearer and dearer, as though the cursed marquise in her grave still gripped the people by the throat.

In reality the Pompadour, even in her lifetime, was only indirectly responsible for the so-called "grain campaign." Her resident physician, Dr Quesnay, had employed his leisure in evolving his theory of "Physiocracy," that high prices for grain were the source of all well-being. The landowner's well-filled money chest, like a healthy heart, pumped blood into the economic circulatory system—such, in brief, was the creed of Dr Quesnay—and Louis XV saw in this desideratum of high grain prices one more means of satisfying his morbid avarice. Commissioners furnished with plenary powers by royal authority commandeered the grain cargoes in all the ports of France, and forcibly prevented private sales in all the markets until the "state" purchases, ostensibly for the needs of the armies, had been effected. So the father of his country enriched himself at the expense of his subjects.

How could a secret that had to be shared by so many persons fail to be exposed in the long run? All France saw God's blessing upon the fields—and this richest of harvests utterly disappeared! Pamphlets surreptitiously circulated exposed this "starvation campaign" of the king against his own people. By the time that the little Marquis de Lafayette had spent two years in Paris and reached his thirteenth year, the fall of Choiseul and the omnipotence of the Comtesse Dubarry had increased the popular hatred and contempt of the Court beyond all bounds; and the boy was ripe to absorb the germs of rebellion.

III. COMTESSE DUBARRY

THE FATE of the Duc de Choiseul was sealed at the banquet that followed the marriage of his arranging between the houses of Habsburg and Bourbon. Refusing to share his power with anyone, he had chosen his own sister, the Duchesse de Grammont, as the Pompadour's successor. His clerical rivals were wiser in their generation. They sent out the panders of

the Parc-aux-Cerfs and found a more competent temptress
for the worn-out voluptuary—the young but admirably
trained Aphrodisian from the gambling hell of the ill-famed
Vicomte Dubarry. The duke made the fatal mistake of imagining that the king's infatuation would not last! He gave orders
to the police to be blind and deaf; and Paris was inundated
with the most outspoken and scurrilous lampoons against the
king's latest darling. An unknown hand daringly placed on
Louis' desk the long list of the names of his fortunate predecessors. In vain.

Choiseul's day was ended when, at the wedding feast, there
sat down in the four seats at the king's own table the king, the
dauphin, the daughter of Maria Theresa—and the Dubarry.

The parvenue "Countess" was not vengeful as the Pompadour had been. She merely took money and presents and in
return would secure from her crowned lover whatever the
givers prompted her to ask. So it is that there hangs to this
day in the Louvre a portrait of Charles I by Vandyck. The
story of the way this picture came to France is entirely characteristic of the last period of the reign of Louis XV. The
Duc d'Aiguillon bought the precious picture as a present for
the Dubarry, for her to hang above the head of her bed. When
the king came into her room she pointed at once to the portrait and reeled off the little passage she had been taught:

"Look, France!" (So she called Louis.) "Have a good look
at that man's picture. He was a king too, and he too let his
Parliament grow a head taller than himself, till it showed its
gratitude by having his head off!"

The Paris Parlement was simply a supreme court of justice,
without legislative power; but the royal decrees needed its
ratification in order to acquire the force of law, and it had been
offering resistance to the insatiability of the Treasury and the
Church. Now the weak king was persuaded to dismiss the
members of the Parlement and install venal placemen in their
stead. Soon there was nothing left in France that could not
be had for money. Louis's own relative, the last scion of the
Catholic house of Stuart, was no longer safe from his Protestant persecutors, even in the Catholic country of "His Most
Christian Majesty." The gold coin of the English government
bought up even the right of asylum. The prince refused to

leave the country voluntarily, and soldiers dragged him from his box at the Opera; he was publicly thrown into a coach and driven off. No official was discoverable as the person responsible for the outrage. Everything was done, indeed, over the heads of the responsible authorities, under verbal instruction accompanied by the clink of good money. A handful of coin made good the absence of official seals.

Amid this universal venality everybody paid his price for what he wanted. The Dubarry kept *lettres de cachet*, ready signed by the king, in her desk, and a stock of money orders —the so-called *acquits comptants*. The buyer entered the sum to be paid and the name of the victim. What was easier than to get rid in this way of a troublesome husband or creditor? There was no remedy against the monarch's "autographed" orders. Every state revenue office honored the king's bills without inquiry. It seemed incredible that the government could be carried on amid such anarchical conditions. *"Ah, la bonne machine, qui va toute seule!"* ("What a grand machine, running all by itself!") wrote Pope Benedict XIV to his legate in Paris.

So far as its own interests were concerned, Rome had every reason for satisfaction with the new régime. The ecclesiastical courts had a free hand once more in France. A Protestant father, an innocent man, was broken on the wheel; an officer, hardly more than a boy, of a good Catholic noble family, was condemned to a dishonorable death on the gallows because the rotted crucifix on an immemorial wooden bridge lay smashed on the parapet one morning, and someone professed to have seen him on the bridge the worse for drink on the previous night.

Soon the young Lafayette could no longer conceal the hatred of injustice and oppression that blazed in his heart. He was more serious-minded than his comrades, and took gloomily to heart the witty sarcasms of M. de Beaumarchais, who had the gift of phrasing his denunciations with a pungent raciness that set the king and the Dubarry laughing over their own obloquy till the tears came. The police could not confiscate the reprints quickly enough to prevent the public from snatching the great bulk of them from the hands of the *colporteurs*. It was the *Figaro* of this same M. de Beaumarchais

that later played the accompaniment to the opening figure of
the great dance of death; as yet he was pillorying only the
servants of the system, the venal judges and officials—fighting
them with the deadliest weapon in France, ridicule.

It was not from any lack of appreciation of wit and humor
that the young Lafayette found no satisfaction in mere laugh-
ter at all this; it was simply because he felt every injustice as
though he himself suffered it. His unusualness was beginning
already to attract the attention of the priests who controlled
the college. The boy was set to write a Latin essay on "The
Superiority of the Spirit of Man to Brute Force, Exemplified
by Horse and Rider": with his innate recalcitrance, he made it
a pæan of praise of the revolutionary spirit of freedom. He
made the proud steed throw his torturer and race off to
"*Liberté.*"

It is a strange thing that this essay, with its subversive line
of argument running deliberately counter to the Church's
authoritarianism, remained unpunished. The prior's disciplin-
ary right extended to the award of twenty-five strokes of the
birch administered by a provost appointed for this special
duty. But there seems to have been something in the glance
and the carriage of the thirteen-year-old boy that revealed to
his priestly masters what General Lafayette tells in his memoirs,
written more than fifteen years later—that he was resolved
to run his little sword into the provost's body or his own rather
than submit to the degradation of that punishment.

Yet it would be a mistake to suppose that the stately environment of his grandfather's palace had no influence on the
young savage from Chavaniac. In the few letters he sent to a
girl in Auvergne, a poorer cousin of his, he reveals only too
plainly his ambition to attain the cynical humor and the air
of superiority of Paris high society:

Our cousin's betrothal has come to grief; there is another on the
tapis, but he must sing smaller indeed; Mlle de Roncherolles has a
place with Mme de Bourbon which brings her a thousand crowns in
the year, and a private fortune of five thousand livres a year—that is
all. As you see, it falls far short of the other matches. Last Thursday's
ball was put off until the 15th, a week from today; . . . if I were
to tell you about some bonnet in the new fashion . . .

And so he goes on, aping grown-ups' turns of speech and smart phrases; every sentence betrays the fine opinion the little writer has of himself as a society chronicler.

This effort to play the perfected Parisian only shows how the young "provincial's" feelings were hurt by his inability to shine among the rest in fine manners and fine talk. For a long time yet his pride had to suffer from his lack of assurance, until success rubbed off these angles.

The "Liberty" which the horse of his Latin essay reconquered, that eternal unknown quantity of human history, assigned a different value by each age and each nation, had already, in the boy's thirteenth year, become the will-o'-the-wisp from which he never afterwards removed his gaze. Every wrong of which he heard, every new encroachment of despotism carried him farther from the aims and outlook prescribed by his noble birth.

IV. THE VOICE OF JACQUES NECKER

THE LITTLE MARQUIS had long ceased to be frightened at night by the noise of the police raids; now, when he visited his mother, he saw the streets swept by the police in broad daylight. The officials in their turn had been hit by the rising cost of living and had to look around for additional sources of income. So the police "mistakes," many of which were no inadvertences but deliberately made, grew alarmingly. The authorities were profuse in their apologies after the event, and ostentatiously reprimanded innocent subordinates, but by then the father or husband of the "little goldfish" had been well "bled"—and what sacrifice would not a prosperous citizen make to extricate his wife or daughter, or perhaps both of them, from a Bridewell? The higher authorities remained deaf to all complaints: live and let live was their motto. Was it not in the best interest of the respectable population that the capital should be freed from the unceasing influx of undesirable elements?

Destitution drove every vagrant into Paris as the snow drives in the wolves. There were regular battles. One day the mob overpowered the guards, stormed the *palais* of the chief magistrate and ransacked its contents. That wave was quickly overcome; but it was a warning twenty years in advance to the victims of the coming deluge.

Prudent people began to prick up their ears. Even in his grandfather's feudal palace the young Lafayette heard talk of starvation and the high price of bread, and no longer merely of good appetite and table delicacies. In all the salons the crisis became a fashionable subject. Everyone who wanted to be in the swim had to show familiarity with political economy. To be of real distinction, ladies had to add to the tortures of monumental coiffures and wasp waists the study of scientific works. It became a matter of good form to discuss economic theories. It was not enough to spend a pleasant hour over amusingly written reactionary books like the *Dialogues sur des blés* (Talks on the Grain Trade) of the Neapolitan Abbé Galiani, full of witty paradoxes; even the authors most difficult to assimilate, even such outspoken enemies of property as Morelly and Mably were patiently plodded through and hotly discussed. The old Voltaire wrote sarcastically to a friend:

The nation has become satiated with poems and dramas in verse and tragedies and sentimental stories, and is now asking for more solid food. Anybody who wants to be read now must write economic dissertations.

Young Lafayette himself listened with keen interest one day when he heard praises of the wonderful, incomparable book of a certain M. Necker. No sensational novel, not even Rousseau's *Nouvelle Héloïse,* not even the publicly burned impieties of Voltaire, no book at all within the memory of man, had ever been received with such universal acclamation as the polemical *Commerce des blés* written over the signature of a simple merchant named Jacques Necker. Every line in this common "self-made man's" book was quoted with a reverence otherwise accorded only to the Bible. Happy was he who was able to read to his friends a few manuscript pages from this book, which had not yet been placed in the hands of the trade. To succeed, without the help of forefathers or any patent of nobility, entirely by one's own abilities, in compelling universal admiration—this was just what the young marquis burned to do; he listened with cheeks afire to all the talk about the famous man.

Jacques Necker, the son of a poor Genevese professor, came to Paris at the age of fifteen with a fortune of three thalers. As a Protestant it was entirely impossible for him to settle there. The all-powerful Pompadour had made an end of the intolerant rule of the ecclesiastical authorities, but the cruel decrees of Louis XIV were still nominally in force, and as the government officials were either left unpaid or paid far in arrear, they had to be allowed to tap the rich reservoir which opens at the closing of an eye. Three thalers would not have sufficed to cover up the entry under "Religion" in the young man's Swiss passport. However, a rich compatriot stood bond for him and took him into his service as a clerk.

The recipe for rising in just fifteen years from a simple clerk to a partner with a fortune of three million francs has remained Necker's secret. When he was about thirty he founded an enterprise of his own. In just ten more years he multiplied his fortune by thirty! Even more astonishing, perhaps, than this acquisition of a hundred millions was the strength of character that enabled Necker to give up so flourishing a business in order to devote the remainder of his life entirely to science. Jacques Necker pronounced the word, "Enough," which is generally excluded from the vocabulary of successful speculators; and he remained faithful to his resolve. Protestant and foreigner as he was, his first book, a historical work, brought him election to the Académie. Thereafter his only dealings with money were in the public interest, from ambition to serve. He became minister of finance. The office had brought great fortunes to all his predecessors. It cost him a good many millions out of his own pocket.

Such rapid advance to fame could not but arouse envy. The book on the grain trade was hotly attacked. It called for sacrifices and renunciation from the rich and charged the possessing classes with callousness. What could be easier than to mock at the converted Saul who only turned Paul the preacher after he had safely put away his own little nest egg of a hundred millions? But cynicism and insinuations failed entirely to shake the young Lafayette's admiring faith. With beating heart he heard such passages as this read aloud in his mother's salon:

Ask the man who drives the plough, ask the poor harvest worker, these labourers who receive the smallest conceivable reward for their labour, whether they want a high price for grain! It is fortunate for them, and still more so for us, that they cannot read and think! When we see how they toil and yet go hungry, we cannot but ask whether the earth was really created for a small minority of privileged persons, invested with the right to shut out their fellow-men with hedges and fences from all the gifts of God. Yet all the new laws made give further protection to the superfluity of the satiated against the needy, to the strong against the weak, instead of the other way round!

Throughout the life of the Marquis de Lafayette those sentences remained graven on his heart. He pondered over them in the college dormitory, and he recalled the dirty, windowless peasant huts of Auvergne, and the timidity and degrading humility of their occupants. He was born into the class of the riders, but he resolved to take sides against his own interests, to take the part of the hard-driven beasts of burden. He would do all he could to wrench from the oppressors the whips and spurs of their privileges! In the unequal battle between the strong and the weak we shall find him always on the side of the weak.

V.   "THERE IS A TIDE——"

POOR LIKE HIS FOREFATHERS, a true "Auvergnat," the young Lafayette had no great desire for wealth and possessions. It may be that, if he had had personal experience of the hardships and humiliations of poverty, he would have reverted to the conventional outlook of the average man. But in a single night the scholar receiving free education at the expense of the state became a rich heir by entail, sole owner of the whole of the landed properties of the Counts of La Rivière. On Sunday he was with his mother, as usual; a week later he entered his grandfather's empty palace as its owner, lord over an estate of three and a half million francs.

Wholesale death was common enough in high society in

those days. The Roi Soleil, Louis XIV, lost all his legitimate children one after another, all his sons-in-law, all his grandsons and great-grandsons, until one only was left, a delicate five-year-old boy, to inherit his throne. Everyone suspected the Duke of Orleans, who as the boy's guardian became regent of the kingdom, of a long series of poisonings, although his own family suffered no less. Since the execution of the woman poisoner Brinvilliers, every death at Court had been suspected of being due to unnatural causes. Yet the conception of cleanliness then prevalent was enough in itself to cut lives short prematurely. The wonder is that a Louis XIV or XV should have succeeded in living to old age. Washing and bathing were processes of which men and women alike had no knowledge. Dressing tables were laden with oils and ointments from the East, but water was taboo. In museum showcases we may still see the wonderfully worked butterflies of brilliants and rubies, set as handles on long knitting needles. Their purpose was to scratch the scalps, eaten by vermin under the tall, full-bottomed wigs! What wonder if whole families were exterminated by epidemics of infectious disease?

So the young Lafayette lost his mother and his grandfather in a single week. Both had been alive and well on Sunday; both were dead by Friday.

An orphan boy with no encumbrances, the bearer of an ancient name, and a millionaire, was no ordinary morsel for a father of marriageable daughters. The Duc d'Ayen-Noailles had no less than five to dispose of, and he precipitately laid hands on this desirable son-in-law. By all means let the marriage take place at once! Lafayette was not quite fourteen years old, the duke's second daughter not quite twelve. Only the energetic protest of her mother prevented this child marriage.

The Duchesse de Noailles was notorious for her piety and domesticity. Well born though she was, she brought up her children herself! She was even faithful to her husband, careless of the ridicule this brought on her—in a society which could not say enough in praise of the Duc de Richelieu for his gentleness towards his wife when he discovered her in her salon in an entirely unambiguous situation. He merely protested:

"Mais, Madame, si quelqu'un vous voyait!" ("But, Madame, suppose somebody saw you!")

Lafayette's future mother-in-law, thoroughly old-fashioned in her outlook on life, had hot quarrels with her husband, who seized every pretext for escaping from the strict atmosphere of his Paris home. On this new issue the two came to a compromise that satisfied both. The marriage should not take place for two years, and meanwhile the two children should live together as brother and sister in the Palais Noailles under the care of the duchess. The mother hoped in this way to accustom the two to one another's ways and so to assure their future happiness; and the duke was relieved of the fear of the splendid match escaping from his grasp.

It would be difficult to imagine a less suitable environment for this young enthusiast for every progressive idea than the strict piety of the duchess's home. Lafayette's interest in the Encyclopedists, his freethinking propensities and his circle of friends who persuaded him when he was no more than sixteen to become a freemason—all those differences of outlook between the boy bridegroom and his mother-in-law would have been likely to play havoc with his straightforwardness but for her tolerance and radiant good-nature. The Duc d'Ayen, too, did what he could to get his future son-in-law away from the influence of crazy women. He obtained an ensigncy for Lafayette in his regiment, and took him with him to parades and inspections. Thus the boy was able at all events to count these two years of waiting as military service. At the same time the duke was able to arrange for Lafayette to receive riding lessons with the youngest brother of the king, the Comte d'Artois, a boy of the same age.

But fate is as willful as a running stream: the surface hardly shows a ripple until the pride of man sets out to dam or to divert it; then it foams wildly past every mark and upsets all calculations. So it happened to the Duc d'Ayen-Noailles. Everything the young ensign saw on parade or in the riding school added to his disgust with the life of Versailles. Every scrap of conversation he caught, wherever he went, confirmed his astonishing discovery that in the richest and most aristocratic stratum of society in France the one subject of conversation was money. Millions of half-starved people watched with amazement and envy the valuable horses and gilded coaches of the elect, who were able to go carelessly in pursuit of pleasure without the humiliating necessity of working for their living. How could the boy of fourteen or fifteen understand the paradox of these spoilt darlings of fortune being as obsessed with thoughts of money as any small shopkeeper? With all their wants amply supplied, they emptied one another's pockets at the gaming tables, envied one another every stroke of luck, haggled with their tenants or the money-lender for every sou of the money which they then squandered, pile after pile.

The young marquis turned away in disgust from the universal money-grabbing. This "Auvergnat," son of the infertile soil whose meager yield trained lord and liege alike in frugality, brought away from this first contact with the sycophantic and avaricious courtiers of Versailles an incurable physical revulsion from every sort of self-seeking. Just as a man may eat too much of one dish and be unable to touch it thereafter, so General Lafayette, greatly to his own disadvantage and often to that of the cause for which he was fighting, fought shy of any sort of collaboration with such men as Mirabeau or Danton, because no talent compensated in his eyes for unclean hands.

Often forgetting his mission in his concern for his own immaculate repute as a man of honor, he let that outweigh all other considerations, unlike the venal but far-seeing Danton, who dismissed all attacks on his personal character with the words:

"Périsse ma mémoire pourvu que la France soit libre!" ("Perish my memory, if only France be free!")

VI. THE NEW KING

THE DUC D'AYEN-NOAILLES was one of the confidants of the Comtesse Dubarry and was thus familiar with the secret miseries of the dauphin's married life. On the wedding night itself the whispering went on unceasingly in the corridors of the château, and every lackey was able to pass on with a smirk the news that the fifteen-year-old bride was passing her wedding night alone, and would probably never be able to be a mother—unless some deputy consummated the marriage.

It is not necessary to carry cynicism to the length of the famous historian who declared that the starting point of the French Revolution is to be sought in a slight infirmity of Louis XVI against which Mohammedans and Jews guard at the birth of a child. But it must be recognized that Marie Antoinette's frivolity and feverish pursuit of pleasure proceeded from a nervous irritation which would unfailingly be produced in the healthiest of peasant women if her husband left her unsatisfied.

At the court of the old libertine, where curious note was taken of every love affair begun or ended, in an atmosphere so overladen with eroticism, how could the dauphin's young wife, pursued by the attentions of every courtier, have any chance of preserving her moral equilibrium? The real culprits were the Duc de Choiseul, who arranged the marriage, and still more Maria Theresa, who replied to all her daughter's complaints with wise exhortations in the style of a pious tract. Not until years later, when the popularity and the reputation of Marie Antoinette were already beyond saving, did the empress send her son, later Joseph II, to look into matters. Of what avail was it for the persuasiveness of his brother-in-law to overcome Louis's fear of the needed operation, and for the queen's first confinement to be heralded by the thunder of cannon a year after Joseph's visit? The malicious and the scandalmongers found ample material in the queen's past for publicly slandering mother and children.

At the time when the young Marquis de Lafayette was laying the foundations of his career at Versailles, his future father-in-law confidently shared the universal belief that the crown of France would fall to a younger brother of Louis XVI. The heir-apparent was the image of his Saxon ancestors on the mother's side, thickset and phlegmatic; he had been carried to bed half-unconscious from his own wedding feast, and his insatiable appetite and growing corpulence had made it more and more probable that he would come to a sudden end. How people would have laughed then over the tragic prophecy that the young insatiable would die suddenly, but on the scaffold and not at table!

The Kings of France would, of course, go on forever, and the Duc de Noailles had only one ambition for his son-in-law, to secure a place for him at Court. At that time the office of chamberlain was no merely honorary distinction: the two noblemen who had to bring His Majesty's *chaise percée* (commode) into his bedroom every morning were required to prove an unbroken line of unblemished ancestry through seventeen generations on both the father's and the mother's side; and their office was regarded as an uncommonly fortunate one, since it guaranteed that they came daily under the king's notice.

Anyone who has ever come late and thoroughly sober into a company well on into the riotously drunken stage will easily appreciate the aversion of the unspoilt young marquis, filled with high ideals, toward the men and manners of Versailles. He arrived at the worst period of all and just had time to become thoroughly acquainted with the moral result of the Dubarry régime; and what he saw did little to inspire him with respect for the royal household.

VII.   AT THE WOODEN SWORD

IF FREE THOUGHT had not been the current craze in good society, the death of Louis XV from infection with a child's disease would have been regarded as outraged heaven's just punishment. One of his victims at last avenged all her ill-used predecessors in the seraglio of the Parc-aux-Cerfs.

Just ten days before the ascension of Louis XVI, Lafayette, then sixteen years old, was married in the chapel of the Palais Noailles in Paris to the second daughter, then fourteen, of the Duc d'Ayen-Noailles. But the hopes his father-in-law had placed in this impatiently awaited marriage were disappointed from the very outset. Instead of installing themselves at Versailles on a footing appropriate to their rank, the young couple remained, at their own desire, in the mother's home, and all the duke's efforts to eliminate the "bad influence" of his unworldly wife were wrecked by his young son-in-law's obstinacy, which now revealed its full strength for the first time.

It was no ordinary event for the honeymoon to be passed under the surveillance of the mother-in-law, and the wits of

Versailles made lively play with the story. Louis XVI, rigidly virtuous and God-fearing, had little in common with his grandfather Louis XV, but the tone of his court was still set by the gallants of Marie Antoinette's entourage, by her women friends and their admirers. The male leader of this society was the Comte d'Artois, the king's youngest brother, and in the general belief his supplanter with his wife. The serious young Lafayette, consumed with a thirst for distinction and with the love of learning, was entirely out of tune with the feverish pleasure-hunting of this circle. His cold reserve and measured manner made him the butt of the wits.

In the Bois de Boulogne, on the way from Paris to Versailles, there was at this time an inn called l'Épée de Bois (the Wooden Sword). It was a nocturnal rendezvous of the associates of the young queen. This was a company not at all to Lafayette's taste. His intimate friends, the young Counts Ségur and La Rochefoucauld, were plowing with him through Rousseau's *Contrat social* and all the new theories and discoveries in natural science. A new youth was beginning to stir: the privileges which their fathers had enjoyed as an inherited and indefeasible right weighed on the sons as complicity in wrong. Here and there men were beginning to realize more and more clearly that privileges of birth were fundamentally indefensible, were imposed by the stronger on the weaker through brute force.

Two trustworthy witnesses testify to Lafayette's isolation in Court society at this period. On one occasion he succeeded in getting tolerably drunk, and the whole way home he implored La Rochefoucauld, who was seeing him safe back, to tell his mockers that this time he had not been merely merry but properly drunk by all the rules! He betrayed under the influence of drink how it hurt his pride to be taken for a crabbed kill-joy. Still more significant is an episode related in the *Mémoires* of the Comte de Ségur. The count committed no indiscretion in publishing it, for it was common knowledge and was published in the gazettes of the time that young Lafayette, in the first year of his married life, was in passionate pursuit of the pretty Comtesse Hunolstein, and that he had no success although the lady was not generally regarded as inaccessible to wooers.

Her indifference to him was due to the influence of the Duc
de Chartres, later "Philippe Égalité," but of this Lafayette had
no knowledge, and he suspected his friend Ségur of being his
successful rival. In the middle of the night he burst into Ségur's
bedroom and tried to make him fight a mortal duel there and
then for the favor of their chosen lady. Day was beginning to
dawn before the Comte de Ségur at last succeeded in freeing
himself of the unjust suspicion, without putting the young
maniac on the right track.

How I laughed to myself [wrote Ségur] when I heard Lafayette described everywhere as a cold pedant, even by those who knew him
best! They were to learn later that ardour was the thing he lacked
least of all!

Blind to Lafayette's true character, his father-in-law proceeded confidently with his plans, until at last events came in
rapid succession to show him his mistake.

VIII. FIRST ESCAPADE

SOMETHING of the black mood of Richard III slumbers in all
second sons of kings. The Comte de Provence, called "Monsieur" by an old tradition, was full of impotent wrath at the
undeserved injury of his belated birth, and when the arrival
of an heir—which he had almost ceased to fear—seemed to
rob Monsieur of all hope of succession to the throne, his dislike of his sister-in-law Marie Antoinette grew into a burning
hatred. Cheated of his chance of the throne, he made capital
out of every flirtation of the queen, every big loss she suffered
at cards, every inadvertent infraction of the rigid court etiquette; he was the secret instigator and paymaster of most of
the defamatory pamphlets, surreptitiously given away, which
undermined the "Austrian woman's" popularity.

In the very act of holding the first-born of the King of
France over the christening font, in the presence of all the
assembled Court dignitaries, he dared publicly to express doubt
as to the child's true parentage. When the Archbishop of Paris
asked what name his godchild was to bear, this tender-hearted
uncle replied significantly:

"Your Eminence has forgotten the first question—the names of the parents!"

Horrified, and blushing crimson, the prelate stammered that in this case the parentage was surely well known. The Comte de Provence, in the father's presence, daringly replied, with a sardonic smile and a shrug of the shoulders:

"Do you think so?"

If the Duc de Noailles had been a better judge of men, he could not have failed to see that his stiff-necked young son-in-law was no fitting member of the suite of this overweening intriguer. Lafayette was bound to the king's youngest brother, the Comte d'Artois, by the memories of their riding lessons together as little boys. The count, as a sort of deputy for his blunt and uncompromising brother, played the part of the "first gentleman" of the kingdom. He was the criterion of the fashions, placed the biggest stakes on the gaming tables, and watched over the prestige of the royal house on occasions when the unimpressive manner of Louis XVI, his shyness and diffidence, would have had a disastrous effect.

If the young Lafayette had been placed in the suite of this extravagant prince, with his almost official function of careless amiability, the boy would at least have shared the prince's lofty contempt of money. But the Comte de Provence was still regarded as the next heir to the throne, and that fact determined the choice made by the Duc de Noailles. To the duke, as a perfect courtier, the officer's uniform was no more than a necessary "livery," which a member of his family would only wear in order to arrive quickly at a place at Court. The profession of a regimental officer was good enough for the petty provincial nobles, whose means were only sufficient to support them in service far from Versailles, the source of favors, with the expectation at best of a Cross of Saint-Louis after, perhaps, twenty years.

These were far from being the ideas of the seventeen-year-old cavalry captain! The Marquises Lafayette had never served their king otherwise than at arms. To fill the degrading office of a prince's chamberlain and lick-spit—no, that was not necessary for the sole inheritor of a fortune of three millions; this young enthusiast, bitten by the virus of philosophy and dreaming of the service of Liberty, had quite other ambitions.

Yet open resistance to the father-in-law's authority would be too dangerous. Improprieties of that sort were cured in the institutions known as *petites maisons*. The society in these communal homes was not of the worst; behind their high walls they were magnificently appointed; but their inhabitants were as dead to the rest of the world as if they lay already in their family vaults. Lafayette, out of respect for this drastic cure for the hunger for liberty, thought out a tactical device. He took advantage of the next Court ball, deliberately set his wig awry so that it revealed a patch of his red hair, and then pursued the Comte de Provence with spiteful chaff until Monsieur lost his patience and shouted at him:

"I shall keep your remarks in mind!"

Lafayette, as though he did not notice that he had been recognized, answered at once:

"Memory is the wit of fools—Shakespeare!"

With that he had assured himself for all time of the ill-will of the prince, who set a good deal of store by his own intellectual and literary gifts. Half a century later, when the Comte de Provence at last ascended the throne as Louis XVIII, he still remembered the insult.

The poor Duc de Noailles hunted in vain for the threads of the intrigue which had robbed his son-in-law of that brilliant post! In face of his sudden disfavor he felt it advisable to let the unsuccessful candidate disappear entirely for a time from the prince's sight. He made arrangements for Lafayette to be recalled to his regiment, then in garrison at Metz. There the young captain could make the acquaintance of his superiors and his brother officers and drill men and horses for a while until the grass had had time to grow over his failure at Versailles.

Lafayette did not wait even for the birth of his first child: regardless of his wife's condition, he hurried away after the bare time necessary for assembling his little caravan of coaches and saddle horses, coachmen and grooms and valets. He left everything that was not indispensable for the journey to follow after him, so great was his impatience to escape from the atmosphere of the Court.

Here let us glance for a moment into Fate's workshop, behind the scenes of the great marionette show. Proud of their privilege of going their own way, men dance like puppets at the end of the threads held by Fate, whom they call "Chance," but who throws them whither she will all through their lives. The ardent young marquis was dreamily riding through the fresh spring landscape on his way to Metz, blind to the humbly bared heads which, after all, were but greeting the chance fortune of his birth, not the heroic services which he was determined to render somehow, somewhere, to all humanity. Meanwhile there trundled toward Metz from the north the train of the Duke of Gloucester. Unconscious of one another's existence, the young marquis from Paris and the brother of the King of England had started on their journey just in time for the one to give the other the cue which would summon him from his vague youthful daydreams to serious deeds on the stage of world history.

IX. THE HEART ENROLLED

METZ, by the new and still unhealed frontier, was occupied by a garrison almost at war strength and placed under the military rule of the Duc de Broglie. To console him for his many reverses in the Seven Years' War the old man had been given the bâton of a Marshal of France; but he was kept at a distance from Versailles, where the cross-grained old swashbuckler would have been out of place. He was better fitted for a camp, where there was no need for him to control his bearishness.

Like all men of his type, he does not fall easily into any category. He could show good-natured indulgence for the frivolities of young officers or a veteran's drunkenness; yet he would grin with satisfaction at the spectacle of an awkward recruit being made to run the gauntlet, with every blow of the iron ramrods tearing the flesh from his bones.

Lafayette, as the son of the fallen comrade who died at Hastenbeck in De Broglie's arms, was ordered by the marshal to sit at his table, a high distinction for the young captain, whose prescribed place was at the table of his regimental commander. This honor done to the fallen father through his son was one more trick of Fate. At the marshal's table, Lafayette was one of the company at the banquet given to the Duke of

Gloucester, which was to change the course of his life. The duke, after drinking more than amply, gave full vent in the company of these officers of noble birth to his disgust at being born only next door to the succession, and with the critical eye of all younger sons of kings for the blunders of their crowned brothers he was merciless in his stories of George III's stupidities.

With no more than a modicum of common sense, said the duke, the Boston rising could have been disposed of without firing a single musket. George III had refused the good fellows the right of all English citizens, won by the blood of their fore-fathers—the right to pay no taxes but those which had been granted by their own elected representatives. A few seats in the Parliament of the mother country, and the emigrants would be satisfied. Instead of this they were to be brought to reason with the bullet and the gallows, because the king's Guelph blood had been roused, and his continental arrogance rebelled against this insular democracy and against any sort of Parliamentary tutelage.

At this exposure of the king's "tyrannical arrogance" by the king's own brother, all Lafayette's explosive enthusiasm for liberty was fired anew. He listened with indignation to the picture the duke painted of the abominable trade in recruits carried on between England and the German princes, who were selling their subjects like cattle at so much a head! On the one side were simple farmers, heroically defending their freedom with worn-out sporting guns; on the other the formidable power of well-armed mercenary forces. To what more honorable purpose could a young nobleman consecrate his sword than the support of the heroic minority?

The Duke of Gloucester was inspecting the fortifications in the company of all the officers of the garrison when an express courier brought him the mails from England. No sooner had he broken the seals than he read out, with the triumphant emphasis of one who had prophesied truly, the Declaration of Independence of the new Congress government. More than ten years after this impressive scene, Lafayette described it at length in his *Mémoires de ma main*. The duke's first words, he writes, in a happy phrase, "Enrolled my heart" (*"mon cœur fut enrôlé"*).

But it was a long way from this "enrollment" to the landing to join the colors on the other side of the ocean! The Marquis de Lafayette had first to vanquish the shades of his ancestors, and many material hindrances, before he was able to make common cause with rebellious subjects for the Liberty which in his own country was called "high treason" and was punished on the gallows.

X. "BARON" KALB

THE DUC DE BROGLIE would gladly have sent Lafayette to fight the English: he would have allied himself with Satan to make them pay for the humiliation France had suffered at their hands. But he could not prudently permit the boy to proceed on his enterprise. If Lafayette came to any harm, the Duc de Noailles might hold him, De Broglie, responsible for a daughter's widowhood. He refused to have anything to do with the adventure. But he passed the young captain on to his old friend "Baron" Kalb, deputy quartermaster general, who was also thinking of going to the New World to fight England.

The "baron" had had an exciting career. He was born in the little village of Hütteldorf, near Bayreuth, and the entry of his birth in the village church register shows him as the second son of Johann Kalb, peasant farmer. The boy had no ambition to be sold into military service to help to keep up the princely state of the Margrave of Bayreuth, and at sixteen he ran away from home. He found employment as waiter in an Alsatian inn; there he learned French and also, as he carried the glasses, studied the ways of officers. Gradually he gained confidence and saved money, until the day came when, on the strength of a forged letter of nobility, he bought a lieutenant's patent from the King of France. At the battle of Rossbach he saved the whole of the army transport of the Duc de Broglie.

In Prussia, as in France, officer's rank was denied to soldiers of humble origin. It would have interested Frederick II to learn that the French officer in captain's uniform who had cheated him of his prey was just a common German peasant.

For this great service Kalb was appointed to the general staff, and on the conclusion of peace he was employed by the

Duc de Choiseul in the diplomatic service. The duke sent him to the New World to study the feeling among the colonists, and especially to ascertain what forces they could assemble in the event of a war with England. The German "baron" carried out his mission with the efficiency expected of him; his confidential reports were found at a later date to be thoroughly well founded. But the Duc de Choiseul was brought down by the intrigues of the beautiful Dubarry; the new masters brought new servants, and "Baron" Kalb returned to regimental duty at Metz. The one thing he had gained was his knowledge of the New World and of the English language. Thus equipped he now intended to enter the service of the Americans against the English.

The "baron" had married the daughter of a rich Dutch merchant, and long ago he had procured a "family" seat, ancestors and all, and domain. He had wealth and title, and the rank of lieutenant colonel. What was it that prevented him from settling down to the enjoyment of his success? He could have lived on his estate, brought up his children, and spent his days with the wife, whom he loved to the point of writing to her every day they were separated—were it not that the malice of fate places a maggot within all the finest fruit. With his courage and intelligence Baron Kalb had overcome the obstacles of his birth; he sacrificed his old age for the satisfaction of a puerile vanity.

As deputy quartermaster he was a titular general, but his substantive rank was only that of lieutenant colonel. He wanted to retire as a real general; for this childish ambition, at nearly sixty years of age, he went out once more to risk his life and all that he had so painfully won. Under the French army regulations officers seconded for service in a foreign army retained the rank they gained in it. For no more than this Kalb went off to America.

As for the young greenhorn planted on him, he accepted that charge with military docility. From his childhood he had been used to the strictest economy, and he asked nothing better than to allow his expenses to Paris to be defrayed by Lafayette.

It was a relief to old Broglie to see the two go off together.

He could not have found a better mentor for his young protégé. He was free of responsibility now; it was for the father-
in-law to look after this adventurous youth.

XI. AN UNEQUAL STRUGGLE

THE TWO TRAVELING COMPANIONS were equally bent on enrolling in the Congress army; but their natures were so different
that the journey to Paris in the young marquis's coach did
nothing to increase their intimacy. Kalb, the peasant's son with
a forged diploma of nobility, was a mercenary of the old type:
courage was just his trade, and he smiled to himself at the
passionate declamations of this high-born young gentleman,
with his great fortune, who could afford to dream of a better
world where the privilege of birth was unknown.

It is not surprising that by the time they reached Paris
Baron Kalb had grown weary of the subject of the liberation
of mankind. If he hesitated to get rid of his young companion
it was less out of consideration for the Duc de Broglie than in
the hope of holding a trump card. The young marquis, as son-
in-law of the Duc de Noailles, was an element of official Versailles. If he publicly took sides with "Boston" it would be
generally inferred that the Court and the king himself favored
the rebels. The boy was thus a recruit of no small value for the
Americans.

Kalb would have liked to come to an understanding with
Lafayette, but the young hothead's naïveté spoiled his plans.
In vain did the experienced man of fifty-odd urge the boy
to be cautious; Lafayette was misled by the apparent popularity of the men of Boston. Benjamin Franklin, the "lightning
tamer," as he was called, had fled from London to Paris on the
outbreak of the war, and the shepherds and shepherdesses of
the Trianon, in their silks and Brussels lace, lionized the old
Puritan with his cotton stockings as though he were a living
illustration out of the pages of Rousseau. The jewelers put his
portrait on snuffboxes and fobs; elegant ladies hung round
their necks miniatures of the Philadelphia paper merchant, set
with precious stones. Only Marie Antoinette's brother, later
Joseph II of Austria, resisted the fashionable infection. A
courtier asked him what he thought of the "man from Bos-

ton." "It is my trade," said the Habsburg prince dryly, "to be a royalist."

But "intellectual" fashions should not be taken too seriously! When the absolute rule of the Roi Soleil was at its worst the Alexandrines of Corneille and Racine were filled with the praises of republicanism and contempt of tyrants. The very courtiers whose elastic backbones could not bend too low before the Pompadour and the Dubarry rewarded with storms of applause the superhuman independence of the heroes of antiquity represented on the stage, just as the small man of the turn of the century, so economical at home, had been filled with enthusiasm at the spectacle of the *bon vivant* carelessly throwing his money out of the window. It is by no means without significance that the curtain falls between play-acting and real life. The soul's longing for the luxury of finer feelings is satisfied in the theater—and then people go home.

There came a cold douche for the inexperienced boy's enthusiasm. His two most intimate friends, Ségur and La Rochefoucauld, burned to go with him to join in the fight for Liberty; but they had not the means. And when they went to their fathers for money the result was startlingly unexpected. The Comte de Maurepas summoned the young marquis to Versailles. On his arrival the count took out of his desk a *lettre de cachet* already signed by Louis XVI. Lafayette, instead of fighting for the liberty of the Americans, was in danger of losing his own.

He did not abandon his project, but waited in patience till a way stood open. At present the forces were too unequal: on one side the whole power of the state; on the other, a blundering youth of nineteen.

Baron Kalb, with no less a recommendation than that of the Duc de Broglie, had been accepted at once; he had read in triumph his letter of introduction:

The fact that Baron de Kalb is prepared to sacrifice his rank in the French army for our cause entirely justifies the preferential treatment I have assured him. I beg you most earnestly to confer on this valorous officer on his arrival the rank of major general.

"At last!" the old fellow sighed.

What a shock for the poor baron when, on the very night

before sailing, he was hauled off the ship with all the other passengers and with the consignment of arms which had been placed on board by M. de Beaumarchais!

That gentleman did not extend his jests to matters of money: he was delivering guns to rebels for profit's sake, not freedom's. Let his *Figaro* concern himself with Liberty; his harlequin's sword would, no doubt, be more effective in support of their premature aspiration than the worn-out shooting irons and rusty sabers his creator was working off on his American customers.

Why did the port police of Le Havre, after they had been duly squared, suddenly discover the smuggled goods which they had themselves been so active in helping through? Poor Kalb only found the clue to the riddle when he reached Paris, once more just lieutenant colonel. Sympathy for the men of Boston had been entirely extinguished by the news that General Washington had suffered a crushing defeat. All that was left of the glorious Congress army was a miserable remnant of scarcely three thousand men.

Friends failed with fortune's reverse. Ministers hastened to convey to Lord Stormont the congratulations of Louis XVI on the English troops' success, and Beaumarchais, in order at least to save his confiscated muskets, went to the police and turned informer. Benjamin Franklin, fêted and lionized but the day before, had now to pay cash day by day for the very purchases for his modest household, so low had the credit of the men of Boston fallen.

Now Baron Kalb discovered the value of enthusiasm. As soon as Lafayette learned of Franklin's troubles he announced that he would buy an ocean-going vessel to transport all the supplies and recruited officers to Boston. What was 100,000 francs when the future of mankind was at issue, the first foothold of freedom on the earth was in jeopardy? "A greathearted offer!" said the baron.

Honest Benjamin Franklin felt bound to advise his young friend strongly against making this great sacrifice. Conscientiously he explained to him how serious was his country's situation; any eavesdropper in the next room unacquainted with the two men would have taken Franklin for the administrator of Lafayette's estate, or the younger man as a pushing

shipowner anxious to foist an unseaworthy vessel on a doubt-
ing buyer. But the most artful swindler could have found no
more effective way of confirming Lafayette in his resolution.
He quickly trumped Franklin's honorably played card and
robbed him of the trick.

"If your cause is in such peril as you say I can only be of
the more service to you. I offered my services when your
countrymen were not so gravely in want of them. How much
more must I stand by you now that help is really needed!"

One condition the young marquis made, and to this he
adhered throughout his life, in whatever situation he was
placed. He would not only sail at his own peril on board his
ship, but would serve the cause without payment or return
of any sort. Others were placing their funds in shares in the
East India Company; he would prefer an enterprise which
was to serve all humanity, to bring freedom and a better future
to the peoples. For him this purchase of a sailing vessel was no
sacrifice, no risk, since he was convinced in his heart that the
good cause would win and that there could be no resisting the
march of progress.

Had not the English won their great victory, Lafayette's
negotiations and plans would not long have remained undis-
covered. But Lord Stormont imagined that the rebellion was
over. He had dispersed the greater part of his espionage organization and no longer required every evening a list of the
visitors received by Franklin and Silas Deane. The danger came
now, indeed, from the other side. The French government was
exerting increased watchfulness in order to gain the good will
of England, and this compelled Lafayette to be exceedingly
cautious. He furnished the needed money; others must do the
rest. When the ship was ready to sail a message from Kalb, in
terms agreed upon, was to summon him on board. Until then
his supreme task would be to do everything to divert any suspicion, whether on his family's part or the government's, from
himself; and he acquitted himself of this task with brilliant
success.

He began by feigning sickness and succeeded in obtaining
temporary release from military duties, so evading the risk of
being charged with desertion. Scarcely had he his certificate of
release in his pocket when he joyfully signed the contract

which had long been prepared. The contract was in precisely the same terms as Kalb's, with the one difference that "Major General the Marquis de Lafayette enters the service of the Congress army *without payment.*"

Partly in order to shorten the period of waiting, partly to get out of the way of his father-in-law, Lafayette had recourse to a trick which enabled him to leave Paris and which at the same time gratified his passionate interest in the progress of science. He had long been a freemason (he happened to be a brother of the same lodge as Baron Kalb), and he was so drawn to every new thing that he resolved to test on his own body the efficacy of the new discovery of protective inoculation against smallpox by vaccination.

To his young wife and the Duchesse de Noailles, it seemed purposeless temerity, a sacrilegious tempting of Providence, deliberately to introduce into the blood the germ of a horrible disease. It was no faith in the achievements of men but their unshakable trust in God that kept them from fear; and they shut themselves up for six weeks with the supposedly infectious invalid, until the consequences of his hardihood had passed.

But the necessity for caution delayed the preparations for the expedition; Lord Stormont's spies were still active in every port. When his quarantine was over Lafayette had recourse to a stratagem of which in any other situation he would not have dreamed. Not to escape from imprisonment or to save his own life from danger would he ever depart by a hair's breadth from the straight path of absolute correctness. But in the struggle for Liberty there were no means that the young marquis did not adjudge to be fair. The Duc de Noailles, the ministers, the king, the whole state imagined themselves entitled to put him under constraint. In this miniature struggle as in the great one into which he was plunging, the blame lay with the oppressor!

XII.   THE LITTLE STRATAGEM

THE BROTHER of the Duc de Noailles was French minister at the Court of St James's. How could he be suspected of harboring a nephew who was waiting to sail across the ocean to become a leader of the rebels? He himself had not the slightest suspicion of his nephew and introduced him in the highest quarters, even securing for him an audience with the king, at a gala performance at Covent Garden in honor of Lord Cornwallis. Here the two future antagonists, shortly to meet on American soil, shook hands as at the outset of a sporting contest. How contemptuously the noble lord would have smiled had anyone prophesied that this young French greenhorn would rob him of the laurels with which he was already being crowned here in advance!

In the midst of the pleasures of this stay in London there came at last the impatiently awaited message from Kalb. Lafayette hurried away at once, explaining to his uncle that he had had bad news of his wife's state of health. To give the impression that he would soon be back, he left his servant and his luggage behind. As soon as he reached Paris he burst like a whirlwind into Ségur's bedroom and woke him with the triumphant shout:

"I am off!"

In vain did the Comte de Ségur urge Lafayette at least to make a short farewell visit to his wife. The poor little woman was just expecting her second baby, and Lafayette made this the ground for sparing her the agitation of a last talk with him. He recalled the example of his father, who had also fallen in battle shortly before his son came into the world; and he had fought only for a caprice of the Pompadour, not for the future of humanity. If their hope should be fulfilled and the second child should be a boy, what grander present could the boy's mother wish for him than the glory of a father who had gone to fight for freedom and justice and, if it must be so, had fallen in the fight? With a heavy heart Ségur realized that it was vain to attempt to alter his friend's resolution.

Lafayette tore out of the room in the same wild enthusiasm with which he had entered and jumped into the simple post chaise that had brought him. He could not stop in Paris during the daytime: a single chance meeting and he would arrive not in America but in the Bastille.

What a trial of patience, with this fever in his blood, to have to wait still two more days at the country seat of the Duc de Broglie because the mails for Congress were not yet ready! At last, as night fell on the third day, the expected coach brought the Americans to the entrance of the château. To the general astonishment Silas Deane helped out of it old Benjamin Franklin: the old man would not forgo the task of once more warning the young marquis before he embarked on his adventurous expedition. But the fatherly warnings rebounded helplessly from the impenetrable armor of the young man's confidence.

The outriders' torches were like open wounds in the black body of the night. At each posting station four fresh relay horses awaited the party. So the two "generals" hastened in the jolting carriage to their common goal and their very different destinies. Leaning against one another in sleep, like a father and son, they dreamed of a triumphant return from a glorious campaign.

At the same moment Franklin and Silas Deane, silent and surrounded with cares, were being driven back to Paris. Would not Congress disavow them and repudiate their promises? The name of Noailles conveyed little to the hard-headed farmers across the ocean! Perhaps in their democratic arrogance they would make light of the young marquis, while the French government, at the instance alike of Lord Stormont and the infuriated Duc d'Ayen, might expel the Americans' representatives as vile corrupters?

Anyone able to glance within the two coaches might have imagined the Americans to be the two husbands who had just left wife and children to hurry off to war, and the two Frenchmen to be the successful representatives of America who had just packed off their sensational capture, the son-in-law of a Marshal of France.

XIII. CUI BONO?

ARRIVED AT BORDEAUX, the two major generals had their baggage and equipment placed at once on board the vessel, which her new owner had confidently christened *Victoire*. In the course of the transfer Baron Kalb made a discovery which wrung from him a wry smile. On all the young marquis's trunks, freshly painted around his coronet, was the device *"Cui bono?"* In a world in which nobody had any other aim but to push himself forward at the expense of his fellow men, in which everyone must watch lest he be trampled on by the rest, what would happen to the poor madman who tried to pursue the service of the community?

It looked as though life meant to give a piece of good advice to the young idealist: his first experiences on board the *Victoire* were a lesson in philosophy. On all sides he heard the question on his baggage, "Who gains?" answered "I!"

The shipping firm of Raimbeaux et Cie had sold the vessel to a certain Motier, Chevalier de Chavaniac. On his arrival Lafayette was told, to begin with, that the ship could not sail for three days, as it would take that time to complete with provisions and fresh water.

Lafayette had not only been told that she was ready to sail; to while away the tedium of waiting on the estate of the Duc de Broglie he had written a letter of farewell to his father-in-law and had sent it back by Franklin's coach to Paris. Within three days he could easily be carried off the ship and put in safe custody. The voyage must be begun instantly, at all costs.

"At all costs" was the most congenial of mottoes for the firm of Raimbeaux et Cie, and equally so for the captain of the *Victoire*, who bore the significant name of Leboursier, "the Speculator." The provisioning could easily be completed in a Spanish port, where long formalities would have to be complied with before the orders from Versailles could be given effect. The captain was quite ready to raise anchor; in twenty hours' time they would reach Los Pasajes, the little Spanish port near San Sebastian. Long before the extradition proceedings could begin in Madrid, the *Victoire* would have placed half the ocean behind her.

Unfortunately there had already been too much delay. The capstan was creaking and the first sails were being hoisted when there appeared a courier, in the livery of the Comtes de Coigny, signaling desperately from the wharf.

Lafayette, to the horror of Baron Kalb, had himself rowed ashore. He ran through his friend's express letter and then made for the nearest tavern.

The news was appalling. Lord Stormont and the Duc de Noailles were furious; an order for Lafayette's arrest, signed by the king, was already on its way to Bordeaux; it was feared at Versailles that there would be reprisals on the part of the

English government, which would be unlikely to credit the Court with innocence of this escapade. If he did not want to cut himself off forever from his country, Lafayette must give up his plan and set out at once for Paris. Perhaps all would then blow over.

The fugitive wrote a hasty letter to the Comte de Coigny, begging him to set all his relations to work and to spare neither trouble nor money on his behalf. It might be that the anger of the king and government was only simulated, in order to soothe the English minister. In any case he felt it was safest to await his friend's reply on the other side of the frontier, so that the king and his ministers might be enabled to give up the pursuit as hopeless if their threats were merely a demonstration. He would await Coigny's reply at Los Pasajes.

The messenger was sent back with a full purse to encourage him to go with speed; and then, at last, on March 27, 1777, toward nightfall the coast of France disappeared astern. It was in depression and uneasiness that the twenty-year-old American general watched the coast of France disappear; but the ill-famed swell of the Bay of Biscay was doing its worst, and gave him enough else to think of. The baron was making his third crossing, but he too groaned in his cabin.

The *Victoire* had no sooner cast anchor next day in harbor at Los Pasajes than the two sick men jumped into the jolly boat to get onto firm ground. But envoys from Versailles were waiting on shore—two officers bringing a bundle of letters, some warning, some furiously threatening, and an official letter from the Comte de Maurepas expressly forbidding the expedition, in His Majesty's name.

Enter into open rebellion against his sovereign's order? Impossible! Hard as it was for Baron Kalb, he could do nothing but advise Lafayette to give way, and the young marquis set off with the messengers to return to Paris. Grinding his teeth, the baron conveyed to Captain Leboursier the order to remain in port and await instructions.

The growing rage of Baron Kalb was a great source of amusement to the ten young officers on board. What was there to worry about? These officers, engaged by Silas Deane, were traveling as Lafayette's guests. The wine cellar on board was splendidly stocked, and the feeding was magnificent. Pay commenced from the date of leaving Paris; each day was a day's leave, and San Sebastian was full of pretty women. The baron must be mad if he was really in any hurry to exchange this pleasant interlude for marches through untracked forest, bitten by poisonous insects, and for all the dangers and hardships of a campaign. All save Kalb—with Raimbeaux et Cie at their head—set themselves to profit by the marquis's lavishness, feasting and reveling on deck with the enthusiasm of Penelope's suitors in the house of Ulysses. Below deck glimmered the fresh-painted motto, *"Cui bono?"*

XIV.   YES OR NO?

IN HIS MEMOIRS Lafayette confesses a little shamefacedly that in his fear of not being accepted he made a great display of his rank and powerful relations, in order to impress Silas Deane. Was he not married into the family of the Duc de Noailles, a nephew of a Marshal of France? How sensational the news must be, and what prestige it must bring the cause!

Alas! the sensation was only too great. He found himself suddenly surrounded by a swarm of threats and warnings— and of messages of approval also; he was inundated with letters and messages; in England as in France the newspapers stirred up public opinion, and polemics raged around his escapade.

The most furious of all was his father-in-law. Lafayette's letter of farewell, begun in London and dated from the French Legation, had the effect rather of a challenge than of an apology:

I am delighted to have so splendid an opportunity of gaining advancement! I have pledged my word of honour, and know you well enough to be certain that if I were to break my word I should forfeit your esteem.

It is not so long a voyage. Rich idlers nowadays are proceeding on longer ones every day merely for pleasure, whereas I am serving a good cause, and shall certainly be worthier of your love on my return than at my departure.

The English newspapers were giving Lord Stormont no less bitter pills to swallow. They regarded it as altogether beyond

belief that a young man like the Marquis de Lafayette should
be ready to bring upon himself the wrath of his king and ruin
his whole career; manifestly the French minister was being
fooled, and the alleged fugitive knew perfectly well that in
reality his enterprise had the warmest approval of the French
government.

The most effective method of making an end of these
suspicions was to arrest the fugitive and place him under lock
and key. Louis XVI ordered the immediate dispatch of the
fastest clipper in his fleet to Martinique, conveying an order
for Lafayette's arrest.

Ten years later Lafayette still remembered vividly the storm
he had brought down upon himself. "The letters from my
family," he writes in his *Mémoires,* "were terrible!" Only his
wife, the one most cruelly affected, whom he had left without
a word of farewell and to whom he had not written to explain
what he was doing, had not a word of reproach for him. She
wrote promising to master her grief for the sake of the innocent being to whom she was to give birth, and only begged
her faithless fugitive not to go deliberately in search of danger,
lest his son should grow up, as he himself had done, without
ever having seen his father. The poor little wife knelt with her
mother in the private chapel of the Noailles' mansion, and the
duchess consoled her daughter with all her native tact and
comprehension. They must only pray to God, she said, to bring
Lafayette back safely from the war in America, not to prevent
him from going, for the love the young man felt for his wife
and child would certainly have held him back if his desire to
serve had not been stronger than himself.

The government's prohibition tempted Lafayette to throw
down the glove to "tyranny"; but the fear of being cut off
forever from returning home determined him to go back with
the two officers to Bordeaux.

There it turned out that the king's order of arrest was little
more than an invitation to a pleasure trip. His majesty commanded the Marquis de Lafayette to make at once for Marseilles, there to await the arrival of his family, who were
about to start a tour in Italy; the young officer was assigned
to his father-in-law, the Duc de Noailles, as aide-de-camp.
Then followed royal commands of a more drastic nature: if

the marquis did not at once set out for Marseilles he was to be arrested and brought to Paris.

Lafayette was able to read between the lines of this: the ministers gave him a breathing space. He ostentatiously hired a post chaise for Marseilles, had his baggage loaded on it, came to the gates of Bordeaux, passed the sentry post and announced that he was leaving for Marseilles. But on the way he changed into the coach of the Vicomte de Maurois, who had also been enrolled by Silas Deane, and was overjoyed at being still able to reach the *Victoire* in time. Like the baggage left at the Legation in London, the baggage in the post chaise parted from its owner; the servant in the marquis's livery accompanied it to Marseilles as innocently as the coachman by his side.

At the last moment, at the inn on the Spanish frontier, disaster threatened once more. The viscount's "courier" had spent the night in the stable between the horses. In the morning a maid came out from the hostelry with his breakfast. Sleepily he reached up for it from the straw—without noticing that his wig was awry, not this time of set purpose as in the ruffle with the Comte de Provence.

The maid opened her eyes wide at the sight of the red hair. *Juste ciel,* was that not the noble French officer who only a few days before——!

Fortunately Lafayette had a full purse lying loose in his pocket. Even a Basque peasant girl could understand the language of the louis d'or. So at last the despairing Kalb saw the owner of the *Victoire,* of whom he had begun to give up all hope, climb on board the ship. That same evening, April 17, 1777, the ship left Europe.

XV. ON PASSAGE

THE NEWS that Lafayette had really got away came as a bombshell. Verses in celebration of his exploit, "written to a familiar melody," were sold in Paris at all the street corners; in the theaters allusions to the hero of the day were greeted with thunders of applause.

Lord Stormont and the English newspapers attributed all this enthusiasm simply to Anglophobia, but they were certainly wrong. And no less certainly such ideas as "Liberty," "Democracy," "the sovereignity of the people," had not yet entered the heads of the mass of the French people. But the issue had arisen over the Bill of Rights, the resistance of the colonists had been over questions of stamp duties and taxation—and the simple news that somewhere in a world a people had chased away the hated tax gatherers, the very idea that it might be possible to tear off these leeches, moved the dull apathy of the crowd as the first breath of a distant storm ripples the smooth surface of a lake.

In the aristocratic salons, where "enlightenment" was the latest fashion, the bold move, of which nobody had imagined the red-haired "sleepyhead" capable, remained the one topic of conversation for days. It was not surprising if debt-ridden officers and younger sons of old families, tired of the hopeless monotony of life in a garrison town, were ready to brave the journey across the ocean and to go on active service in the pay of a nation of shopkeepers. But a Marquis de Lafayette—the son-in-law of the Duc de Noailles! There were those who suspected love troubles or secret scandals. But the bold step was none the less appreciated, partly out of hatred for the English, the hereditary enemy, and partly because an awakening public opinion saw in every reverse suffered by absolute governments a promise of better times to come.

Only in the bigoted circles of the provincial nobility, hermetically sealed off from every new idea, where at the name of Voltaire or Diderot people made the sign of the cross, was there indignation. A young Chevalier de Marais wrote to his mother in the provinces:

All Paris is talking of nothing else but the escapade of a young officer who has left his pretty young wife, a niece of Marshal Noailles, with her two children, in order to fight in America on the side of the rebels. He stands well at Versailles and has an income of at least 50,000 crowns, and might have had a splendid life and a fine career at Court if he had not rushed off to help the insurgents in the New World. He is the Marquis de Lafayette.

One can imagine the expression of stony horror on the old lady's face as she wrote her indignant letter in reply:

What new sort of folly is this, my son? I am happy to see that in spite of your youth you recognize and condemn the extravagance of such behaviour. How sorry I am for the poor mother of the young adventurer!

While these conflicting opinions raged round his act, the mountainous waves of the Atlantic saw to Lafayette's due punishment. For weeks the *Victoire* danced and gyrated on the storm-tossed seas, and her thirteen passengers had to be tied into their hammocks to prevent being pitched out and breaking their necks. Not until the end of the third week did the storm calm down and the officers crawl one after another up to the deck.

Instead of joining the eleven young comrades who were his guests on board, Lafayette passed the days alone with Kalb, wrestling with the English language from morning to night. With his determination and conscientiousness he soon overtook his master and continued his study independently, in the intervals of writing a full report of the voyage to the wife he had forsaken.

It was a strange monologue that thus grew day by day as the ship went on towards a far-sunk horizon. Lafayette had no knowledge whether he was the father of a son or of a second daughter, he did not even know whether his young wife had lived through her confinement. Each day's addition to the record had to be written three or four times over, since the English privateers were confiscating all the postbags from America and a single copy would have little chance of getting through. The letter is headed: "Begun on board the *Victoire*, May 30, 1777." No fewer than forty-three days of journeying through storms and suffering horribly from seasickness had spread their thick veil over the memory of his wife's face when the writer began his report!

It is from far away that I am writing to you, my dear heart, and on top of this cruel distance there is the still more dreadful uncertainty as to when I shall be able to have news of you. Still I hope that I may have some soon; among all the other reasons for which I long to arrive in port, none makes me so impatient as this. What fears and anxieties I have, joined to the grief, still so keen, of the separation from all that is most dear to me! How will you have taken my departure? Will you love me less because of it? Will you have forgiven me? Will you have seen that in any case I had to be separated from you, wandering in Italy, and leading an idle life in the midst of the people most opposed to my projects and to my way of thinking?

All these reflections did not prevent me from feeling a frightful sensation in those terrible moments when the ship was taking me away from shore. Your regrets, those of my friends, our little Henriette,—it was all heartbreaking. If you only knew all that I have suffered, the sad days that have passed in fleeing from everything that I love in the world! Shall I have to add to this misfortune that of learning that you do not pardon me? In truth, my heart, I should be in need of pity.

But the feeling that he was to blame fell more and more into the background; the apologist made way for the soldier:

Do not be afraid that I run any real danger in the occupations ahead of me. You know I am going as Major General, and the position of staff officer has always been regarded as a patent of immortality. As for the service in store for me, you will certainly agree yourself, my dear heart, that it will be an altogether different sort from idling and pleasure-going in France! As a defender of the Liberty which I adore, and free myself more than anybody, in coming as a friend to offer my services to this interesting republic, I am bringing nothing but my genuine goodwill, no ambition, no personal interest. In working for my glory I am working for their happiness.

Adieu! it is getting dark and I cannot go on, for I have strictly prohibited any light on board since birds have brought us the promise that we are nearing the coast. If my heart will guide my pen a little I shall need no light to tell you that I love you and shall love you all my life.

XVI. ARRIVAL

BETWEEN THE EMOTION of this tender conclusion and the postscript added on land, Lafayette passed in silence over the only exciting incident of the voyage. All the passengers were already in the rigging looking out for a sight of land when a ship came into view and set her course for the *Victoire*. There could be no thought of defence with nothing but two rusty little cannon; it was merely as a stratagem that Lafayette ordered all on deck on the chance of intimidating the enemy. If the worst came he gave Captain Leboursier the heroic order to send the *Victoire* into the air with all on board rather than let her fall into the hands of the English.

The order was little to the taste of the more commercially

minded captain, but he was saved the necessity of playing any heroic part, for the supposed English blockading ship proved to be an American trading vessel, captured soon afterwards by the English. It had done the *Victoire* the service of diverting attention from her until she had safely run the blockade.

On the morning following this false alarm the coast of America came at last in sight, and toward the evening of the same day, June 15, 1777, the *Victoire* dropped anchor in a small creek of South Carolina, not far from the little town of Charleston. The captain energetically refused to sail up the river without a pilot familiar with the soundings. But his passengers had already been fifty-nine days on board and had no desire at all to pass a sixtieth. After a long wrangle the two "generals," Kalb and Lafayette, were taken ashore in the jolly boat with the two next senior officers.

But South Carolina a century and a half ago was very sparsely inhabited and mostly virgin forest. The sailors rowed on and on upstream without finding a single human habitation. In their innocence the Frenchmen tried to cut their way inland with their little officers' swords; the attempt was quickly abandoned at the cost of one or two broken weapons. Already the inky southern night was falling over the treetops, and the sailors were refusing to go any farther, when at last dark figures were observed running from a sand bank. They were Negro slaves who had been collecting oysters for their masters.

Once more Lafayette's ducats did their duty as the best of all interpreters. The Negroes allowed themselves to be persuaded to conduct these white strangers in their unfamiliar uniforms to their master's summer residence. The sailors spent the night on the boat in midstream; the four officers went with the Negroes through the dark forest.

If Lafayette had not been too intoxicated with joy at being at last on the soil of the Land of Freedom, he might have found food for reflection in the fact that neither money nor persuasion would induce the Negroes to go ahead with their torches as guides. Their experience of Europeans had taught them never to turn their backs on them if they could help it. The four officers had accordingly to stumble on uphill, falling every now and then over stumps of trees, until lights and the barking of dogs indicated that they were nearing their goal.

They were received with bullets whistling past their ears; Baron Kalb had to bring out all his English to induce the inhabitants of the house to stop firing.

The owner of this little summer residence was a Mr Huger, of Charleston, himself a major in the Congress army. He gave the newcomers a cordial welcome and explained the reason of their hot initial reception. The forests were full of German deserters, peasants from Anhalt, Ansbach, Brunswick and the original home country of Baron Kalb. Their princes had been paid in good English guineas to send them out to a death fit for heroes, but they had shirked their part of the contract. They were pushing through the forest in the hope of reaching the coast and finding a ship that would take them home again. If the English caught them, they hanged them. The farmers would have been glad to let them alone, but the poor devils were driven by hunger to rob hen roosts and flocks, and so they were hunted like wild animals by both sides.

But the strangeness of all around him masked for Lafayette such deeper realities as this grim balancing of sheep and hens against human lives. Like a runaway schoolboy revelling in his conquest over distance, he found everything strange and interesting, from the mosquito curtains thrown like a veil over his bed, and the tall palms seen under the blue southern sky from his window, to the dazzling white teeth of the grinning Negro who brought strange fruits to his bedside when he woke up. After he had seen no more than this little summer pavilion and Major Huger's small farm, Lafayette hastened to add this postscript to his long story of the journey:

People here are simple and honest, in every respect worthy of the country that has been sanctified by the noble name of Liberty!

In the afternoon Kalb and Lafayette rode to Charleston on horses lent by Major Huger. The host could only lend native guides to the two other officers; they lost their way, and in the end, disfigured by insect bites and with their uniforms torn beyond recognition, were seized as marauders and placed under lock and key. They spoke a strange language and a stranger English; and the police placed no faith in their story of baggage on its way on board a ship making for Charleston.

While the Marquis de Lafayette and Baron Kalb were being
entertained by the authorities as guests of honor the two
"tramps" sat in prison on bread-and-water diet, until a word
from Lafayette freed his comrades from the suspicion of
having landed without visible means of subsistence.

Before we pursue further the fortunes of the reunited company of officers, let us return to Major Huger's summer residence, where Lafayette was gratefully bidding farewell to his
host. A little American gentleman of five, the major's son,
planted himself inquiringly in front of the mysterious stranger, gazing full of respectful admiration at the gold lace and
golden sword-hilt of this fairy prince who had sprung out of
the ocean in the darkness of the night. It was merely an
automatic courtesy that Lafayette bent down and patted the
boy's blushing cheek; yet this almost unconscious gesture
struck root like a seed of corn in the child's receptive heart.
When he was twenty years older and Lafayette sat helpless in
prison in Olmütz, young Huger, then a student of medicine,
risked his life in a daring rescue of the famous man who once
patted him on the cheek when he was a baby.

Chance? Yes, just chance—for we have no other name for
the good will and the malice of the all-powerful Director whose
mood determines the marionette dance of our earthly existence. But was not the whole of Lafayette's seventy-six years
of life one long chain of circumstances like this, unforeseen
and mocking all calculations? His own rich inheritance, the
possessions of the wife he had married, all the real and personal
estate of the family was swept away by the tornado of the
Revolution, with the single exception of the sums squandered
on the liberation of America! The shrewdest speculators were
beggared, every prudent calculation was made mock of by the
most disordered half century in European history. Only the
money sacrificed, "written off," for the ideal of Liberty proved
a safe capital investment and assured Lafayette an adequate
pension in his last years.

XVII. DREAMS AND AN AWAKENING

THE WELCOME in Charleston exceeded Lafayette's boldest expectations. One of his comrades reported that the marquis had

been fêted like a Marshal of France. The Governor of South Carolina himself hastened back to town from his summer seat in order to preside at the banquet given in honor of the young hero from Versailles. Anyone who was ready to cross the ocean at his own expense and on board his own ship in order to defend the rights of a foreign nation was something of a curiosity in the New World as well as the Old. The governor had difficulty enough in inducing even his own militiamen to follow the colors or to make any material sacrifice for their own country.

The news of his wealth proved of great assistance to Lafayette when he proceeded to the equipment of his "expedition" to Philadelphia. There was astonishing readiness to supply him with vehicles and horses, to press on him all conceivable supplies. It was of great assistance also to the twelve comrades traveling with him, who were his guests as far as the Congress building: on the strength of the pay promised them as from the day of enrollment, and payable on reaching Philadelphia, the young gentlemen had already got rid in Spain of the whole of their modest traveling expenses. Meanwhile Lafayette was robbed with expert skill by Captain Leboursier; the young marquis bought horses and wagons and tents from anywhere and of any quality with unfailing gratitude to his adviser.

Amid all his impatience to get ahead, and all the business of preparation, he did not forget his promise to send full reports to his *"cher cœur"* about the country and the people:

I made the acquaintance of the country life at Major Huger's, and now I am seeing the town life here.

It will be remembered that his stay in the countryside, including a good night's sleep, amounted to about twenty hours! What he has to say about the town life shows hardly more penetration:

People here are as charming as my enthusiasm figured them. Simplicity of manners, readiness to help, obligingness, love of their country and independence of thought are the common characteristics of all the inhabitants. There is no difference between poor and rich. In spite of the enormous landed properties of some people here, I should like to see the man who could estimate people's relative wealth by their behaviour to one another! . . . In America there are no poor at all, not even what we in France should call peasants. Every citizen has at least sufficient to live well, and enjoys the same rights as the richest landowner in the country.

This letter went to Europe, with a substantial parcel of bills to be met, two days after Lafayette left Charleston. Only half a week after his arrival he started his long overland journey, equipped more like the manager of a traveling circus than a future army commander.

One of the participants has painted a humorous picture of the departure of this caravan. It was headed by Lafayette's valet in French hussar's uniform; in a little dogcart sat the two generals, Kalb and Lafayette; the only solidly built coach was occupied by four officers. The best off were the five comrades on horseback, until, one after another, they had to change to coach horses or pack animals that had not been lamed. They were nearly a month on the way, forced as a rule to spend the nights in the open, plagued by mosquitoes through the night and by the unaccustomed heat during the day, and approaching their goal more and more slowly, because at last they had to take it in turn to go on foot, until finally the last of the baggage horses had gone lame.

It is not wonderful that the company grew depressed, with the exception of Lafayette, who was indifferent to all troubles amid his continually growing enthusiasm for the marvels of this justly named New World. How different was everything in this land of freedom from his exploited, impoverished, oppressed France! For a whole month the little caravan had been traversing inhabited and uninhabited regions, and nowhere did a fortress stand threateningly above a valley; nowhere by ford or bridge did servants of a feudal lord claim toll; nowhere were hollow cheeks gray with hunger to be seen, nowhere the dull peasants, living hardly better than animals, who greeted their unfeeling masters with a humility which it used to madden him to witness. No one with his heart in the right place could see hunting and fishing and access to all of nature's wealth the common right of all men, without thinking with blazing indignation of the conditions in the Old World, and above all in France.

The way from Charleston to Philadelphia led through the territory of three states. Everywhere men were free; the product of the work of their hands was not dissipated by idlers, at the card table or in perfumed boudoirs. Every citizen enjoyed the protection of the authorities, whom he himself had set in their place instead of having them imposed upon him by "divine right."

All the promise that Necker and Rousseau had held out for a future as yet nebulous and far off, Lafayette found, in his twentieth year, realized in the New World. The dreams had become everyday realities. For thousands of years in every social structure the lowest stratum had supported the whole burden: the young Marquis de Lafayette and his peers were no more than ornaments on the summit of the roof. In this young continent, still too thinly populated, he found, as in an enchanted realm, a superfluity of forests and fields, counties and kingdoms unpossessed—a wealth of unclaimed possessions and an actual shortage of owners. There were not enough people to gather in the fruits, the gifts of God were rotting in the fields, while in France men were starving!

Carried away by all he had seen, Lafayette arrived in Philadelphia on July 22, 1777, redhot, like an overheated boiler, from the daily stoking he had received with new fuel for his conviction that the protection of this earthly paradise of humanity against the destruction with which it was menaced was a most sacred duty. Like the founder of his line, who had received the Villa Faya with its forests and fields as a marquisate for his services in a holy war, this last male survivor of the line felt himself to be a crusader, in the new, modern, progressive sense. He was out to free his fellow men from the burden of their earthly cross.

Nothing but this fanaticism can explain how it was that Lafayette's *amour propre*, so vulnerable at other times, stood the test of the crushing blow of his reception in Philadelphia. He had hastened there like a pilgrim, and now the perils and labors and obstacles, the sacrifices and struggles of the pilgrimage were forgotten as he stood at last before the Congress building, the very shrine of the wonder-working power that had created all the marvels witnessed on the way. At no other moment of his life would the marquis have put up with the treatment he now received, treatment which all his comrades felt to be a gross offence.

Hastily brushing up their uniforms and repowdering their wigs, and stopping to take no more than the edge off their hunger, the ten officers hurried to join Lafayette, and less than two hours after reaching Philadelphia the party were in the Congress building.

The very first meeting—it cannot be called a reception—threw an ice-cold douche over their happy excitement. A Mr Lovell, president of the Committee for Foreign Affairs, was called out of the Congress hall; in the lobby, without any superfluous courtesies of greeting, he collected the agreements and letters of recommendation prepared by Silas Deane. He performed his office in the surly spirit of a man dealing with troublesome petitioners; and then he dismissed the gentlemen, requesting them to return at the same hour on the following day. Meanwhile Congress would examine their "requests."

Unceremoniously the little group were left standing in the lobby, petrified with amazement. Had they crossed the ocean to be summarily dealt with like lackeys in an anteroom by a puffed-up commoner, whose greeting they would not even have acknowledged in France—officers as they were of noble birth?

But there was still worse to come. Next day at the appointed hour the little troop presented themselves again in the Congress building, with Lafayette and Kalb at their head. Once more they were allowed to wait in the lobby like lackeys. Finally, when Mr Lovell condescended at last to receive these troublesome people, he had the two leaders informed that he was afraid their business had very little chance of success. Under the circumstances they would be best advised to return as soon as they could to Europe.

Fortunately this reply was of such incredible grossness that Lafayette felt there must be some misunderstanding. He suspected, rightly, as it appeared, that Congress had not even taken the trouble to read the documents he had presented. Accordingly he made the modest request of Mr Lovell that he should at least put himself out so much as to read the letters from Silas Deane and Benjamin Franklin and inform the Assembly of their contents.

With that he took his leave and returned to his inn with his exasperated comrades. On reaching it, he addressed this request in writing to Congress:

After the sacrifices that I have made in this cause, I have the right to ask two favours at your hands: the one is, to serve without pay, at my own expense; and the other, that I be allowed to serve at first as a volunteer in the ranks.

This very unusual offer was so utterly in contrast with the covetous and pretentious letters received every day from the many European candidates, that the whole Congress listened in surprise. Franklin's information about the rank and the influence at the French Court of the house of Noailles made an impression on the members, and it was resolved to look more closely into the strange case of this enthusiast, who had expended a large sum in order to be permitted to serve. So, once more, all turned out for the best for Lafayette. He succeeded even in getting the agreement with the one and only Baron Kalb ratified. A messenger rode after the gallant general and fetched him back, at the moment when he had almost escaped the hero's grave that awaited him in the forests of South Carolina.

XVIII. THE STATE OF THE NEW WORLD

THE AMERICAN GOVERNMENT had had its good reasons for the very unfriendly reception of the Frenchmen. At the moment when the small party of officers arrived in Philadelphia the front had come perilously close to Congress. News might come any day from Washington that with his few ill-armed and exhausted troops he was no longer able to withstand General Howe's superior forces, and that the assembly must flee to a remoter city. The full significance of the enemy's approach is best shown by the letter sent by an influential English politician to the two commanders-in-chief, the brothers Admiral Lord Howe and General Sir William Howe:

It will be incumbent upon you to use the powers with which you are intrusted in such a manner that those persons, who shall have shown themselves undeserving of the royal mercy, may not escape that punishment, which is due to their crimes, and which it will be expedient to inflict for the sake of example to futurity.

To consider any question while in such uncomfortable proximity to the gallows is a severe trial of the nerves. The approaching enemy was plentifully supplied with reinforcements, munitions, and foodstuffs, while the resources of Congress were trickling in more and more meagerly, and it had not the power to hasten the dilatory contingents and the agreed supplies of stores from the states it represented. All the states wanted to be free of the English "yoke," but their governments and citizens alike wanted to keep down to the minimum the price of their independence. In strong contrast to Lafayette's sublime idealism, there was much more haggling over grants of recruits and money than enthusiastic emulation in combating tyranny. The new Republic, just like France, was constantly short of money, and the smallest loan would have been more welcome than the proudest procession of fighting cocks from Europe.

Silas Deane was better acquainted than his superiors with the conditions in France, and rightly regarded it as his principal task to promote friendly feeling towards America in Versailles and Paris. Had it not been for the reluctance of Louis XVI to enter into an alliance with rebellious subjects, his ministers, Counts Maurepas and Vergennes, might already have secured French intervention in the war. To gain so powerful an ally, Silas Deane considered the creation of a few dozen or even some hundreds of redundant officers' posts to be a trifling sacrifice. The families of the nobles enrolled strengthened the phalanx of public opinion, and this in turn strengthened the ministers' backbone. Two years later, when France's powerful fleets were protecting the American coast and French landing parties hastening the final decision, the shortsighted grumblers in Congress began to see light!

At the time of Lafayette's arrival, however, Philadelphia was still full of indignation over Silas Deane's inexcusable proceedings. Instead of confining himself to the engagement of the needed engineers, he was sending over shiploads of greedy adventurers and conceited dandies, who looked down with contempt on the "civilians in fancy dress" who made up the American corps of officers. As professional soldiers they regarded General Washington himself as a mere farmer's son "elected" as commander-in-chief by semi-peasants and traders of his own sort. They were doing a good deal in accepting his command, and to regard the militia officers as of substantive rank would have been a denial of the tradition which was the backbone and the justification of their existence.

Congress, tired of the continual complaints about these lordly foreigners, resolved to annul the agreements which Silas Deane had concluded. It made an exception in the special case of the Marquis de Lafayette and approved his commission as major general, as promised, partly out of respect for the money he had sacrificed, partly out of respect for Benjamin Franklin. The rest of the dozen were invited to make themselves scarce. To prevent any recurrence of awkward situations of this sort, the incorrigible Silas Deane was sent a letter recalling him to America.

Imagine the rage of the eleven French officers at the simple repudiation of their contracts by Congress and its cool invitation to them to go back to Europe, as though they had hopped across from the next village! The majority, in expectation of the pay promised them, amounting now to a pretty little sum, had spent their last sou. Now, instead of giving them what was due, they were invited to pay out of their own pockets, their empty pockets, the heavy cost of the return journey. And the ridicule! The ridicule when they returned as failures, chased off like bad servants by a crowd of common shopkeepers!

Kalb, as their senior, put in a protest, and in it he gave free rein to the wrath that moved him. His letter gave Congress food for thought: it would not be wise to let these desperadoes go back to blacken the reputation of America. On the other hand, the general officers in the army, from the least senior to Washington himself, had protested too often and too emphatically against any further enlistment of professional soldiers from Europe to be overridden now. After long deliberation it was resolved to meet the expenses of the return journey out of public funds.

Lafayette was greatly troubled by his comrades' misfortune. He did his utmost for them, but secured no more than the permission to retain the Vicomte de Maurois as his aide-de-camp, at his own expense.

Strange as it may seem, the exception made by this democratic assembly in favor of Lafayette is expressly defended in the minutes of proceedings on the ground of his "illustrious family" and his "high social relations." M. le Marquis de Lafayette, who had come to America to fight against the obsolete notions of aristocratic régimes, was enrolled in the Congress army purely out of regard for his birth. Kalb, the peasant's son, the experienced soldier of fifty-six, who had fought his own way up to lieutenant colonel, would have been rejected, in spite of all his technical ability, by the first democratic assembly in the world if his twenty-year-old protector, of "illustrious family," had not exerted his influence to keep him.

XIX. THE "POSTHUMOUS" FATHER

JUST A YEAR after Providence had brought the Duke of Gloucester to the banqueting table at Metz, Congress summoned General Washington to Philadelphia for a deliberation. At the farewell banquet given by Congress before his return to his headquarters the commander-in-chief met the new Benjamin among his generals.

Washington was deeply displeased by the presence of this general of the age of a lieutenant. Had he not often enough asked that there should be a definite end of the enrollment of European professional officers? His own officers were ill fed, ill equipped, ill paid; if they were deprived even of the normal recognition of promotion, if every adventurer from Europe was held of more account than the men with the most brilliant record in his own camp, how could the supreme commander, surrounded by wronged and exasperated officers, continue to withstand superior forces that were continually increasing?

The members of Congress hastened to show the commander-in-chief the strong recommendations that had come from Franklin and from Silas Deane, and smoothed away his displeasure with the assurance that the general's commission was no more than a political demonstration, a sort of honorary title.

From the very beginning the war for independence had been carried on in confident expectation of French assistance. With the continually changing and inadequately equipped troops it was impossible to withstand the strong English fleet and the regularly dispatched, faultlessly trained reinforcements, and no one without Washington's entire self-abnegation would have consented to remain a general constantly on the run and constantly put off with empty promises. For a year he had had to content himself with surprise attacks and with rearguard skirmishes made at the price of strenuous night marches. If ever he succeeded in cutting off a commissariat column, his soldiers were able for once in a way to eat their fill; but the next transport made good the English loss; they were driving him farther and farther inland, and the very victories of the Americans were trumpeted all over Europe as defeats.

The only things that enabled Washington to persevere in his thankless task were his faith in the justice of his cause and his hope of French intervention. Shortly after Benjamin Franklin reached Versailles he reported a statement made by Louis XVI which could not have sounded more promising. All purchases and transports were to be permitted and even assisted by the French authorities, so long as the English minister to the court of Versailles was unable to prove anything to the French ministers, unable to charge the French government with aiding the rebels.

It was characteristic of Louis XVI that his ministers, the Comte de Maurepas and the Comte de Vergennes, were required to undertake only to read this royal promise to the American representatives and not to hand it to them. If the arrangement came to the ears of the English, His Majesty must be able to deny its existence without the embarrassment of written evidence against him in the Americans' hands!

In view of the king's vacillation, Franklin and Deane in their letters urged that French public opinion should be humored. It would not do at all to let a member of the house of Noailles return with a grievance. Accordingly Washington, consoled with the assurance that the high rank was granted only as a courtesy, decided to invite the baby general to visit his headquarters.

It would be difficult to find two more dissimilar natures than that of the self-contained, authoritarian, secretive Puritan and his French guest, nearly twenty-five years younger than he. Washington was the only son of a rich farmer; at seventeen he became a land surveyor. This choice of profession shows that even as a young man he was drawn to the opportunity of a solitary and reflective life in the still uninhabited territories, away from the turmoil of the towns. The war between France and England for Canada brought him to the assistance of the "mother country." In the course of the seven years' struggle in both hemispheres he attained the rank of a colonel in the British army; he quitted the service as soon as the Peace of Paris made an end of French rule in America.

Placed by the thirteen rebellious states at the head of their combined forces, he supported with really superhuman patience the double task of holding out against the superior English forces and against the inevitable sniping from the thirteen states. The Congress had not the means of enforcing the supply of the army's needs; Washington's so-called army, ill equipped and ill fed, was but an untrained horde which would have disintegrated at once had not its supreme commander shared all its privations. A gulf separated the American, with his ripened knowledge of life and his simple unsentimental devotion to duty, from the exuberance of the young French nobleman, who declaimed the abstract philosophical ideas of Rousseau in the style of the literary salons of Paris, and imagined the calculating, haggling members of Congress to be noble-minded followers of the Savoyard preacher. He must have seemed to General Washington even more callow than he really was. But the keen and experienced glance of the older man soon recognized the nobility of the wine that was fermenting in the younger one; and the officers at headquarters found it easier to forgive the absurdly high rank of the dreamer who was fighting as an unpaid volunteer than the exasperating arrogance of his fellow countrymen who had only come over in order to pocket big pay.

Lafayette's modest and amiable manner also contrasted favorably with the behavior of his predecessors. When Washington showed him the camp and the troops distributed around it he prefaced the inspection with an apology: he was ashamed, he said, to show an officer of the French army his poor, ragged soldiers. Lafayette replied: "I am here, Sir, to learn and not to teach."

Just as the finest, rosiest apples show the mark of the spot on which they have been resting, so Lafayette bore the unhealed scars of the first wounds to his self-esteem suffered in the Epée de Bois and at Court balls. Washington had the psychological insight to realize that the young man's impatience to win public recognition was an outcome not merely of youthful vanity but also of the reaction of the stiff and awkward red-haired Auvergnat to undeserved slights from frivolous scoffers.

Just at the critical period of his life, when the casting was still malleable, still answered to formative pressure, Providence sent the posthumous boy, who had grown up without guidance, a "posthumous" father in Washington, to shape him and to purify the fine metal from the slag of immature ambitions.

XX. THE FIRST TASTE OF "GLORY"

A CENTURY AND A HALF AGO the newspapers were no more particular than they are today in their handling of sensations, and the "hero's" fame in Europe went ahead of his deeds. Lafayette landed in America on June 15, 1777; it took him thirty-seven days to reach Philadelphia; his general's patent bears the date July 31, and on the following evening, August 1, he first made the acquaintance of Washington. That did not prevent the editors of the *Courrier de l'Europe* and the *Gazette d'Amsterdam* from publishing a month earlier full reports of his ceremonial welcome, or even from reporting his first victory before he had set foot in the New World. One newspaper stated that Congress had placed its illustrious guest at the head of a brigade of militia; another that the marquis had equipped six thousand men at his own expense and was carrying on an independent campaign against the English, with success at the first blow.

The occasion for these rumors was the confinement of the Marquise de Lafayette. On July 1 she gave birth to a second daughter, not knowing at that moment where her thoughts could join the baby's father. On July 25, shortly after Lafayette reached Philadelphia, she received the first news of his landing in America, and the little daughter was three months old when he learned of her birth.

If everything had gone as Lafayette wanted, even the newspapers in Europe would never have been prompt enough to prevent their reports from straggling far behind his exploits. In his eagerness he took Washington's invitation, which had been no more than an act of courtesy, for a military order which would be followed at once by the assignment of a command. His impatience to be given an opportunity to distinguish himself is revealed by Washington's despairing appeal to Congress for assistance. Every sentence of the letter betrays the commander-in-chief's embarrassment at the importunity of his young guest:

If I did not misunderstand what you or some other member of Congress said to me, respecting the appointment of the Marquis de Lafayette, he has misconceived the design of his appointment, or Congress did not understand the extent of his views; for certain it is, that I understood him, that he does not conceive his commission as merely honorary, but given with a view to command a division of this army. It is true he has said, that he is young and inexperienced, but at the same time has always accompanied it with a hint, that, so soon as I shall think him fit for the command of a division, he shall be ready to enter upon the duties of it, and in the mean time has offered his service for a smaller command. . . . Let me beseech you then, my good Sir, to give me the sentiments of Congress on this matter. . . . The Marquis is actually in Philadelphia.

This letter happened to be sent off to Philadelphia at a moment when Lafayette was away from headquarters. On the order of Louis XVI the French ministers had written to Franklin to ask him to prevent Congress from enrolling the marquis. But it was impossible to annul Lafayette's nomination without some grave reason, and this fact saved Maurepas and Vergennes from the unpleasant duty of punishing the hero whom all France was acclaiming. Moreover, Vergennes and Maurepas had let plenty of time pass before informing Franklin of the king's request; Franklin took time in his turn, and Congress was able to see that there was no need to take his message seriously. As for the marquis, if he troubled at all about the consequences of his flight from France there was nothing to worry about in so tardy an intervention. He returned in entire tranquillity to headquarters.

Great was Washington's disappointment to find, when his guest came back, that he was still without any knowledge of the purely ornamental character of his rank. The gentlemen of Philadelphia had turned a deaf ear, and instead of taking advantage of the young officer's presence in their midst to explain things to him as Washington had suggested, they contented themselves with writing to Washington to confirm that the nomination of the young general was purely formal. In any case, the two armies would soon go into winter quarters.

Lafayette would thus have had to hold his energies in leash had not the indolent General Howe been replaced by a new opponent, the Lord Cornwallis whom Lafayette had seen fêted as a hero at Covent Garden and had met there. Cornwallis was determined to make an end of the somnolent strategy of Sir William Howe, who had been content with an occasional skirmish. He would not suspend hostilities for the winter without having first achieved a striking success to signalize his assumption of command under Howe. He would capture Philadelphia and have no more of the provocative proximity of the rebel government to the English army.

This renewed energy on the English side brought Lafayette nearer to his baptism of fire. On the day after his return to headquarters the marquis took part, for the first time in his young life, in a council of war. In the uniform, one might almost have said the disguise, of a major general of the Congress army, the young marquis sat silently at the council table, as became his youth. But no power could hold him back when it was unanimously resolved, on Washington's proposal, not to abandon the seat of Congress to the enemy without an attempt at resistance. A lost battle would be less demoralizing to the troops than the eternal retreats, which destroyed all confidence. The resolution was no sooner adopted than Lafayette, no longer concerned either for rank or for command, asked simply to be placed in the front line, and this eagerness to risk his life won him universal forgiveness for his earlier importunities.

The frightened population of Philadelphia saw the town

already in the enemy's hands. To prevent panic, Washington ordered his whole force to march through the streets. The illusion it conveyed of an immense army of defence comforted the timorous members of the public, and the soldiers' pride in the acclamations they received completed the restoration of confidence and enthusiasm at which he aimed. Smartened up and with green foliage in the soldiers' caps, the little army made a procession that took an hour to pass through the long rows of onlookers, with the commander-in-chief and Lafayette at its head. How could the sight of the rich French "count," who had voluntarily abandoned all the magnificence of the Court of Versailles in order to fight for American freedom, fail to make an impression on the crowd, who saw in him the first swallow that heralded the hoped-for armed assistance from France? The scene had been cleverly staged and had its effect on the population. As for Lafayette, for weeks his letters were full of this march through Philadelphia.

But his panegyric of the supreme commander and his human and soldierly virtues reached the poor marquise at the same time as the first news that her husband lay wounded in the little town of Bethlehem. Blind to his peril, when the battle at Brandywine Creek was already lost, and the fate of Philadelphia sealed, Lafayette had tried to stop the flight of the militia troops. The glittering gold braid of his brand-new general's uniform drew upon him the fire of the enemy sharp-shooters, and a bullet penetrated the upper part of his thigh. In the heat of the action he took no notice of it; only when the blood began to fill his riding boot did he allow his comrades to persuade him to dismount. Ambulance men carried him on a stretcher to the village near by, where a few decades later his fellow countryman and friend Comte Dupont de Nemours started the first works of what is now the Bethlehem Steel Company.

The shot had passed through the flesh without touching the bone, but the leg became enormously and painfully swollen, necessitating several weeks' lying in bed. The inaction was a sore trial for Lafayette in his impatience to do great deeds. He sent endless letters to his wife, full of conjugal affection. He made light of his "wound," declaring that he only gave it so pompous a name in order to make himself interesting; and he did his utmost to allay his wife's fears. Each letter he sent in triplicate or quadruplicate:

So as to be read not only by King George of England, whose vessels are capturing all true reports so that the English generals' panegyrics of themselves may obtain credence in Europe.

He writes of Washington:

This honourable man, whose talents and virtues I admire and whom I venerate the more the better I become acquainted with him, has done me the honour to be my intimate friend. When he learned that I had been wounded he sent me his own medical attendant, urging him to treat me with as much care as if I were not only the commander-in-chief's friend but his son.

Without waiting for the complete healing of his wound, he arrived unexpectedly, leaning on a stick and still limping, at Valley Forge, an inhospitable spot in which the American troops, after suffering a fresh defeat at Germantown, were forced to spend the winter amid great privations. Insufficiently clothed even for summer, and precariously protected by tents and rough wooden huts against the inclemency of the weather, officers and men endured in this wild valley the worst period of the whole War of Independence. Washington shared their hardships instead of retiring to his estate: that was a necessary sacrifice in order to keep within limits the discontent in the army. But a foreigner? The sight of the limping marquis, who had voluntarily shed his blood for America and now hurried, before he was really well again, to the snowed-up camp, impatient to expose his life anew in their cause—this sight turned the last remaining envy and uncharitableness into admiration. The letters sent by officers and militiamen alike from Valley Forge to their homes all told the story of Lafayette, this French noble and millionaire, and his astonishing self-abnegation; his name became familiar all over the Union. Less than six months after his landing from the *Victoire*, General Washington's twenty-year-old "friend" had seized hold of the popular imagination, and the foundation had been laid of an unexampled popularity. Never, perhaps, has a foreigner so captured the hearts of an entire nation as this French "hero," scarcely yet arrived at manhood.

Washington's paternal affection was more and more strengthened by his admiration for the young dreamer's bravery. As an unpaid volunteer, Lafayette was entitled to choose the detachment to which he would like to be assigned. As soon as he learned that General Green's brigade was to advance against the enemy he begged Washington to allow him to join the expedition. A new army, formed of English soldiers with grenadiers provided under contract by the Duke of Hesse-Cassel, was pushing southward from Canada to effect a junction with General Howe's troops. It was important for Washington to prevent this if possible. He gave way to his young French friend's importunity and placed him in charge of the small advance guard. Scarcely ten weeks after his wounding, Lafayette with his 300 men came into contact with an advance guard of 350 Hessians. With "true French fury," as the American reports tell, he threw his force against the enemy in the dark. Taken by surprise in the trackless forest, part of the enemy force were cut down, part capitulated.

This little skirmish gained increased significance through the victory won just afterward by General Greene. The whole of the English reinforcements that had landed in Canada, 6,000 men, surrendered with their cannon, muskets and food supplies. This sensational news became known in Europe at the same time as Lafayette's skirmish which had preceded it. In America, from that day, nobody troubled any more about the youth of the brave French major general! At Washington's express request, a resolution of Congress placed the Marquis de Lafayette, "in recognition of the military talents of which he has just given brilliant evidence," in command of a brigade.

Scarcely three months had passed since the commander-in-chief had appealed to Congress for support against the boundless ambition of the young titular general, and now he was bringing his whole influence to bear to help his "guest" to a command. The moment he had in his hands the authority for this, granted in terms most flattering to Lafayette, he left it to his protégé to choose what troops he would like to lead. Lafayette's choice fell on the contingent from the state of Virginia, who with their southern temperament were more closely related to the French than the brave and tenacious but cold and matter-of-fact Puritans of the north. The young general, overjoyed, wrote to his *cher cœur:*

> I have never before seen soldiers so cheerful, so enthusiastic, and so impatient to attack without asking the enemy's strength. My brigade is small, even measured on the small scale of the whole army. The poor soldiers are half-naked, and ill-shod or even without boots; but I am promised cloth from which I shall make them uniforms, and recruits out of whom I shall have to make soldiers.

Thus he had to pay out of his own pocket even for the uniforms of his troops! The states were not eager to risk yet more money for a cause virtually lost, and Lafayette was not the man to let his soldiers go barefoot and only half clothed. Soon his 1,200 Virginians were the best equipped in the militia, and their young general's notes of hand were piling up with banks and merchants. He even met the troops' arrears of pay out of his own pocket.

What wonder that the name of Lafayette enjoyed almost the popularity of that of the commander-in-chief! Everybody forgot the difference in age between the two "friends," who might well have been father and son. At Mount Vernon, Washington's estate, Lafayette was at home as though it were Chavaniac. His wound and his first success were the talk of the New World and the Old alike, and the first day of the new year 1778, in the course of which he attained the age of twenty-one, found him at the summit of a military career and famous, like his great teacher, on both sides of the ocean.

XXI. CONWAY'S CABAL

THERE HAD LONG been back-biting in Congress against the supreme commander, and charges that he showed insufficient enterprise. Washington's wise cautiousness, doubly justified by the superior strength of the enemy and by the demoralization of his troops, was complained of as "irresolution" by his opponents, and they succeeded in launching against the great leader the intrigue which is known in the history of the War of Independence as "Conway's Cabal." One day Washington,

who was well aware of the conspiracy, handed to Lafayette a
letter from Congress, saying with assumed indifference:

If anyone is to be entrusted with this task, I would rather that it
should be you.

It is greatly to Lafayette's credit that not even the subtly
calculated temptation the letter contained could shake for a
moment his loyalty to Washington. The letter ordered him to
proceed at once to Congress, to receive from the head of its
military office detailed instructions concerning an expedition
against Canada which he was to command as its independent
and supreme leader. An expedition against Canada, the territory that had been stolen from France! It was a wily temptation, and the reserve with which Lafayette, with his boundless
ambition, received the order is the more noteworthy. He accepted the commission subject to one proviso: that as leader
of this "independent" expedition, far from the actual theater
of war, he should still remain under Washington's supreme
command. He would gladly assume the responsibility of the
enterprise but was not prepared to be regarded as independent
of the commander-in-chief. It would be unpardonable ingratitude to elude the authority of his instructor, to do anything
that might savor of an attempt to outshine the man to whom
he was so indebted.

His loyalty cost him dearly. For two months he waited at
Albany, sending messenger after messenger with vain appeals
for the promised troops with their winter equipment. The few
men sent to him received neither pay nor provisions and were
kept uselessly exposed to the hardships of the severe winter.
The one thing achieved during the long period of waiting was
an arrangement with chiefs of neighboring Indian tribes who
had been bribed by the English to fight against the Americans.
Some of them were won over by the bounty of the "Great
Kayevla," as they called Lafayette.

Lafayette's letters to Washington were appeals for help:

Your Excellency may judge that I am very distressed by this disappointment. My being appointed to the command of the expedition is known throughout the continent, it will soon be known in

Europe, as I have been desired, by members of Congress, to write to my friends; my being at the head of an army, people will be in great expectations, and what shall I answer? I am afraid it will reflect on my reputation, and I shall be laughed at.

Washington's replies were full of sympathy and solicitude; but words alone could not solace this general without an army. How he had hastened to tell his wife and his friends in Europe of the great task that had been entrusted to him! At the first news of it French officers had come forward from all parts; experienced campaigners like old Baron Kalb waited patiently in readiness to place themselves under the orders of their youngest comrade in arms in order to drive the hereditary enemy out of Canada.

Only at the end of three months did Lafayette realize that he had been duped. He gave expression to his astonishment with touching naïveté: could there be intriguers, men of ill will, men capable of underhand dealings, in the Land of Liberty?

In the end he realized that the Cabal had been trying to exploit his ambition against the great man whom he revered. After that a bombardment of proposals and inquiries rained down on Congress and on the generalissimo: had not General Putnam just been recalled? Was not General Arnold planning a thrust against New York but too ill to carry out the plan at present? He wrote in appealing humility to his friend and mentor:

I would choose to become again only a volunteer, unless Congress offers the means of mending this ugly business by some glorious operation, but I am very far from giving to them the least notice upon that matter. I should be happy if something was proposed to me in that way, but I will never ask, nor even seem desirous, of anything directly from Congress; for you, dear general, I know very well, that you will do everything to procure me the only thing I am ambitious of—glory!

But of what avail could suggestions be, however transparently advanced? The superiority of the English forces was increasing too rapidly to permit any secondary expeditions. There remained nothing for the young general but to return

in the spring to Valley Forge. Conway, the instigator of the
Cabal, had to make a public apology and disappeared from the
scene. Meanwhile Providence and Washington united to help
Lafayette to forget his misfortune. While he was negotiating
with painted Iroquois and Oneida chiefs, Congress learned of
the coming of help of vastly greater importance. The fastest
ship in the French navy brought the Franco-American treaty
whose conclusion marked a turning point in the history of
mankind. It was perhaps for the first time since great states
had existed that a treaty bore the names of signatories of such
unequal birth as His Christian Majesty Louis XVI of France
and the ex-bookseller Benjamin Franklin, a plain man without
predicate or title. A treaty of alliance for defence and offence
had been concluded in the name of a king and in the name of
an assembly of rebel tradesmen!

Between the lines of this agreement there lay the capitulation of the old order before the new. The anointed of heaven
had committed lèse-majesté against himself. The crowned successor of Saint Louis, by promising them loyal assistance at
arms, had recognized common mortals as his equals.

XXII. THE "HERO OF TWO WORLDS"

LAFAYETTE had done his honest share in bringing the alliance
into being—the alliance which had built the bridge to the New
World over the fathomless ocean of prejudice. The news of
France's entry into the war reached him just as he returned
from the Canadian border; and it came to him like a message
from heaven.

The sensation it caused did more than divert the attention
of the world from his misfortune: he was no sooner back at
headquarters than Washington himself applied a plaster to the
wound his protégé had suffered from Conway's Cabal. On May
9, 1778, there was a military parade with fireworks, followed
by a banquet of no fewer than nine courses, with endless
speeches and toasts: to His Christian Majesty of France, to the
chivalrous French nation, to its great poets and thinkers, and
to its bravery, which now offered the surest of guarantees of
American freedom! Less inflammable natures than that of the
young marquis would have been unable to hear such praises of

their country without forgetting all about recent humiliations.

A few days later Washington held a council of war. He had no intention of letting the time that remained before the arrival of the French be passed in inactivity, and the whole of his staff agreed. The first thing necessary was to ascertain the enemy's intentions, and Major General Lafayette was ordered to reconnoiter in the direction of the advance guards around Philadelphia. He was to beware of enemy surprises, and to harass the enemy by sudden raids. Washington himself helped him to choose his division of 2,500 men, with whom he marched out of Valley Forge on May 18, 1778. Two American generals were attached to his division, to serve under this twenty-year-old commander.

When the English generals learned from their spies that the perfidious young French greenhorn, who had obtained an introduction to the English Court as nephew of the French minister, was advancing with a reconnoitering division, it was resolved at once to capture His Impudence. General Sir William Howe put off his departure for England in order to help to hunt this rare bird. All the English generals took part in the game. The new commander-in-chief, Sir Henry Clinton, personally directed the encircling movement, and Admiral Lord Howe voluntarily came in to assist.

But the strategists spread their net in vain. Lafayette had learned from Washington that bravery is not enough for an army commander. He prudently retired in time to escape the trap set for him. What news it would have been for all the newspapers of Europe if the canary who had set out like an eagle to cross the ocean had been brought back in a cage! The failure of the English sportsmen added fresh laurels to the fame of this novice who could defeat the wiles of the best of England's generals.

But Fate exacted her toll for his pride and satisfaction in this success. On his return to headquarters Lafayette found letters awaiting him which told of the death of his elder daughter. He had not yet seen the younger, and his conscience pricked him at the thought that his wife, his "dear heart," had given birth to the two children in his absence and had not even had the comfort and support of his presence at their child's deathbed.

Washington found the means of dispelling some of this sadness. He formed a division of 5,000 picked men from his best regiments and placed Lafayette in command of them. This time it was to be no mere reconnaissance. The new British commander-in-chief, Sir Henry Clinton, conceived his mission very differently from his less energetic predecessor. He evacuated Philadelphia and went along the Delaware River to march on New York. To permit the enemy to move about in the states of the Union as he chose would be an open admission of impotence and would have the worst effect on the new ally. On Washington's advice the council of war resolved to give battle to the enemy at the first opportunity.

Lafayette's task as commander of the advance guard was to harass the enemy and to draw them across the front of Washington's army. But this time his star had paled; then came a period of disappointments. To begin with, General Lee, Washington's deputy and so the second officer in the American army, refused to be placed under Lafayette's orders. He had been born in England and had spent his earliest years there; he was a Tory at heart and secretly stood less in fear of American defeat than of American victory. On the strength of his rank he protested against the allocation of troops that had given the young Frenchman the pick of the army; he claimed half of the corps for himself, with the command of the whole.

What did it avail if after the loss of the battle of Monmouth Lee was court-martialed and deprived of his rank? At the eleventh hour Washington had come up and had stopped the retreat of his troops, but the English remained in possession of the field of battle; and Lafayette saw himself cheated of glory, like a child who has lost a butterfly already almost netted.

His discontent was further increased with the coming of France into the war. He was continually asking himself whether the rank and reputation he had won in America would not serve him better in his own country. He sent off letters in all directions in his fear that others might rob him of the leadership of a direct attack on England.

This entry of France into the war constituted a complete justification of the "deserter." The Duc d'Ayen-Noailles, who at first would gladly have sent his son-in-law to the Bastille, was now delighted with the intelligent foresight the boy had shown in divining His Majesty's intentions. He was full of anxiety that Lafayette should not "prematurely" return to France, of tender concern lest he should abandon too soon the position he had won.

The young marquis's own feelings were just the opposite of this. As soon as Admiral d'Estaing's fleet appeared in the estuary of the Delaware, Lafayette's French heart beat proudly under his American uniform. He might have been destined to be the link uniting the two nations, but unconsciously he became their buffer. The enthusiasm that had driven him over the ocean evaporated in the face of the inevitable differences born of collaboration on land and sea between two nations. He thought less and less of his high mission of installing a home for Liberty on the earth. Why fight another nation's battles when he could be fighting for the glory of France?

XXIII. DISAPPOINTMENT AND RETURN

ADMIRAL CHARLES HENRI THÉODAT, Comte d'Estaing, was an Auvergnat like Lafayette. The two families were, indeed, related by some sort of cousinship, like the whole of the old nobility of their poor and infertile province. The admiral was a capable sailor who gave loyal and disinterested service to his royal master. He was unconcerned with the Americans' political aims, and the conceptions of Freedom and Democracy which had lured his young relative across the ocean were quite foreign to him. He left Toulon harbor on April 13, 1778, with a strong fleet and some thousands of troops, ostensibly to relieve the garrison of Martinique. The real purpose of the voyage was known to him alone. The commanding officers of the units of his fleet had received autographed instructions signed by the king and placed under quintuple seals, which they were not to open until the order was signaled from the admiral's ship.

At sea, three days after sailing, the king's message was read to officers and crews: France was entering the war on the side of the "men of Boston." The strictest secrecy had been observed in order to assure the success of the expedition. France meant at last to have a reckoning with her hereditary enemy and to avenge all the losses and humiliations of the two last dictated treaties. The news was received with enthusiasm on board all the ships of the fleet.

But a stowaway had crept on board the admiral's ship—Misfortune! Never, perhaps, had a warlike enterprise, begun under such good omens, been so obstinately pursued by ill fortune as this first French expedition to the United States. All the forces of nature seemed to have conspired to illustrate by the example of the Comte d'Estaing the impotence of the will of man. The passage across was itself a regular Odyssey. Instead of the usual three to four weeks, the ships pitched and tossed on the raging ocean for nearly three months—eighty-five days. The two months lost upset all the military calculations. When the fleet arrived, Philadelphia had already been long evacuated, and the French fleet appeared in the estuary of the Delaware to capture an English fleet which was already anchored off New York in the sheltered upper reaches of the estuary of the Hudson. The poor Comte d'Estaing could do no more than land the first French minister, whom Congress received with all due ceremony. The fleet then took to sea again and sailed northward to blockade New York.

All the experts of his day were loud in praise of the seamanship of Admiral Comte d'Estaing in bringing his ships safely through their three months' ordeal without the loss of a vessel or of a single human life. But those who have Fortune's ill will against them may accomplish prodigies of heroism and do their duty a thousand times over, and still the stigma of unsuccess will cling to them.

The admiral's fleet anchored off Sandy Hook. It was impossible for the enemy to escape past him. He held victory in his hand—but his ships drew too much water. Even the much smaller English units had had to land their guns one by one in order to lessen their draft and so be able to enter the Hudson. The admiral offered 150,000 francs to any pilot who would bring his vessels within range of the English fleet—in vain: ultimately he had to accept defeat at the hands of Destiny. After eleven days had been uselessly frittered away, he gave up the attempt to capture New York.

It might seem surprising that a fortnight should pass after the arrival of the French fleet without the young Marquis de Lafayette, so ardent and precipitate on much smaller occasions, taking the opportunity to go on board and meet his kinsman. But a week passed before he learned of the fleet's arrival; and then his tact forbade him to go uninvited and place the admiral in the embarrassing situation of receiving an officer for whose arrest a warrant was out. Officially that sword of Damocles was still suspended above his head; in spite of the fame he had won since his flight there had been no pardon. Consequently he contented himself at first with writing his cousin a letter of welcome a yard long.

Destiny loves playing with coincidences. This first letter to the Comte d'Estaing, written from camp at Paramus, was dated *"Ce quatorze Juillet"*—July 14th, the date that was later to be the zenith of Lafayette's career and was to become the national festival of France.

Every line of this lengthy letter expressed the young man's scarcely controlled impatience to meet the admiral. It is an excited collection of military news, personal ambitions, plans, hopes, fears, and official communications from Washington, thrown together pell-mell like the clothes frantically stuffed into a bag by a fugitive from persecution.

Consider the high hopes which all America set on the aid of this mighty ally! If the French fleet had captured Lord Howe in Delaware Bay the war would at once have been lost for England! The disappointment was equally acute for both of the allies.

"Can you believe it?" wrote Lafayette, in the utmost indignation, in a letter to D'Estaing. "I was summoned to a council where a protest was made against a measure taken by a French fleet!"

The Americans went a good deal farther. But what matters in judging Lafayette's attitude is not so much to discover the truth in regard to these accusations as to understand the conduct of the Americans. Admiral d'Estaing had defeated Lord Howe's fleet and landed French infantry to attack Newport as soon as his ships were repaired in Boston. It was not his fault that his ships were once more dispersed by a storm and that he was unable to appear off Newport at the prearranged time; it is not surprising that he was indignant when he found the American camp broken up. On the other hand, it is possible to sympathize with the American officers' irritation at the

romantic way in which the French made war. According to
the reports to Congress, the French commanders "talked like
women disputing precedence in a country dance," contesting
every place for the attack, because the honor of their flag demanded that they, not their ally, should occupy the most
dangerous posts.

On the whole the practical result of this great expedition,
embarked on at such enormous cost, amounted to nothing.
But the poor Comte d'Estaing had never been defeated by the
enemy, though continually by the elements, and was quite
unjustly accused. He was so upset that in the end he offered
to renounce his rank and to serve on shore as a simple militia-
man in General Sullivan's forces, in order to prove to his de-
tractors that he was entirely uninfluenced by personal motives
or vanity.

Imagine the situation of the young Marquis de Lafayette,
caught as intermediary between these contending parties, and
torn between his conflicting allegiances as American officer and
French nobleman! In vain did Washington do his best. With
the most honorable impartiality he defended Admiral
d'Estaing's correct attitude against the furious attacks from
his own subordinates. Congress, at all events, expressed
America's gratitude to the parting admiral in the most
generous terms. It also unanimously resolved to express in
writing to Major General Lafayette its appreciation of the services he had rendered as liaison officer. But the fires of his enthusiasm were extinguished, and it was remarkable that amid
his feelings of almost intolerable ill usage this volunteer officer,
who was at liberty to retire from service at any moment, was
able to see the French fleet set sail without giving way to his
nostalgia and going as well. "If you undertake an attack
on England and land troops and I am not there with you, I
shall hang myself!"—so Lafayette wrote in his letter of farewell to the Comte d'Estaing.

The extent to which his national feeling had been roused is
shown by his disregard even of Washington's paternal advice.
Lord Carlisle had opened negotiations with Congress on be-
half of the King of England, and his lordship described the
French attack without a declaration of war as "perfidy."
Lafayette at once asked Washington whether he should chal-

lenge Carlisle to a duel. Without waiting for the prompt reply, he was so indiscreet as to send to the English an intimation that he would "chastise the noble lord in the presence of the English and American armies." As Washington predicted in his letter, this "gesture of an out-of-date chivalry" only aroused the derision of the English.

Buffeted to and fro for weeks, entrusted by both sides with the conveyance of unpleasant messages, Lafayette was so thoroughly disillusioned that he wrote:

> I am beginning to realize that in my blind enthusiasm I have made a ghastly mistake in leaving everything and rushing to America.

Why, then, did he still remain months longer? Here, as always, he was ruled by his unconquerable ambition. He was unwilling to leave the country so long as he risked missing an opportunity of military distinction. But all his efforts to obtain authority from Washington, or from Congress, to carry out the winter attack on Canada which had been abandoned the year before, were without avail. The ministers in Versailles were equally deaf to every proposal for an attack on the British West Indies, and Count Bouillé, Lafayette's cousin, showed not the slightest inclination to lend the young marquis his Martinique garrison for independent operations. So the autumn of 1778 passed, and his twenty-first birthday. After a regretful farewell to Washington at Mount Vernon, Lafayette set out for Boston to sail home to France.

But now, after the long series of bickerings and the tension and physical strain of these months, he broke down. On the way to the coast he developed a high fever and lay for weeks between life and death.

As soon as the news reached Mount Vernon, Washington hurried to his friend's bedside and stayed anxiously watching over him during his delirium. These long hours of disquiet were perhaps the source of the tender and almost melancholy affection for Lafayette which thereafter filled the old man's heart, in spite of all differences of opinion, to his last day.

The sick man nearly succumbed to a hemorrhage, but it saved his life. He passed his convalescence on Washington's estate, and then, completely restored to health, went to Philadelphia and at once presented to Congress a request for leave to visit Europe. In Philadelphia, fêted and sought after, he had a foretaste of the joys that awaited him in his mother country. He had left surreptitiously like an adventurous schoolboy: after less than two years he was returning home as a successful general and a famous fighter for freedom.

The French minister in America, Gérard de Rayneval, wrote to the Comte de Vergennes at Versailles:

I must not conclude this long report [on the regrettable differences between Admiral d'Estaing and General Sullivan] without rendering due justice to the discernment and ability shown by M. le Marquis de Lafayette in these discussions. He used the authority with which his friendships and his services invested him here to give the most salutary advice. It is my duty to state that his conduct, alike prudent, courageous and amiable, has made him the idol of Congress, the army, and the whole population. His military abilities are rated very highly in this country. You know how little inclined I am to flattery, but I should be committing an injustice if I did not convey to you the admiration felt for him by everybody here.

General Washington wrote to Benjamin Franklin, the accredited minister of the United States in France:

The generous motives, which first induced him to cross the Atlantic, the tribute which he payed to gallantry at the Brandywine, his success in Jersey before he had recovered from his wounds, . . . his services against British grenadiers and against Rhode Island; are such proofs of his zeal, military ardor, and talents, as have endeared him to America, and must greatly recommend him to his Prince.

Coming with so many titles to claim your esteem, it were needless for any other purpose, than to indulge my own feelings to add, that I have a very particular friendship for him, and that whatever services you may have it in your power to render him, will confer an obligation on, . . .

The President of Congress sent Lafayette the approval of the leave requested, the period to be for the general himself to determine, and sent, in addition to his own most flattering expressions of gratitude, copies of two resolutions unanimously passed by the representatives of the thirteen states in public session, and minuted as follows:

Resolved,
That the president will write a letter to the marquis de La Fayette returning him the thanks of Congress, for that distinterested zeal, which led him to America, and for the services he hath rendered to the United States by the exertion of his courage and abilities on many signal occasions.
Resolved,
That the minister plenipotentiary of the United States of America at the Court of Versailles be directed to cause an elegant sword, with proper devices, to be made and presented, in the name of the United States, to the marquis de La Fayette.

The Congress also unanimously passed this resolution:

Resolved,
That there be written to His Majesty the King of France the following letter, in order to recommend to him the Marquis de Lafayette: To our great, faithful, and beloved friend and ally
      LOUIS THE SIXTEENTH, King of France and Navarre.
The Marquis de Lafayette having obtained our leave to return to his native country, we could not suffer him to depart without testifying our deep sense of his zeal, courage, and attachment. We have advanced him to the rank of major general in our armies, which, as well by his prudent as spirited conduct, he has manifestly merited. We recommend this young nobleman to your majesty's notice, as one whom we know to be wise in council, gallant in the field, and patient under the hardships of war. His devotion to his sovereign has led him in all things to demean himself as an American, acquiring thereby the confidence of these United States, your good and faithful friends and allies, and the affection of their citizens. We pray God to keep your majesty in his holy protection.
Done at Philadelphia, the 22nd day of October, 1788, by the congress of the United States of North America, your good friends and allies.
                                        HENRY LAURENS,
                                                President.

This communication from an assembly of shopkeepers, farmers and lawyers, addressed to the King of France, is swarming with repetitions of the word "friend," like bacilli in infected blood. So it smuggled into the luggage of the Marquis de Lafayette the germ of the new plague which was to degrade the anointed rulers "by divine right" to the rank of simple mortals, and to accord to every citizen, without distinction of birth or title, the right to rule if his compatriots placed their trust in him!

Rarely in all history has a young man of twenty-one years looked forward to returning to his country with such recommendations and achievements to his credit. Yet Lafayette allowed two more months to pass, still hoping that in the end Congress might entrust him with the leadership of an invasion of Canada! Christmas had passed before a definite and unambiguous rejection of the plan reached him in Boston.

After this nothing could keep him any longer in America. He was burning to leave for Europe now that on this side of the ocean there were no more laurels to be plucked, while on the other side there was war between France and England, with the opportunity of brilliant deeds at arms! He agitated for his departure with an impatience almost amounting to discourtesy. Congress once more asked him to work for the interests of the United States, and also gave him an official communication to old Benjamin Franklin, instructing Franklin as minister to consult the young Marquis de Lafayette in all negotiations with the government of its royal ally. Then one of the fastest sailing vessels of the American navy was ordered to Boston, and the illustrious guest who had come uninvited to America in his *Victoire* went on board a warship, christened *Alliance* in his own honor and France's, for his homeward journey.

On January 11, 1779, just before the ship weighed anchor, Lafayette added a last sentence to his letter of farewell to Washington:

Farewell, my dear general: I hope your French friend will ever be dear to you; I hope I shall soon see you again, and tell you myself with what emotion I now leave the coast you inhabit, and with what affection and respect I am for ever, my dear general, your respectful and sincere Friend, etc.

Like all officers going home, Lafayette took with him a whole mail entrusted to him by his brother officers. Kalb, serving for pay, could not leave when he liked, and gloomily watched from the shore as the sails of the *Alliance* took the wind. When the marquis returned a year later to America, Kalb was already lying in his grave in the virgin forest of the south. He had died a hero's death, covered with wounds, beaten by the same Cornwallis who later was to surrender to Lafayette. Fate took a cruel revenge on the baron and all his race for his forged patent of nobility. His two sons, brought up as aristocrats, emigrated at the outbreak of the Revolution. One died fighting the Republic in the ranks of the émigré nobles. The other's death had not even that dignity. He discovered somehow that he was neither of noble origin nor French and hurried to Paris to demand, as a simple plebeian, the return of his father's confiscated property. But the revolutionary tribunal refused to accept the German identity papers he produced, and the "aristocrat" "Baron Kalb" joined a tumbrel-load of his peers and was guillotined as a *"ci-devant."*

Only the baron's daughter remained alive, but she lived to endure wretched poverty, for she was never able to secure her American heritage. Congress recognized her claims to be just if she could prove them. She was entitled to the arrears of her father's pay, and to the national gratuity due to the general. But in the absence of documents she could obtain nothing: her only inheritance was the misfortune that had dogged her family.

Yet when he left Boston harbor the young Marquis de Lafayette was much nearer to death than the sexagenarian Kalb who had remained behind. All the passengers on board the *Alliance* were in mortal peril, from which only a chance saved them.

Lafayette had been in too great haste to get away. There had not been time to assemble a reliable crew. It was against the principles of this fighter for freedom to resort to the customary press gang, and the only remaining expedient was to man the ship with English sailors who had been taken prisoner in the war, with a few American seamen as officers. The crew were little attracted by the prospect of returning to prison in France, and much more by the reward paid by the English government for every captured enemy ship. They loaded cannon by night in readiness to shoot down the officers as soon

as the coast of Europe came into sight. Then they would throw
the corpses overboard and make for the nearest English port.

One hour before the signal was to be given, one of the
American sailors, who had joined the mutineers, repented, and
warned Lafayette. The rest were overpowered, and on February 6, 1779, nearly two years after the *Victoire's* secret departure, the *Alliance* anchored in Brest harbor.

Two days later Lafayette took coach to Versailles, where he
presented himself before the minister, the Comte de Vergennes, whose warrant had pursued him two years before.

This haste to go to Court even before seeing his wife and
child led the newspapers into retailing all sorts of innuendoes
about the marquis. His incursion with naked sword into the
Comte de Ségur's room at night was recalled, and it was suggested that the hero was now hurrying to receive his reward
from his mistress.

There is no denying that throughout his life the search for
conquests of gallantry was a component of Lafayette's inordi-
nate ambition. The red-haired young marquis had not the
exterior of a breaker of hearts, and as a dancer and a drawing-
room lion he had had no success at all, but as a "hero" he was
all-conquering; it was well known that even the demure
beauty for whom the life of his best friend had not seemed
to him too high a price to pay was altogether kindly disposed
towards him on his return.

Louis XVI received his insubordinate officer with a gracious
smile and condemned him to a week's domiciliary arrest, to be
passed in the Noailles mansion with his wife and child. Even
the queen, who once had given up the attempt to dance with
her awkward partner, exclaiming, "No! it is impossible," took
the first opportunity after the "domiciliary arrest" was over
to open the Court ball with the *"héros des deux mondes."* Admired, sought after, spoiled by the women, this young man of
twenty-one was fêted like a victorious commander. The bourgeoisie and the common people saw in him the hero who had
shed his blood for their liberation, and had preferred the perils
and hardships of war in the inhospitable virgin forest to the
drone's life of a fawning courtier at Versailles. One evening
it became known that the Marquis de Lafayette and his wife
were to be present at the first night of a new drama at the

Comédie Française. In the midst of the play the most popular actress in the royal troupe advanced to the footlights, held out a laurel wreath in the direction of his box and declaimed a few neat Alexandrines added for the occasion.

How intoxicating it must have been for this supremely ambitious young man to be called again and again to the front of his box to receive the never ending applause of that distinguished audience! The day came when a discreet hint was actually conveyed to him from the highest quarter to restrict his appearances in public to a minimum, because his enormous popularity was unduly diverting public attention from the princes of the blood royal!

Behind these innocent displays of joy, and as yet masked by them, there flickered and flashed already the distant lightnings of the dangerous problem which was to convulse the future: the issue between personal merit and birth. Destiny was preparing for the Marquis de Lafayette, without his knowledge or desire, the rôle it had assigned him of idol of the people and upsetter of thrones.

XXIV. A YEAR AT HOME

LAFAYETTE'S RECEPTION at Court had surpassed his wildest hopes. But he had come ashore in France in the uniform of a French captain, not an American general. Here he was not "on leave" but discharged indefinitely, and now he sought for an independent command in his own country, after his three months of vain endeavor at Boston. Thanks to the influence of the queen herself, he was appointed colonel; and he was able to buy for 80,000 francs the command of a regiment of the king's Dragoons.

But for this general who had commanded brigades of four to five thousand men, what was an ornamental post of regimental commander? The hero of Washington's general staff had not returned to his own country merely to rest on his laurels and direct parades! During his year in France his plans and proposals and memoranda piled up mountainously on the desk of his patron, the old Comte de Vergennes.

In order to get round the obstacle of financial stringency with which he was constantly met, he first proposed to work in collaboration with the famous Paul Jones, a mixture of adventurer, pirate, and naval commander, a man of remarkable bravery but doubtful reputation. He pursued this Leatherstocking idea with the utmost energy and with entire seriousness, enlisting the help of Sartines, minister of police, in discovering the captain's haunt. The Comte de Vergennes had to promise him the leadership of a more important expedition in order to induce him to abandon this unduly adventurous project.

This more important expedition was itself Lafayette's idea. He proposed to exploit the discontent of the Irish to launch a revolution, with the aid of an expeditionary force of a thousand men. Other negotiations were carried on, with Baron de Staël, the Swedish minister, who was later to be made famous by his marriage with Jacques Necker's daughter. The negotiations were concerned with the chartering of some Swedish warships for service with the United States, and the correspondence concerning this plan produced the following offer from Lafayette to the minister:

The ships would enter our ports under the Swedish flag and would hoist the American flag on sailing; France would not come into the matter in any way. The only question would be whether France would undertake financial liability under the charter party and give assistance in completing with stores. Even this expenditure would only fall on the state in so far as the amount of the guarantee might exceed the total amount of my private fortune.

We must not run ahead of events, but it is only just to give Lafayette, who at a later date was the subject of so much calumny, credit for this bold and generous offer. We shall see that he was unable to understand that poverty is the worst sort of slavery, and that the problem of freedom is an economic one. But the infatuation of this man who was ready to sacrifice the whole of his wealth must be placed in an entirely different category from the moral indignation of those feudal lords and ecclesiastical princes who fought so furiously to maintain their own privileges and revenues, regarding every attempt to shake off the crushing burden of poverty as the worst of all crimes, to be suppressed with the gallows and the ax.

For the moment Lafayette did not lose his millions; but his escape was not of his own contriving. Benjamin Franklin made no secret to him of the threatened financial collapse of the United States. As in all countries and at all times, the Americans were readier to sacrifice their lives than their money; and their distrust of their own bank notes so destroyed their credit in Europe that with all his efforts Lafayette was unable to secure any loan for his friends. France's exchequer was already seriously depleted, and was being vigilantly defended by old Jacques Necker, who, though himself full of enthusiasm for the Americans' democratic ideal, felt bound, as the minister responsible for the conduct of the French finances, to prevent any large expenditure in support of France's ally. If he was to banish the specter of state bankruptcy, the crushing burden of debt must not be increased through either economic or military assistance to America. "For what concerns the present situation and the designs of our ministry, I will only speak to your excellency about that great article: money. It gave me much trouble, and I insisted upon it so much, that the director of finances looks upon me as a devil!"—so Lafayette wrote to Washington; and he certainly was not exaggerating, for in all his reports Franklin himself attested that the Marquis de Lafayette was fighting for the interests of the country of his adoption with all the zeal of a native-born American.

Lafayette was fortunate in having as his patron so old and experienced a minister as the Comte de Vergennes. Instead of proposing petty raids, the count advocated a large-scale enterprise which would hold out the prospect of big profits to army contractors, and of decorations and important missions to generals and diplomats. The more interests were engaged in the enterprise, the better would be the prospect of breaking down the resistance of the minister of finance. Accordingly the effort was made to win over the Spanish minister, the Conde Florida Blanca, to the idea of a joint expedition under the protection of the French and Spanish fleets.

With this division of responsibility, Louis XVI also was less afraid of the enterprise, and after the usual diplomatic delays there emerged at last the definite plan of a combined attack on England, now that she was denuded of troops.

No sooner did the first news of this reach Lafayette than

he began to bombard the Comte de Vergennes with questions,
demands and exhortations:

Everybody is talking of an impending expedition, and I find my
worst apprehensions confirmed—still no definite summons! I should
not be showing due candour if I failed to say that my blood is boiling
in my veins. In my imagination I see myself penetrating into England
at the head of an independent advance column of grenadiers, dragoons, and light infantrymen. Perhaps you will think me too hot-
headed, but please do not forget how I have been spoilt for two years
with high commands. My confidence in my abilities and the flattering
reception accorded to me by my country make it incumbent upon
me . . .

And so on. Soon Lafayette appeared personally at Court to
lay siege to ministers and to all his influential friends. He
threatened that he would buy a vessel from the East India
Company and work in association with Captain Jones rather
than let his fame be tarnished by accepting a subordinate command. To get rid of this importunate petitioner it was decided
at Versailles to send the young colonel to Le Havre as deputy
quartermaster general, to supervise the equipment of the expeditionary force.

Just at this moment of discontent, as though sent by Providence, there appeared at Le Havre Benjamin Franklin's grandson, to deliver to the "deputy quartermaster general" the
sword of honor promised by Congress. On its golden hilt were
reliefs showing the scene of his wounding at the Brandywine,
and other heroic incidents, executed by a master hand.

The preparations were dragging on in such a manner as to
make the realization of the expedition more and more doubtful, and with the growing doubt the golden hilt of the sword
of honor glittered more and more temptingly. Lafayette began to long for the country of his triumphs.

Both Congress and his friend Washington had impressed
upon him that in view of the differences in temperament between the two nations it was not desired to repeat the experiment of a French expedition which had so thoroughly failed.
Lafayette, however, now went deliberately against his instructions. He urged on the Comte de Vergennes a plan for dis-
patching to America a small expeditionary corps of at most

three to four thousand men. Too honest to dissimulate his motives, he revealed in his letters, with charming simplicity, the "secret" ambition that consumed him:

If the command of the expedition were entrusted to me, you need have no anxieties at all, M. le Comte, for I am too well known to the Americans to inspire them with any doubts. If some other leader were appointed it would be necessary to take steps to avert any undesirable affect on American opinion. It would be inconceivable to the Americans that anyone but myself should be entrusted with the leadership, so that in that event it would be necessary for me to go over in advance and broadcast the explanation that it had been my own preference to command a brigade of the militia as an American major general.

It might have been supposed that there was nothing more to be said on that subject, but Lafayette quickly followed up his letter with a personal visit in order to urge his new plan. He continually emphasized that there need be no repetition of an expedition on a grand scale, no strong escort of warships, and no great expense.

To help the ally in his difficulties at no great sacrifice—how attractive a prospect! The plan might have tempted the king's ministers, and especially Louis XVI himself; unfortunately there was equal unanimity in hesitating to appoint an officer of barely twenty-two to command the expedition. That might be possible in the improvised army of an infant nation of shopkeepers, but not in France!

Even before the devastating knowledge of this came to Lafayette, he was pressing for a recall to America, scenting the coming trouble. His hints multiplied themselves in his active correspondence with Washington. Could the general induce Congress officially to request Versailles to set him free to resume his service as an American major general?

Nothing could make me so delighted as the happiness of finishing the war under your orders. That, I think, if asked by you, will be granted to congress and your excellency.

There was not the slightest desire in France to stand in the way of a glorious career for the young marquis in the American backwoods. On the contrary, the idea was welcomed as a means of softening the blow to the boy—for the leadership of the expedition was entrusted to General Rochambeau. The Comte de Rochambeau was thirty years older than Lafayette, and had won distinction by his bravery in the Seven Years' War; his appointment added to the prestige of the enterprise. Only a small expedition was being sent, and the value of the assistance rendered would have seemed still less if the command had been entrusted to a child.

"M. le Marquis de Lafayette is returning to America to resume his service as major general with our allies," wrote the Comte de Vergennes dryly to his colleagues in the ministry; but to please public opinion, and still more for Lafayette's own sake, his seconding was given the color of an honorable mission. A frigate of the royal navy, the *Hermione,* received from Louis XVI the order to hold herself in readiness in the port of La Rochelle to take her orders from the marquis. The French nobleman in the uniform of an American general was to sail on board a French warship, in the service of the French and American governments and as the friend of General Washington, to convey in the name of His Most Christian Majesty the news of the expedition, and to make all necessary preparations for the landing of the troops and for their commissariat.

Lafayette had landed at Le Havre on February 6, 1779; he left La Rochelle on March 13, 1780, to return to America. During the year in his homeland he had been unable to add to the number of his deeds at arms so much as a single skirmish at the head of French troops. He had come home in the hope of gaining new laurels; now he was returning ruefully to Washington, who was able to show a proper appreciation of his abilities without troubling about his youthfulness.

But if the year had been lost in a military sense, it had not been lost for his family, whose head was not this time exposing himself to the perils of war without the assurance of a successor. On December 24, 1779, Mme de Lafayette presented to her husband as a Christmas gift the long-hoped-for son and heir. On Christmas Day the boy was christened—Georges Washington. He was to prove a worthy godson of the great American. This boy was the only member of his family who escaped hardship and imprisonment in the Revolution. He was taken across the ocean by his clerical tutor and lived peacefully in the childless home of old George Washington and his wife, inhaling and assimilating the free atmosphere of America under the roof of his famous godfather.

When, years later, he returned home, he had acquired a thoroughly American indifference to external honors. He called himself simply Georges Washington de Lafayette; and he continued to play in his father's life the part his godfather had once played. As the silent companion of his father's eventful career, he shared all its dangers, demanding nothing for himself, as though he were no more than the shade of Washington watching over the marquis. He was himself growing old when the great Lafayette died, and continued thereafter to serve the memory of his famous father. With the devotion of a faithful servant he collected and ordered all his father's records, his speeches and letters and documents, and attentively watched the anti-Lafayette press of the Citizen King, to protest against every misrepresentation. So he preserved the brilliance of the name of Lafayette, not because it was his own, but because it was that of his illustrious father.

BOOK II
Fame

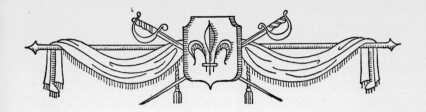

I. A LETTER FOR WASHINGTON

THE PASSAGE in the *Hermione* lasted four weeks. Let us profit by this period of forced inactivity to consider impartially Lafayette's avidity for glory, which was so constant a subject of mockery on the part of his contemporaries and subsequently of historians. The present writer cannot be charged with attempting to conceal it.

It was not the cause of his rapid rise, but its consequence. Instead of being spread over his life, his rich gifts from Fortune were concentrated within the narrow limits of his early manhood. First millionaire, then an officer, while still a boy; married at sixteen, a father at eighteen, a general at twenty! How could so amazing a progress fail to have its effect on Lafayette's character?

Every momentary halt in his progress seemed to him a downfall; the fear of losing his precocious fame spurred on his ambition; he had arrived at the summit at a bound, without the normal long years of apprenticeship, and he wanted to climb yet higher out of fear of the descent of unknown slopes.

Everyone knows the hectic thirst for life of the consumptive, already doomed, who frenziedly uses up his vital forces as though forewarned by some instinct. This element is not confined to the incurable consumptive. The functioning of this mysterious "metronome" can be observed in athletes of herculean build. And the exceptionally long life of which it has been difficult to compress the story into this single volume was

87

also ruled by a special law. Banished from public life by the
Revolution and by Napoleon, hated more than ever by the
royalist reaction of the Restoration, Lafayette passed the best
years of his manhood and more than half of his life in inactivity. It may well be that the thirst for glory which drove
the youngster of twenty to and fro across the ocean, now in
American uniform, now in French, was the unrest of the soldier oppressed by a foreboding that his career was to come
to a premature end. Only once, when he was not yet twenty-
four, did the young general draw the great prize of a real
victory; then suddenly his military career was over; no other
opportunity came of distinguishing himself on the field of
battle. What wonder that he went in search of opportunity
with feverish impatience?

When, on April 27, 1780, the *Hermione* dropped anchor off
Boston, the news that the Marquis de Lafayette had returned
brought half the town to its feet. His two years in America
had made this young and valiant foreigner universally popular. And the English had for years been so confidently pre-
dicting the impending collapse of the rising and the prediction
had come so close to realization, that Lafayette could not
dream how opportunely the French reinforcements, which had
been so energetically declined at the time of his departure for
Europe, were now coming.

Intimate friends of Washington relate that the commander-
in-chief read with tears in his eyes the lines his young friend
had written him in advance of his arrival. The friendship of
these two famous men was no more than a brief episode in
their lives. Yet they were united by a rare affection, springing
in part from the very contrast between their natures. The letter of welcome which Washington sent by one of his staff
officers to his guest reveals all a father's solicitude and joy
over the coming reunion:

Unhappily you do not tell me the route you are taking across the
state of New York; otherwise I should certainly have sent an escort
of cavalry to meet you, since you will be passing estates owned by
"Tories." In any case, Major Gibbs will meet you at the parting of
the ways. I most sincerely congratulate you upon your safe arrival
in America, and shall embrace you with all the warmth of an affec-

tionate friend when you come to headquarters, where a bed is prepared for you.

Not until all the presents he had brought with him, the
swords and plumes and spurs, had been distributed, and the
two friends remained alone, did Lafayette reveal to Washington the true reason of his coming. By the flickering light of a
candle he read to Washington the autograph letter from
Louis XVI which placed the whole of the French auxiliary
forces, military and naval, under the supreme command of the
American generalissimo.

This evening interview marked a change of rôles. At Versailles it had been Lafayette who fought for Washington; now,
in Philadelphia, Washington fought for his young friend, to
save him from loss of prestige in the eyes of his compatriots.
For the ragged horde that was all that was left of the Congress
army would excite the derision of the French. The currency
had so depreciated that the month's pay of a captain would no
longer buy a pair of boots. The state governments were turning a deaf ear to all demands on them, and after a whole winter
of starvation the best of the soldiers were losing their willing-
ness to be further compromised by continuing the rebellion.
Only the fear that the English might penetrate into states
which had not yet been pillaged, and the fear of reprisals when
the Congress troops returned, prevented the population from
open advocacy of capitulation.

Under these tragic circumstances the assistance announced
by Lafayette was of inestimable value; but it demanded an
equal effort from America. The French king's envoy, not yet
twenty-three years old, found himself faced with a task which
would have taxed the shrewdest of diplomats. To report the
whole truth to Versailles would have been to give the signal
for the immediate return of the French expedition and so to
seal the fate of American liberty. Yet in this case the truth
was bound to be revealed very quickly, for as soon as the
Comte de Rochambeau arrived, the first letters sent home by
his officers would disclose the true situation, painted in the
vivid colors of disappointment and malice.

Lafayette very adroitly avoided either telling or suppressing
the truth: he only mentioned the troubles to show at once the

remedy for them. He explained the shrinkage in Washington's army and its inadequate equipment as the results of the currency depreciation of which everybody knew in Europe, and went on at once to remark that the cash payments to be made by the French troops would quickly remove these evils.

But rose-colored reports of this sort would not alone be of any avail; it was necessary that America should make capital out of the anticipated French assistance. The prospect of supplies to be paid for in good money attracted the traders, and the failing confidence in ultimate victory was galvanized into new strength with praises of the mighty ally. Washington sent letter after letter to spur on the patriotic ambition of Congress; Lafayette himself wrote also, appealing to the public self-esteem and urging that the American soldiers should not be exposed to the ridicule of foreign troops. That for his own part he ran up to his ears in debt, himself clothed and fed and often paid his regiments, was to be expected from this despiser of money; but he also succeeded in enlisting the interest of the ladies of Philadelphia and the other towns in raising funds. At the head of each list he entered his wife's name for a large sum, which set the pace for those who followed. The activity of society ladies in providing comforts for soldiers, so often subsequently degraded into a craze, was also Lafayette's idea. All over America the highest circles of society competed in worthily clothing the half-naked fighters for freedom.

Time would have been all too short before the arrival of the French expedition, which sailed a week after Lafayette had landed in Boston, had not its passage been exceptionally protracted, taking no less than seventy days.

The necessity of constantly keeping in touch with all the transports, and the inevitable difficulties of every naval expedition, not only delayed arrival but frayed the nerves of Admiral de Ternay and the Comte de Rochambeau; both of whom, like their officers and crews, reached America exhausted and not in the best of humor. Meanwhile Lafayette, under constant pressure, had been putting on paper endless advice and opinions and demands as they occurred to him. The first pilot boat took the Comte de Rochambeau no fewer than three long epistles. The count acknowledged them only on July 12, 1780, four days after landing, without any remark on their contents. Meanwhile, in his first official report to the Comte de Vergennes he gave plain expression to his annoyance:

On my arrival I found letters from the Marquis de Lafayette awaiting me; they are too voluminous for copies to be sent, and they contain a mass of excited and rather incoherent proposals.

Under the influence of the failure of the first expedition, and in order to prevent a repetition of the earlier friction with Admiral d'Estaing, Louis XVI had ordered that his ships and regiments were unreservedly to obey the orders of the rebel generalissimo, as elements of the Congress army. For Lafayette personally there was no difficulty in this; he was already wearing American uniform. But the order was felt as a humiliation by the French officers, in the aristocratic pride of their Old-World outlook. Only the compelling personality of Washington induced them gradually to forget the injury to their self-esteem.

II. THE FRENCH IN AMERICA

THE KING'S ORDER conferring on Washington the right of supreme command was accepted. But it was quite another matter with the twenty-three-year-old compatriot who was able, as the reward of his immature enthusiasm, to play the part almost of a commander-in-chief. It was natural that Rochambeau and Admiral de Ternay should press for an interview with Washington. Washington himself had no thought for the susceptibilities he was in danger of injuring; the gentlemen from France spoke only their own language, and at the American headquarters neither the commander-in-chief nor any of his older staff officers spoke French. The obvious solution was to make use of Lafayette, and Washington did so without troubling about his youth. He was, in any case, transmitting questions rather than commands to Rochambeau and the admiral.

But the result was that Lafayette came once more, this time in entire innocence, under suspicion of being too importunate and interfering. Rochambeau had been ordered by Louis XVI to press on with the siege of New York and to capture the city. Washington and Congress had been occupied with the same plan. Nothing could be more fatal to the prestige of the English than to be driven out of the estuary of the Hudson. But the seventy days' passage from France once more upset the plans of the allies.

In carrying out the instruction from his friend and revered leader to propose an attack on New York, Lafayette once more showed undue energy! In vain did the Comte de Rochambeau object on the strength of his long experience; the young Frenchman in American uniform would not permit his country to be denied the opportunity of delivering this great and perhaps decisive blow; relying in part on Washington's authority, he tried to counter the objections advanced. Even the good-natured Rochambeau began to grow annoyed.

The private comments of the two disputants are revealing and make amusing reading. In a communication addressed jointly to the count and the admiral, Lafayette apologized for his unseemly excess of zeal, and he followed this with a second letter to Rochambeau asking his forgiveness and assuring him of his regrets and his respectful affection. But on the same day he sent his wife this account of the conflict:

Through a little excess of plain speaking I have got into a slight controversy with the two gentlemen. As I could see that there was no possibility of winning them over to my view, and as it is in the interest of the common cause that we should remain good friends, I have roundly declared that everything I said was wrong, have repentantly acknowledged my errors and formally asked pardon, which has had such a wonderful effect on both the gentlemen that we are all on much better terms than ever before.

The Comte de Rochambeau's reply opened with these sentences:

Permit an old father, my dear Marquis, to reply to you as to a tender son whom he loves and infinitely esteems. You know me well enough to believe that I have no need to be incited, that at my age, when one has been forced by circumstances to reach a decision founded on military and state reasons, all the instigations possible can not make me change without express orders of my general.

But in spite of all this fatherliness Rochambeau had not overcome his irritation, as is evident from his insistence on a personal meeting with Washington. Accordingly a council of war was held at Hartford (Connecticut) on September 20, 1780, and here at last Admiral de Ternay, General Rochambeau, and the general's chief of staff, the Comte de Chastellux, met Washington. But the "unwelcome intermediary" was still there, as interpreter for the commander-in-chief. General Knox was also present.

The council of war was entirely abortive. It was agreed on both sides that the preponderance of the English at sea made it out of the question to embark on any enterprise of importance. Unless France would provide strong naval reinforcements and would supply on credit the required uniforms, boots, and guns, the existing combined forces could undertake no serious offensive. There remained, therefore, nothing that the French could do but arrange good and carefully fortified winter quarters, and anchor their ships in safe harborage, until Versailles sent the necessary reinforcements, and primarily a real fleet of warships, either from France or from the Antilles. The son of the Comte de Rochambeau was sent to Europe, with General Lawrence representing Congress, to try to persuade Louis XVI to make these further sacrifices.

With this the activities of the French expedition in the year of its arrival came to an end, without a shot being fired. Until the spring of 1781 Washington had to depend on his own troops. This result could have been attained without making him proceed personally to Hartford.

But the Comte de Rochambeau and the admiral were but pawns pushed forward by Providence, for a purpose quickly and astonishingly revealed. Since he had come away from headquarters and had already lost much time, General Washington made a small detour on his return journey, to the new forts on the banks of the Hudson at West Point. He informed General Arnold, the constructor of the forts, that he would come with his party to lunch with him. On his arrival Mrs Arnold was found unconscious on her bedroom floor. While Lafayette and others were tending her a messenger arrived and handed Washington papers that had been seized on an English spy who had just been caught. They were plans of the new outer forts and a receipt from the traitor—Arnold. The unhappy wife was seized with fits of hysterical shrieking and had to be removed to an institution. The officers, deeply shocked, placed the unhappy woman, herself completely innocent, in the carriage that bore her away.

Only then did Washington give vent to his bitter despair: "Who is there that we can still trust?" he exclaimed, and ordered the pursuit of the traitor. But Arnold had ridden along the river bank to a boat lying hidden in undergrowth. He waited awhile in vain for his accomplice; then, making for the English warship *Vulture*, he reached New York unharmed. His less guilty partner, the English Major André, who had risked his life in patriotism and not for money, suffered the full penalty. The American court-martial condemned him as a spy to the dishonor of death by hanging. The brave officer was not allowed to be shot, although he had not sinned like Judas for thirty pieces of silver, had not sinned against his oath and his country like Arnold, who became an English general. Lafayette himself, in a letter home, wrote of the Englishman's attractive personality: his candor and fortitude had won him the sympathy of the whole of the court that had condemned him.

His death, the other's career, the saving of the Hudson forts as American defences, all these were consequences of Rochambeau's insistence on a meeting with Washington. His roused *amour-propre* brought Washington, against his will, at the critical moment away from headquarters to the danger spot—a working of Providence which a story-teller might have hesitated to invent.

On his return to Valley Forge, Lafayette received a new proof of Washington's regard, by way of compensation for his compatriots' slights. Two battalions of riflemen, each a thousand strong, were formed from among the sharpshooters on the Canadian border and placed under Lafayette's command. He was proud of his riflemen, and they had every reason to appreciate their commander. With the aid of a loan of ten thousand crowns, shared between several banks, he provided handsome uniforms for his men; he succeeded in drawing stores for them from the French army supplies, and only failed in trying to induce Washington to give him the command he eagerly awaited to lead his troops at once into the firing line.

Almost all the officers of Rochambeau's expedition were of most distinguished origin. There was scarcely a family of the old feudal nobility of France that was not represented in America; they had come as if to a Court ball. It may well be that Lafayette's own enthusiastic and overdrawn accounts had contributed something to attracting his young friends across the ocean; but the night of August 4 was to prove that these modern Argonauts, these Crusaders for Democracy, were not fighting simply to be in the fashion or merely in a spirit of adventure.

The forced inactivity during the winter drew the fine flower of the Court of Versailles into the embryo cities of the New World, and the letters sent home by these aristocrats give a picturesque account of the first attempts at contact between two forms of society poles apart. There was no lack of beautiful women and girls in America; but how could young French noblemen who had learned to treat such conceptions as "conjugal fidelity," or "the comforts of home," still more such appallingly bourgeois ideas as those of industry and economy, with nothing but contempt, find their way out of their own world of superficial brilliance and formal courtesies and nothing else, and adapt themselves to the puritan world of the virtuous wives and daughters of these sober and hard-fisted farmers and shopkeepers? The Marquis de Chastellux relates that one Sunday, with Lafayette and his brother-in-law, the Vicomte de Noailles, the Comte de Montesquieu, Comte de Damas, and Comte Duplessis, he visited a Mrs Shippen in Philadelphia. A Miss Rutledge played to them on the harpsichord; the daughter of the house sang timidly but with a pleasant voice; finally the Vicomte de Noailles cut off some of the strings of Mrs Shippen's harp, strung them on his violin, and played for the rest to dance:

This was the first time I had heard music in America and been present at any sort of social gathering. If the inhabitants of this New World awake to a sense of the fine arts and learn to be gay and social without formal invitations and stiff introductory ceremonial, they will not need to envy us anything.

Ten years after this optimistic prophecy the Marquis de Chastellux had the opportunity of observing the actual effect of the manners of Versailles on these unpolished Americans. The times were hard; French money had heavily depreciated. A Mr Morris, member of Congress, was visiting Versailles with his good American dollars, and was a welcome caller in the boudoirs of the most distinguished ladies at Court.

And what was the result of these intimate visits in "the best society"? Mr Morris, like the Marquis de Chastellux, kept a diary—a diary, moreover, filled with venomous references to Lafayette. In it Mr Morris, with the indignation and the arrogance of a *grand seigneur,* ridiculed these "fools of democrats," lackeys of the populace, who were out to suppress the most sacred traditions. He resentfully noted the progress of the anti-monarchical revolution. Incidentally, with the precision of a respectable trader, he entered the expenses incurred in his daily visits to princesses, duchesses and marchionesses.

The Marquise de Chastellux was in her bath when I arrived. But she poured into the water the contents of a bottle of perfume, which made the water milky, and then she went on chatting as unconcernedly as if we had been sitting in her *salon.*

The fact that Mr Morris did not remove intimate details like this from his text before printing his diary on his return to America is refutation enough of the optimistic forecast made by the Marquis de Chastellux. Not until the French Revolution had brought down the century-old divisions between social classes could the great English exposer of human weaknesses, Thackeray, give universal currency to the pregnant word "snob" for people of the type of Mr Morris.

For the young French nobles, on the contrary, this winter of traveling through the States was an unforgettable experience, in spite of, or perhaps in consequence of, the primitive surroundings. They had been accustomed to think lightly of the money which bailiffs and tax-gatherers and customs officials procured for them away from their sight; here in America they were able to learn how labor is the whole life of millions of men. On their return to France they were to "discover" the people, and to be unable any longer to squander the fruit of men's labor with a clear conscience. Thus England unconsciously revenged herself in advance for the loss of her principal colony. As the barbarian hordes of the great migrations through Europe had succumbed to the infection of the civilization of settled communities, so the French were infected in America with the democratic ideal and outlook.

III. "THE BOY"

THE LONG INACTIVITY of the winter greatly helped General Washington. Tied to the north with his best troops through the presence of the English commander-in-chief, who had occupied New York with forty thousand men and the principal units of the English fleet, he was in danger of losing his munition stores and magazines in the south, where the traitor Arnold, now a general in the English army, was utilizing against his own country his knowledge of the position of the principal munition depots. All the supplies in southern Virginia would be lost if resistance was not offered to this Judas. He would be able afterwards to effect a junction with Lord Cornwallis and to drive the weak and dispersed American units before him like wild game, in the forests he knew so well, until they were exterminated.

This infamous desertion made Washington's blood boil. Indifferent to the great superiority of the English forces, seeing only the scoundrel who was leading them, he detached some thousands of men from his army and placed Lafayette at their head with orders to capture the traitor dead or alive.

A protest was now made for the first time against the marked favor which the commander-in-chief was showing to the young foreigner. The expedition demanded a great deal of strategical skill, and great importance was attached to it. Was there no one among the country's own generals, men of riper years, who would be better able to cope with the difficulties of the enterprise? But Washington replied:

It is my opinion that the command of the troops cannot be in better hands than the marquis's. He possesses uncommon military talents: is of a quick and sound judgement; persevering and enterprising, without rashness; and besides these, he is of a very conciliating temper and perfectly sober,—which are qualities that rarely combine in the same person. And were I to add that some men will gain as much experience in the course of three or four years, as some others will in ten or a dozen, you cannot deny the fact and attack me upon that ground.

Lafayette's task reduced itself to a sort of man-hunt; the single objective was the capture of Arnold himself at all costs. The months that followed were full of incident. Once Lafayette imagined that he was on the point of achieving his objective: a strong fleet accompanied by transports came upstream and anchored. Unhappily, it was not the expected French support, but English reinforcements, which destroyed all hope of capturing the traitor; for Arnold was recalled to New York, his place being taken by an officer senior to him, General Phillip.

This General Phillip was the same man who twenty-four years before, as a major of artillery, had shot down at Hastenbeck the French cavalry regiment commanded by Lafayette's father. General Phillip now paid at the son's hands for the father's death: he succumbed to malaria in the depths of the American forest into which he had been lured by his victim's son.

The death of the enemy commander was of little practical moment for Lafayette; there was nothing that he could do with his exhausted and starving troops. The spectacle of the well-nourished English army, drawing its supplies without trouble by water, discouraged and exasperated the American troops, whose ranks were daily thinned by desertions. Lafayette tried first to combat the movement with severity, and had all deserters who were caught hanged, but the result was a mutiny in his camp. An appeal to the sense of honor succeeded better. Instead of hunting down deserters he assembled the troops and told them that he was leading them against superior forces. Those who were afraid of the unequal struggle, if they would say so, would be given a safe-conduct to headquarters and would be assured of impunity. But those who did not avail themselves of the offer must remain true to their comrades and their leader.

In this situation the soldiers had no choice. It was a simple matter to desert in secrecy; but who would openly come forward before the rest and say he was leaving them in the lurch? Nobody had the melancholy courage to confess to such cowardice. Lafayette procured food supplies out of his own resources and met the worst of the need. The moment came when a sick noncommissioned officer, to prevent being left behind, had himself carried on a stretcher by Redskins.

For a long time all sacrifices seemed to be in vain. The son of the Comte de Rochambeau returned from France with money and a cargo of uniforms, but Versailles refused any new naval expedition. The hopelessness and precariousness of Lafayette's situation in Virginia are evidenced by Washington's and Rochambeau's concern; the latter wrote, on receiving the news of a small success achieved by General Greene in Carolina:

I should rather hear of Greene's junction with the Marquis de Lafayette in the defence of Virginia than of all the success in the world in Carolina.

What Lord Cornwallis said, in a cheerful report to England, was:

The boy can not escape me!

But at this desperate moment the fortunes of war turned. A powerful French fleet, from the Antilles, entered Chesapeake Bay and cut off Cornwallis's access to the sea, and consequently his supplies. Cornwallis had pushed as far as Yorktown and had entrenched himself there. At the same time a new French corps of three thousand men was disembarked, under the command of the Comte de Saint-Simon. At a stroke Lord Cornwallis, instead of capturing the "boy," was himself entrapped.

At this chance opportunity, dearly bought by semi-starvation, Lafayette showed himself more than ever worthy of Washington's confidence. The French admiral, the Comte de Grasse, wanted to return quickly to the Antilles, to escape the risk of being blockaded and destroyed by a concentration of the whole English fleet. The Comte de Saint-Simon was pressing for the investment of Yorktown before France's American ally could share the glory of capturing the town. But Lafayette, with all his natural impatience and ambition,

36

EMORY & HENRY LIBRARY

Lafayette, who was never tired of working out the most adventurous plans, clung desperately to his orders to await the arrival of Washington, who, with Rochambeau, was bringing six thousand men from the north by forced marches.

It was only with endless difficulty that he succeeded in keeping the Comte de Grasse with him; the admiral spoke every day of weighing anchor. But in the end Lafayette's self-denial won its reward; the arrival of the troops from the north compelled Yorktown to capitulate unconditionally. How many human lives his patience had saved, without any diminution of the triumph! The six thousand men under Lord Cornwallis marched out of the town, company by company, to lay down their arms; only the noble lord announced that he was ill, and had his sword conveyed to Washington by one of his aides-de-camp. On the following day he invited Lafayette to lunch, to make excuses to the "boy" for his defeat.

The elements themselves now came over to the side of the conquerors. The Comte de Lauzun's ship flew before favoring winds across the ocean to Europe in just three weeks, and the unhoped-for triumph aroused no less delight in France than in America.

The capitulation was a severe blow to British prestige. It is said that Lord North, the British prime minister, staggered as though he had been struck by a bullet, "robbed of all self-control by this frightful catastrophe." Immediately after the arrival of the news of the victory a list of distinctions conferred by Louis XVI was issued from Versailles. He deprived the Marquis de Lafayette of his regiment of dragoons, and promoted him *maréchal de camp* (brigadier general) as from the date of the capture of Yorktown, October 19, 1781.

On December 23, 1781, Lafayette embarked in Boston harbor, homeward bound. Once more his last farewell was addressed, as the anchor was being weighed, to his friend General Washington. This time the *Alliance* reached Lorient in twenty-three days. When the news of his landing reached Paris the Marquise de Lafayette was at the Hôtel de Ville, the Paris City Hall, where a brilliant gathering was celebrating the birth of the long awaited dauphin. Marie Antoinette, who was present, left the company at once in order to take Mme de Lafayette to

the Hôtel de Noailles. The news had already spread throughout
the city, and at the gates of the Hôtel de Noailles the *dames de
la halle*, the famous market women of Paris, were waiting with
a laurel wreath. Not until they had crowned Lafayette and embraced him in turn did they let him go at last to his wife,
who fell fainting into the queen's arms when she heard her
husband's voice as he approached the room.

The weeks and months that followed were one long series
of triumphs and ovations. The newspapers throughout
Europe fed their readers with news of Lafayette. He was
called the "Liberator of America" and "Washington's savior";
it was not his fault if there were many tasteless panegyrics
that bordered on the ridiculous. French national pride had
been infinitely flattered, and the humiliating treaties of peace
imposed by England on the Roi Soleil and Louis XV had been
avenged.

An achievement which caused even more furore than his
American victory was Lafayette's conquest of the Comtesse de
Simiane, the famous beauty queen of Versailles. The Duc de
Richelieu, still notorious as "Marshal Cupid," and the old
Duc de Lavalle, solemnly declared that it was a more glorious
achievement to win the favor of Mme de Simiane than to
storm the proudest fortresses, and the newspapers hastened to
inform their readers of these expert pronouncements. It is
curious that Lafayette was so quickly at home again in the
French atmosphere of gallantry after his return from America.
It is here that we note for the first time the double nature of
this sincere reformer, always unshakably faithful to the democratic ideal, but never able to slough off his *grand seigneur's*
skin. He was deeply imbued with the political principles of the
New World but was uninfluenced by the puritan austerity of
his American friends. In appearance and manners he was a
French nobleman to the fingertips, but he was entirely in
sympathy, heart and soul, with the oppressed masses; and so
he was hated by the plebeian leaders of the Revolution as an
"aristocrat," and by those of his own rank as an agitator and
renegade. All the sudden disasters, the precipitous crashes in
his life were mainly consequences of this duality in his character as politician and private individual.

IV. OVERTAKEN BY PEACE

LAFAYETTE COULD NOT KNOW that his second return home was to mark his farewell to the trade of soldiering and to begin a period of seven lean years. Until the Revolution called him, after July 14, 1789, to be its leader in its own home, his sword of honor rusted in its scabbard; and when once more he wanted to draw it, not merely in peaceful ceremonies or parades, but for serious work in the struggle against his country's enemies, this same Revolution no longer trusted him and struck his sword out of his hand.

All the things of which other young men of his age dreamed as far-off objectives fell into Lafayette's lap at the outset of his career. The very morning after his arrival he was summoned to Versailles, received personally in audience by Louis XVI, and treated with all the honors of a victorious army commander. The famous portrait painter to Marie Antoinette, the beautiful Mme Vigée-Lebrun, begged the famous champion of Liberty for the favor of a sitting. Marshal the Duc de Richelieu invited all the Marshals of France to a banquet, to honor their country's latest victor in the name of her glorious past. Even the unalterable laws of freemasonry were set aside in Lafayette's honor; the Paris Grand Lodge of the Scots unanimously proclaimed its illustrious guest a "Master," against the sacrosanct principle that a secret ballot is obligatory even for princes.

No one had less sympathy for the American rebels than the queen, Marie Antoinette, but even she fought down her pride, and chose the most public opportunity to show to all the world how highly she regarded Lafayette's services to the honor of French arms. When the "Comte du Nord," the future Czar Paul I, son of the great Empress Catherine, made his farewell visit to Versailles, it was to the awkward dancer of the Epée de Bois that the queen gave her hand for the first quadrille in the Court ball.

Since Necker's fall into disfavor the specter of bankruptcy had stalked through France; and Louis XVI could not forget the warning words of his dismissed minister of finance. Now that the national pride of his country and its thirst for ven-

geance against England had been satisfied, he saw no reason
for making further sacrifices merely to help the rebels. His
fleet had returned to the Antilles; orders were now issued to
the Comte de Rochambeau to expedite the return home of the
victorious troops.

France's war-weariness aroused the hope in London of the
conclusion of a separate peace, which would be fatal for the
rebels. The English Cabinet hastened to send envoys to Versailles to open negotiations. No one at Court but Lafayette
ventured to interpose on behalf of the Union. Benjamin Franklin, in his reports to Congress, repeated again and again that
no American could have defended his country's interests with
more energy and perseverance than the French marquis had
shown. The minister, the Comte de Vergennes, allowed his
protégé to persuade him to advance a loan of six millions in
metal coin. It was also entirely due to Lafayette's urgency that
the discussion of the half-forgotten plan of a joint Franco-
Spanish expedition was reopened.

Washington's appreciation of Lafayette's energy and loyalty
found expression in the gift of a life-size portrait of the
general and his wife, which was brought over from America
by the diplomatic courier and taken to the Hôtel de Noailles
for Lafayette. The marquis's declarations of friendship may
sometimes seem too flowery and too perfectly turned, but this
must be set down to the fashion of the day. The way the cult
of good taste was pursued to the point of bad taste is strikingly
shown in the insipidity of the family group which Lafayette
had painted as a return gift for "his dear General." The marquise was approaching another confinement; in order to mask
her condition the artist placed her two children on her right
and left, leaning towards one another over their seated
mother's knees. But, not satisfied with showing her husband at
the back of the group in his American general's uniform, the
artist showed Mme de Lafayette holding a tiny American officer's tunic in front of her and helping her little son to put
it on. The newspapers, in their descriptions, dwelt on the
"charming detail" of "the joy and surprise that light up the
father's eyes as he watches the proceedings in approving
pride." To his last day General Washington had to see his

godson slipping on his tunic and Lafayette looking down at the boy in perpetual surprise!

The group had become incomplete long before it crossed the ocean; for in the year of his return home, on October 10, 1782, another daughter was born to Lafayette. She was christened Virginie, in honor of the state in which the marquis won his first great victory. Once again the marquise had to content herself with a short visit from her husband; he had but time for a hasty glance at the baby in its cradle, for preparations had already begun for the Franco-Spanish expedition.

Admiral d'Estaing, who was placed in supreme command of the combined fleets, was burning to avenge the failure of his first expedition. He wrote to the minister of war asking that the Marquis de Lafayette should be allowed to accompany him. Lafayette's new rank in the French army corresponded to that of a major general in America; and on joining the French fleet, which was awaiting the departure of the Spaniards at Cadiz, the French *maréchal de camp* embarked in his Congress uniform, to emphasize that Washington was still his superior officer.

On New Year's Day, 1783, he wrote home from Cadiz letters still overflowing with warlike ardor. Three weeks later, on January 20, the representatives of France, America, and England signed the peace preliminaries of Paris. The war was at an end.

V. THE NEW STATE

WHEN HE HEARD the great news, Lafayette begged a ship from the admiral, so that he might be the means of sending the first announcement to Washington and Congress. With his liking for symbolic names he chose the light frigate *La Triomphe*. She was a fast sailer, and reached America long before the official news. The optimistic name of the *Victoire* was being justified, with the aid of the *Alliance*, by the *Triomphe*.

Had it not been for the short intermezzo of a Whig government in England, a great deal of blood would still have been shed in the American seat of war. The Tories, in the obstinacy of their pride, would not so easily have renounced either the

chastisement of the rebel farmers, or this great and promising
colonial territory. But the cutting short of the war was very
far from cutting short Lafayette's fame. On the contrary, it
was only now, with their final liberation from English taxes
and duties, that the American merchants and farmers did
full justice to the services their leaders had performed. Thus,
in the eyes of the whole nation the mad Frenchman who had
voluntarily endured the hardships of the American backwoods,
instead of enjoying life at the Court of Versailles, was turned
by the victory into the glorious national hero who had shed
his blood for Freedom.

If the frigate *La Triomphe* had brought not only his letters,
but Lafayette himself, as the herald of victory, the country's
guest would have been whirled from town to town through
the whole Union by a cyclone of public enthusiasm. But he
allowed a full year and a half to pass before visiting America to
gather his laurels and to visit Washington. The delay was fresh
evidence of his loyalty.

Congress had need of him in France. These eighteen months
were devoted from the first to the firm establishment of the
new state. It was not easy to secure the recognition of a state
of such doubtful origin as the American "Republic" by the
conservative European governments. His very first step showed
Lafayette how much had still to be done in Europe. The King
of Spain was afraid of the effect of the bad example of these
victorious rebels on his own rich colonies in South America.
He refused to receive the plebeian representatives of the
Congress government. The actual representative of Congress
had already thrown up his post and left the country in face
of the transparent pretexts with which he had been put off
and the humiliations he had suffered; the chargé d'affaires
whom he left behind would have had no better success if
Lafayette had not come to his aid. In vain did the Spanish
minister, Count Florida Blanca, try to wriggle out; in vain
did the king invite to his table the fêted and respectably born
"hero of two worlds." Lafayette refused to appear at Court
except in his American uniform and in the company of the
American representative. His demonstrative support of their
"ally" was so awkward for the proud gentleman of Madrid
that they hurriedly gave way, even entering into a commercial

treaty with this state without a ruler, in order to get the coroneted "Republican" out of the country.

On his return to Paris the French *maréchal de camp* had to bid a final farewell to his beloved American uniform. The war was over, the guns had said their say, and what now remained to be done would be settled in tedious negotiations behind closed doors. Instead of blood, only ink flowed now, and it was no congenial task for the young hero with his crown of glory, who knew that a liberated nation on the other side of the ocean was waiting to acclaim him, to argue such questions as debt service and amortization, import duties, and commercial privileges. Lafayette learned to haggle in the interest of his American friends in a way he would never have demeaned himself to do in his own interest, and so ably that no one unacquainted with him would have recognized the rich and open-handed officer in this obstinately unyielding agent.

It would be tedious even to summarize the story of the long-drawn-out negotiations which Lafayette had to carry on, in addition to a busy correspondence. One of his mortal political enemies during the Revolution, Brissot, later a Girondist, writes in his *La France et les États-Unis* in admiration of the unique example furnished by Lafayette of the high-born aristocrat and famous general, devoted entirely to soldiering during the war, who at its end was able to turn his attention with success to the economic exploitation of the victory, concerned throughout both periods of activity for the freedom and well-being of humanity, and stirred to glorious deeds at arms only as a means to that end.

This praise from a later opponent was thoroughly well earned, for it would scarcely have been possible to discover, among all the higher officers in France, another one who would have condescended to enter into the complicated commercial negotiations—quite apart from his capacity to do so, which, indeed, was not always adequate in Lafayette's case. He had, for instance, to learn from his friend Washington the meaning of the term "free port"—a term of which the definition was, indeed, still a controversial matter—in order to present a case. But no sooner did he know the sort of privileges that were sought than he secured the grant of no less than four free ports on the French coast, by dint of pressing the tempt-

ing argument that everything done to promote American
trade would hasten the return to the exchequer of the money
that had been lent.

But amid all the exertions and the time absorbed by this
struggle for the existence of the new state, Lafayette's interest
in every advance of science was too keen for him to let slip
the opportunity of acquainting himself with any new discovery
and achievement. It was the period of the mystics, the al-
chemists and the magicians. In the ruins of the orthodox be-
liefs which Voltaire and the Encyclopedists had undermined
there sheltered the adventurers who exploited human stupidity, greed of gain and fanaticism. It was precisely the "enlightened" members of the best society who swarmed in blind
credulity around charlatans and mountebanks of the type of
the "divine" Cagliostro. Lafayette did not follow these
fashions; his desire was for knowledge and light; the obscur-
antism of these cults of an unexplained magic had no attraction for him. But when he heard of the wonderful cures
effected by the Viennese physician Mesmer, through the new
force of magnetism, he threw himself into the study of this
alleged science with all his natural impetuosity.

Here he imagined that the torch of scientific research was
lighting up a secret of creation hitherto buried in darkness.
Mesmer's teaching touched all that was noblest in him: it
fired the spirit of the boy who went forth against the werewolf, of the volunteer adversary of oppression, of the helper
who to the last years of his old age was always ready to fight
to free human beings from suffering and injustice, of the
benefactor in Lafayette: he was fired by the prospect of
soothing pain, of healing the sick. He took lessons from this
master, and his joy in the anticipation of making the lame
walk irradiated his report to Washington:

A German doctor, called Mesmer, having made the greatest discovery upon animal magnetism, he has instructed scholars, among
whom your humble servant is called one of the most enthusiastic.
I know as much as any conjuror ever did, which reminds me of our
old friend's at Fishkill interview with the devil, that made us laugh
so much, at his house, and before I go, I will get leave to let you into
the secret of Mesmer, which, you may depend upon, is a grand
philosophical discovery.

In Lafayette's correspondence with his "dear General" there are many other evidences of his constant alertness to be of service to his fellow creatures, his sensitiveness in the face of all human suffering. Amid the blind folly of the nationalisms and racial hatreds of our world of today, it is instructive and moving to see in these yellowing letters of a century and a half ago the humanity and generosity, now buried fathoms deep, by which these two friends, so different in all externals, were both inspired.

Where in this year of grace 1935 are the travelers on pleasure bent who can turn, even for a moment, from their admiration of the overpowering spectacle of the skyscrapers and the hustle of American life to trouble about a Negro's maltreatment or even a lynching? Yet all this is nearer to us today; the innocent victim's body is scarcely cold when the sensation is served up, still hot, on the breakfast tables of all the world. Things were not so simple for General the Marquis de Lafayette. Rich and famous, hedged in always by his adjutants and his friends and admirers, he was almost hermetically sealed from the martyrdom of the colored slaves. But he had scarcely recovered time to breathe when he sent this proposal to Washington:

At present, my dear General, when you are going to enjoy some little repose, permit me to propose to you a plan that may become generally useful to the black portion of the human race. Let us unite in purchasing a small estate, where we may try the experiment to free the negroes and use them only as tenants. Such an example as yours shall render it a general practice, and if we succeed in America, I will cheerfully devote a part of my time to render the method fashionable in the West Indies. If it be a wild scheme, I had rather be mad that way than to be thought wise on the other tack.

And that was not a momentary bee in his bonnet! Years later, though Washington was against the project, Lafayette was not to be deterred from attempting to carry out his plan alone, at his own cost.

A visit he had had to make to Chavaniac, some time before this, showed that his sympathies did not need the striking contrast between white and black in order to be stirred. His bailiff proudly showed him the piled-up stores of grain and said:

"I think, M. le Marquis, the time has come to sell. Corn is worth its weight in gold, there is such scarcity."

"Then, sir," growled Lafayette, "the time has come to give." And he himself watched over the opening of the granaries to his half-starved peasants. Soon deputations came from all sides, attracted by the astonishing news; and the benefactor's carriage was accompanied to the borders of Auvergne by shouts of "Vive Lafayette!"

VI. CINCINNATUS

ON HIS RETURN to Paris with his old aunt, Lafayette at last left the Hôtel de Noailles, and realized the desire he had long had to set up a home of his own. By the time when all was ready and his family had moved in, eighteen months had passed since the conclusion of the preliminaries of peace; but the victor of Yorktown was still in Paris, held there by Franklin's negotiations over commercial treaties. In order to advance American interests, Lafayette urged Washington to pay a visit to Europe. Washington refused; he could not but refuse. As he grew older his dislike of social gatherings increased; triumphal processions, banquets, toasts and lionizings were torture to him. Scarcely had the last English warship left the port of New York when the victorious commander-in-chief returned his commission to Congress, only too glad to be able to resume his simple and peaceful existence at Mount Vernon.

A French historian has well said that Washington's letters to his young friend Lafayette are the finest monument that this truly great man could have set up to his own memory.

I wish to banish from my letters the word "war." I wish to see the young people of this world at peace, all busy and happy in fulfilling the first and great commandment: Increase and multiply. As an encouragement, we have opened the fertile plains of Ohio to the poor, the unfortunate, the oppressed of the earth. All those who are overladen, broken down, seeking a soil to cultivate, may come and find the promised land flowing with milk and honey.

Who in our day would venture to attribute words like these to a great soldier, who in fifteen years of war had given ample evidence of his personal courage, and as commander-in-chief had carried to a victorious conclusion the unequal struggle against England's immense superiority? Lafayette replies worthily in the course of a private family letter written from off Cadiz:

I am content! America is assured of her independence. Mankind has won its cause; Liberty is no longer homeless on the earth.

Lafayette was certainly not of the type of the average French aristocrat of 1783, and Washington's letters are not typical of the American farmer of his day. But the popularity that both enjoyed shows that a man's worth was valued in their time by a different measure from our own.

At length, my dear Marquis, I am become a private citizen on the banks of the Potomac; and under the shadow of my own vine and fig-tree, free from the bustle of a camp, and the busy scenes of public life, I am solacing myself with those tranquil enjoyments, of which the soldier, who is ever in pursuit of fame, the statesman, whose watchful days and sleepless nights are spent in devising schemes to promote the welfare of his own, perhaps the ruin of other countries, as if this globe was insufficient for us all, and the courtier, who is always watching the countenance of his prince, in hopes of catching a gracious smile, can have very little conception.
I have not only retired from all public employments, but I am retiring within myself, and shall be able to view the solitary walk and tread the paths of private life, with a heartfelt satisfaction. Envious of none, I am determined to be pleased with all, and this, my dear friend, being the order of my march, I will move gently down the stream of life, until I sleep with my fathers.

In order to do honor, in spite of himself, to this generalissimo who had hung up his sword to return to the plow, Congress decided to create an Order of Cincinnatus, to be conferred on all the officers who had won special distinction in the War of Independence. Washington charged Lafayette with the selection of the French officers to be given the order, and no less than six months of his life were devoted to the difficult decision. Horace Walpole, tickled by the story of this vanity fair, wrote to his friends that Versailles had been consulting all the calendars to discover St Cinnatus (*Saint-Cinnate*) and ascertain the virtues to which he owed his canonization.

VII. A LAST FAREWELL

HAVING AT LAST brought to an end this labor of Hercules, Lafayette was able to fix July 1, 1784, for his long-delayed departure for America.

The mightiest of monarchs could not have been given a more triumphal reception. In every state from the Canadian border to South Carolina, in every principal town and in the smallest villages he had passed through during his campaigns, he was met by ceremonious processions and accompanied by them on his departure. Everywhere the church bells rang in his honor in greeting and farewell. No sheriff within possible reach of his route would miss the rare opportunity of greeting a true "hero." In thousands of toasts and more than a hundred banquets the Liberator was told of America's eternal gratitude. Simple taciturn farmers discovered their gift of speech, and through a hundred and twenty days Lafayette untiringly emptied glass after glass, sometimes in two townships on the same day, to Freedom, to the solidarity of the partners in the new state, to Congress and to the health of his revered friend Washington.

But there was more than mere speeches and toasts. All the honors that are generally paid to great men only during the lives of their descendants were showered on Lafayette, at twenty-seven years of age, during his triumphal progress. Every village named a street after him; cities and states presented him with their freedom; and finally Congress, in the name of the whole nation, conferred by its vote on the Marquis de Lafayette and all his male descendants hereditary citizenship of the Union. In the north, two adjoining territories were named Lafayette and Washington, so that the map should perpetuate the memory of the friendship of the country's two liberators, as the map of the skies commemorates Castor and Pollux!

Lafayette's long stay on the Canadian border at the time of Conway's Cabal against Washington, of which he had been a victim, had brought him the friendship of some of the Indian tribes; and a visit to them made a picturesque break in the monotony of these celebrations. Some of the Redskins had retained their arms after the conclusion of peace, and the new Tory government in England observed with no displeasure that their raids were continuing.

These sons of nature had plenty of discernment and could differentiate between the open-handed French nobleman and the average cold-hearted "Pale-face." To the Sioux, the Oneidas, the Iroquois and other tribes Lafayette was still "the great Kayevla" and a popular figure. Soon after his arrival in America he made use of this sympathy in the service of the American government. After a short stay with Washington and the first official festivities in his honor, he set out at the request of Congress to visit his Indian friends. Furnished with a few bales of colored cloth and, above all, with some small casks of "fire water," the small expedition departed for the palaver, which was to be held in the neighborhood of one of the American frontier forts. The "fort" was a tiny blockhouse which scarcely sufficed to shelter Lafayette and his aide-de-camp; several French nobles had accompanied him, but had to sleep in the open.

Next to the spirit, the most convincing argument in Lafayette's possession was the accuracy of his past prophecy of the defeat of the English. He reminded the Redskins that he had warned them to range themselves on the side of the friends of the powerful King of France and not of the English, and this reminder had its effect. The "great Kayevla" was assured that "his children" would always follow his wise advice, and the treaty of friendship was concluded.

In his diary the Chevalier de Marbois tells the strange story of the meeting of the deputation with an old "Indian" of the Oneida tribe, who listened attentively for several days to the words of the French officers and then addressed them in faultless Provençal! During the Seven Years' War he had been taken prisoner and had seen six of his fellow prisoners roasted on an open fire. He had himself been smeared with the fat which was to add succulence to his flesh when he was claimed by a chief's daughter, whose heart spoke for him louder than her stomach. Twice he had attempted flight from his drunken and

unattractive spouse; but both times he was caught and set
down again among his adoptive tribe. He was now the father
of seven children and the grandfather of some more. He was
offered a passage home to France, but declined it with thanks.
Twenty years in the virgin forest had driven out his memories
of his native country; his relations and friends in Provence
were dead or had forgotten him; the life of the Indians, skin
and paint and feathers and all else, had become second nature
to him. At the end of the palaver he looked on with calm indifference as his countrymen went away.

After this last service, Lafayette was received by Congress
at an extraordinary session held in his honor. The representatives of the thirteen federated states listened standing and
bareheaded as the President expressed the undying gratitude
of this nation of ten million souls for the services rendered by
the young hero, who had sacrificed a fortune and shed his
blood for the liberation of the country. Lafayette concluded
his reply with these eloquent words:

> May this immense Temple of Freedom ever stand a lesson to op-
> pressors, an example to the oppressed, and a sanctuary for the rights
> of mankind! And may these happy United States attain that complete
> splendour and prosperity which will illustrate the blessings of their
> government, and in ages to come rejoice the departed souls of their
> founders.

The treaty of peace with the Indians had been the overture
to Lafayette's six months' stay in America; its finale, tinged
with melancholy, was a farewell visit to Washington's estate.
These two quiet and peaceful weeks in Washington's home were
in strong contrast to the months Lafayette had just passed in
the whirl of processions and festivities. When the hour for
leaving came, Washington found it difficult to part from his
guest. He accompanied him for several days on his journey
before, with a heavy heart, he decided to return to his solitude.
A cloud of dust on the horizon finally hid the departing friend
from view.

> In the moment of our separation, upon the road as I travelled,
> and every hour since, I have felt all that love, respect, and attach-
> ment for you, with which length of years, close connection, and your

merits have inspired me. I often asked myself, as our carriages separated, whether that was the last sight I ever should have of you. And though I wished to say no, my fears answered yes. I called to mind the days of my youth, and found they had long since fled, to return no more; that I was descending the hill I had been fifty-two years climbing, and that, though I was blest with a good constitution, I was of a short-lived family, and might soon expect to be entombed in the mansion of my fathers. These thoughts darkened the shades and gave a gloom to the picture, and consequently to my prospect of seeing you again.

But I will not repine; I have had my day! . . .

The light touch of melancholy in these words of farewell was natural to the older man who sees youth riding off to the Promised Land. Like the symbolic father and leader in the Scriptures, Washington imagined himself to be left behind at the frontier of a new world which had no more use for his wisdom and experience. But this time again he was mistaken. It was the older man, head of a state which his sword had created, who remained actively engaged in public duties for fourteen years more. The younger one was on his way to imprisonment in the casemates of Olmütz.

The two friends never met again. For fourteen years life kept them apart, until Washington's death called him to his fathers.

VIII. SIGNS OF STORM

ONCE MORE the departure from America coincided with the Christmas festival, and the arrival in France with the opening of the new year, as though the passage from the New World to the Old was a crossing of the threshold of time. In America a salute of thirteen guns was fired as the hero departed. A month later, on January 20, 1785, Lafayette landed at Brest, attracting scarcely more attention than any other officer returning home.

And yet the moment he landed he found that in his own country men had changed. Everywhere there were public meetings of protest and denunciation; subjects denied all rights were beginning to turn into citizens with wills of their own; he felt almost as if he had got back again to the New World.

The nobles of the province of Brittany were assembled at Rennes and asked him to take part in their deliberations. He joined them at once. He would have been denying his past and his reputation if he had hesitated to postpone his return to his family at the call of the public interest.

If the editors of the newspapers of Europe could have looked at the land registers of Brittany they would have found there a refutation of the sensational news they spread. They declared that Lafayette had received enormous territories in the New World as a reward for his services. The truth was that he had had to sacrifice to his passion for freedom, one after the other, the five finest and most extensive of the domains he had inherited in Brittany from his mother. It was only a small remaining property that entitled him to his place in the provincial council.

The Bretons, proud and defiant, like the cliffs on their shores, were known in France as the most recalcitrant of the country's subjects. They were the best possible instructors for acquainting Lafayette with the abuses, the oppression and the injustices of the arbitrary rule of Versailles.

Since the birth of his first child, Louis XVI had been his wife's bondsman. At Marie Antoinette's bidding, or at that of the nobles and clergy who prompted her, he had dismissed Necker and put the Comte de Calonne in his place. Calonne had been about two years in office when Lafayette returned from America. The count had long been a member of the dissolute group who had taken pride in their nickname of Louis XV's "roués"; and his one and only concern was to satisfy every influential favorite at Court. Instead of protesting, like the miserly kill-joy Necker, against the queen's extravagances and lavishness, the new minister gave his support to every request for the grant of new sinecures, as though the exchequer were overflowing with gold. The Duchesse de Lamballe, daughter-in-law of the richest feudal lord in France, lost a million francs one night to Marie Antoinette. As compensation there was created for her a special office of Surintendante du Lit de la Reine (Mistress of the Queen's Bed), with an annual salary equal to her one day's loss! Members and friends of the house of Polignac received for various similar "services" nearly three millions a year, and Lafayette's own relations, the Noailles family, received 1,800,000 francs a year in "pensions," quite apart from ordinary salaries and payments in respect of official posts and dignities.

Lafayette himself renounced a pension of 750 francs which Louis XV had granted to meet the cost of the education of this heir to three millions. Is it not eloquent of the extravagance at Court that this pension would otherwise have continued to be paid year after year? He renounced it in favor of a poor widow and a famished invalid. He would have been wiser to accept the money and pass it on to the two beneficiaries through his own bailiff; for his written renunciation made a bad impression at Court. It was a point of honor at Versailles to make the most of their majesties' liberality. Even the richest competed in demonstrating the extent of their enjoyment of royal favor.

"What are a few thousand francs more or less to the king?" said the courtiers, with a shrug of the shoulders.

"The sweat of a whole village," replied Lafayette. He had not forgotten the readings from Necker's book nor the scenes of poverty he had witnessed as a boy in Auvergne.

Extreme language of this sort was not to the taste of the society of Versailles. Indeed, it was not quite gentlemanly even to mention money! Lafayette himself avoided discussing mere money questions. His money was always at the service of those in need; but he felt no call to struggle against the existence of poverty; he was concerned for the "higher" problem of spiritual oppression. He had scarcely been two months in France after his return when he wrote to Washington:

Protestants in France are under intolerable despotism. Although open persecution does not now exist, yet it depends upon the whim of the King, queen, parliament, or any of the ministry. Marriages are not legal among them; their wills have no force by law; their children are to be bastards; their persons to be hanged. I have put it into my head to be a leader in that affair, and to have their situation changed. With that view I am going, under other pretences, to visit their chief places of abode, with the consent of M. de Castries and another. I will afterwards endeavour to gain M. de Vergennes and the parliament, with the keeper of the seals, who acts as chancellor.

It is a work of time and of some danger to me, because none of them would give me a scrap of paper, or countenance whatsoever;

but I run my chance. M. de Castries could only receive the secret from me, because it is not in his department. Do not answer me about it, only that you had my cyphered letter by Mr. Adams. But when, in the course of the fall, or winter, you hear of something that way, I wanted you to know I had a hand in it.

This request for caution reveals the fanatical intolerance from which the country was suffering, in spite of Voltaire and the Encyclopedists, even under the much-extolled benevolence of Louis XVI. Were it not for his world-wide fame, Lafayette might have had to pay dearly for the tour he undertook of the districts inhabited by Protestants, his friendly intercourse with Protestant clergymen, and his inquiries concerning persecution and abuses on the part of the ecclesiastical authorities. He was left alone only because it would have been impolitic to harm a man who was a welcome guest with every sovereign in Europe.

The first monarch to express a desire to meet the young conqueror was Frederick II of Prussia, the old freemason and atheist. Lafayette wrote with intelligible pride to Washington that he had been invited to maneuvers of picked troops under Frederick's personal command.

IX. WITH FREDERICK THE GREAT

BENJAMIN FRANKLIN, then seventy-nine, left France at the same time as Lafayette. It is significant of Lafayette's standing that the octogenarian statesman took back with him to America this recommendation from Lafayette to Washington in favor of Franklin's grandson:

. . . a very deserving young man, who wishes to be introduced by me to you, and whom I beg leave to recommend to your attention. He has been much employed in public service: got nothing by it, and as the doctor loves him better than any one in the world, I think he ought to have the satisfaction to see him noticed by congress.

In Lafayette's full life the few months spent on this tour to Potsdam, Vienna and some of the smaller European courts, marks a sort of zenith; it is the period of the bringing in of the rich harvest of his youth.

On his way, at Cassel, he saw once more the Hessian soldiers whom he had only seen before in rags, scratched and torn by the thickets of America's virgin forests. And at the king's table at Sanssouci, the royal palace near Potsdam, he had as his neighbor, of all men, Lord Cornwallis—this time not without his sword, as after the capitulation at Yorktown. Without question Frederick's gouty fingers had sorted the cards that produced this situation. A sardonic smile must have passed over the thin lips of the "crowned philosopher" at the forced courtesies of the two former adversaries. How many thousand soldiers had cut one another down at the command of these two neighbors at dinner! How admirable an illustration of the biting sarcasms the king used to utter concerning affairs of state, wars, the morality of princes, and the stupidity of their exploited subjects!

For Lafayette this meeting with the most famous man of his day, friend of Voltaire and renowned soldier, was an unforgettable experience. He draws a picturesque portrait of the monarch in a letter to Washington:

In spite of all that I heard about him, I could not help being struck with the figure of an old, decrepit and dirty corporal, all covered with snuff, his head almost lying on one shoulder, and his fingers nearly dislocated by the gout. But what surprised me much more, was the fire and sometimes the softness of the most beautiful eyes that I ever saw, which gave to his face an expression as charming as it can be rude and menacing when he is at the head of his army.

Frederick himself, then seventy-three, observed Lafayette with the keenness of an adversary in the ring. He saw in him the forerunner of the new time of which, as a king concerned for his dynasty, he could have nothing but apprehension. Freemason and Voltairean though he was, and familiar with every progressive idea, the old king was a skeptic and a misanthrope (*"cette maudite race, à laquelle nous appartenons"*), and had no faith in the realization of democratic theories. Just as he liked to sun his old body but would shade his eyes from the rays, so the "philosopher of Sanssouci" only blinked now and then at the distant horizon which Lafayette described to him. He listened patiently to his young guest's enthusiastic talk of constitutions, franchise and the legislative

power of assembled representatives of the people, and contented himself with replying dryly, when the propagandist
had finished:

"I used to know a young man who spoke as you have done.
Do you know what happened to him?"

"No, Your Majesty," stammered Lafayette, taken aback.

"Why, sir, he was hanged!"

If Frederick offered this story as a warning, he was to be
justified in time. Not quite ten years after his visit to the Prussian court Lafayette was to make the acquaintance of the
Prussian prisons and to come very close to the gallows.

The marquis reaped a better harvest as a soldier than as a
commercial traveler for democracy; he described the Prussian
maneuvers to Washington with unrestrained admiration.

His visit to Vienna, to the second crowned freethinker of his
day, Joseph II, was again only a qualified success. The monarch
listened to a detailed report, given at his own request, on the
novel state; but he was too convinced an autocrat not to be
shocked at Lafayette's advocacy.

The tour of Europe lasted nearly six months, with visits to
Cassel, Brunswick, Potsdam, Prague, Dresden, Breslau, Vienna,
and then once more to Berlin and Potsdam on the way back to
Paris. The fêted "hero of two worlds" saw nothing on the
whole tour, as he writes to Washington, but "princes, regiments, and post-horses."

On his return home in the late autumn of 1785 he found the
country in an uproar over the Diamond Necklace affair, which
marked a turning point in the queen's life.

After a hundred and fifty years this affair remains a mystery. Marie Antoinette was constantly in want of money, and
driven to put off the creditors for her unending purchases of
jewels and finery rather than approach the king. When Boeh-
mer at Bassange, the Court jewelers, first offered her the
precious necklace for 800,000 francs she refused it, exclaiming:
"You must find a richer customer." But why did she throw
into the fire at once the letter demanding payment of the
first installment? If she knew nothing of the deal made in
her name by Cardinal de Rohan, ought she not to have paid
more attention to an improper claim for 200,000 francs?
Finally, Rohan's secretary rode a horse to death on his way to

burn the letters from the queen which had been "forged" by the Comtesse de La Motte, the cardinal's mistress, while the countess, after being publicly whipped and branded and condemned to confinement for life in a nunnery, was helped to escape by the Duchesse de Lamballe, the queen's most intimate friend!

It may be that the whole story subsequently published by the Comtesse de La Motte in London was a pack of lies. But whether Marie Antoinette had played any guilty part in the affair or not, all France believed that she had done. So far had the daughter of Maria Theresa lost repute.

Lafayette attached little importance to this sensational case. In his long letters to Washington he only mentioned the affair once, in telling his friend that the cardinal had been liberated.

X. AT HOME

LAFAYETTE CONTINUED loyally at work in America's service. He used his brilliant reception at the courts of Europe as a further lever for raising the prestige of the new state. Everywhere he endeavored to push through favorable commercial treaties, and on his return to France he persuaded Calonne to set up a commission of farmers of taxes and prominent financiers, worked out a plan for the reduction of the high duty on tobacco, and put in front of the reluctant *fermiers généraux* detailed figures to show that the increased turnover resulting from lower prices would increase their revenues. He was a *grand seigneur* too generous and too careless of money to grind his own bailiffs, but succeeded in beating down these bloodsuckers of state concessionaires. The American farmers sent him in token of gratitude a cheese weighing 500 lbs.

Destiny made strange play with another gift voted by the parliament of the state of Virginia to the country's liberator. Old Franklin had been accompanied by a sculptor sent to America by Lafayette at his own cost to make a bust of General Washington for the château of Chavaniac. The government of Virginia took the opportunity of the artist's presence to order two busts of Lafayette, one for its own assembly hall and the other for the Hôtel de Ville in Paris. Jefferson, Benjamin Franklin's successor at the Legation in Paris, subsequently American President, was entrusted with the formal presentation of the second bust.

Three years later, after the storming of the Bastille, when the citizens of Paris, in mortal terror at the sight of heads carried up and down the streets on pikestaffs, were in search of a leader who could inspire confidence in the armed people, somebody pointed to the bust of the champion of American independence, and the cry of "Vive Lafayette!" was taken up and thundered through the streets of Paris in confirmation of the happy choice.

These American tributes were not the only signs of Lafayette's worldwide popularity. The Empress Catherine of Russia, who had not been afraid to summon the free-thinking Diderot to her Court, expressed the desire to meet also the famous champion of Liberty. Nature had set in the queen's insatiable body an active mind and a keen thirst for knowledge, and this most absolute monarch of her epoch was interested to learn from Lafayette the results of the experiment in popular government. The French ambassador in St Petersburg, himself a Noailles and a relation of Lafayette, transmitted the invitation, with a special request from the Czarina that he should not delay his journey, as she had to inspect the Crimea in the coming spring and would be away for a long time. After "so many post-horses and uniforms," Lafayette was far less interested in seeing St Petersburg than in traveling through the storied lands on the shores of the Black Sea in the Czarina's entourage. He asked and received permission to travel via Constantinople and join Catherine's suite in the spring of 1787. His letters to Washington were full of enthusiasm at the hope of soon visiting the fascinating countries of the Near East.

Only "hope," for, since the fall of Necker and the conclusion of the burdensome alliance with America, France's financial situation had daily grown worse. All the hopes of the country rested in the dismissed minister, who was living in exile. His daughter, Mme de Staël, the celebrated wife of the ambassador of the King of Sweden, assembled in her literary salon the society which, if it could, would have gathered round the throne, especially in such disturbed times. On his return from the royal hunt at Fontainebleau Lafayette visited her house, at the risk of disgrace at Court.

Things had reached such a pitch under Calonne's malad-
ministration that an English traveler noted with astonishment a thoroughly subversive demonstration in the royal
theater at Versailles: rounds of applause interrupted the performance of a play of Voltaire's when an actor declaimed a
line to the effect that he loved freedom and "held kings in
horror." The growing discontent made even Calonne appre-
hensive; as a last resource, he advised the king to convoke an
assembly of notables. It might be that a united effort of the
best heads in the country could still avert the threatening
state bankruptcy.

On learning of this decision, Lafayette at once canceled his
visit to the Czarina. He felt that the moment had now come
in France for making an end of the appalling abuses of
"tyranny."

A last ray of royal favor fell on him at the opening of the
assembly of notables on February 22, 1787. Of the 144 members of the assembly, twenty were housed in the royal palace,
and Lafayette was one of these twenty.

The first sight of the assembly was a shock to the nobles.
Among those present were the mayors of the principal cities of
France; the prelates and the high aristocrats were in the
minority; these two privileged classes observed with alarm that
their united forces failed to outnumber those of the bourgeois
representatives. A dramatic surprise had been secretly prepared
for them. Marie Antoinette herself had been given no hint of
it, for fear of intervention.

It was discovered now that Calonne, with his easy-going
prodigality, had been of no more service than his dreadful
predecessor. The minister was careful not to disclose the total
amount of the deficit; with all his desire to damage Necker,
he did not dare to reveal the frightful depth of the abyss. He
tried to absolve himself and the king by throwing all blame on
the past. For a full century, he explained, the state had been
living on credit. For decades past each year had begun with
the revenues of three years to come already expended. In
order to cover themselves against failures of crops, floods, and
other disasters, the farmers of taxes had made advances to the
state at enormous rates of discount. The growing impoverish-
ment of the country was making the collection of taxes more

and more costly; administrative expenses were beginning to swallow up the whole revenue. Of the money extracted from the half-starved people only one tenth was reaching the exchequer. France was being bled to death, and yet the king was compelled continually to contract fresh debts because the ordinary revenues no longer sufficed even to cover interest payments.

This tale had been heard before from Necker, and from Turgot before him; both of them had dared to point the moral and to bring forward the monstrous proposal to interfere with the freedom from taxation of the two privileged classes, the nobility and the clergy, and both of them had been turned out for doing so. Now the same demand fell like a bomb at the end of Calonne's speech. Nine tenths of the soil of France, he said, was free of all taxation, and the possessors of the remaining one tenth had to maintain the rich!

Never before had anyone ventured in the presence of the King of France to describe as "abuses" these traditional rights of the great spiritual and secular dignitaries of the kingdom. Calonne's speech was his undoing. The "mainstays of the throne," trembling for their rights, took refuge behind the queen. Calonne was forced to declare the actual figure of the deficit. He admitted no more than a milliard and a quarter, scarcely more than half of the true figure; but a panic broke out all over the country. Louis XVI himself went into one of his frequent fits of rage: he smashed the first chair that came to his hand as he shouted, "That villain Calonne! I ought to have him hanged!"

Among the masses, led by their instincts, the revelation of the enormous figure of the debt let loose the hatred that had long been accumulating against "the Austrian woman"; Marie Antoinette could scarcely show herself anywhere without hearing her new nickname of "Madame Déficit." Too vain not to be wounded by her unpopularity, too proud to allow herself to be intimidated, she further provoked public opinion by her arrogance. Backed by the Comte d'Artois, the Polignacs and their noble friends, she urged the king to resist all innovators, regarding any appeal to the notables as an abandonment of the royal prerogative. The king, undecided by nature, would have asked nothing better than to sound the retreat; but the

144 counselors were now in session. They divided into seven commissions, each under the presidency of a prince of the blood royal. Lafayette was assigned to the commission of the Comte d'Artois, but the memory of their riding lessons together could not diminish their hostility.

So long as nothing more was at issue than the fate of the Protestants, there were no serious differences. The princes were too frivolous to be fanatical and were in favor of tolerance, and the king himself was soft-hearted. But out of respect for his ancestors he modified only the severest laws. Lafayette only began to make himself seriously unpopular when he attacked the *fermiers généraux,* the farmers-general of taxes and exposed the dishonest means by which they enriched themselves at the expense of the defenceless taxpayers. He did not content himself with vague allusions, but gave details and went straight to the point. The Comte d'Artois was not prepared for this tone. Sentimental regrets for the poverty of the lowest grades of society, private disparagement of men who had enriched themselves as farmers of taxes—all this was good form and evidence of a modern outlook. But public denunciation of the authorities, innuendos pressed as far as the king's immediate entourage! When Louis XVI learned of this from his brother he flew once more into a rage and told the Comte d'Artois to warn Lafayette that anyone bringing forward such grave charges must have the courage to submit them in writing over his own signature.

The taunt was unjust, if only because of the inequality of the opposing forces—the royal omnipotence on one side and the isolation on the other of the accuser, who ran the risk of being thrown into the Bastille. Nevertheless, Lafayette had the minutes of the assembly transmitted to him, and calmly placed at the foot of the text of his speech his signature: "Gilbert du Motier, Marquis de Lafayette, *maréchal de camp* of the king's armies." This was provocative enough, but he went further: he took advantage of the king's "permission" to add to his charges this statement:

The millions that are being dissipated are raised by taxes, and taxes can be justified only by the real needs of the state. All these millions abandoned to depredation or cupidity are the price of the

sweat, the tears, and it may be the blood of the people, and the reckoning of misery caused by the raising of these sums so lightly
thrown away is a terrifying reflection on the justice and goodness
which we know to be the natural sentiments of His Majesty.

Under the shelter of this compliment, Lafayette, signing his
name in full, took the liberty to address very humbly to the
king a petition for a strict inquiry, by persons in whom
absolute trust could be placed, into all the accounts of the
administrators of the royal domains, and the farmers of taxes
and duties, with an examination of the allocation of pensions
and the conveyances of land.

If after this Louis XVI did not have this pert disturber of
the peace thrown into the Bastille, it was less because of his
natural indecision than because his conscience was not clear.
He was too familiar with the shameful details of the financial
administration to dare to have them made public knowledge.
He took advantage of the intervening period between the fall
of Calonne and the entry into office of the new minister to
destroy with his own hand the most compromising documents.
But to appease his conscience he set a good example by cutting
down his own expenditure and compelled the queen to make
a great reduction in her extravagant budget.

But once more, just as after earlier accessions of energy of
this sort, he feebly gave way before his wife's stronger will.
Marie Antoinette had a fatal incapacity for putting the right
man in the right place. Under the influence of courtiers concerned for their own privileges, who affected only to be
anxious to maintain the royal authority, she persuaded the
weak-willed king to show that he was not to be moved by
the impertinent meddling of the notables, and she secured the
appointment of Loménie de Brienne, Archbishop of Toulouse,
as minister of finance in Calonne's place. The bishop hastened
to do the will of his exalted patroness by sending home the
144 notables.

At the final meeting of the assembly the Marquis de Lafayette and the Comte d'Artois came once more into collision;
for in regard to the principal question the result achieved by
the assembly amounted to nothing. The Protestants had been
recommended to the king's favor, and a resolution had been

passed advocating the reintroduction of elected provincial assemblies in place of official nominees, as a guarantee of stricter control. But the exchequer was still empty; the attack on the immunity of the rich from taxation had failed, and no new sources of revenue had been discovered. The thing that all clear-sighted observers had predicted had come to pass: the wisdom of the monarch by divine right permitted no challenge from the limited knowledge of lesser mortals.

But the energetic Lafayette was not to be deterred from making yet another demand. He called for the entry of this petition in the minutes of the assembly:

> We humbly beg His Majesty now to fix a date when he will himself assume control of all operations, and assure a happy result thereof for all time, through the convocation of a National Assembly.

"A National Assembly"—the phrase could not but sound strange in the ears of the Comte d'Artois, who knew only of three estates and, outside them, peasants and populace, and for whom even these did not make up a community, since the people changed their masters with every inheritance, marriage, and conquest. He had heard of an institution in the past history of the country, now almost forgotten, called the États-Généraux. The crown used to summon this assembly when there was urgent need of money; all three estates, the lords temporal and spiritual and even common citizens, had the right freely to elect representatives, furnished with written instructions by those who elected them, in order to vote the king new taxes in return for such concessions as could be obtained. For two centuries there had been none of this haggling between the crown and its own subjects: absolutism had deprived them of all rights and made them the property of their crowned master. The Comte d'Artois did not trouble his head long over so bizarre a word as "nation." The cool proposal to turn back the clock two hundred years and degrade the crown once more to the level of a party to a deal was itself provocative enough.

"What!" he exclaimed, in amazement, "do you want to demand the summoning of the États-Généraux?"

"Yes, monseigneur," Lafayette replied with an ambiguous smile, "and perhaps even something better."

He had no illusions as to the effect his intervention could have. He wrote to Washington on May 5, 1787:

The king, his family, and the high personages of his entourage, with the exception of a few friends, do not forgive the liberty I have taken. But it is above all my popularity among the other classes of the nation that they grudge me.

This popularity was indeed the cause of great concern at Court. There were plenty of voluntary spies who observed every public appearance of Lafayette in Auvergne, and every coming and going of his guests when he stayed at Chavaniac, and who then dispatched malevolent stories of the noxious influence of this "agitator." Not that the other provinces showed any less unrest than Auvergne; but through all the ages rulers have made the same mistake as the bad physician who tries to cure a sickness by merely attacking its symptoms. They imagine that they have only to wring the necks of the cocks who crow loudest in order to prevent the sun from rising. Their error is as old as the world.

XI. "LITTLE BY LITTLE"

WHEN LAFAYETTE began "agitating," as the reports called it, a century had already passed since in England the king by divine right had been beheaded for refusing to submit to the control of his subjects or to allow the amount of his expenditure to be dictated to him. But now news from America was beginning to filter into France; it was spread by returning officers' servants and by sailors in the mercantile marine. There the rich merchant, the shipowner, the silk manufacturer needed no "agitator" to persuade them to ask themselves why they should eternally be fleeced for the benefit of high-born idlers. The French middle-class man, regarded as an inferior and excluded from all honors and places, was now beginning himself to lay claim to rights and was no longer content to bear the whole burden of the state for the benefit of noble gentlemen who had merely taken the trouble to be born!

Beaumarchais's *Figaro* had popularized the difficult philosophy of the great thinkers, Diderot, Rousseau, Voltaire. The bourgeoisie itself undertook the "enlightenment" of the poorest classes, hungry, homeless, ragged and down-trodden. The dangerous game that regularly precedes every revolution then began: the desperate masses were whipped up with the aid of the aroma of the roasting chestnuts. Once the victory had been won the masses would be left with their burns, the whippers-up would have the chestnuts.

The notables had managed to secure permission to convoke provincial assemblies once more, and in these assemblies the general discontent was everywhere voiced. Lafayette wrote cheerfully to Washington that the nation was slowly awakening to the consciousness of its strength. He himself went ahead of this evolution, careless of the fact that he was alienating the last sympathies for a connection of the house of Noailles. The popular enthusiasm saved him from any annoyance; in all the towns of Auvergne he was received with such acclamation that he might have imagined himself to be back in America. An ecclesiastical chronicler sought for excuses for this popularity, which was almost going beyond the bounds of decency: "It was the first opportunity the people had had of seeing a real 'hero,' and the crowd were never tired of gazing at him."

Lafayette, as always, underestimated the difficulties to be faced. He wrote confidently to Washington that events would bring France

Little by little, without a great convulsion, to an independent representation and, consequently, to a diminution of the royal authority. But it is a matter of time, and will proceed the more slowly that the interests of powerful men will clog the wheels.

"Little by little, without a great convulsion"! Within two years the first heads were carried round Paris on pikes! But Lafayette was consumed with impatience:

The people, my dear General, are so apathetic in this country that the doctors have had to open a vein to save me from the consequences of my annoyance.

XII. IN DISGRACE

THE GOOD EFFECTS, if any, of this blood-letting were assisted for a time by unrest in Holland. A rising against the tyranny

of the Stadhouder gave Lafayette the opportunity of helping
the oppressed Netherlanders, if not with his sword, at least
with his money; but the arrival of Prussian troops made any
further resistance hopeless. Lafayette had no resource left during this time of waiting but to resume his service in the French
army. The Court was only too glad to accede to his request for
permission to return to duty; it was a satisfaction to know
that this troublesome politician would be under military discipline.

But his absence from the scene did not end the protests
against the new taxation. During the latter half of 1788 the
resistance grew alarmingly. The provincial assembly of Brittany
followed the example of Auvergne, refusing in its turn to
agree to the new taxes. And among the signatories to its protest was the Marquis de Lafayette!

This filled the cup to overflowing. Marie Antoinette took
the first opportunity to ask the marquis what Breton questions
had to do with an Auvergnat seigneur. Lafayette retorted,
with more readiness than discretion, with a question of his
own:

"Is not Your Majesty Queen of France and also a member of
the house of Austria?"

This reply was a declaration of war. The next day the king
ordered Lafayette through the Minister of War to return his
diploma of *maréchal de camp;* he no longer required the services of a disrespectful officer. Incidentally, of course, he restored
Lafayette's freedom of political action. The king would have
been wiser to recognize the growing peril and not to thin
the ranks of his loyal courtiers; but the daughter of Maria
Theresa considered that it was beneath the dignity of a queen
of France to exercise caution. Mirabeau said later with justice
that Marie Antoinette was the only man at Court.

To satisfy the high protectress who had set him in the saddle, Loménie de Brienne advised the king to act with energy.
New taxes were imposed, provoking the most bitter opposition from the bourgeoisie and the legal profession. All certificates, consignment notes, receipts, documents, commercial
contracts, ledgers, newspapers, and printed sheets of music
were made subject to a stamp duty which affected all classes
and all occupations. It was clear now how unjust and puerile

it had been to accuse Lafayette and other "agitators" of his sort of stirring up the population. This time the whole of the members of the Paris Parlement unanimously refused to register the new law. Louis XVI, urged on by his wife and his advisers, summoned the Parlement to Versailles and repeated in person his order for the new edicts to be registered. But the magistrates stood firm. They knew that they had the whole country behind them. They registered the decrees in favor of the Protestants, and other concessions which the king had made, but not the new fiscal laws.

In this desperate situation Louis XVI resolved on a supreme concession. He pledged his word as a king that he would summon the États-Généraux, the States-General, within five years! The new edicts, providing a way out of the financial difficulties, were to have force only for five years, and then the great assembly, freely elected and representative of all three estates, should reorganize the whole of the public administration from top to bottom.

Unfortunately it was too late; no trust was placed any longer in the king's promises; the cross-currents at Court and the disastrous influence of Marie Antoinette were too widely known. However sincere the king might be in making his promise, everybody knew that the queen and her camarilla would get it revoked, not in five years, but in five days.

Louis then took a further step. He came to the Parlement in Paris and ordered that the decrees should be registered there and then in his presence. The intransigents of Versailles forgot that a century had passed, the century of Voltaire and of "Enlightenment," since the Roi Soleil had come to that Parlement whip in hand to compel the magistrates to do his will. The poor king, awkward and ill at ease, was almost a pitiful figure when, red in the face and with great beads of sweat on his forehead, he demanded, in a carefully rehearsed tone of command, the immediate registration of the decrees. Were it not for his fear of his wife's wrath, he would scarcely have been able to resist the orator who implored him on his knees to convoke the States-General not in five years but at once.

It was on this occasion that the Duke of Orleans, the future Philippe Égalité, for the first time took the people's side against his cousin, the anointed ruler. His support emboldened the magistrates of the Parlement to append to the registration a declaration that it had not been a voluntary act, but had been wrung from them by the threat of force. The day after this the king issued orders for the arrest of the "ringleaders" and the banishment of the Duke of Orleans.

All the Court achieved by this was to make martyrs who were a fresh strength to the opposition. When the Duke of Orleans left the Palais Royal he was acclaimed like a victorious commander. One of the king's ministers, the Baron de Breteuil, had been commissioned by the king to accompany the duke as far as his place of exile. The duke, shrugging his shoulders, and pointing to the board on which the lackeys stood, said to the minister:

"Very well, get up behind."

"The Turkish despotism of the régime," wrote Lafayette to Washington, "is maddening me." Yet he might well have rejoiced at it; for each new provocation from the Court cost the king a year out of the five he had given himself. Loménie de Brienne, as though stricken with blindness, allowed himself to be pushed into more and more fatal measures, without noticing how he was isolating the throne and driving the whole country into the opposition camp. Chained to his bed by a grave malady, he carried on the hopeless struggle from his sickroom. Every breath of opposition was punished by imprisonment. The Marquis d'Agout had to go twice with his soldiers from Versailles to Paris and back again to make the Parlement deliver up the two magistrates condemned as "ringleaders"; on his order for the delivery of the culprits the whole of the members present rose in a body and declared that they were all responsible. Finally the king dissolved the Parlement and replaced it by a curious supreme court ("Cour Plénière") composed of princes, high dignitaries, and the most hated of the intriguers in Marie Antoinette's entourage. The Parisians were held down by a strong garrison, and contented themselves for the time with exercising their wit over the lord high steward, whose duty was to hold the ink bottle, and the Master of the Horse, who pumiced the parchment. But in the provinces the first victims began to fall. Petitions protesting against the royal decrees had a menacing air; and at Rennes the king's envoy, as he was enforcing the dissolution of the Breton Parlement with the aid of soldiery, was wounded by a stone thrown at him.

It was about this time that the American Morris, of whom mention has already been made, arrived in Paris. (His Christian name was "Gouverneur," as others might be called James or John; it was a name which might give rise to misapprehension.) Morris, filled with pride at the distinction of the people he was meeting, spoke only with lofty irony of the "democratic" protectors of the plebs. To avoid giving offence to Washington he passed lightly over his visit to Lafayette, simply saying that the general's family spoke English well, and the eldest daughter had even sung to him an American popular song; he scarcely mentioned the marquis's political attitude. But the official report from the minister, Jefferson, gave sufficient ground for anxiety:

The marquis has drawn upon himself the enmity of the whole court; on the other hand, his credit is growing among the nation. But for some time I have trembled for his liberty.

XIII.   THE STATES-GENERAL

As FOR LAFAYETTE himself, he saw the day of triumph dawning; for all the decrees and banishments and arrests could not fill the empty exchequer. The first thing necessary for rule by violence, as for war, is money. Praetorian Guards will only shoot down the people if they are paid for it. The sick minister's friends would not hear of personal sacrifices. The rich archbishops declared from their pulpits that their wealth belonged to heaven and that it would be sacrilege to tax it.

Brienne's inability to procure money was the end of his ministry. The queen wept for rage when she had to let him go, and Louis XVI complained that "they are making me bring back Necker; he will do me no good." And indeed, the unhappy king found nothing to temper his misfortunes. With the return of the bourgeois heretic from Geneva the confidence of the capitalists also returned, and credit with it. At the same time the promised ultimate convocation of the States-General had to be advanced four years. The date for their opening was fixed at—May 1, 1789.

Lafayette wrote in triumph to his friend Washington of this victory of the good cause. His faith in the panacea of a freely elected popular assembly was absolute; he saw a completely cloudless future. Once more, on November 6, 1788, he took his seat as a notable, in the Comte d'Artois's committee for laying down the procedure in the impending elections. If the high dignitaries of the Church had had their way the elections would have been held on the same basis as for the States-General of two centuries earlier. But the specter of state bankruptcy was at the door; the speculation in grain, pleasantly named "free trade," had driven prices so high that the peasants could not even afford to buy their seed corn. Shortage of money, high rates of interest, and vanishing purchasing power had crippled trade and industry. In order to prevent new rivals from setting up in business, the guilds imposed prohibitive apprenticeship fees; every carpenter's bench, every cobbler's or tailor's workshop, every general store became an entailed property.

The tilled land was so burdened with dues that it scarcely provided food for the tiller, and there was no trade to which he could turn. Innumerable beggars covered the country like a swarm of locusts, and the state was compelled to organize a sort of barrack system for them: anyone found to be wandering without means of subsistence was required to be lodged at once in the nearest institution, and the institutions were always filled to overflowing. Crowded in hundreds into dark and verminous rooms, squeezed together, sick and healthy alike, as many as five or six on the same half-rotted straw palliasse, the inmates of these institutions were dying like flies every night, and yet for every vacant place there were two waiting at the door, to receive the plateful of watery soup provided out of the payment the concessionnaire received from the state. That payment had to cover not only his own profit but the bribes he had given in order to secure his contract.

Jacques Necker was realist enough to be well aware that, although all this misery existed cheek by jowl with the extravagant living of the two privileged estates, there was no possibility of securing any adequate remedy through voluntary concessions on their part. And everybody knew that his recall meant that the king intended to make use of the States-General for the suppression of the fiscal exemptions of the privileged classes. Moreover, in disregard of the most sacred traditions, the third estate was now to be assured of representation equal to that of the two other estates together. Accordingly, the notables representing the Church and the nobility took refuge behind the demand that the voting for bills must be decided not by the counting of heads but of orders! If the issue had been only over mere questions of money, these *grands seigneurs* would have blushed to haggle over it with their opponents, as they did, for five weeks. But they claimed, as always in such cases, to be defending a sacred principle—the principle that it is the first duty of every nobleman, and still more of every father of the Church, to pass on his inheritance intact to the next generation. All the protests and arguments of Lafayette and his friends were in vain. By a majority of votes it was declared that the procedure, the regulations and the statutes of the États-Généraux of 1614 must be observed in every respect.

After this open declaration of war on the people from the loyal supporters of the throne, the king sent the notables home, and the election campaign began. At once, as if every Frenchman had had a glimpse of the future, the whole country was in a fever. The people knew in their hearts that the struggle about to take place was one of life and death. Like a giant enchained, the whole nation of thirty millions summoned up its forces to free its limbs by a single wrench from the rusted chains of the past.

Lafayette hurried away from Paris to open his campaign in Auvergne. He made no secret of his determination to work for a reform of the law, cost what it might. He wrote plainly to Washington:

For my part, I am satisfied with the thought that before long I shall be in an assembly of representatives of the French nation, or—at Mt. Vernon.

XIV. THE GIANT STIRS

"LITTLE BY LITTLE, without a great convulsion"—so, wrote Lafayette in his letter to Washington, the people would awaken to the consciousness of their rights. In the resistance of the

two threatened classes he saw only the application of the brake
which would preserve the car from destruction through too
headlong a course. He cheerfully imagined that all that was
needed was to turn the peaceful streamlet of drawing-room
philosophy into the broader bed of parliamentary debate in
order that the mills of eloquence might grind out flour to feed
the famished millions. At Versailles and in Necker's ministry
there was the same illusion; it was supposed that a little arith-
metical operation would do all that was needed. At Christmas
a crown council was held, the queen herself attending; and it
was demonstrated to her that the number of bourgeois representatives must be doubled in order to carry through the
imposition of taxation on the nobility and the clergy.

The blindness of the Court could not be shown more plainly
than in the protest sent to Louis XVI by all the princes of the
blood, at the instance of the Comte d'Artois. In this fatal
document the nearest relatives of the sovereign, as the "proper
counsellors of the crown," voiced their warning against "every
attempt to interfere with old and tried institutions which for
centuries have provided the power and prestige of the kingdom." The Comte d'Artois, the Princes Condé and Conti, and
the Dukes of Enghien and Bourbon were unable to conceal
their alarm at the presumption of the third estate! They even
threatened that, if the third estate should use its doubled
representation to exploit the higher estates through the suppression of their fiscal privileges, the result might be open war-
fare. Degradation, humiliation, ignominy, spoliation—all the
wealth of the French language in forcible synonyms was poured
forth in the indignant denunciation of the attack on the
money bags as an outrage upon tradition. Even the provincial
Parlements of the lesser nobility and the legal gentry, who
shortly before had been of so revolutionary a temper that they
had refused to be intimidated by arrests, now registered the
convocation of the States-General only with the express addition of the proviso that it should take place in the same forms
as those observed in 1614; that is to say, without the doubling
of the bourgeois representation. The twenty-nine millions of
plain Frenchmen were not even to be allowed the same number
of representatives as the few hundred thousand privileged persons.

Only thirty dukes and princes had the good sense to offer voluntarily to dispense with the most burdensome of their feudal privileges. No one among the privileged classes dreamed that there might be other issues besides the question of money. They were dumbfounded when six millions of Frenchmen began to clamor insistently to be allowed to exercise their right to cast an indirect vote!

Six millions! Poor Necker was in the case of the sorcerer's apprentice. He had summoned the bourgeoisie, and the whole nation had been set in motion. It was not as though only the enlightened town population were proceeding to the polls; but the ignorant beasts of burden from the fields, who had always been put off with the Church's reminder of the life to come, were streaming into the villages to give their votes for delegates familiar with their wretched condition. The fear grew that this unexpected intrusion of the lowest strata would have its effect on the drafting of the so-called *cahiers* (the instructions each electoral committee had to give to its elected delegates), and that revolutionary demands would find their way into them.

The "nomination" of the delegates for Paris was reserved to the king. The Paris populace, "corrupted" by newspapers and pamphlets, was thus excluded from influence on the issue of the elections. What was not realized until too late was that the rest of the country had also been infected by the poison of "enlightenment."

The French people of 1789, unable to read, had seen the first thin rays of light penetrate into their prison chamber, as through the cracks and breaches in an undermined wall. The Pompadour said once, as she drove past the frozen and half-starved peasants: *"Le peuple est bien bon."* But she was mistaken. The quality she took for "goodness" was merely lack of imagination, the common human incapacity to imagine different conditions from those of everyday existence. Once this fatalism of the masses is disturbed, it is replaced by the active force of the eternal dream of happiness, a force not to be arrested by a few pounds of bread.

Here we find Lafayette for the first time on the wrong track. His place should not have been on the side of the privileged class. As the herald of equality of rights, he should not have come forward as one of the candidates of the nobility, but should have put himself at the head of the bourgeoisie and of the masses. His mistake was fully exploited against him by Right and Left alike. But no candidate from among the nobility, however progressive in views, went so far as to deny his class, with the single exception of the Comte de Mirabeau, who in seeking the votes of the bourgeois electors was guided by feelings of vengeance, by the rancor of a Coriolanus.

Mirabeau was the eldest son of a neurotic father who, under the pseudonym of "*L'Ami des Hommes*," preached loving-kindness in his works, but who had thrown his wife into a lunatic asylum, had driven his daughter to suicide and hunted his son and heir from prison to prison. This son was predestined to a career which was the exact opposite of Lafayette's; he was one of Fortune's victims; in his youth he had gone from disaster to disaster as Lafayette had gone from success to success. Like the marquis he was an officer at seventeen; but he began his career with a scandal, and at his own father's desire was confined in the casemates of the Île de Ré, until the Corsican war enabled him to recover his freedom. He fought in the war with distinction, but had scarcely returned from it when he found himself in danger of being imprisoned again as "unmanageable" if he did not marry the rich heiress his father had chosen for him. The young woman's parents were themselves opposed to the marriage on account of his evil reputation; to overcome their resistance Mirabeau appeared one morning on the girl's balcony in a dressing gown and with his hair in disorder, to the terror of the poor girl, who was compromised by his act and lost the whole of her dowry when she married this frenzied gambler. Later she obtained a separation from him, and his father once more had him thrown into prison. The daughter of the prison governor fell in love with the young count, helped him to escape and fled with him.

After this Mirabeau, with the rage of a lion demolishing his cage, threw himself against despotism in a book exposing the disgraceful traffic in *lettres de cachet* which was being carried on in France. This work made him known, and, driven by necessity, he worked with his pen for his daily bread and that of his mistress, writing whatever the publishers of Amsterdam and Hamburg might demand—politics or pornography; he was ready to publish the most intimate details of any scandal if he could find no other means of earning money. "My son the phrase merchant"—so his father called him, and he had the young couple arrested abroad; the lady was shut up in a convent and young Mirabeau in the Château d'If.

Four times a captive, and with his sight nearly destroyed through writing in the gloom of his cell at Vincennes, Mirabeau regained his liberty only after his father's death. He was eight years older than Lafayette, but they were eight years completely lost, which had left him nothing but a frantic thirst for what life had to offer. With his health undermined by his vices and his frame worn to the bone by the chain of poverty which made him the slave of unsatisfied desires, he bounded onto the political scene like an unknown provincial actor who seizes the chance of at last displaying his talent before the public of a capital. Like Lafayette, he needed to secure a seat at the election; but unlike him he was unshackled by any sort of conviction or family consideration. The provincial nobles were so imprudent as to contest the right of this dangerous man to be elected among them when he had no entailed property; the result was that the "phrase merchant" sold his eloquence to the bourgeois leaders, who felt deeply honored by their association with M. le comte, and hastened to provide him with a mandate. For some days he had this sign put up over an empty shop:

COUNT MIRABEAU   CLOTHIER

and the credulous public thereafter swore by this high-born aristocrat who had vowed to do battle for the rights of the poor.

Now the "phrase merchant" could at last hope to gain more by his eloquence than the poor fees of a scribbler! He felt that he had at his back millions of followers whom he could lash into fury with his voice of thunder and lead where he would. Already he counted with confidence on obtaining at least a ministerial portfolio. To make sure of winning his campaign, he started a newspaper and gathered round himself the whole of the literary advance guard of the militant revolutionaries, a talented but unscrupulous group.

Lafayette was ready for any sacrifice in his sincere enthusiasm for ideals which Mirabeau jingled like a bunch of skeleton keys. The two men could not fail to become mortal enemies. How could Lafayette descend like the other to the level of the *canaille?* If he had ever dreamed of coming forward as a representative of the lower orders, the repulsive example of Mirabeau would have been enough to deter him from doing so, quite apart from the opposition of all his family and friends.

The square of turf surrounded by the arcades of the Palais Royal, today so peaceful, was the witches' cauldron of the election of 1789, the fevered heart of Paris, sending out into the furthermost arteries of the faubourgs the wildest of lampoons and rumors and popular songs. Under the arcades was the *marché aux amours,* the teeming assemblage of prostitutes. The cafés and restaurants and gaming dens in the upper story brought the Duke of Orleans, the king's nephew—who was always in debt in spite of his immense wealth—an income which, if hardly in keeping with his dignity as a prince of the blood, was at least respectable in size. Was it without intention that this ill-famed spot was called the Palais Royal, instead of being named Palais d'Orléans after its owner? Was there not some underlying desire to compromise the title "royal"?

The owner, the future "Philippe Égalité," was a roué too worn out and indifferent to have any ambition left when the Revolution came. But all the dissatisfied, all those who had been left in the cold, all the pushing politicians and journalists made him a pretender against his will, in order to become his paladins if he should succeed to the throne. In this quarter Lafayette was hated even more violently than at Court, for he was regarded here as the most dangerous of rivals, one who might easily get all the best pickings when the struggle really began in the arena of the States-General.

XV. THE THIRD ESTATE

ONLY A CHANCE technical complication prevented the States-General from being opened on the appointed day, May 1. The solemn Te Deum was not chanted until the fourth; the opening came on the following day. When the procession was on its way to church from the Palace of Versailles, the elections had already begun in Paris. The city was to send 600 deputies to Versailles, 150 each chosen by the nobility and clergy and 300 representing the bourgeoisie. These latter were not elected by the people, as in every province, but nominated by the king; yet these 300 citizens of Paris, chosen by the monarch as the most "reliable," at once repudiated their mandatory and began to discuss the *cahiers* only after they had roundly declared that they regarded themselves as the representatives of the people and not of the Court.

This seditious resolution, passed by the most loyal citizens who could be discovered, ought to have been a warning to the monarchy to agree to small, superficial concessions which would strengthen its position. Blood had already flowed in many of the provinces, and the bourgeois deputies had brought with them in their *cahiers* energetic demands for equality of rights. A wise diplomacy would have sought to calm down this agitation.

In the working-class faubourgs of Paris a rumor suddenly spread that Réveillon, the rich upholsterer, one of the delegate electors of the Third Estate, had demanded a general reduction of wages! Nobody had heard him make this demand; but some groups of ragged vagabonds, men of a very doubtful type, moved among the workers and roused them against him, as an inhuman wretch for whom the poverty of the workers was still not dire enough.

Preparations for a riot went on with clockwork precision. The very elements seemed to be in the plot. An exceptional drought had destroyed the hopes placed in the season's crops. And secretly, without the knowledge of the king, who would not have tolerated "starvation campaigns" against his own subjects as his grandfather had done, enormous stocks of grain had been bought and shipped to Jersey, Guernsey, and even the New World.

Le Noir, ex-lieutenant of police, and De Sartines, his worthy successor, had protected this profitable operation, which was at the same time a political machination. In vain did Necker assemble all the principal grain merchants around Paris; they had scarcely received from the minister orders to hold their reserves at the disposition of the capital when there arrived at their offices a formal prohibition, signed by Necker himself, of all supplies to Paris. For producing these forged orders there were plenty of official seals in the desks of the former agents of the Pompadour and the Dubarry.

On top of the prohibitive price of bread there came the further misery of a winter of unusual rigor. Great bonfires were lighted outside the nobles' houses. When the cold was over, its place was taken by hunger; poor people were dying in the streets.

M. de Berthier, commandant of the garrison of Paris, warned the captain of the watch, in a letter which is still extant, that the mob had decided to sack and burn Réveillon's house on the morrow. But the watch did not appear until the afternoon, when the vandals had already carried away valuables, thrown the furniture out of the windows, and set the house on fire. Meanwhile patient queues of famished Parisians waited outside the bakers' shops; no food shop was pillaged, and no other private house was attacked. If it had been, the excuse would undoubtedly have been seized for suspending the Paris elections and dissolving the Assembly.

But the people had become clear-sighted. They saw through the maneuver of the *agents provocateurs* with a sure instinct. They placed all their hopes in the demands of the States-General; and they had learned more in this short period than in preceding centuries. The sensational pamphlet by the Abbé Sieyès, *Qu'est-ce que le Tiers État?* had become a sort of new evangel; his denunciation of the ignorant, indolent, heartless idlers who lived on the people was passed from lip to lip. Day and night the arcades beneath the Palais Royal rang with the shrill cries of the *camelots* hawking it. Those persons who could not read listened attentively to groups in debate. The new ideas filled the minds of the people and permeated throughout France, and even beyond her borders.

And what did Versailles do to prepare against the coming storm?

The narrowest of wrong-headed champions of tradition had wormed their way through all the old documents, to make sure that not the slightest alteration should be made in the procedure followed centuries before, and not the slightest account taken of the changed times. The externals of the procession to church on May 4, and of the opening ceremony on the next day, were themselves eloquent indications of the inevitably approaching catastrophe.

The magnificent procession was headed by the Tiers État, the Third Estate, humiliated by the same sumptuary clauses as 175 years before. Its representatives were permitted to be dressed only in black cloth, without any silk trimmings, and without buttons or any sort of decoration on their hats, the ribbons of which were not allowed even to have a bow at the side. This black, funereal procession was followed, in provocative contrast, by the nobles in flowing silk mantles, the buckles of which were studded with precious stones; underneath these were white satin coats covered with gold braid and decorations; precious stones sparkled on the feathered hats and the sword hilts. The reply of the Second Estate to the demand for equality was to march through the lines of spectators like a troop of peacocks with fans spread.

Only the Duke of Orleans, perhaps rehearsing his future role as Philippe Égalité, walked, as though by inadvertence, so far in front of his peers that he seemed to be following the Third Estate instead of leading the Second. He was loudly acclaimed by the crowd all along the route, as was the lion-headed Mirabeau. Lafayette, lost in the flamboyant procession of the nobles, said nothing; but Mirabeau's cheaply won popularity must have been a bitter pill to him. Which of the two was the one who had rendered genuine service and made genuine sacrifices for Liberty?

In his sermon the Bishop of Nancy, himself no revolutionary, described the intolerable poverty of the peasants and the indifference of the rich, and the shameless extortions of the farmers of taxes, "who commit their barbarous exactions in the name of a just and good king." At this, in this house of God and in the monarch's presence, there was loud applause. When before had such a thing been known? But this clap of thunder passed in its turn unheard by the Court intriguers.

Next day, at the royal opening of the session in the great Salle des Menus at Versailles, in the presence of two thousand invited spectators of the highest ranks of society, the black-coated men of the Third Estate were herded into a sort of hen coop, a wooden shed hurriedly improvised as a lobby. This had been put up outside the narrow back door through which the elected representatives of the "nation," already over five hundred in number, were to pass into the hall. For two-and-a-half hours the delegates of the king's twenty-nine million subjects had to wait here, standing packed together, while the carriages drove up to the front entrance and the Chief Master of Ceremonies, with his staff, assigned places in due order of precedence. Only when this had been done was the little back door opened, for the tired crowd of the Third Estate to struggle through under the ironic glances of the high society present.

After a short opening speech the king sat on his throne and put on his big feather hat, ornamented for the occasion with the famous "Pit," the biggest of the crown diamonds. The representatives of the two higher estates hastened to take advantage of their privilege of putting on their hats when the king did so. But, to their horror, the bourgeois crowd did the same. A great battle would have been lost, the foundations of the state would have been shaken, if Louis XVI had not had the surprising presence of mind to take off his hat again. He wiped his forehead, as though he were too hot, and held his hat in his hand until the end of the sitting, for three whole hours, so that nobody else in the hall should put his hat on. This was the first act of state of the new era, which was to make a clean sweep of so many of the injustices of the past.

Only the eyes of the Comte de Mirabeau, bleared with drinking and deep sunk in his swollen flesh, were sharp enough to read the future. This human ruin whose worn-out frame was, two years later, to be the first to be laid in the Panthéon, indicated with a motion of his head the sunburned, vigorous, corpulent king, and said to his neighbor:

"Voilà la victime!"

XVI.   THE RIGHTS OF MAN

AND THE Marquis de Lafayette? Where was this ardent protagonist of Democracy, who had crossed the ocean when he was little more than a boy in order to fight for the ideals of Liberty and Equality? Was he now, at thirty-two, denying all the glory of his youth so far as to smile with his peers at the shameful game the privileged classes were playing with the men who had the confidence of France's twenty-nine millions?

No—if he was a silent witness of this arrogant trifling, he was far from applauding it. But the instructions in his *cahier*, that of the Auvergnat nobility, left him no freedom of action, even when matters more serious than the child's play of hats on and hats off were at issue. He was bound by oath to defend the vote by orders and not by heads. No one could be more sincere in his desire to see joint discussions and voting on an equal basis, or more keenly alive to the indefensibility of giving more weight to the vote of a brainless noble or an intolerant prelate than to that of an able man of the Third Estate. His situation was indeed both trying and compromising: in his heart he condemned the privileges of birth; outwardly he had to defend them. Among his own class he was nevertheless in bad odor, for he made no secret of his sympathies. The good Jefferson said to him: "Your principles would plainly throw you into the arms of the people, but your instructions hold you back. I am very disturbed about your position."

The only way of emerging from this equivocal situation, this double apostasy, would have been to throw up his mandate from the nobility. Few as were the seats of the Third Estate falling vacant through deaths, resignations or contested election results, one would certainly have been found for the champion of liberty. The correspondence, the private diaries, even the accusations of his contemporaries, provide ample evidence that as the Court grew more and more reactionary Lafayette became more and more determined to resign his mandate; but events moved too rapidly.

The beginning of the electoral campaign in France coincided with the election of Washington as the first President of the American Republic. The temporary lull in the correspondence which had been so actively carried on between the two friends was, no doubt, a consequence of the disturbed times; but on Lafayette's side it was also due to a temporary infatuation. During the critical weeks of the assembly he was writing to his flame not only daily but often several times in the course of a few hours. These letters have been included in his collected correspondence without mention of the name of the lady, but this discretion only adds to the credibility of the text, which is too confidential not to be sincere:

At nineteen I devoted myself to the liberation of mankind and the destruction of despotism, in so far as a single weak individual like myself could achieve anything. I left for the New World, against universal opposition and aided by no one. I have tried everything except civil war, on which I could have entered but did not, because I dreaded its horrors. You can imagine, then, how delighted I cannot but be at anything that helps on a revolution.

All this stuff I can write to nobody but you, not because I flatter myself that your judgment will be favourable but because I know I can count on your discretion. I swear to you that if I have made many mistakes I owe not a few of them to other people's caution.

Just as Lafayette blamed that caution, and with equal justice, the poor king might have attributed a large portion of his worst mistakes to other people's lack of caution. The Duchesse de Polignac took advantage of her unbounded influence over the queen to incite her against Necker and against allowing the crown to be humiliated by accepting the public degradation of its only sure supports, the clergy and the nobility, in face of the deputies of the Third Estate.

"Troops! We want troops!" cried the queen, wringing her hands in shame and exasperation at her husband's feebleness.

But things had scarcely reached this stage when there came a change. It is pathetic to observe how quickly the whole of the progressive section of the National Assembly, as the Third Estate had named itself, proceeded to eat humble pie when an iron ring of mercenary troops began to close round Versailles and Paris. Day by day the addresses from the deputations grew more submissive and the replies more arrogant; the deputies could only appeal to His Majesty's "gentle heart," and Louis XVI dealt more shortly and sharply with them as each new regiment arrived.

Only the populace of Paris refused to be intimidated. It showed itself alarmingly well informed. Dr Marat, formerly veterinary surgeon to the Comte d'Artois, had struck up an acquaintance with his master's grooms at the same time as with his horses. The *camelots* who shouted the doctor's newspaper in the streets announced a royalist coup d'état for July 15. The

names of the "strong men" were known, and it was known that
Necker was to be driven out. It was said that the old Maréchal
de Broglie (who once had received the young Lafayette so cordially at Metz) was to be appointed minister of war. Twelve
revolutionary ringleaders were to be publicly hanged; the list
was headed by Lafayette and Mirabeau!

Mystery, repeated again and again—neither of the imperilled
idols of the people dreamed of taking shelter behind the bastion
of the hundreds of thousands of the Paris populace, who were
already prepared to go to extremes! Necker, too, waited at
home for his dismissal and the decree of banishment while his
name was being acclaimed throughout the capital. Even Mirabeau, for all his thunders, feared to cast in his lot with the
unwashed mob more than he feared the executioner.

The progressive deputies, caught between perils from below
and above, confined themselves to desperate efforts to find
safety in new laws. Decrees were issued granting personal immunity to the representatives of the people and providing that
taxes should be levied only after approval by Parliament; with
these and other equally illusory ramparts the deputies sought
to defend themselves against the old marshal's regiments.

Only one man was unconcerned for the protection of his
own person and unprepared to remain fatalistically inactive,
merely awaiting the issue of events—the Marquis de Lafayette.
His one concern was to save from the threatening collapse such
elements of progress as could be saved. On July 11, with
Necker on the eve of dismissal and exile, and with De Broglie's
regiments ready to march into Paris to punish the populace
and turn out the National Assembly—at this hour of supreme
danger, when many men were looking round for any hole into
which to creep for safety, Lafayette mounted the tribune and
read out the Declaration of the Rights of Man:

Nature has made men free and equal; the necessary distinctions in
the social order are based only on general utility.

Every man is born with inalienable and imprescriptible rights;
these are the freedom of his opinions, the care for his honour and his
life, the right of property, the entire disposition of his person, his
industry, and all his faculties, the communication of his thoughts by
every possible means, the pursuit of well-being, and resistance to
oppression.

The individual's exercise of his natural rights has no limits save
those which assure the enjoyment of the same rights to the other
members of society.

No man may be made subject to laws other than those agreed to
by him or his representatives, promulgated in advance, and legally
applied.

The principle of all sovereignty resides in the nation. No corpora-
tion and no individual can have an authority which does not expressly
emanate therefrom.

All government has for its sole purpose the common good. This
requires that the legislative, executive, and judiciary powers shall be
distinct and defined, and that their organization shall assure the free
representation of the citizens, the responsibility of the agents, and
the impartiality of the judges.

The laws must be clear, precise, and uniform for all citizens.

Subsidies must be freely agreed to and proportionally distributed.

And since the introduction of abuses, and the right of succeeding
generations, necessitate the revision of every human establishment,
it must be possible for the nation to have, in certain cases, an extraordinary convocation of deputies, the sole object of which shall
be to examine and correct, if it is necessary, the vices of the Constitution.

The Comte de Lally Tolendal followed Lafayette and declared that the marquis had spoken for liberty as he had defended it on the field of battle; but—for all their agreement in
"principle," none of the representatives ventured to vote for
the rights of unarmed humanity with the latest of many deputations waiting at that moment in the palace to convey the
most submissive of petitions to the king for the withdrawal of
his troops.

If it is a small blemish in Lafayette's life that he took so
long to decide to go over from the reactionary nobility to the
bourgeoisie, his intrepid attempt, at this moment of supreme
danger, to save the germ of liberty for future generations, this
resolute stand in face of the shadow of the gallows, is ample
compensation.

XVII. "TO ARMS!"

DESPOTISM IS BLIND to warnings; were it not, the simple fact
that it had been necessary to employ foreign mercenaries

should have given the Court food for grave concern. Were there no French regiments in Paris? Men who were to become the most famous captains of the Revolution were serving as corporals in the Gardes Françaises—Lazare Hoche, the groom's son, for instance, and Masséna, the cooper's son; most of the future marshals of the empire were serving in the ranks of the king's army. Now the men were confined to barracks; and those who had not managed to get out were fraternizing with the crowd from the barrack windows. The hatred of the privileged classes had already penetrated deeply everywhere.

The Parisians knew nothing as yet of Lafayette's Declaration of the Rights of Man; he had read it out on the evening of Saturday July 11, 1789, and it had not had time to influence the events of the Sunday morning. But the wheel of history began to race at full speed on this 12th of July. Placards had been posted in the night bidding the population, in the king's name, to remain calm and commit no imprudences, and stating that the concentration of troops was a simple precaution for the protection of the capital against approaching "hordes of brigands." No one had seen any sign of these brigands; but rumors spread that grain convoys had been stopped. The troops at the gates of Paris were cutting off the city's food supplies!

About noon the first messenger breathlessly told the crowd assembled in the garden of the Palais Royal that Necker had been dismissed and a new, arch-reactionary ministry appointed. At this the wrath of the people exploded like a bomb. A young and unknown man, Camille Desmoulins, jumped on a café table and shouted, "*Aux armes!*" The cry spread instantaneously to the remotest suburbs. The armorers' shops were broken open and looted, and a human avalanche, collected from all classes of society, reached the Hôtel de Ville, where the electoral delegates were still sitting.

The *prévot des marchands,* the chief official in the Paris magistracy, a M. de Flesselles, was sent to calm the crowd and put them off until the troops could converge on the center of the city. "Gain time" was his order, and M. de Flesselles did his best. At one moment he told the crowd that there was a store of arms in the cellar of one of the Paris convents; at another moment he sent off the impatient masses to the opposite end of

the city. He had no fear, for he was confident of the success of
the coup d'état fixed for the morning of July 15. Without any
hesitation he sent to the governor of the Bastille a written order to hold out for three days. This order, accompanied by
ironic remarks on the way the people had been fooled and
which was found a little later on the governor's dead body,
cost Flesselles his life.

Finally 50,000 muskets were discovered in the cellars of the
Invalides. The crowds poured into the store over the trampled
bodies of its own forerunners; and on the evening of July 13,
1789, there were more armed citizens in Paris than soldiers
in the camps around the city. Candles were kept burning all
night in every window; ragged, barefooted, emaciated figures,
with hollow cheeks and sunken eyes, patrolled in front of the
shops and dwellings of the bourgeoisie, with muskets on their
shoulders and their pockets filled with powder and cartridges.
The few isolated attempts at fishing in the troubled waters were
repressed by the crowd itself with draconic severity; a poor
devil who was caught with his hand in his neighbor's pocket
was strung up at the nearest lamppost. The people were protecting their rising from calumny.

Monday's sitting of the National Assembly revealed growing embarrassment. The Court had no definite knowledge of
the purposes of the rising, and none of the members of the
Assembly was ready to compromise himself. The deputy Guillotin, a philanthropic physician who was to incur unmerited
ill-fame through his machine, urged in the name of the
Parisians whom he represented that a "reliable" guard should
be armed; the meeker spirits were still for a fresh appeal to
the "well-known good-heartedness" of Louis XVI. The Assembly resolved that "Necker carries with him the esteem and
the regrets of the nation."

But resolutions were but empty words. It was impossible to
close the sitting and go home to bed while the capital was in
the throes of revolt. Some 150 delegates declared themselves
ready to spend the night in the assembly hall. It was necessary to give some relief to the aged president of the Assembly,
and Lafayette was chosen on account of his courageous declaration of two days before; he acted as vice-president for the two
critical nights of July 13–14 and 14–15. In the dimly lit hall

the delegates lay on benches and tables; above them, in the
president's armchair, the hero of American independence
watched the feverish body of his country painfully giving birth
to the new era.

XVIII. THE FALL OF THE BASTILLE

WHEN THE MORNING of July 14, 1789, dawned over some
sixty thousand armed Parisians, was there still nobody in the
whole city who could say against whom their muskets should
be directed? A winter of bitter deprivation had severely tested
the endurance of the poor; now at last the foodshops and the
bakeries could have been pillaged, and the hungry could have
eaten their fill at the cost of a bourgeoisie paralyzed by terror! Yet where did the crowd go?

Someone, nobody knows who, cried: *"À la Bastille!"*

The word was enough. The starving, ragged, barefooted
crowd threw themselves against that stone monster, which,
from as far back as memory could go, had held no other
prisoners but men of birth and spirit who had given displeasure to the crown.

What was the explanation of this mysterious selection, by
the ignorant, suffering masses, of the only prison which had
had no terrors for them? If they had rushed to open the ordinary prisons, or if they had simply set out to fill their empty
stomachs, so ordinary a revolt might perhaps have been suppressed. It would not have aroused sufficiently widespread
enthusiasm. But the very symbol of despotism, the Bastille,
succumbed in a few hours to the fury of the people, taken
without siege guns, almost with bare hands. Thus consternation paralyzed all the powers of the previous day, and the designs of Providence were accomplished.

The instrument of Providence, who at the price of unspeak-
able suffering whipped up the dull masses at the critical moment and led them, an unseen standard bearer, against the
Bastille, was a country gentleman of small means, Henri Masers
de Latude, whom in the days of Louis XV the Marquise de
Pompadour had had arrested and thrown into the Bastille on
account of an indiscreet letter he had written. He was then

twenty-two years old. He petitioned for release; the Pompadour replied with the single word *"Jamais!"* He fainted when the decision was communicated to him.

Thereafter he had but one interest, to struggle against this inhuman cruelty. He and his sole companion pulled threads out of their bed linen and wove them into rope. For nine years he worked on a rope ladder, a hundred yards long, and succeeded against all probability, and at the cost of pains and perils beyond description, in escaping.

The Pompadour had stolen ten years of his life, and still she was not satisfied. He had fled to Amsterdam. There her myrmidons seized the poor fellow, in broad daylight, and brought him back to the Bastille. He was thrown into a punishment cell, windowless, above the sewers. The bitter winter cold froze his gums so that all his teeth fell out.

But no cruelties availed against his will to live. He pricked the fingers of his left hand with fishbones, in order to write a petition with his blood on a sort of paper of his own making. The Pompadour was dead; the petition came to Sartines, the minister of police, who complained that this agitator was never content. Twice again Latude performed the feat of breaking out of the strongest prisons. Finally he was shut up in the lunatic asylum of Bicêtre.

Latude had been a prisoner for thirty-two years, forgotten by his friends, and condemned to a slow death from hunger so that at last he might give no more trouble, when, through collecting crusts of bread from a heap of garbage, he contracted scurvy. On a bed in the asylum hospital, shared with three or four other unfortunates, he struggled for months against death. All round him patients were dying one after another; only this one bundle of misery, scarcely human in appearance, defeated death through its invincible will. Latude recovered and went back to his lunatic's cell. He performed all sorts of small services in order to procure paper and ink. Finally he was able to bribe one of the attendants to smuggle out of the asylum his long and horrible story of thirty-three years of martyrdom. The attendant promised to place the document in the hands of a former protector of Latude.

But was this protector still living? Would he undertake a

dangerous duel with the police for the sake of a forgotten victim? It was too hopeless a matter. The attendant got drunk and lost the document.

It was picked up in the market by the young wife of an artisan; she took it home in her shopping basket.

Poor and ailing, and expecting her first baby, this unknown Mme Legros read Latude's frightful story with tears in her eyes. She begged her husband to allow her to make an effort to get the unfortunate victim set free. She succeeded in arousing the compassion of the Cardinal de Rohan of the diamond necklace affair, a vain and foolish old man, but good-natured. The cardinal interested the wife of Jacques Necker, who was then in power. But the police refused to move, showing medical certificates of the man's condition.

Brave Mme Legros, too poor to hire a carriage, went on foot to Versailles and back. In vain did the minister of police threaten to throw her too into prison; she succeeded in touching the king's heart. Louis XVI sent for the papers. But once more, after thirty-three years, the king merely repeated the Pompadour's word—"*Jamais!*" Set free a dangerous maniac? Never!

After this all the influential gentlemen and ladies she had interested advised Mme Legros to abandon her efforts. Mme Necker contented herself with sending money and clothes and food. Only the poor artisan's wife refused to put up with injustice. She went on petitioning, pestering, fighting—until at last, after thirty-five years of imprisonment, Henri Masers de Latude was freed from captivity and came back into life.

The Académie des Sciences awarded Mme Legros its gold medal for virtue. But it was not allowed to state on the accompanying diploma what the action was that had gained her this high distinction. Louis XVI in his simplicity had imposed this condition of silence, out of a consideration for the memory of his grandfather. But the more faithfully Latude kept his promise never to appear in public, and the harder the authorities worked to hush up the affair, the more the story of this innocent victim, his thirty-five tragic years of wrongful imprisonment and his three vain escapes, excited the imagination of the people of Paris. Nobody could look in passing at the tall and menacing towers of the Bastille without recalling the martyrdom Latude had suffered and picturing the spectral company of innocent victims confined forever within the accursed walls of that gigantic tomb. For days after the capture of the Bastille, groups armed with spades and pickaxes went through all the corridors and dungeons, testing the walls and tearing open the vaults, for fear that some poor victim might still be there, buried alive.

XIX.   ALARM AT VERSAILLES

WHILE THE CANNON were thundering in Paris, all was uncertainty at Versailles. Neither at Court nor in the National Assembly was anything known about the progress of the fighting in the streets of the capital. The barriers of the city had been closed, to prevent any courier from summoning the foreign mercenaries. Not until late at night, when the miracle of the storming of the Bastille had been completed, and the governor and part of the garrison lynched, did the first eyewitnesses bring news from Paris to the king and the Assembly. Flesselles had paid with his life for fooling the people; his head and that of the governor of the Bastille were being carried through the streets as trophies.

This news filled the National Assembly with horror. It decided to send a new deputation to the king at once, and the bourgeois representatives were the most urgent of all in calling for the organization of armed defence against the "populace."

Nearly a hundred and fifty years have passed since that July 14 without any modification of the conventional picture of the storming of the Bastille. The hundred-odd victims—98 dead and 63 gravely wounded—who, ragged and hungry, sacrificed their lives in the storming of the prison of the nobility, these sublime madmen of the "populace," are forgotten; history mourns only the twenty "murdered" men of the garrison.

Mirabeau was the only one who rightly appraised the decisive nature of the popular victory and who did not forget where the blame really lay. Instead of merely denouncing the ferocity of the people, he fulminated against the princes and princesses and Court minions who on the night before had been entertaining the foreign mercenaries, pressing money and wine on them and inciting them to prepare a new St Bartholomew for the nation and its representatives.

But any provocation of the ruling power at so critical a time was not to the taste of the majority. The Assembly sent a deputation to the king to express its deep horror at what had happened. In order not to compromise itself on either side, it asked its vice-president, the Marquis de Lafayette, to lead the deputation, leaving, it said, "to the orator's judgment the choice of the phrases that may appeal to the king." But just as the deputation was starting the lord high steward brought the news that Louis XVI was coming to "visit" the elected of the nation, to seek counsel and comfort from them. With no escort, accompanied only by his two brothers, the king appeared in the hall as a petitioner rather than the stern master who but a day before had so haughtily rejected any interference in his sphere of authority.

The extremists of the Right seemed like reeds bent after a storm and still trembling. Their mouthpiece, the Comte d'Artois, came in with pale and drawn features. How this world had changed! Louis XVI indignantly declared that it was a calumny to suggest that he could have approved the use of armed force against his beloved people. To dissipate this abominable misconception he had already ordered the troops around Paris and Versailles to retire. The new ministry had been dismissed, and an express courier was on his way to Belgium to induce Necker to return. The unrest in his good city of Paris so troubled His Majesty that he had hastened to come to convey personally to the National Assembly his desire that a strong deputation should proceed at once to Paris. It should solemnly declare in the name of the crown that the ugly rumors which had worked such havoc in the capital were baseless.

Louis XVI then returned with his brothers across the square to his palace. The deputies, regardless of rank or party, streamed out of the National Assembly to escort their good king across, as though they had not had a moment's suspicion of the intentions of the mercenaries assembled outside their city gates. Those nearest the monarch joined hands and formed a ring round him, to protect his person from the pressure of the enthusiastic crowds in the square. Marie Antoinette appeared with her children on the balcony of the palace, and a tremor of joy passed through all Versailles. On returning to the hall the Assembly hastened to comply with the royal command and entrusted eighty-eight of its members with the pacification of the capital. Once more Lafayette was chosen to lead the deputation. Instead of going as a petitioner to the palace, he was to go as a messenger of peace to Paris.

The Comte d'Artois did not wait to see the outcome of this capitulation—he departed in haste; and with him went Marshal de Broglie, to put his white head into safety. Traveling in ordinary hackney carriages, behind curtained windows, the leading extremists began the emigration, without concerning themselves about the fate of the king and queen whom their advice had brought into peril.

Bravery and cowardice are inborn qualities, and there are plenty of timid people who, possessing rare talents, have done more for humanity than all the Hectors put together. Lafayette feared the reproach of cowardice more than death; the Comte d'Artois left his brother and sister and sister-in-law to die under the guillotine, after his advice had brought down on them the wrath of the people. Charrette, the royalist leader, who later was shot, wrote in his last testament that "His Royal Highness's cowardice" had brought about his downfall and that of all his party.

But this "cowardice" is a needed accessory in the great puppet play for which Providence cuts out and paints its dolls to fit them for their allotted parts. It was Providence that filled the petty squire Henri Masers de Latude with an incredible tenacity in boundless misfortune and gave the poor artisan's wife the soul of a heroine in order to weave out of the two a story which by its profound effect on its hearers should bring down like a pack of cards one of the strongest fortresses in Europe.

Similarly we shall see the Comte d'Artois and Lafayette alternately on the stage of world history through half a century, like the two dolls of the old-fashioned weather cottage, one coming out in rainy weather and the other in sunshine. They were both seventy-three when the storm of July, 1830, shattered the mechanism and the two old opponents came to the end of their political careers.

XX. THE REBELS' GENERAL

THE DUEL between the two began when the Comte d'Artois hastily fled from France on July 16, 1789, while Lafayette, as leader of the deputation to Paris, went with the eighty-eight deputies as bearer of a conciliatory declaration from the National Assembly. The deputation was received in the Hôtel de Ville, in the hall in which there stood the bust of Lafayette which had been sent as a thank-offering from the citizens of Virginia. It arrived in the midst of a discussion concerning the setting up of a civic guard; those present were trying to find a commander for this body whose authority would be sufficient to prevent the people from resorting to further bloodshed.

The post was not to everyone's taste. The human sea surging round the Hôtel de Ville had brought Flesselles out of that hall and hanged him at once from the nearest lamppost. The first candidates proposed for the post of commandant of the guard preferred to renounce the dangerous honor. At that point a hand was suddenly raised, pointing to the bust on the wall. Not a word had been necessary; there was no spoken proposal; after a few seconds of silence the shout rose of "Vive Lafayette!" and thundered round the hall. It passed out of the open windows and was taken up in the Place by countless throats. The name of the new commander was shouted from street to street to the farthest limits of the city.

Without a moment's hesitation, Lafayette drew his sword and replied to this shout of popular confidence with the declaration that he would defend the newly won liberties, even at the cost of his life.

Was not this oath an act of high treason? The king alone disposed of the forces of the state, and it was his prerogative alone to distribute commands. In accepting the post entrusted to him Lafayette took sides with the rebels and against the monarchy; from that moment he was himself a rebel in the eyes of the Court. Anyone else might have waited to receive the king's assent to the choice; but that would have been to deny the "sovereignty of the people" of which the marquis himself was the foremost advocate. He ostentatiously con-

tented himself with a hurriedly scrawled note to the National
Assembly to explain that his new duties made it impossible for
him to continue to carry out those of its vice-president.

The people of Paris had been treacherously cut off from
their sources of food supply; the mercenary hordes around the
city had been withdrawn a little, but still surrounded it; Paris
was virtually beleaguered. The starving people imagined spies
everywhere. On the morning of July 17 Lafayette arrived in
the Place de l'Hôtel de Ville just in time to save the life of an
innocent abbé around whose neck a rope had already been
placed; and twice again on the same day his popularity enabled
him to prevent the shedding of blood. His endurance was
superhuman; after two sleepless nights in the presidential
chair, and after the unending fatigues and excitements of these
days, he was tireless in riding again and again through the
streets of Paris on his white horse. The unbounded popular
confidence in him helped him everywhere to prevent excesses.

Meanwhile he was holding endless discussions on the organization of the new civic guard, which on his proposal was
christened "Garde Nationale de Paris." Gradually he cleared
it of doubtful elements, disarming them and putting in their
place soldiers of the Gardes Françaises; this regiment had
been disbanded by the king for the part it had played in the
storming of the Bastille. The men were distributed between
the thirty subdivisions of the Paris National Guard, whose
officers were elected by the rank and file.

After he had thus had to remove his own troops, Louis XVI
was forced to be a passive witness of Lafayette's organization
of an excellently equipped force of 50,000 men, a power in the
state which was able to impose its will on the crowned ruler.
Already on July 16 mounted trumpeters had proclaimed at
every point in the city a decision which Lafayette had made
on his own responsibility, without consulting anyone—the
Bastille was to be demolished, razed to the ground. Thousands
of idle hands here found work; the destruction of this blot
on the past provided food for thousands of hungry families.

Lafayette was too busy to keep actively in touch with Versailles and heard no more than a faint echo of the fury he was
arousing at Court. His order for the destruction of an ancient
royal prison, without consulting its legal owner, was more

than even the fat, sleepy, phlegmatic Louis could endure in silence. When the news was brought to him he shouted indignantly: *"Ah! cela c'est fort!"* ("What insolence!")

But the king had to put a pleasant face on a great deal that was even more "insolent." He had even to pay a visit to the rebellious city and to return with a smile the acclamations of its criminal people.

The flight of the Comte d'Artois had made it possible to create the official fiction of a misunderstanding between the misled king and his loyal and unjustly maligned subjects, and so to gloss over the sanguinary events of these days. In the hall of the Hôtel de Ville, packed from door to door, Louis XVI had to listen, dumb and perspiring, to eulogies of himself which were at the same time insults to him as the heir to an absolute monarchy. To crown it all he had to allow a cockade of blue and red, the colors of the city, and the badge of the rebels, to be stuck in his hat, and to show himself to the crowd, thus decorated, from the balcony of the Hôtel de Ville.

The people, in their childish credulity, were roused to enthusiasm by this facile concession. The king drove away surrounded by acclamations that suggested a beloved father of the people, through this city whose inhabitants his mercenaries were waiting to cut down.

In spite of his agitation, the king did not forget to emphasize his nominal authority; while Lafayette escorted him with drawn sword to the waiting carriage, he graciously confirmed the marquis's appointment as commander.

On his arrival at Versailles the queen fell on his neck, weeping. Then she caught sight of the unfamiliar cockade and asked what it meant. In answer the king tore it from his hat and furiously trod it underfoot. So he was to be until he reached the scaffold—docile though fuming, insincere to the point of mendacity.

In vain did Lafayette constantly protect Louis and his family with a magnanimity bordering on simplicity. The general's uprightness, his candor and unfailing consistency, only put the king in a more unfavorable light; and Marie Antoinette's hatred of him grew deeper the more deeply she felt herself to be indebted to his self-sacrificing labors.

Lafayette held his new post for exactly a week. He then

resigned it and refused to resume it on any terms. On the morning of July 22 he was unable, for the first time, to hold the maddened crowd in check, and to prevent them from lynching the seventy-four-year-old *fermier général* Foulon, who was dragged from the hall of the Hôtel de Ville under his very eyes; a few minutes later Foulon's head was being paraded on a pike. The unfortunate man was alleged to have said that the people might eat grass if they could not afford bread; he may never have spoken the phrase, but he owed his great wealth entirely to speculations in grain. His son-in-law, Colonel Berthier, who was equally hated and with equally good reason, was summarily executed by the mob on the same day.

It is not surprising that Lafayette, *grand seigneur* by birth, should have refused to become the leader of a bloodthirsty band of murderers who were carrying the heads of their victims as trophies through the streets. Yet this same Place de l'Hôtel de Ville had witnessed many similar executions in the past, the only difference being that the victims had been broken on the wheel, or hanged, drawn and quartered, in the name of King Louis XVI. It was not surprising if the distinction was too fine for the masses to comprehend.

For the authorities and the whole of the bourgeoisie of Paris, Lafayette's resignation was a calamity. His popularity was the only existing defence against uncontrolled popular passions while the organization of the civil guards was still incomplete. For two days the new city council besieged him with vain appeals; at last he was induced to withdraw his resignation by a declaration, drawn up, in humble and repentant terms, in the name of the whole population, promising blind obedience in future. But the tone of his private correspondence reveals his sense of the thanklessness of his task:

> I cannot leave the citizens in the lurch when they have put their whole trust in me; yet, if I remain, I am in the terrible situation of witnessing evils which I am powerless to prevent.

No more than a week after his resumption of the command, it became plain that there was some reason for the mistrust that underlay the mob violence. It had been suspected that Foulon and his son were to be imprisoned merely in order to enable them to escape in secret. On July 30 there came strong reinforcement of this suspicion. On that day Jacques Necker and his wife returned to Paris, with their daughter, Madame de Staël. The popular faith in his sense of justice and financial talent gave the hungry people of Paris confidence that there would be substantial relief from taxation for the poor and that there would once more be food in plenty—the granaries full and bread at a price within reach! Necker had to remain for hours on the balcony of the Hôtel de Ville to receive the ovations of a vast crowd; his wife and daughter wept with emotion at the spectacle.

But what use did Necker make of the influence this boundless popular gratitude gave him? He demanded the liberation of Baron Besenval from prison. The enthusiastic crowd did not hesitate for a moment; his request was granted, and so, thanks to his intervention, there was released the supreme leader of the coup that had been planned against the people of Paris, the man who had been waiting to shoot them down. By the time Marat, Desmoulins, and Mirabeau had revealed to the citizens how their magnanimity had been abused, the author of the plan of massacre was safely out of the country.

Those same argus eyes of the growing number of revolutionary ringleaders were also suspiciously watching Lafayette himself, as a man too high-born to be trusted as a popular leader. When he secured the liberation of his relative and former protector the Maréchal de Castries, the popular trust in him began to wane.

Yet, on the very day of Necker's visit, Lafayette inscribed his name for all time in the memory of his nation. As we know, it was at his instance that the citizen guards took the name of Garde Nationale de Paris, and that all the towns and villages of France were invited to recruit independent subdivisions of the new "national guards," to watch over the liberties of the people. The Paris colors were not available for general use, and Lafayette added between the blue and the red the white of the Bourbon fleur-de-lis. He handed this "tricolor" badge to the city council on July 30, 1789, with these words:

I bring you here a new cockade, which will go round the world as the symbol of an institution, both civic and military, which must triumph over the antiquated tactics of Europe, because it will leave the autocratic governments only the choice between being beaten by external powers if they do not imitate it, or overthrown if they do.

His prophecy was to be fulfilled. Not even Napoleon I ventured to replace the tricolored flag of the Revolution by an imperial standard. The interval of Bourbon rule was of short duration and was easily swept away by the collateral branch of the house of Orleans, largely because the new aspirant to the throne hastened to take shelter beneath the famous colors of the Revolution.

But Lafayette's cares were by no means confined to such bagatelles as the choice of the colors of a cockade. He succeeded, at the cost of great efforts, in imposing on the new municipality the provision for the equipment of the Paris Guards. The money had to be raised through gentle pressure put by all the leading personalities on the rich bourgeoisie. Amid the general uncertainty it was no easy matter to get purses opened. Lafayette set an example by refusing the annual salary of 120,000 francs offered him, but even that did little to encourage the rest.

It may even be that it would have been more politic of him not to decline the salary. The Comte de Mirabeau, always short of money and harassed by his creditors, was bound to be full of jealousy of the immense popularity of a rival who could allow himself the luxury of refusing 10,000 francs a month. The same hostility was aroused among future leaders who were still struggling to emerge from obscurity. Camille Desmoulins wrote one begging letter after another to his father, in vain; Danton, rake and voluptuary, had to content himself with cheap meals in suburban cafés. It was only human that these impatient spirits should exercise their sharp wits on the idolized "hero of two worlds," who was able to enjoy everything that made life worth living, wealth, power, glory, the favor of women of fashion and an unexampled popularity.

XXI. THE "AUSTRIAN WOMAN'S" GUERRILLA WAR

WHILE HIS POPULARITY was thus being sapped from below, Lafayette was also being attacked by Court intrigues. In vain did he seize every opportunity of demonstratively showing his loyalty to the crown. In vain did the enlightened section of the nobles among the deputies point, with Lafayette, to the century-old constitutional régime of the United Kingdom, in evidence that the sovereignty of the people was entirely compatible with a monarchical régime. In the eyes of Marie Antoinette, of her husband, and of all *gens de bien*, all "right-minded people," every new paragraph of the Constitution drawn up by the National Assembly did criminal violence to the royal prerogatives. And although Lafayette's duties in Paris in the maintenance of order and the prevention of speculation left him little time to take part in the deliberations of the National Assembly, it was well known at Court that he was constantly inviting his American friends and his party comrades to his table, and, from time to time, discussing with them half through the night the means of abolishing arbitrary rule.

He was not able to be present at the famous session of the night of August 4, which definitely made an end of feudal privileges; but he hastened to approve his friends' decision. All privileges of birth, all titles and hereditary distinctions, all economic exemptions of the nobility and the clergy, inequalities and wrongs of which the people had borne the burden through many centuries, disappeared in that single night. In a burst of magnanimity which many subsequently regretted, an end was made of the second Bastille, the citadel of parchments and paragraphs which had crushed the life out of the people.

When it was learned at the Palace of Versailles that the nobles had taken part in their own disinheriting, there was the utmost alarm and anger. What is a court without the jingling of titles, the bedizenment of great names? Mirabeau, as a tribune of the people, could not vote against this bill, but as soon as he got home he exclaimed to his valet:

"I hope that for you I shall always remain Monsieur le Comte, young man!"

The Marquis de Lafayette, on the contrary, never again, during forty years of changing governments, called himself anything but "General Lafayette." How different he was in this respect from his inveterate enemy Bonaparte, who was less disturbed by the millions of deaths with which his career was strewn than by the refusal of the governor of St Helena to give him the title of "Majesty."

It is easier to understand and to find excuses for the feelings of the daughter of Maria Theresa at the disappearance of external honors. Yet it was her hatred of Lafayette, and of all the sincere men and women who tried to persuade her to renounce absolute power, that was the destruction of herself and her husband. She had no means of resorting to violence against the "rebel," but she gave her approval to many underhand maneuvers and conspiracies which later recoiled on herself.

On the king's name day, August 17, Lafayette led to Versailles those of his men who already had their equipment, and communicated to the king the good wishes of all the National Guards of the capital. He was insistently offered the command of the National Guard of Versailles, but categorically refused to accept it, because of his sense of the dangers of excess of authority. In spite of this, the Court did not forgive him for his presence at the banquet given by the Guards of Versailles in the open air, near the palace, to their comrades of Paris. Even when he publicly and energetically refused to be appointed to the command of the whole of the National Guards of the entire country, and warned his countrymen of the dangers of placing too much confidence in military leaders, he remained in the eyes of the Court the "rebel" who was working to bring the crown to destruction.

Decaying governments have one unchanging device for taming their adversaries. Twice the king endeavored to impose on the marquis the title of "constable," the highest military rank he could confer. This post of honor at Court would have cost the general his popularity, without which nothing would have remained of the constable but a discredited scarecrow which every sparrow of Versailles could mock. How many idols of the people have fallen victims to their greed for titles and dignities and possessions, and so, through their subservience to a tottering power, have enabled it to rivet once more on the people the bonds they had burst. If hatred were not so bad an adviser, it should have been clear at Versailles that the man who would not allow himself to be placed in command of the

whole of the National Guards of France was not likely to be
tempted by the brilliant-studded sword of the *Connétable*.

No better success attended an attempt to turn the wrath
of the Parisians into mistaken channels. At the end of August
a circular was brought to Lafayette. It forbade the millers
around Paris to sell flour to the bakers of the city, and bore
his own well-forged signature!

The royalist newspapers declared every day that bread was
so dear because the twelve hundred kings of the National
Assembly had now to be supported, instead of the single king
on the throne. But the Parisians were not so easily to be deceived: they were kept too well informed by Marat. They
learned, moreover, that the palace guards had been secretly
doubled and that the Flanders regiment had been brought up
to replace the disbanded guards whom Lafayette had distributed among the National Guard of Paris.

While intrigues were thus being hatched at Court and the
growing destitution in Paris was rousing popular exasperation,
Lafayette brought before the National Assembly a bill to
abolish the medieval penal code. No longer should there be
breaking on the wheel and quartering and tortures either in
public or in prison cells! But even the most progressive of his
colleagues found this reform inopportune, at a time when the
temper of the people was a menace to public security. Lafayette contended that the way to counter mob violence was not
by inhuman punishments but by justice and the prevention
of destitution; but he found no support.

To the Court, too, violence was the one remedy for re-
belliousness. It set to work to incite the young officers and the
provincial nobles against the Parisians. A fête was organized
for the last night of September, in honor of the newly arrived
Flanders regiment; it was a reunion of the elements loyal to
the king, and it was hoped to assure their cohesion and make of
them a reliable force. The organizers in their blindness invited
even the officers of the National Guard of Versailles. It occurred, apparently, to no one that the uniformed lawyers and
shopkeepers and wigmakers would not properly appreciate the
undeserved distinction conferred on them, still less that the
condescension of the great might be rewarded, out of loyalty
to the mob now christened "the nation," by "high treason."

The banquet was furnished by the best contractor in Versailles, at 210 francs a head, wines not included; the wines came from the royal cellars and were poured out so freely that the guests were thoroughly intoxicated by the time the royal family and the whole suite made the round of the tables. Marie Antoinette led her children by the hand; the handsome boy whose protection she confided to her faithful nobles aroused great enthusiasm. Military bands played patriotic tunes, and emotions were worked up to frenzy. Officers who had grown gray in the service wept like children; half-drunken hotheads jumped onto the front of the boxes to follow the retiring Court. The guests assembled drew their swords and swore to chastise the mob for its humiliation of the king; the bullets in their cartridge bags were referred to as "plums for the Parisians," and the tricolor cockades were pulled off the hats of the invited officers of the Versailles National Guard and trampled underfoot.

That same night, in the somber streets of the faubourgs, long queues of poor mothers were waiting at the door of every baker's shop to buy a pound of bread for their children. Yet in Versailles it was possible to provide a banquet at 210 francs a head.

XXII.   THE MARCH ON VERSAILLES

WHAT NEED was there to look for conspirators and ringleaders when, on the morning of October 5, 1789, a simple woman of the people took a drum from a guardroom and went through the streets beating it and calling on every mother to march with her to Versailles? Let the royal family and all the Court be brought to Paris; then their superfluity would follow them to the capital. The argument sounded logical, and soon a first troop of some hundreds of women set off for Versailles.

Women are always the best advance guard; it is not so easy to decide to shoot them down. Tens of thousands of women followed in batches; men dressed up as women helped to fill their ranks. Some were armed with muskets, pikes, scythes, and even a few guns, though nobody knew how to serve them. The regularly armed National Guard was under military discipline; it could not set off like the crowd without an order; but the church bells sounded the tocsin, and the armed troops assembled in the Place de l'Hôtel de Ville; they were roused by the challenge of the women to come and avenge the insult to the tricolor, and the fury that had been pent up for days now exploded.

For hours Lafayette held them back with a courage worthy of all admiration. True to himself at all times, he held fast to the principle of submission to the authority of the civil power; he was ready to obey, but of the three hundred city councilors not one would venture to take the responsibility of unloosing civil war. Pressed on all sides by a raging sea of humanity, Lafayette, on horseback, held his ground, concerned alike for the fate of the royal family and for the people, whom he wanted to protect from their own bloodthirsty fury. A hundred times muskets were pointed at him, he was threatened with hanging from a lamppost, as Flesselles and Foulon and others had been hanged already for betraying the people; he remained firm, from morning until late afternoon, every moment in danger of being torn from his horse and trampled underfoot.

"We do not think you a traitor, my general," exclaimed an old grenadier, "but you yourself are being deceived!"

Finally, about 4 P.M., the councilors in the hall above began to fear for their own lives; the crowd was threatening to storm the Hôtel de Ville—and a written order was sent to the commandant to march his troops to Versailles. Lafayette turned pale as he read these lines; he knew that the councilors were sending him off only to save themselves; but he obeyed the order. Shortly before reaching Versailles he halted his troops and exacted once more from every company an oath of absolute obedience. Only then, towards 11 P.M., did he enter the threatened town—to save it.

Rain had been pouring down incessantly and had driven the women who first arrived to take refuge in the hall of the National Assembly. There were too many for the accommodation in the galleries, and they had squeezed their way in among the deputies. Their shouts made the debates impossible; instead of chattering there, they cried, the deputies should be getting bread for them.

The same cry—"*Du pain! Du pain!*"—was raised by the

crowd outside the royal palace. Small deputations were taken
before Louis XVI, but the crowd outside refused to be content
with promises and fine phrases; drenched to the skin, they still
remained outside the palace, incessantly calling for bread. Only
the venal beauties of the Palais Royal found a more effective
occupation; they slipped between the horses and applied all
their seductiveness to inciting the men against their officers.
The sight of these famished and drenched women robbed even
the "absolutely reliable" Flanders regiment of all inclination
to march against the people; as for the Versailles National
Guards, they were filled with resentment against the aristocratic bodyguard which had defiled their colors and now, with
the Swiss mercenaries, alone remained on guard behind the
closed doors of the palace. One blow would have broken down
the slender defence they represented against this tidal wave, if
the disciplined columns of the Paris National Guard had not
arrived at the critical moment.

Lafayette, careless of his own popularity, had the crowd
driven back, and went up alone, without any aide-de-camp, to
the king. As he entered the room there was a murmur of *"Voilà
Cromwell!"* from the courtiers around him. He turned to them
and retorted with a smile:

"Cromwell, gentlemen, would not have come alone!"

But of what avail could sense and sincerity be against men
of such ingrained prejudice that, even at the moment of supreme peril, the chief marshal of the Court hurried up to
Lafayette and shouted to the "intruder" as he came upstairs:

"His Majesty gives you permission to enter the *petits appartements.*"

Think of the gross violation of etiquette if the rescuer, who
had only the right to enter the anterooms, came unbidden into
the *petits appartements*, the rooms in which the suite were
waiting, crowded together in perplexity! The moment it had
been learned that Paris was marching against Versailles, messengers had been sent to bring back the king, who was hunting. Hours had passed; the Council of Ministers, presided over
by His Majesty, had sat until night and still had come to no
decision; for all but Necker were urging him to flee to Rambouillet, and Louis XVI went up and down the room wringing
his hands and moaning in irresolution: "A king in flight! A

king in flight!"—until in the end Marie Antoinette added her voice and persuaded him to accept the advice.

XXIII. GENERAL MORPHEUS

IT WAS MAINLY against Marie Antoinette that the hatred of the people was directed. The *"Autrichienne,"* the "Austrian woman," had been the one who had urged on her husband against the people; she was lost if the palace was stormed. At dusk the king sent out two carriages, with some of the chambermaids in them, to see whether, under military escort, they could make their way through the crowd. But the attempt failed miserably, and only revealed the complete impotence of the bodyguards. Might it not have been supposed that the arrival of superior forces would now be welcomed with joy by the besieged Court?

"I have come," said Lafayette, "to protect Your Majesties, if necessary at the price of my life."

But the king could not inflict on his aristocratic defenders the humiliation of serving alongside uniformed shopkeepers. Lafayette's troops were assigned the external defence of the palace. Accordingly, on the king's command he organized an active service of patrols round the park, placed strong posts at the important points, and stationed the rest of his troops, as well as he could, in churches and in the porches and stables of the neighboring nobles' palaces.

At last the long day of effort and tension, begun with hours facing a menacing crowd in Paris, in peril of his life, in front of the Hôtel de Ville, was over. Now, in the early hours of the morning, with not a dry spot on his body, he lay down in his clothes for a short rest, to be equal to the demands of the coming day.

This short sleep, after a day of superhuman exertions, was counted against him as an unpardonable crime. In the hours and months and years that followed he was to risk his life again and again in the defence of the thankless queen and her family; yet the nickname "General Morpheus" stuck to him. The real culprits were the gentlemen of the bodyguard who had declined to serve alongside "shopkeepers." In their excitement they had forgotten to bolt and guard a small side door. At dawn, as the rain began to abate, some Parisians wandering past discovered the open door, and the awakening crowd, impelled by hunger and curiosity rather than by any lust of blood, swarmed through after the first intruders.

Two persons—some versions of the story say three—were the first to notice the movement under the palace windows. A young officer of the aristocratic bodyguard took aim from a window and killed a Paris workman. At that the fury of the people was at once unloosed. The corpse was laid at the top of the entrance steps, and the blood flowing from it glowed like fire on the marble. A human flood poured through the palace, overpowering the few guards who defended the entrance and the upper stories, and rushed from room to room in search of the "Austrian woman."

Is there any truth in the story that Marie Antoinette had in her bedchamber the handsome Swedish Count Fersen? She was certainly the first to hear voices in the court of the palace and rang for her ladies-in-waiting. Her children's governess wrote in her memoirs that the "handsome Axel" had to be disguised and got away by a remote staircase before the queen would think of her own safety. Her guards resisted the crowd at door after door; the last shouted into the room behind him as he fell: "For God's sake, save the queen!" Marie Antoinette had not even time to put on her slippers; barefooted and in her nightdress, she reached her husband's room by a secret passage.

Every eyewitness of the events of that morning of bloodshed has a different story to tell. According to one version it was Lazare Hoche, then a noncommissioned officer of the Gardes Françaises, and three years later a famous general, who saved the queen. But whatever may be the truth as to these details, it is certain that without Lafayette's overwhelming forces the bodyguards would not have been able to hold back the crowd or to save Marie Antoinette. Her bed was transfixed with pikes and cut to pieces with knives; then, to make up for the vengeance of which they had been deprived, the women in their rain-soaked rags tried the "whore's" bed and relieved their feelings with coarse jests.

"General Morpheus," who had hastened to the scene at the first news, was now permitted to guard the palace within and without with his plebeian troops. The dead bodies of their comrades strewn over stairs and landings had broken the pride of the bodyguards. When the news of these events reached the National Assembly, the delegates of the nobility, who on the opening day had paraded so proudly in their brilliant costumes, demanded that there should be uniform clothing for all members!

XXIV. THE MOVE TO PARIS

AND THE KING? His faithful suite were busy around him writing on small slips of paper the message that "The king is going to Paris." These were being thrown out of the windows. But the crowd refused to be reassured until the king himself came to the balcony to confirm the news: in deference to the wishes of his good Parisians, he was coming to live in their midst.

There remained the most difficult problem—the queen. The crowd demanded to see her; her suite held her back. But the crowd had its way; for once it was able to command! Marie Antoinette crossed herself and went with her two children onto the balcony.

"Not the children!" shouted the crowd from below—"only the queen!" And muskets pointed at her, and signs imitating the hangman and the headsman at work told plainly enough the fate that menaced her. At this Lafayette came forward, bowed to her and said:

"Come, madame."

"Have you not seen the horrible signs they are making?" said the queen, hesitating.

But Lafayette took her by the hand, led her out and then, as no human voice could have dominated the howls and shouts of the many thousands in front of the palace, bent over her hand and deferentially kissed it.

This symbolic guarantee from the popular general was enough for the crowd. There were shouts of *"Vive Lafayette! Vive la Reine!"*

There remained the problem of reconciliation between the people and the bodyguards, and this miracle also was demanded of Lafayette.

"Our poor guards! Will you not do something for them?" urged the king and queen.

Lafayette took the tricolor from his own cap and placed it

over the white cockade of an officer of the bodyguards. Then
he took the adversary so decorated onto the balcony and there
embraced him. The tens of thousands in the Place would not
have been Frenchmen if they had not broken into shouts of
enthusiasm at that scene of reconciliation. *"Vive messieurs les
gardes du corps,"* was shouted in every street. Bodyguards and
National Guards exchanged caps and embraced; and there remained nothing to prevent the Court from being transferred
to Paris; nor could the transfer be safely delayed any longer.

There is no truth in the story that the king's carriage was
preceded by the heads, carried on pikes, of the guards who
had been killed in the palace that morning. The Court carriages
went, surrounded by a strong detachment of the Paris National Guard; Lafayette rode his horse alongside the queen's
carriage. It was impossible, however, to keep out of hearing of
the royal family the deafening noise made by the women returning on the guns or on the sacks of flour which had been
brought away from the Versailles granaries. The people naïvely
assumed that with the arrival of the Court in Paris there would
be a return of plenty.

No less evident than the jubilation of the crowd was the
anxiety of the Court. For monarchs have no longer memories
than their peoples. With the disappearance of the mortal peril,
the memory of the services rendered by "General Morpheus"
was also effaced; and Marie Antoinette saw now in the protector who rode by her carriage only a jailer carrying her to
captivity in Paris.

Lafayette, so much more popular than the king that he had
had to protect him from his people, had reached a summit
which was too narrow to hold two persons. All the painful and
humiliating memories of the last day in Versailles were inseparably associated with his person. He was suspected of
conspiring to dethrone the king and succeed him!

The necessity of feigning joy made the trial yet harder for
the king to bear. All Paris was illuminated; the people were
wildly jubilant; in their blind trust in the king and queen and
dauphin they came out to meet them shouting acclamations of
"the baker, the baker's wife, and the baker's boy." Not until
the king and queen reached the dusty, dismal rooms of the
Tuileries, where not a bed and not a candle was in readiness for

them, could they drop their mask of cheerfulness. The little dauphin, tired out by the long ride between the marching soldiers, clung to his mother's dress and wailed: "Mummy, I'm hungry!"

So the first act of the tragedy ended on its keynote.

XXV.   "THE MOST SACRED DUTY"

THE NATIONAL ASSEMBLY soon followed the Court to Paris, and the political arena was thus brought entirely under Lafayette's protection. In the center of this city of many hundred thousands the rhetorical battle was continued between the royalists and the revolutionary innovators, and the popular leader with his voluntarily enlisted guards was constantly on the watch to prevent any outbreak of violence: to see that not a hair on the head of the most provocative orator should be harmed when he came out of Parliament into the streets where passions still ran high.

Watched by the Court and by his political opponents, with both sides on the alert for any opportunity of injuring him, Lafayette would not have retained his popularity even through the autumn but for the fear of the masses which was common to all three estates—the masses whom no one but Lafayette could control and whom in case of necessity he was able to hold in check with his civic guard.

Frederick the Great declares in his testament that in politics there is no field for character. Lafayette's fatal error was that he resolutely refused to have anything to do with men even of the foremost importance if their public life did not come up to his moral standards. His very first step was a disastrous blunder. There is a huge volume that contains the depositions of three hundred and eighty-eight witnesses in the case against those held responsible for the march on Versailles. It had been rumored that the Duke of Orleans had had money given to the women who were loudest in shouting "À Versailles!" and that ladies with delicate hands covered with rings had fomented the rising, disguised as fishwives. Not one of the depositions on oath offers the slightest evidence of all this, but before the case was even opened, on the strength of simple rumors, Lafayette had the duke banished.

This stirring up of the great wasps' nest of the "Orleanists" was worse than indiscreet. The duke was very popular among the lower stratum of the population. To men of the type of Mirabeau and Danton, the duke's exile meant a grave weakening of their party, which was not yet strong enough to endure such blows. But Lafayette had no fear either of Mirabeau or of Danton. There was too deep a gulf between these venal gladiators of the political arena and the man who kept Washington's shining example always before his eyes for any understanding to be possible between them.

These rivals of Lafayette's, with their greed for money and power, found support in the secret intrigues of the queen and Court, in Marat's venomous accusations, in the biting sarcasms of Camille Desmoulins, and in the perturbed criticisms of Loustalot, a sincere idealist whose daily leading article reached two hundred thousand eager readers. Lafayette faced continual risks for the safety of the Court, but he remained none the less in the eyes of the royalists a criminal who was holding his king captive; while the masses, driven into demonstrations by their hunger and impatience, and also, very probably, by agents provocateurs, gradually lost sympathy with this supposed people's general on whom the municipality was imposing the duties of a lieutenant of police. And the soldiers of the National Guard, who had put on their uniforms as defenders of liberty, went out unwillingly against the people.

Lafayette himself knew well how much injury he suffered in undertaking the thankless task of the preservation of public order; but as the slave of his conscience he did his duty. Mirabeau, in his secret reports to the queen, transmitted by the Comte de Lamarck, urged that there should be no attempt at violence against Lafayette. Martyrdom would restore his popularity; instead, he should be allowed to wear it out. Every street demonstration broken up would saw a good piece off his stilts!

Lafayette saw the danger well enough. Several times he refused to allow his Guards to be misused for police duties by the municipality; but the mayor with his three hundred councilors could always make use of the general, for Lafayette saw in the subordination of the armed forces to the civil power too crucial a dogma of democracy for him not to act on orders given. On one occasion he sprang out of the saddle and seized an agitator himself.

The municipality became responsible for his first defeat when it instructed him to arrest Marat. Marat, *"l'ami du peuple,"* had taken refuge in the most revolutionary quarter of Paris and had placed himself under the protection of the committee presided over by Danton, who had been elected captain of the National Guard of the district. Two battalions of this force resisted the attempt to seize Marat, and Lafayette, rather than let loose a regular civil war over a single journalist, capitulated before the opposition. His withdrawal meant the loss of his authority, but he had avoided bloodshed. Had he not so firmly believed that once the Constitution had been enacted there would be no further injustices and resentments, and consequently no more disorders in the streets, he would have resigned long ere this.

About this time Benjamin Franklin died in America. In a letter to Washington Lafayette opened his heart to him:

How often, my well beloved General, have I longed for your wise counsels and your friendly support!

It was just the qualities in Lafayette which had won Washington's heart that unfitted him for the atmosphere of hatred and intrigue in Paris. He was not used to weighing every word, and he had the misfortune to let slip a phrase which his enemies afterwards used against him throughout his life. In the spring of 1790 the resistance of the royalists against any sharing of power between crown and Constitution had resulted in disorders and bloodshed in the provinces. Lafayette made a speech to his troops in which he condemned violence and called for absolute respect for the law as the expression of the will of the majority. He was thinking of the provisions of the new Constitution, and uttered a phrase which was to be accounted his worst crime:

For the Revolution disorders were necessary; the old order was nothing more than slavery, and in such a case insurrection is the most sacred of duties; but under the Constitution it is essential that order shall be consolidated.

"L'insurrection le plus saint des devoirs!" This phrase, malignantly falsified by detachment from its context and isolation from the second half of his antithesis, which demanded obedience to the just laws of the Constitution, cost Lafayette years of imprisonment and pursued him even beyond the grave.

With justifiable pride he rejected the warnings of his friends, as in this declaration to the young Comte de la Rochefoucauld:

"I have beaten the King of England in his might, the King of France in his authority, the people in their fury; certainly I shall not yield to M. Mirabeau."

The boundless hatred of Lafayette in aristocratic quarters was shown by the plot of the Marquis de Favras. The marquis was to put the inconvenient "democrat" out of the way, rumor said at the instance of Monsieur, the king's brother. It was established that before his arrest Favras negotiated a loan of two millions with the prince's banker. The unfortunate officer was the first person in France to be made to feel the equality of all before the law. In spite of his title of marquis and his officer's rank he was hanged. He was not interrogated, however, in public, but in his cell, and the records of the interrogation disappeared—was it feared that he might betray the source of his commission? In any case the affair had a strange sequel: the brother of the reigning monarch hastened, on his own initiative, to the Hôtel de Ville in order to make a solemn affirmation of his innocence before the shopkeeper councilors there assembled!

Whether or not it had actually been intended to murder Lafayette, the plot to get him out of the way was a complete failure; the peril to which he had been exposed did much to restore his popularity.

XXVI. OATH AND FALSE OATH

THE COURT and the Court party had good reason to tremble at the approach of the national festivities which were to celebrate the first anniversary of the storming of the Bastille. Necker's star was declining; the hopes the Parisians had placed in "the baker, the baker's wife, and the baker's boy" had been disappointed; the presence of the Court in Paris had done nothing to make an end of destitution. It may be that it was in a desperate effort to take the wind out of the sails of the dreaded "Cromwell" that Louis XVI made a totally unexpected appearance in the National Assembly one morning. The monarch had come unescorted, entirely on his own initiative, in order to give an oath of loyalty to the still far from complete Constitution —which was being secretly sabotaged. He not only took the oath in his own name, but added:

"I will do yet more. In agreement with the queen, who shares all my sentiments, I shall prepare my son's heart and mind in good time for the new order of things which circumstances have brought about."

After this voluntary oath from the King of France, how could a man of honor like Lafayette have any doubt of the sincerity of his crowned master? It was impossible that a monarch should make, quite gratuitously, promises which he was secretly determined not to keep!

The new oath prescribed by law bound those who took it to give loyal service to "the nation, the law, and the king." To accept the last place in this way when actually the first was a sacrifice worthy of recognition! The members enthusiastically applauded the king, and after his departure they mounted the tribune one by one to repeat the oath. Open refusal would have been suicidal; some of those who were unable to slip away quietly committed deliberate perjury. The Abbé Maury, for all that he was a servant of God, whispered to his neighbor the famous alexandrine:

"*Le parjure est vertu, quand le serment fut crime*" ("Perjury is a virtue when the oath was a sin").

In vain did Marat warn his readers not to place exaggerated trust in the king's promises. An epidemic of eagerness to swear the oath of loyalty spread all over France. It was administered in every office, even in the streets; fathers held up the little hands of their new-born babes and bound them by oath to be loyal throughout their lives to the nation, the law, and the king. No lane in the suburbs was too poor to resound in those days with shouts of "*Vive le roi!*" Only in the secret letters from Marie Antoinette to the Court of Vienna was this "degra-

dation of the crown," the insolent farce that made the king
the servant of his subjects, denounced as intolerable.

His failure to see through this falsity, and the part he played
in consequence, in all innocence, in betraying the people, was
Lafayette's greatest and most fatal mistake; he was to pay
dearly for it. But before this, before his decline, he was able
to sun himself in the glory such as few sovereigns have enjoyed. It was nothing but his own selflessness that prevented
him from setting the crown of France on his own head as Napoleon did later. On July 14, 1790, he need only have stooped
to pick it up, so entirely did his presence throw the king into
eclipse.

For the people this festival of Fédération was much more
than a mere ceremony. The new Constitution had suppressed
the internal barriers, and with them the hated customs houses
which had been a worse burden on the country than a foreign
garrison would have been. The *gabelle,* the salt tax, varying
from province to province, had been a standing temptation to
the miserably poor countryfolk to engage in smuggling, which,
in the interest of the farmers of taxes, was punished as a capital
crime. The prohibition of the transport of grain without an
official permit even from one side of a streamlet to the other,
where a hailstorm had perhaps destroyed the crop, made their
work easy for the speculators who drove up prices. The "fed-
eration," the unification of the kingdom, thus brought enormous relief to the people.

History, like a sheet of water, inverts the picture of revolutions. Why should the poor, the masses, once they are given
their freedom, are relieved of the burdens they have borne
so long, grow cruel? Revolutions become sanguinary only when
the attempt is made to wrest from these grown-up children the
gift to which they are clinging. At the time of the Fédération
a long interval of two years, sown with perjury, avarice,
chicanery and open war, still separated the people from the
Terror and the king from the scaffold.

At the clean sweep of all the medieval privileges and taxes
and *corvée* obligations there were unparalleled rejoicings all
over France. A new realm had been born; from the North Sea
to the Mediterranean, from the Rhine to the estuary of the
Rhone, all the barriers had been thrown down; thirty mil-

lions of Frenchmen felt themselves free of their whole country, instead of their province only. As though a tidal wave had lifted them over every bank and reef, they had won freedom of movement over roads and bridges and fords. And now, like children long parted from their mother, the delegates of the National Guard came from every corner of the country to fraternize in Paris.

XXVII.   THE RIDER ON THE RAINBOW

NEVER HAS THE WORLD witnessed a spectacle to compare with the reunion on the Champ de Mars on July 14, 1790. A colossal amphitheater had had to be erected around the whole great field, seating 250,000 spectators to view the evolutions of the 200,000 National Guards in the central ellipse. In the middle of the field, on a mound, stood the "altar of the fatherland," up to which the Bishop of Autun, M. de Talleyrand-Périgord, was to limp, with something satanical about him even in his canonicals. No one could yet dream that this high prelate was to be untrue not only to his priestly vows but to every sworn obligation of his long career. Dragging his leg, a cynical smile on his lips, he stood in the center of the tremendous assembly like the devil in disguise, whose sacrilegious prayer was to call down on the nation the curse of the coming years of bloodshed.

At the beginning of July it had seemed impossible that the central elliptical plateau and the surrounding terraced seats should be completed in time. The municipality exhausted its financial resources, but hired hands alone could not complete this labor of Hercules. Yet it was essential that all should be ready by July 14, 1790, the first anniversary of the great popular victory. The enthusiasm of the Parisians performed the miracle. Armies of voluntary laborers came daily to the Champ de Mars. At the end of their long days' work the poor devoted the bright summer evenings to helping in the great task. As soon as the evening meal was over, whole families set out to join in the work. The mother dug, the father wheeled the heavy barrow, and the boys and girls stamped flat the earthen terraces. Rich men of leisure, fine ladies, business men, artisans, soldiers and officers, all grades of society fell in with the fashion. The Paris actors' guild arrived with musicians leading them and threw themselves into the work; delicate bejeweled hands swung beribboned spades and shovels; elegant cavaliers threw their jackets and embroidered vests carelessly on the ground, regardless of their precious watches (it was good form at the time to carry two). Barefooted workers dug side by side with these dandies, but not a single theft was reported.

All Paris felt itself to be host, and the preparations for the festival of fraternity and the confidence in the future effaced the memory of past quarrels. The crowds chanted in chorus the refrain of the new popular song, *"Ça ira, ça ira, ça ira!"* ("It'll get done, it'll get done, it'll get done!") No matter how big the job might be, *ça ira, ça ira, ça ira!*

Two years had scarcely passed after this, when the "guillotine hyaenas" began chanting to the same melody: *"Ça ira, ça ira, ça ira, Les aristocrates on les pendra"* ("We will hang them, the aristocrats"). The gentlemen with the two watches in the gold-embroidered waistcoats then had the hands that had so busily swung spades and shovels bound behind their backs, and their former fellow workers of the Champ de Mars crowded alongside their tumbrils. Who had effected that transformation? Who had turned the happy workers of the Fédération into the cruel hordes of the Terror? Woe to those who betray the people's trust!

The guests streamed in, gay and trustful as children on holiday. On foot, dusty and laden; the more prosperous ones by post chaise or in their own carriages—the "brothers," National Guards in their uniforms, poured in from every town and village of France, into the friendly, decorated, beflagged capital. Their hosts waited in crowds in front of the Hôtel de Ville. Whoever had an empty cellar or attic moved into it in order to give up his best room to the visitor from the country. No one would be outdone; hosts were in competition for guests. For the first time Paris had become the true capital, the best room of this great family of thirty million souls. Not an inn or hostel had a bed unoccupied. Nobody would miss the wonderful spectacle to be presented by the fraternization of half a million of the people of France.

Only at Court was there a dull refusal to take advantage of

the unique opportunity. In vain did Lafayette urge the king
and queen to show themselves in the streets, so that the in-
coming tide of humanity, when it receded again, might carry
to every corner of the country the message of their popularity.
Mirabeau seconded his efforts less disinterestedly, green with
envy of the acclamations that everywhere greeted the popular
rider on the white horse. But the timid and indolent monarch
would not be persuaded to enter into competition with
Lafayette or to abandon the hunt, his great passion; and Marie
Antoinette was too haughty to sue for the favor of the
populace. Instead of visiting the busy workers on the Champ
de Mars, the Court merely permitted the steadfastly royalist
detachments, which had asked for this high honor, to carry
out a torchlight procession in the evening. The queen watched
gloomily as these soldiers of Lafayette's filed past, and brightened only when she heard some German words of command;
she sent for the German battalion leaders, accorded them the
favor of a lengthy audience and waved to their troops as they
passed on. As though she were not hated enough already, she
allowed her pleasure in the interview to be observed by all,
plucked her husband's sleeve and said aloud to him: "There go
your faithful Lorrainers!"

As the responsible guardian of public order Lafayette had
no choice but to be moving about Paris from an early hour
until late at night. Tables were spread in the open air along
the streets, at which sat the guests of the various districts;
there was feasting and dancing and drinking; he had to protect the country people from their own good thirsts and to
keep the merriment within bounds without damping it.

The Bastille, which was being demolished by his order, was
as yet only half destroyed. Restaurant proprietors had put up
tents by the entry to the ruins, and over the archway which
had swallowed so many existences forever was a big trans-
parency that bore the legend: *"Ici l'on danse"* ("Dancing").

On the morning of the great day there were deluges of rain.
Only the high dignitaries were able to save their gala uniforms
by sheltering under the king's purple canopy. More than a
quarter of a million spectators were at the mercy of the rain
as they sat on the terraces of the enormous amphitheater. The
uniformed host in the center, the serried mass of almost as

many National Guards, had to wait patiently like the public
for the ending of the downpour; even the divine service on the
"autel de la patrie" was unable to avert the wrath of the
heavens.

Only when Lafayette advanced to take the oath in the name
of the assembled National Guards did the hot July sun at last
break through the clouds, as if by command! A rainbow
spread over the enormous arena; millions of brass buttons
shone; and even the hundred guns of the adjoining Military
School thundered less loudly than the shouts from half a million throats when the famous white horse galloped up to the
altar. A spectator among the members of Parliament whispered
to his neighbor:

"Violà M. de Lafayette qui galope dans les siècles à venir"
("Look at Lafayette galloping down the ages to come").

The masses broke into indescribable jubilation as Lafayette
dismounted and went up the steps of the altar in the center of
the amphitheater. The blade of his American sword of honor
flashed as he drew it from its scabbard and touched the altar
with its point, while the firmly spoken words of the oath re-
sounded in the sudden silence.

Even the most fanatical royalists, however infuriated by the
spectacle, have described in detail, however scornfully, the un-
precedented tornado of enthusiasm which now broke out in
this gigantic basin of humanity. Separated from his horse,
swallowed up defencelessly in the maelstrom that raged around
him, now engulfing him, now lifting him above its waves on
the shoulders of those nearest him, amid a sea of applause,
Lafayette was helpless against his own popularity. When at
last he succeeded in getting back into the saddle he was surrounded by people who covered his coat-tails, his boots, his
spurs, his stirrups and even his horse with kisses. This great
mass of people centered their joy and their hopes on the person
of the "Liberator."

Louis XVI felt instinctively that it would be fatal to drag
his own fat and flabby body before the same altar; he confined
himself to holding out his arm where he stood under the royal
canopy and so taking the oath, which in his own eyes and his
wife's was no more than an enforced perjury. In vain did Marie
Antoinette lift up her little boy and show him to the crowd;

in vain did the nobles around her shout themselves hoarse with protesting cries of *"Vive le roi! Vive la reine!"*—the enthusiastic crowd had no eyes for anything but its favorite.

At this summit of his career, amid all this frenzied acclamation, Lafayette no longer stood on firm ground. A less haughty queen than Marie Antoinette, any queen at all, would never have pardoned the subject who in this way thrust her husband and herself into the background. The crowd who raised Lafayette onto their shoulders broke the bonds that united him with the Court to which his family had belonged for centuries, offering him no better support in return than the narrow pedestal of an ephemeral popularity. Worse still, at the very moment when he was being thus fêted, his popularity was being sapped. On the day following the festival on the Champ de Mars, Marat headed his article: *"C'en est fait de nous!"* ("We are undone!") He saw in the popular enthusiasm for the marquis, who nevertheless had the instincts of his class and, moreover, had "been bought by the crown," the destruction of liberty. It was, Marat added, only the *petits bourgeois* of the country towns who, in their pride at wearing the same uniform as Lafayette, had been carried off their feet.

The great mass of the Parisians had already lost faith in Lafayette. Marat was not the only one to put his readers on their guard against this man who, at critical moments, always defended the throne against the people. By his sudden appeals to the generosity of the crowd he had saved the queen and the bodyguards; but in doing so he had lost the confidence of the people, without conciliating the Court.

So, suspected by the people, hated at Court, Lafayette rode, borne only by his own faith, on the bright rainbow of his dreams, doomed already to disaster at the moment when he imagined himself and his whole nation to be nearest to the goal of their pursuit.

BOOK III
Downfall

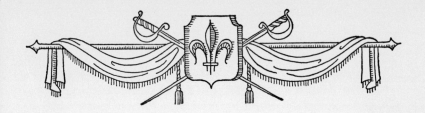

I. THE FIRST FALSE STEP

LIKE MOST OF THE ÉMIGRÉS, the Marquis de Bouillé sought to make money out of his Memoirs. To do him justice, he made no secret of his disloyalty towards his dear cousin Lafayette. He had been Governor of the Antilles when the twenty-year-old marquis asked for his help and met with an icy refusal. Bouillé, an old soldier and a man of the old school, saw in the "hero of two worlds" only an officer who took the part of the rebels for the sake of notoriety.

Lafayette's triumph made even the queen cautious for a while, but Bouillé did not change. In his arch-conservatism he was as much of a Quixote as his progressive cousin. Both were victims of the tragic optical illusion of the Knight of the Rueful Countenance. Lafayette, honored while no more than a boy by the friendship of Washington, intoxicated by the enormous difference he found between a France riddled with abuses and the magic land of justice and freedom, imagined a France made happy under wise and generous rulers through a few reasonable laws. The same optical illusion showed Bouillé, in place of the real Louis, narrow and indolent, eating, hunting and sleeping, drawing revenues from his people and bound to them in no other way whatever, "the king," the heir of Saint Louis, incarnating in virtue of his birth all the qualities that Lafayette found in Washington.

Both equally unteachable, because the picture each painted for himself hid the real world from him, Bouillé and his rebel cousin were predestined to be mortal adversaries. Bouillé, fifty years old, and with thirty-five years of soldiering behind him, was not the man to give way before a mob of insurgents. The fall of the Bastille and his cousin's treasonable leadership of the armed mob merely awakened in him a feeling that it was his duty to rescue his king from a desperate situation.

The transfer of the Court to Paris on October 6, 1789, interfered with the plan of rescue. It would be necessary to have patience, to lull the people and Lafayette, the jailer of the royal family, into a sense of security. Then, on the pretext of a departure for a holiday, it would be possible to bring Louis XVI into a safe refuge. Meanwhile Bouillé purged his troops of all doubtful elements, removed the infected civilians, and awaited the moment when ultimately it should be possible to take his royal master back to Paris and settle accounts with the rebels. The fact that the vain simpleton who had gone over to the populace, and was being acclaimed by every guttersnipe, could boast his relationship with the house of Bouillé, added to the old soldier's venom and made every device permissible in his eyes.

Lafayette, so sincere himself, refused to doubt either his cousin or his king.

The precipitate fall from throne to scaffold has thrown an aura of martyrdom round the heads of Louis XVI and Marie Antoinette; but in 1790 they were not yet pitiable victims; they were building scaffolds themselves, treacherously and pitilessly, for their adversaries. Even more than Bouillé, they regarded all means as justified, any disingenuousness, any breach of confidence, any perjury that helped to gain time.

Marie Antoinette was even less able than her husband to endure a capitulation to the rebels. The hope of aid from Bouillé was not enough; she corresponded secretly with her brother, Joseph II of Austria, and negotiated with almost every monarch in Europe, without the slightest sense that she was committing high treason. Unhappily for her, these secret relations were at once revealed to the public; it might have been supposed that the walls of the Tuileries were transparent. The queen found her most secret letters reproduced almost word for word in the anti-monarchical news sheets and pamphlets published by Marat. And it was in vain that the garrisons and fortresses were weakened along the whole of the northern frontier; instead of soldiers, there came from Vienna only formal words of consolation. Meanwhile the *camelots* shouted beneath the queen's very windows: "Read the Austrian woman's latest treason!" or: "Parisians, make an end of the plots of the Austrian committee!"

All these shouts drew down upon Lafayette the queen's hatred: she held him to be the instigator of the attacks on her. Was he not the champion of the liberty of the press?

Fortune was not kind to Marie Antoinette. Her favorite brother, Joseph, died in the spring of 1790, just when she most needed him. Her brother Leopold, until then Grand Duke of Tuscany, had been much more interested in art and philosophy than in political affairs. And before thinking of helping his sister, he devoted himself now to his own empire. The change of sovereign in Austria thus drove her to place all her hopes in Bouillé.

She would have shown even more impatience but for her husband's superstition. Destiny had placed a sign in his room in which he read a warning against precipitancy. This was the portrait of Charles I of England, by Vandyck, which after the death of Louis XV had been transferred from the Dubarry's bedroom into that of Louis XVI. Whether through the suggestive influence of the portrait or through some unexplained presentiment, the king, usually so lacking in intellectual curiosity, had conceived a keen interest in the fate of Charles I. He had sent for the new book by the famous historian David Hume, and had become engrossed in it. It had lain next his book of devotions in his bedroom at Versailles, and had been on the short list of things for his personal use for which he asked after the removal to Paris; it followed him, with the Vandyck portrait, to the Tuileries, and finally accompanied him to the Temple prison.

Through his mystical interest in this sovereign who had been decapitated by his subjects, Louis learned that it had been Charles's attempt to reconquer his capital by force that had cost him his life. Louis would have been glad to recover the power that was being taken from him bit by bit; but there was that warning sign on the wall. Probably he knew little of the schemes that were being hatched behind his back by the queen and the Marquis de Bouillé.

The plan of a forcible restoration was carefully concealed from Lafayette; but his respectful attitude towards the Court made it easy for his adversaries to charge him with complicity.

Years later, when the king and queen had long been decapitated, and Lafayette had emerged from his Austrian prison, General Bouillé regretted his deception of his cousin. Ten years of exile in England, under a constitutional monarchy, had changed the general's view of his cousin's "high treason." Had the two met, would the course of events have been changed, as the general imagined in retrospect? It is very doubtful. Had not Lafayette introduced into the National Guard the free election of officers by the troops? Did not the new Constitution grant civic rights to soldiers and an appeal against "injustice" at the hands of their superiors? How could an autocrat of Bouillé's type have made terms with such pretensions?

The Swiss remained under the draconic régime of their own country, and the new rights accorded to the French soldiers did not apply to them. Consequently, Bouillé refused these concessions to all his regiments. He had taken the new oath at the king's urgent request, apparently because otherwise the supreme command of the frontier troops would have had to be taken away from him. But he had no intention of entering into argument with his soldiers—anyone who asked for "civil rights" would be discharged with *la cartouche jaune*, in disgrace, with a "yellow card," and might starve; for he would find no employment with any landowner or public authority and would be too old to learn a new trade.

The soldiers were concerned above all to make an end of the old abuse of imposing fines on them, which subsequently were gambled away by the officers in their club. Their request was rejected in such offensive terms that two regiments in their wrath forcibly carried off the regimental chests into their barracks; and they wrote from Nancy to the National Assembly requesting the dispatch of an impartial arbitrator.

An arbitrator was appointed; but the choice was deliberately made of the most arrogant and most unpopular officer in Nancy; and he so thoroughly maddened the soldiers that they indulged in acts of indiscipline. Frightened by their own audacity, the poor fellows then sent deputation after deputation to say that they were ready even to hand over the chests if demanded. Unfortunately, Bouillé was only too glad of the opportunity of "making an example." He painted the affair in such vivid colors, and so spiced his report with instances of breach of discipline, that the officer in his trustful cousin came to the surface. Lafayette was already beset in his turn by a swarm of undisciplined critics—Marat, Desmoulins, and the rest of the Left-wing publicists—and was longing for a clean sweep of his own; and he allowed himself to be carried away by Bouillé into an indiscreet phrase—*"Frappez un grand coup!"*—"Strike hard!" This phrase, in his own hand, was a mortal weapon against him in the hands of his adversaries.

Bouillé did not ask for this advice to be repeated. With his German, Croat and Swedish regiments he shot down the two French ones, and he had all the prisoners hanged. For this shameful massacre Lafayette, whose instruction had been busily circulated, had to bear some of the responsibility. And when the Parisians crowded to the doors of the National Assembly to protest against the "massacre at Nancy," it was Lafayette again who had to set his "most reliable" National Guards against the "mob." He had been deluded by Bouillé, and now with his own hands rooted his name out of the hearts of the people of Paris.

II. AN AMBUSH

BUT THE INTRIGUING was not confined to efforts to destroy his reputation as a friend of the people. It was no discovery of the Revolution that the safest way to get rid of enemies was through death! World history is a textbook all too rich in examples of the preference for this definite settlement. It was never clearly established whether the hanged Marquis de Favras, poor and indebted as he was, was really hired by the king's brother to make an end of Lafayette. The attempt now made on his life was undertaken more cautiously, not through an aristocratic officer but through obscure and venal assassins.

The action began in front of the house of the rich brewer Santerre. On the morning of February 2, 1791, he was awakened by the rolling of the drums of the National Guard of the

Faubourg Saint-Antoine. He had been elected commandant
of this section, but was not the man to dominate the will of
his subordinates. He docilely accompanied them to Vincennes,
where they were going to demolish the fortress and raze it to
the ground.

Why February 2 rather than any other day? The casemates
had been out of use since the storming of the Bastille. To
seize the empty fortress, some distance from Paris, in the midst
of the winter was not an idea likely to occur to the small
shopkeepers and artisans, or to appeal irresistibly to them. Who
made the suggestion? Nobody knows. Unless some "clinking"
arguments had been brought to bear, it would not have been
easy to induce these poor people of the faubourg to forego
their day's earnings simply in order to wield their picks, in a
sudden access of enthusiasm for liberty, on the frozen walls of
this fortress.

The noisy procession of these columns armed with picks and
shovels was a provocation of the authorities, who could not sit
with arms folded while a royal possession was being pulled
down. About midday Lafayette was ordered to prevent this
senseless destruction, and he marched out of Paris with a detachment of Guards.

Could any more unsuitable mission have been devised for
this man, who on the day after the fall of the Bastille was
proclaimed head of the National Guard, and himself gave the
order for the destruction of that hated fortress? Lafayette had
been the first to praise the heroism of the conquerors of the
Bastille: now he was leading his bayonets against the men who
had set out to continue his work at Vincennes.

As at so many critical moments, he was saved by his own
courage. Santerre's troops and his own stood face to face, clad
in the same uniform. A single overhasty command, a single ill-
considered shot, and there would have been a repetition of the
massacre of Nancy. But the good brewer was no more than a
fat swaggerer. He submitted with a few grunts, and his soldiers
with him. There remained the crowd who had followed them
with their shovels and pickaxes. Lafayette went alone to face
them, and his intrepidity won the day. They shouldered their
implements and started off home.

On the way home there came a check. Lafayette found the

gates of the Faubourg Saint-Antoine closed and had to advance his guns before they were opened. Then, as he rode through the dark labyrinth of lanes, there suddenly came shots from all sides, and bullets whistled past his ears. At a street corner his horse shied at a wire stretched across, and only a bayonet thrust made in the nick of time by one of his loyal Guards saved him from the poniards of assassins, who escaped under cover of the darkness.

Was it simply an ambuscade of criminals of the faubourgs with some grudge against the marquis?

As far as the Tuileries it was possible for Lafayette to assume that this was all. But there the adventures of the detachment he had left to guard the gates of the royal palace threw a different light on the affair. While he was known to be safely out of the way at Vincennes, men in black clothes had streamed into the palace grounds through the various entrances. Each sentry knew only of the guests who had passed through the gate he was guarding, and so several hundred noble "visitors," furnished with the prescribed cards of admission by the *premier gentilhomme de la chambre*, were able to assemble in their majesties' private apartments. With pistols and swords, sword-sticks and daggers concealed under their black silk cloaks, the noblemen thus smuggled in made up a force strong enough to overcome the guards and cover the departure of the royal family before Lafayette, alive or dead, returned with his troops from Vincennes. The plot was frustrated by the imprudence of a hothead, drunk with arrogance or wine, who flourished a couple of pistols in the face of one of the sentries. The National Guards forced their way into the private apartments, found them full of men, disarmed the conspirators, and held them prisoners in the palace until Lafayette's return.

The embarrassed king denied all complicity in the affair. He stammeringly complained to Lafayette that his supporters' excess of zeal was more fatal to him than his opponents' hatred. The future was to justify the assertion; at the moment, for all that, it could not have been entirely sincere, for arms were discovered in cupboards and empty rooms and concealed behind all sorts of furniture—hidden there for the next opportunity.

This attempt at flight, accompanied by the ambush, re-

habilitated Lafayette in the eyes of the people. Even Marat
and his colleagues admitted that the general was stupid rather
than machiavellian. They forgot when they said so that he was
not receiving, like them, regular information from palace
lackeys, but only from Bouillé's son, who came, perhaps, a
little too frequently on leave from the frontier. Every day the
Paris papers revealed new plans of flight of the "Austrian
woman"; anonymous warnings piled up on the mayor's desk;
often in the middle of the night excited messengers would
come to burden Lafayette with news which subsequently
proved false. Was it forged in order to lure him into a sense
of security? Had he not the word of his king?

The extent of his trustfulness was shown at Easter, when the
Court publicly announced its intention to go for a change of
air to Saint-Cloud. The carriages of the royal family and the
suite were ostentatiously brought out of the mews and the
horses harnessed to them; Louis XVI and his family waited in
their carriage for hours watching Lafayette's vain struggle
against the raging crowd and his own insubordinate National
Guards.

The time was to come when the Court, seriously determined
to flee, took secret steps of quite a different nature. Neither
Bouillé nor Marie Antoinette was naïve enough to make the
attempt publicly. This frustrated departure had simply been
intended as a demonstration that the King of France was not
free. When Lafayette's orders and threats and attempts at persuasion had alike failed, when the horses were sent back to the
stables and the carriages to the coach houses, the faces of the
king and queen and courtiers were radiant with ironic satisfaction. What a check for the "dictator," nominally guardian of
public order and of the throne, but in reality the prisoner of
this populace, who derided his orders and dictated their will
to him! He could do no more than turn, deathly pale, to the
mayor and tender his resignation; then he fainted.

This fainting attack showed how Lafayette took to heart the
Guards' refusal of obedience. Had he had the slightest suspicion that his royal master could break his word, would he
have shown such indignation against the masses? For days he
was besieged by deputations; all the authorities implored him
not to abandon them; ultimately he withdrew his resignation,

but he certainly told the simple truth when he wrote to Washington that he had done so only in the interest of the public order and of the safety of his fellow citizens.

III. VARENNES

ON QUIETLY THINKING it over, the simplest dweller in the faubourgs had to tell himself that the Court was not likely, if it made a serious attempt at flight, to announce it publicly in advance—that the enterprise would not be attempted in broad daylight and with a maximum of display.

As always, it was Marie Antoinette who was mainly responsible for the attempt when it was made, on June 20, to 21, 1791, and for its failure. This is clear from the fact that the Comte de Provence successfully escaped on the same night on which the royal couple failed. The count left Paris at the same time as his brother, but he took only his wife with him, and made the journey in an ordinary hired carriage, which was able to pass every posting station to the Belgian frontier unnoticed. So the future Louis XVIII assured to himself the succession to the throne of France, for which he was so eager, at the cost of a single night's discomfort.

For the daughter of Maria Theresa a complete trousseau of underlinen was prepared at Brussels and sent to Metz. Her lover, the handsome Axel von Fersen, disposed of some jewelry in Belgium to cover the cost of the preparations, which had to be ceremonious and magnificent: they were for the flight of a queen!

It was this lover's attentions that brought destruction to Louis XVI and his family. The count's care for the comfort of his beloved cost the monarch, who was himself so easily satisfied, his crown and his head. In his efforts to spare her discomfort and risk, the gallant organizer of the journey forgot all the rules of prudence which a sovereign should observe if he wants to get safely out of his own country. A sort of unshapely ark was specially built, to contain comfortably the six fugitives: the king, his sister, the queen, the two children, and their governess. This vehicle inevitably aroused curiosity at every relay station; it was bound to awaken suspicion—a negligible detail in the eyes of Fersen, that perfect courtier, who could not condescend to take account of the existence of staring plebeians. Were their majesties to be incommoded out of consideration for a pack of gaping shopkeepers?

No enterprise is free from risk. But instead of organizing the flight as discreetly as possible, Fersen and Bouillé—as a matter of prudence!—drew public attention to the ark's voyage; they advertised it! The rumor was spread that a transport of gold, for the payment of the troops, had left Paris for Metz. To protect this precious convoy, patrols awaited it at every relay station as far as Châlons. Could any rumor have been better calculated to arouse curiosity along the whole route?

In spite of all these ostentatious preparations, the ark might have arrived in port if the Marquis de Bouillé himself had not been more preoccupied with giving his illustrious visitors a proper reception than with insuring their safety. But he did not venture on such an occasion to place the patrols under old and experienced noncommissioned officers, who would have sat on the benches of the village inns and chatted over a bottle with the postmaster. He chose his youngest officers, so long as they had great names: the Marquis de Choiseul, the Comte de Damas, his own son, and other stars of the aristocratic firmament.

Worst of all, an unpardonable fault in any risky enterprise, no account was taken of the possibility of failure. Greve (Count) Axel von Fersen was an officer; but neither he nor the Marquis de Bouillé gave thought to the possibility of an enforced return of the travelers to the capital. Instead of a pseudonym worthy of the King of France, the passport was made out in the name of a Baronne de Korff and her suite. Louis XVI was not entered by any name: he wore the livery of a *valet de chambre!* The head anointed with the sacred oil, the crowned head of the heir of Saint Louis, wore a menial's cap!

It is well known how the king was recognized on the way to the frontier by the landlord of a posting house. The landlord, Drouet, had served in the dragoons, and the memory of the humiliations he had suffered as a common soldier had been revived since the new laws had proclaimed human dignity to be the right of every Frenchman. Now he ran in and out of his door all day long, wounded both in his pride as a republican

and in his pocket. He did not mind paying his rent to the
state. But that young aristocrat the Comte de Goguelat, who
had come to the village in charge of the patrol, had put up
at the inn across the road! Nothing was good enough for these
young sparks!

The enormous coach which came past at midday also
stopped, of course, in front of the officer's inn. There was
something suspicious, too, about its impressive escort: why so
many and such distinguished officers merely for a convoy of
coin? He loitered curiously around the carriage—until there
appeared at its window a fleshy and suspiciously familiar face.

Immediately he was reminded of a passage in Marat's passionate appeal to the Parisians in the *Ami du Peuple,* then lying in
his own bar:

He is to be smuggled out of the country, on the pretext that his
cause is the common cause of all the rulers of Europe! Parisians, you
idiots, I am tired of repeating to you, watch the king and the
dauphin, and put the *Autrichienne* under lock and key. The loss of a
single day may cost the lives of three million Frenchmen!

Mais oui, du diable, it was the very same crook in the fleshy
nose, the very nose of the Bourbons! One glance at the
assignats for fifty francs, which had the king's head on them,
and Drouet was sure of it.

He allowed the carriage to start off without a word: he had
too much sense to get himself cut to pieces by the hussars.
But before that six-horsed chariot could reach the next relay
station, at Varennes, he had time to cover the distance twice
over. In a moment his best horse was saddled, and he set off
for Varennes by the bridle path.

But the solitary rider aroused the suspicion of the young
Comte de Goguelat. Where was the fellow going at that break-
neck speed? Too many precautions were better than too few.
The two best riders of his patrol were ordered to follow the
suspect and bring him back alive or dead.

Here were three cavaliers of destiny racing to decide the
future of France and of Europe, the fate of the whole of the
century shortly to dawn. They rode as though they knew, at
all events, that the lives of a king and queen were at stake.
The monarchy and all of France's past traditions were mounted

behind Sergeant Major Rémy, a simple peasant's son. Behind Drouet there floated invisibly the tricolor, the standard of the Revolution; the "Marseillaise" was drumming, as yet unheard, in his ears. The course of history was determined at this moment not by generals or ambassadors or ministers but by two peasants on horseback. If the sergeant major caught the innkeeper, Louis XVI would reach Bouillé's army. The thirty thousand men on the frontier, trusted regiments of picked troops, would be joined by the nobles who had emigrated or were still in the country; success, fear, loyalty, habit would make their appeal to men's hearts and reopen the gates of the country to its crowned head.

How many victims' lives would have been saved on the fields of battle of the Revolution and of Bonaparte if Drouet had not been so familiar with every turn of his bridle path? Amid the gloom of an impenetrable forest he reached Varennes long before the king's carriage, blocked the road by overturning a hay cart, and himself sounded the tocsin. The signal was taken up by belfry after belfry in the neighborhood, and the National Guards poured in from all the villages around. After a few hours the little house of the grocer who as Mayor of Varennes gave shelter to the royal family presented the aspect of a beleaguered citadel.

If Louis XVI had had the spirit of the man who returned from Elba with a handful of soldiers to conquer France, his case would not have been hopeless even at Varennes. Toward midnight the Duc de Choiseul came up to the room in which were the royal family and their small suite. Two peasants were on guard outside the door, armed with scythes. The duke flicked aside these instruments of death, entered the room, and declared that as yet there were only a few hundred men outside, armed with nothing better than pitchforks. The French soldiers under Goguelat and Damas had mutinied, but the duke's German hussars did not understand the mutineers' language, were not fraternizing with the people, and were waiting in their saddles, with drawn swords, ready to cut their way through. The duke proposed that seven horses should be taken from their riders, one for the king and the dauphin, one for Madame, the king's sister, one for the queen, one for the little princess, one for her governess, and one for each of the gentlemen in waiting. Defended by forty-three swords and by the pistols of three officers, their majesties would still be able to break through the weak cordon of besiegers before the crowds coming up from around made any attempt at escape impossible.

His Majesty considered for a long time. When at last he opened his mouth, it was not the king speaking, but a fat, placid lackey, sitting there in front of a bottle of Bordeaux and a piece of cheese, taking his supper in a grocer's shop.

"Can you guarantee," he said, "that in this unequal combat between a handful of men and seven or eight hundred peasants, some bullet will not hit my wife, my sister, or one of my children?"

A guarantee of success? But the price of every spirited effort is the acceptance of the possibility of failure! When Napoleon stepped out with his cloak open, challenging the first regiment sent to meet him, a single shot would have been answer enough! When there is a crown to be regained, chances must be taken. In a single year Lafayette was to risk his life three times to save Louis XVI and Marie Antoinette; he was to leave his own wife alone in France, in danger of the Terror and of the guillotine, compromised by his efforts to save the royal family!

Every occupation has its advantages and its risks. Millions of men win their scanty daily bread by the sweat of their brow and the sacrifice of their health in the bowels of the earth, their lungs full of coal dust, threatened every day by fire damp, by falls of earth, by the black death of the miner. Every day in excavations, or on scaffolding, countless men, to gain a meager living, risk their lives for the comfort and enrichment of a small fortunate class. The man who wants to be enthroned at the summit of this human pyramid, to live in idle elegance and luxury, must not hesitate if history demands of him that he shall risk his life to preserve the renown of his ancestors and the heritage of his posterity.

Least of all could Louis XVI, in his situation, afford to hesitate. The longer he did so, the less chance he had of escaping from the terrible necessity of returning to Paris through half of his kingdom in the livery of a lackey. Historians have sought excuses for him in his unwillingness to risk bloodshed; they forget that he concentrated regiments of foreign mercenaries around Paris and Versailles in order to restore his absolute power at the cost of sanguinary repression. In the end he mounted the scaffold without fear. He knew how to submit to the inevitable; he had a passive courage but not the courage of the fighter.

Without thinking of the disastrous consequences to the royal authority which might follow his appearance in his undignified disguise, he comforted himself with the prospect of aid from Bouillé. He built up hopes on illusory calculations, and underestimated distances and obstacles in his effort to justify the expectation of assistance from without. So he spent the whole night chattering cheerfully with the shopkeeper who held him prisoner, as though he were really the lackey whose livery he was wearing.

Next morning Lafayette's aide-de-camp arrived at Varennes with the order from the National Assembly for the arrest of the perjured king, who had fled in order to return as a conqueror, armed against his own people.

What a return along the high road in the great "ark," surrounded by thousands of National Guards! For three interminable days, amid the dust raised by the crowds escorting it, the coach rumbled on toward Paris. Its occupants were enacting the interment of the monarchy; the sight of the fat valet behind the carriage window destroyed the imposing image of the royal majesty which the king's subjects had had before them and revered all their lives. As ships at the bottom of the sea are gradually encrusted, so crests and crowns, thrones and banners are covered by a thick deposit of tradition. Past ages of respect had thus given a protective coating to the empty carcase of the French monarchy; it still took fourteen months before the rotted throne finally collapsed. But the destiny of Louis XVI was already sealed when he had to enter his capital in a lackey's livery. It was not a crowned head that fell under the guillotine but a head in the cap of a flunkey.

IV. DOWNHILL

AT ELEVEN O'CLOCK on the evening of the flight Lafayette, carrying out the prescribed round, had found the royal couple at cards with the Comte and Comtesse de Provence. At mid-

night Bailly, the mayor, who was in constant alarm, compelled
him to go once more to the Tuileries, because, among the heap
of anonymous denunciations which reached him day by day,
he had found some letters declaring positively that the king
intended to flee that very night.

For months news of this sort had been reaching either the
mayor or the commandant of the National Guard every day.
Lafayette unwillingly made this second journey to the palace;
there he found Commandant de Gouvion Saint-Cyr, his friend
and aide-de-camp, sleeping on a chair put against the door of
the queen's bedroom.

It took all his amiability not to give a rough welcome to
four wildly excited citizens who came at 2 A.M. to drag him
out of bed, obstinately declaring that the king had left the
palace.

It was Marat's constant prophecies of a new St Bartholomew,
which would restore absolutism through the extermination of
the patriots, if the king escaped and subsequently returned
with Bouillé's troops, that were making it impossible for Paris
to sleep. The city was filled with panic when it was learned,
early in the morning of June 21, 1791, that the king had fled.
As on the morning of the 6th of October, which had unjustly
won him the nickname of "General Morpheus," Lafayette once
more learned the sensational news in bed, about 8 A.M. Soon
the open spaces in front of the Hôtel de Ville, the Tuileries
and the National Assembly were packed with people, and the
excited crowds coming up from the faubourgs were blocking
all the main streets.

"Impossible!" stammered Lafayette as he hurried into his
uniform. Without waiting for his white horse to be saddled
he went on foot to the Tuileries.

"Impossible?" The many secret passages and hidden stair-
cases made it easy enough to escape from the palace. But it
was not his trust in bolts and bars and sentries that had made
Lafayette regard the flight as "impossible": he had the king's
promise, the king's pledged word! He should have read his
Machiavelli.

Marie Antoinette knew that Lafayette had assumed responsibility to the Parisians for the safe custody of the king, and
that his life was forfeit if the flight succeeded. Yet, as she her-

self related, it was with a smile that, as she stood under one of the entrances of the Tuileries, shortly after midnight, she saw Lafayette with his torchbearers passing by. And at Varennes she was unable to suppress an indiscreet question when she saw Lafayette's signature at the foot of the warrant of arrest: How was it that the general was still at his post?

Her surprise was only too well justified, for a good many heads had already been carried round Paris on pikes. Lafayette would have met the same fate if he had not been saved, as always, by his intrepidity. In his unshaken confidence, with no other protection than his own presence of mind, he was perhaps the only person in this innumerable crowd who showed not a trace of apprehension. For the very men who two years before had fearlessly gone to the assault of the impregnable bastions of the Bastille were now unnerved, like children in the dark, by Marat's prophecies. Incapable of independent judgment, they would be intimidated or roused with equal ease by anyone who knew how to deal with them; and, fortunately, Lafayette knew how to stimulate in them the consciousness of their own strength. Wherever he passed, faces brightened, and his own rallies were a better protection for him than bayonets.

"Let us be cheerful!" he said chaffingly. "There are twenty-five millions of us paying taxes, and so we shall save twenty sous apiece every year on the civil list!" At another corner he asked a downcast group who was really worse off, the people, who could live quite well without their king, or the king, who was nothing at all without his nation.

This jesting Lafayette, carrying his forfeited head fearlessly as he passed through the crowd, might have been able to prevent many evils if he had been able to show the same lofty contempt for other people's influence and advice as for perils. He reached the Tuileries undisturbed in mind, but there he met Bailly and the Duc de Brissac, who were awaiting him with faces livid with fear. At once these two newcomers almost broke the spell. Both were in terror of the populace.

Yet the fury of the populace had not yet broken out. The clumsy giant, left to himself, was as yet merely satisfying his childish curiosity by wandering through the abandoned apartments of the royal family; he was particularly attracted by the "Austrian woman's" rooms. A fruit hawker had the idea of displaying her cherries on the queen's bed; her "stall" was sold out in no time. The queen's enormous wardrobe created amusement, but nothing was stolen or spoiled. The crowd watched operations keenly; several people were searched and even made to take off their clothes.

The mayor and the Duc de Brissac were not entirely at their ease in this vulgar assembly. They took Lafayette with them to the Hôtel de Ville—a piece of great good fortune for Major Gouvion Saint-Cyr, who would have been hanged in a few moments if his commanding officer had not arrived just in time to rescue him from his executioners. To prevent lynching, the volunteer detachments of the National Guard were summoned from all the thirty districts of the city; with the 8,000 men of the regular guards Lafayette had a force of nearly 70,000 muskets at his disposal, while Bouillé had probably a more experienced force, but one of only half the strength.

When Lafayette and his companions reached the Hôtel de Ville, they found there the president of the National Assembly, the Vicomte de Beauharnais, who on the king's flight had become the highest authority in the nation. Beauharnais was in a state of consternation. He had duly issued orders for the drums to be beaten to assemble the deputies, but it was necessary to wait for a quorum, and he was afraid that before it was got together the fugitives would have so long a start that there would be no hope of overtaking them. The municipal council would not venture to fire the alarm guns until the National Guards had arrived in sufficient strength to prevent the crowds from committing excesses—yet with every minute's delay the responsibility of the authorities for the king's escape was growing.

The only one who was not afraid to take a decision at once was General Lafayette. He himself relates in his memoirs how he asked those present in the Hôtel de Ville:

"Are you all convinced that it would be better for France if the king were brought back to Paris?"

There was a unanimous reply of "Yes."

"Then," he said, "I will take the responsibility for it"; and he drew up at once a warrant of arrest, signed by himself alone. Romeuf, his aide-de-camp, rushed off with the document.

As he was riding out of the city, Romeuf was stopped by the suspicious crowd and brought back to the National Assembly, where Lafayette had just arrived with the mayor and Gouvion Saint-Cyr, to report his action. The Assembly immediately furnished the aide-de-camp with credentials, to prevent him from being again interfered with. Then he rushed to the pursuit of his royal quarry.

His game licence referred "in error" to a kidnaped, not an escaped, quarry. Why did Lafayette invent the story of "conspirators and enemies of the people" who had "kidnaped" His Majesty? His reason remains obscure. Probably he wanted to avoid the painful task of signing an order for the arrest of the King of France. Moreover, when he signed it he knew nothing of a letter which Louis XVI had addressed to the National Assembly and left on his desk in the palace. With the dubious courage of the debtor who has fled and imagines himself to be out of reach of his creditors, Louis revoked all his oaths and assurances as exacted from him under duress and therefore null and void.

The ministers listened apprehensively to the reading of this letter, which abandoned them to the wrath of the people. It was fortunate for the old Comte de Montmorin that he was able to prove that he had made out the passport used by the fugitives—for a supposed Baroness de Korff, with her children, governess, and lackey—in good faith, at the request of the Russian minister. The minister of justice read out the royal prohibition of delivery of the seals to the Assembly and of compliance with its decrees!

The deputies, now that in the course of the night they had become so many kings, took over the reins of state with dignity and decision. An unhoped-for chance enabled them to take shelter behind the myth of the "kidnaping" which Lafayette had invented. Hated by the throne, ignored by the people, the remains of this assembly which had aroused such hopes were suspended in the void, denied support from above or below. Only Lafayette's armed citizen troops bore the burden of its defence against the duped masses of the people.

If the Court and the nobility had been more reasonable, the seven hundred deputies of the Third Estate would have been ready to make many sacrifices to assure their conquests. On the morning of June 21, 1791, the future was still obscure, and nobody could say what it would bring. If the king was successfully brought back, his crown must be preserved intact; there must be no talk either of perjury or of cowardice. The "kidnaped" king of Lafayette's invention must be brought back, not the fugitive of the king's own letter.

Destiny had granted Lafayette a minute for reflection. When he had learned the contents of the king's letter he still had time to repair his error, to correct his falsification of the facts. But his pride as a gentleman closed his mouth.

Scarcely had he come into the presence of the Assembly when Robespierre, a provincial lawyer, shouted into his face: "Traitor to the people! Accomplice!"

The whole assembly, nobles and bourgeoisie alike, rose as one man to defend the commander of the National Guard, their one defender against the dreaded Paris populace. Even men like Barnave, themselves jealous of him, showed their respect for the spotless escutcheon of the hero of Liberty, whom his actions no less than his words raised high above any suspicion of complicity with the plotters who had tried to plunge France back into the slavery of the past.

Thus acclaimed, thus defended by the framers of the Constitution, could Lafayette break with them? Could he deny what they affirmed, as though he feared the howls of the pack of Jacobins whom Robespierre held in leash? It was not enough for him to have silenced his denouncer in a place where Robespierre counted for nothing. He would show that he had no fear of him even in the place where he was all-powerful. That same evening he went in search of the wolf in his lair—at the club of the Jacobins.

This society, founded at an early date by Lafayette, Mirabeau, the Comte de Lameth, and the other popular leaders of what was then the advanced party, under the name of "Society of Friends of the Constitution," now met every evening in the chapel of the former monastery of the Jacobins; it had become a rallying center for the demagogues. The bourgeoisie had parted from the common people, once the "heroes of the

Bastille," but now, in 1791, "the populace" and "the agitators." The poorer population, in turn, would no longer have anything to do with the Assembly. So it was that Robespierre, on the strength of his authority as a deputy, succeeded in becoming the leader of the "Jacobins' " club, where his speeches carried much farther than from the rostrum of the Assembly.

All over France, as in Paris, the retainers of the émigrés and the people who had gained their living out of the luxury of the rich were now workless. They were a body of discontented persons scattered over the whole country, and their condition drove them to extremes; they crystallized around the Jacobin center in Paris as their parent society and became a power in the state. They showed ability in organizing branches, found everywhere zealous propagandists and put into circulation in the country the formulas and instructions sent out from Paris. The sittings of the National Assembly were rarely attended by more than 250 out of the 1200 deputies; the great hall of the Jacobins, with 2000 seats, was so packed every evening that late-comers formed a queue at the doors like those in front of the bakers' shops. Robespierre would launch over this fervent audience his fiery tirades carefully seasoned with disturbing prophecies; Danton would precipitate into the hall brief speeches like an avalanche of rocks; and every telling argument against the reviled Assembly was printed at the expense of the central club and sent out for propagation among its branches. The vast number of illiterates who were unable to follow the newspaper reports of the debates in the National Assembly profited by the rhetoric of the leaders of the Paris club, thundered into their ears at second hand by their local Demosthenes.

In condescending to defend himself in the forum of the Jacobins against the charge that he had been an accomplice in the king's flight, Lafayette was making a concession to his party; his friends feared the influence of the club on public opinion. The sensational event of the morning had filled the chapel to the roof; the crowd, with no fixed judgment of its own, had come in order to learn the opinion of Robespierre, its oracle, on the significance of the king's flight and the consequences of this treason. The announcement that Lafayette was coming prompted all the speakers to launch violent attacks

against the only power still strong enough to hold the crowd in
leash, and the attitude of the Assembly in persisting in the im-
probable story of a "kidnaping" made it easy for them to
demonstrate that the marquis had deserted to the enemies of
the people.

Too proud to exercise caution, Lafayette only arrived at the
club after his evening inspection. It was nearly eleven o'clock
when he tried to enter, followed by two hundred deputies of
the constitutional party. He was unable to make his way to
the platform and was obliged to stop in the midst of the
crowd, who had already been worked up against him and continually interrupted his short speech with hostile remarks.

At the moment when he turned to go, Danton rushed up to
him like a lion let loose. The "Mirabeau of the faubourgs"
thundered against the "unmasked" hero, who eyed his unworthy adversary with the utmost contempt. For Lafayette
had in his pocket a receipt signed by the lion, a bit of paper
which could easily have closed the immense jaws which threatened him. In order to win over this dangerous shouter to the
side of the Court, the Comte de Montmorin, on instructions
from the king, had bought Danton's legal practice at ten times
its value. His profit of 90,000 francs was more than sufficient
to compromise the tribune of the people irredeemably.

"Monsieur de Lafayette," roared Danton, "you have pledged
your head for the king. Do you call that paying your debts?
If you are not a traitor, you are an imbecile. In either case you
are unworthy to command the National Guard of Paris."

The amazing thing about this meeting is that Danton knew
very well that the receipt he had signed was in Lafayette's
pocket. But Danton was not the man to be intimidated by the
paper. He knew that Montmorin had sent it to Lafayette for
use as a crushing weapon. But he also knew—his knowledge of
men told him so—that this man was incapable of exposing
Montmorin in order to justify himself.

The grand seigneur was stronger in Lafayette than the politician. He ought to have seen that in Danton he was affronting
an adversary on whom it is impossible to turn one's back with
impunity. Yet he left the hall, with his following, without
clearing himself of the suspicion of having assisted the king's
flight. Next day Marat, foaming with rage, demanded that he

should pay the price with his head, and he would not long have been safe, even in the midst of the bayonets of the National Guard, if the news of the king's arrest had not arrived in time to save him.

V. ASTRAY

IT WAS LAFAYETTE's fatal and entirely unmerited misfortune that he could neither call into existence a strong republican party to which he could turn for support, nor demand the appointment of a regent until the dauphin attained his majority. In either case he would lay himself open to the suspicion of coveting the leadership. Perhaps, although he never allowed the slightest allusion to the subject to escape him—perhaps he may really have been tempted to become, like Washington, the first protector of the liberties he had helped to win. He need only, like Napoleon, have looked around him; he could have found pretexts enough for stilling his conscience by dressing up a desire for power as a sense of patriotic duty.

Lafayette made no secret, either from Washington or from his party friends, of the fact that the restoration of this king who was an enemy of the Constitution was not to his taste, although these latter had certainly rallied to the throne which they had for two years been destroying. The incestuous alliance between the advance guard who had now arrived in power and the beaten beneficiaries of the old régime, a process constantly repeated throughout the ages, left the upright and selfless dreamer himself uprooted.

The four long days up to the king's entry into Paris were fatal both to Lafayette and to the monarch. The peasants hurried across the fields from the most distant villages to demonstrate against Louis XVI as he passed along the high road. None of them would miss the opportunity; for the very thought of the king transformed them at once into furious revolutionaries. At last, after long years of famine, there was promise of a rich harvest, which this time could no longer be taken from them in the name of hereditary "rights"; and at this moment the King of France had fled secretly in order to bring up his soldiers to restore the old "order" of tithes and capitations and corvées! Throughout the four days fists were shaken at the windows and oaths and threats were shouted at the king and queen.

The four days were ably exploited in Paris by Marat and the Jacobins. The working population of the faubourgs, and the masses of the starving unemployed, flamed up in indignation when they were told that the perjurer, who in fleeing had declared war on all the conquests of the Revolution, was to be reimposed on them as the first personage in the country. And while the "ark" trundled back with the wretched remnants of the French monarchy over the bumpy high road, in Paris Lafayette too was a target for universal hatred. Less than a year before, thousands had been crowding forward to kiss his boots; now insults were heaped on his name. Before long the charge of being a "Fayettist" was to become sufficient for a sentence of death. The bourgeois section of the National Guard feared and detested the populace; and the poor of the faubourgs, who eleven months before had been contending for the honor of defending a "protector of liberty," now called the National Guards "Lafayette's spies." The guards were no longer safe if they went about alone in their uniform.

Yet Lafayette was doing no more than his impartial duty. He was not trying to turn the reëntry of the fugitives into a triumphal procession. At all the street corners placards announced that "Anyone who acclaims the king will be arrested; anyone who insults him will be caned." A double row of bayonets lined the main road to the palace. Meanwhile Lafayette turned the little procession into side streets and so led it to the gate of the Tuileries.

On arrival there, Marie Antoinette was unable to refrain from demonstrating her hatred of this man who had just protected her for the second time from the wrath of the people and whose life she had herself cheerfully jeopardized. She petulantly threw down the keys of her baggage, telling him to search anything he wanted to. Twice he had to return the bunch of keys to her.

The poor king tried to laugh away the awkwardness of the moment. His first request, as always, was for something to eat, and he greeted his valet with pleasantries:

"Ah! There you are! And here am I. Everybody does stupid things at times, and why not the king?"

Lafayette saved the royal dignity which Louis XVI could not himself preserve. Bowing low and redoubling his marks of respect for his sovereign in his misfortune, he reminded him that he had often urged him, both by word of mouth and in writing, to turn away from an effete nobility and clergy and to accept the love of the nation and the power of the new laws as the chosen supports of his throne:

"I have never concealed from Your Majesty that if I were placed in the dilemma of having to choose between serving the nation or your person, I should not hesitate to remain faithful to the nation."

The king's reply showed that, when away from his wife's influence, he was not deaf to the voice of reason. He recognized that Lafayette had always openly proclaimed his principles. "It is a matter of party," he said, adding:

"I must admit that I felt confident, until now, that I was being misled by a small group of men whose interests were leading them to give me a wrong picture of public opinion. My journey has shown me that I was mistaken."

Fear is a bad adviser. The fear of anarchy led the National Assembly into servile complaisance toward the king. Cowering behind Lafayette's bayonets, it wounded the people's sense of justice by ill-advised decisions which only increased the popular hostility to the throne. Thus three deputies were appointed to take "evidence" from the king and queen concerning the unknown "kidnapers." For a nation just enfranchised and by no means inclined to be treated as mentally deficient, this story of "conspirators" was too transparent an invention. Marie Antoinette, true to her system, used even this opportunity to weaken the position, already precarious, of men who were honestly concerned to protect her from the popular fury. When the deputation from the Assembly appeared, at the time she herself had appointed, to hear her evidence, the queen sent a message that she was having a bath; would the gentlemen come some other time! A mortal enemy could not have discovered better food for the suspicion, spread by Marat, that the queen was so confident of the help she was expecting from abroad that she was merely trying to gain time.

Louis XVI had fled on June 20, 1791, and returned to the Tuileries on the 25th. The choice of date, so near to the anniversary of the great Fédération, further excited the indignation of the Parisians. What had become of the oath sworn on the Champ de Mars? This inevitable question made a conflict certain between the people and their representatives. The Assembly had, indeed, completed its main task, of giving France a Constitution. All that was now needed was the king's sanction. But the king could not be asked to swear fidelity to its provisions without having examined a single line of it. He was therefore accorded a certain time for studying it. The authority of the crown was suspended, meanwhile, by decree of the Assembly, until the day the Constitution was adopted. That done, the power would revert to the king, whose oath sufficiently guaranteed respect for the Constitution—as the past had shown!

The only persons charged in connection with the flight were the three nobles who had accompanied the fugitives, the children's governess, and the queen's ladies of the bedchamber. As Robespierre said, with some reason—the small people had been struck at in order to protect the great.

To protect itself from the threatened consequences of this farce, the Assembly decreed special measures against unlawful assembly and rioting. A law directed unmistakably against the people of Paris gave the mayor the right to declare a state of siege by hoisting a red flag over the Hôtel de Ville. The very representatives of the people who two years earlier were saved from the gallows, imprisonment, or banishment by the popular rising and the storming of the Bastille, celebrated the second anniversary of their deliverance by voting a sanguinary law against their liberators. And it was on Lafayette, the head of the armed forces, that the duty of this suppression fell. On the very spot where, a year before, he had sworn to protect the rights of the nation, he was now to pour out the blood of his fellow citizens.

VI. THE MASSACRE ON THE CHAMP DE MARS

BEFORE THINGS CAME to this pass Providence granted him one last opportunity, magnificent and unforgettable, for proudly recalling that he counted among the creators of the new France. On the second anniversary of the popular victory the mortal remains of Voltaire were brought to Paris, to be laid alongside those of Mirabeau in the new Pantheon of the nation. All Paris came out when the coffin reached the capital on July 10, 1791. It was received at the city gates with princely honors; the coffin was borne on the shoulders of the most eminent men of the country. Lafayette preceded it on horse-back as far as the place where two years earlier the cyclopean building of the Bastille had stood.

Voltaire had himself been twice a captive within those gloomy walls, but it was not for that reason that his body was to remain through the night on the spot where the tomb of free thought had stood. It rested there as a symbol, but a symbol that bore the stamp of the French genius, with its innate respect for the grandeur of thought. This homage to the remains of Voltaire was perhaps the finest that has ever been rendered to the power of the human intellect.

In the midst of the great open space on the edge of the Faubourg Saint-Antoine, Voltaire's coffin was placed between lighted candelabra, and the population of the great city filed in an unending column past its "Liberator." For that was the inner meaning of this nocturnal ceremony: it was not even the conquering people, nor Lafayette, who two years ago de-molished this rampart of tyranny; it was your great intellect, Voltaire, that brought about this prodigious achievement!

The dead man slept under the open sky on the spot where for centuries the power of darkness had kept its victims chained, cut off from air and light.

But this night, devoted to the honoring of the invincible mind of man, was followed immediately by one more act of dull tyranny. What a caprice of Destiny! And what blindness of men!

The people were unable to forget the king's perjury. They demanded the abdication of Louis XVI, and the more the Assembly tried to protect him the more insistent became the demand. But however bitter might be this contest between the people and their representatives, there should have been no necessity for bloodshed in the new France, whose laws recog-nized the right of every citizen to petition the National Assembly. This right of petition could also be exercized jointly by all the inhabitants of whole districts or towns, if their meeting was duly announced to the authorities three days in advance.

This provision was properly complied with. Brissot and Danton drew up the text of the Parisians' petition demanding the deposition of Louis XVI. The petition was to lie on the *Autel de la Patrie*, the "altar of the fatherland," on the afternoon of Sunday July 17, 1791, for signature by "every good patriot." The written permission of the authorities had been handed, duly stamped, to the organizers of the petition.

At this point that secret power which men call "chance," and which flits about the world like Shakespeare's Puck, arranged for its own amusement a sanguinary farce. One of the many wigmakers who had lost their employment, a man accustomed to carrying the latest scandal from one half-dressed customer to another, sought an *"ersatz"* for the libertine atmosphere of which he was feeling the loss. The idea occurred to him of getting underneath the platform of the Autel de la Patrie. There he promised himself a great deal of enjoyment from the spectacle presented from below by the long procession of crinolines. A wooden-legged friend was attracted by the idea, and at dawn of day the two were already on the Champ de Mars. They had brought ample provisions with them, including a little cask of wine. On arrival at the altar they lifted a plank of the platform, got through, put it back above them, and set to work piercing peepholes. Who would be likely so early on a Sunday morning to be anywhere near this scaffolding in the middle of the Champ de Mars?

Contrary to all expectation, a poor fruit hawker, anxious to find a good pitch, came at this early hour onto the scene. To pass the time she came up to the altar and reverently examined the inscriptions and symbolic ornaments on it; and she happened to set her foot on the very spot at which the wigmaker was boring, at the very moment when his gimlet came through!

Her cry of alarm brought up other people who were beginning to arrive. Someone ran to fetch the nearest guards, and the two "conspirators," pulled out of their hiding place, found themselves transformed at once into bribed assassins, preparing to blow up the crowd of good patriots. There was their barrel—obviously of gunpowder! The temper of the people had already been sufficiently roused of late, and very soon the heads of the two unfortunate men were being promenaded on pikestaffs among the Sunday crowds of the faubourgs.

This precipitate act of vengeance took place about seven o'clock in the morning. There was no connection whatever between the murderers and the crowd that assembled in the afternoon around the Autel de la Patrie to exercise their legal rights of petition and assembly. But the promenading of the two heads as far as the center of the city had taken time, and the same nervous tension that had converted a barrel of wine into a powder cask, now invaded the whole of the Assembly. Without troubling greatly about details, an impatient cry was raised for "an example" to be made. The mayor and the commandant of the National Guard were summoned at once, and the representatives of the people issued an order for the red flag to be hoisted over the Hôtel de Ville in declaration of martial law and for action to be taken against the "murderous horde" on the Champ de Mars.

Poor Bailly, who was very far from being a bloodthirsty tyrant, was to be laden three years later with board after board of his scaffold, and to carry it bit by bit to the Champ de Mars, to expiate his "murderous rage" under the guillotine on the scene of his "crime." In reality he was no more guilty than Lafayette, who also had only executed his orders, misled by his own party.

The sun was already getting low in the west, and eleven hours had passed since the morning's crime, when troops marched from two sides against the peaceful and totally unsuspecting crowd of signatories. There is nothing to be gained by attempting to reconstruct the actual course of the collision out of the mass of contradictory evidence. Does it matter, in any case, whether the three prescribed warnings were given or not? According to Marat, over a thousand corpses were secretly buried that night; the official total of dead was fifteen. But human lives are not to be counted like sacks of potatoes; each one of us suffers the cruelty of his own death, and the atrocity is not less real if the figure is smaller.

In vain did Lafayette try to prevent the mischief when the spectacle of the peaceful and unarmed crowd showed him that there had been a mistake. His "reliable" soldiers were well-to-do citizens, easy-going in their everyday duties, but all the more impatient now to have a stern reckoning with the eternal disturbers of the peace who were the ruin of trade. Lafayette rode his horse in front of the loaded cannon at the risk of being blown to pieces; but nothing availed against the suggestive influence of what had happened.

It was no longer the Lafayette of the Fédération who returned to the city on the evening of July 17, 1791. The past had disappeared, had foundered in the blood shed on the Champ de Mars; that was seen to by the new leaders of the people, Marat, Camille Desmoulins, Danton, Robespierre—and by the day's dead.

Detested by the people of his own rank and at Court, attacked with equal venom by the royalist and the Jacobin newspapers, Lafayette sighed with relief when at last, on September 4, 1791, Louis XVI accepted the Constitution and swore to respect it. Once more the whole of the Paris Guard marched to the Champ de Mars to take the oath to the Constitution before their commander. The popular wit found scope for bitter comments in this "theatrical humbug." Oaths now sounded like false coin since the king had given the example of perjury and since Lafayette had shed the blood of the people in order to protect the perjurer.

On the 8th of October, a week after the National Assembly had dissolved, Lafayette placed his resignation in the hands of the mayor. Like his friend and exemplar, Washington, he meant in future to live the life of a plain citizen. Did he, perhaps, secretly hope that a day might come, much later, when he would return like Washington to public life? The ambition of a Lafayette would scarcely be extinguished at thirty-four. But at the moment of this farewell he certainly took his retirement very seriously. Hatred and ingratitude had made it easy for him.

Only the bourgeoisie insisted on paying their tribute to the fallen idol. The customary speeches, a second sword of honor, and a marble bust of Washington were to indemnify Lafayette for his lost popularity and for two years of public service which had made inroads on his great fortune.

For two women his departure from Paris brought contentment. Marie Antoinette's hatred feasted on the fall of the man whom she regarded as her mortal enemy. And at Chavaniac Mme de Lafayette was waiting to shower her affection on the husband who was at last restored to her. Without a word of complaint she had seen herself abandoned for glory, and often also for more terrestrial rivals; she was none the less attached to her husband with all her heart.

His consolation in retirement was his castle in the air, the new, completely reconstructed state, the constitutional monarchy which would reconcile people and throne and would assure to the country, after its great trials, a period of peace and prosperity.

His letters to Washington reported his happy return home and breathed his unshakable confidence:

As to me, I enjoy, with the rapture of a lover of liberty and equality, this complete change, which has placed all citizens on the same footing, and which respects only legal authorities. I cannot express with what feelings of delight I bow down before a village mayor. A person must be somewhat of an enthusiast to enjoy all this as I do. I do not ask you to enjoy it with me, but at least enjoy it for me. They who believe that I came hither to achieve a revolution, are great fools.

I take as much pleasure and perhaps as much *amour propre* in an absolute repose as I have taken in fifteen years in that action which, always directed towards the same end and crowned by success, leaves me no rôle but that of a labourer.*

VII. DISASTER

MARIE ANTOINETTE's fatal talent of always getting the opposite of what she wanted left the new "countryman" scarcely a month in his rôle of Cincinnatus. He had just come to an agreement with the architect and the painter in regard to the repairs and decoration of the old château of Chavaniac, in order to turn it into a fitting and comfortable home, when the French declaration of war against Austria recalled him to Paris.

For a long time the Emperor Leopold had remained deaf to the appeals from his sister, who tried to win him to the project of a general crusade of monarchs against the peril of the new

*I.e. *laboureur*, plowman. TRANSLATOR'S NOTE.

ideas. Since the carefree period of his reign over Tuscany, the emperor had remained in touch with all the intellectual currents of his time; he had not forgotten to take the works of the great philosophers with him to Vienna. He was well acquainted with the traditional abuses of the French Court and was not greatly moved by his sister's outbursts of rage at even the wisest reforms.

The queen had no better success in Berlin. Only Gustave III, the "chivalrous" King of Sweden, influenced by the liaison between his favorite Axel de Fersen and the Queen of France, regarded her liberation as a romantic mission. But he was not strong enough to undertake so costly a campaign unaided and resisted the temptation until the Emperor Leopold, fearing for his sister's life after the failure of the attempt at flight, decided to organize an offensive alliance against France. In August, 1791, while Louis XVI was busily studying the new Constitution, there was concluded at Pillnitz the pact which was to enable it to be abolished. The French émigré officers and nobles got together a small army against their country, commanded by Condé, and the two brothers of the King of France persuaded the allied sovereigns that the march on Paris would be nothing more than a promenade through a country which would receive its saviors with open arms.

Marie Antoinette clung to the idea of this royalist crusade. She was not intimidated by the memory of the peasants' fists that had roughly menaced her. She had too much contempt for the "populace," too much faith in the superiority of professional armies, to doubt for a moment that she would be saved if only the first troops crossed the frontier. The storming of the Bastille? It was due to the governor's cowardice. Bouillé's failure? A piece of bad luck. Would the people put up any serious resistance? Would they brave all Europe, would they touch their sovereigns while punishment was already on its way? Never! The queen did not dream of it for an instant. Her one idea was to rid herself of the detested Constitution. She said so to the bourgeois ministers whom her weak husband accepted; she said to their faces:

"Do you really imagine that we are going to tolerate this for long? Nothing of all this can last!"

Accepted by the king, openly repudiated by the queen,

hotly criticized as insufficient by the great mass of the nation, ignored by authorities with royalist sympathies, the Constitution no longer offered any solid guarantee. In the new Parliament, the Legislative Assembly, the ill turn done by Robespierre was bearing fruit; it was seen that he had calculated extremely well when he induced the National Assembly to decree that none of its members should have a place in the coming Parliament. Personally he lost nothing; he had his own rostrum at the Jacobin club, where he could make his voice heard all over France without any need for a member's mandate. Emigration had considerably thinned the ranks of the royalists, and the suppression of classes facilitated the elimination of representatives of the nobility and clergy. If on top of this all the popular members of the first assembly, who had already proved their worth, were got rid of, the benches of the Legislative Assembly would be invaded by an army of new men amenable to popular pressure.

Robespierre's calculation was only too sound. The new Assembly reflected the new France; but the center, representing the well-to-do bourgeoisie, was caught between the ultra-royalists and the extremists of the Left and was doomed to succumb to the pressure of the clubs and the population of Paris. In these straits the Gironde, the representatives of the liberal and cultivated section, resorted to the desperate remedy so often employed as a safety valve for popular passions: it worked for war.

The queen was delighted, after all the intriguing and appeals to monarchs abroad for a punitive expedition, that now war was forced on her vacillating husband by the hated Parliament, which signed its own death warrant in doing so. Marie Antoinette and the thinned circle of her followers waited in the Tuileries like unsuspecting saloon passengers in a sinking ship and counted the days before their liberators could cross the frontier and reach Paris.

The bourgeois majority of the newly elected Legislative Assembly rested its hopes on the enthusiasm that would carry all patriots to the threatened frontiers and would rid Paris of the dangerous elements. But the people had well-informed instructors; day by day they read in the newspapers of the latest decisions of the "Austrian committee," which was engaged in treason under the queen's leadership, sending the enemy cipher letters communicating the strength and disposition of the French troops, and preventing the equipment of the French army and the frontier fortresses.

Two of the three French armies were to be commanded by senile, septuagenarian marshals. The third was to be placed under Lafayette—a decision in which it was certainly not easy for the king to concur. But he had allowed Mme de Staël, Necker's brilliant daughter and the wife of the very important Swedish minister, to persuade him to appoint as minister of war the handsome young Comte de Narbonne. And it was her voice and her knowledge of men that spoke through the mouth of Narbonne:

"If Your Majesty does not voluntarily appoint M. de Lafayette today, the people will compel his appointment tomorrow."

Mme de Staël was well aware that the king was anxious to maintain at least the appearance of authority. In this way she helped Lafayette, the playmate of her youth, into the saddle, as later she helped Prince Talleyrand, Benjamin Constant, and many others.

Christmas Eve seemed to be the regular date for the critical events in Lafayette's life. His appointment to the command was handed to him at an audience at noon on December 24, 1791. As it was laid down in the Constitution that the crown had to secure the assent of Parliament to the appointment of army commanders, Lafayette presented himself in the evening before the Legislative Assembly and thanked it for its confidence, which he hoped to justify. This act of courtesy reawakened the hatred of him at Court, where the Constitution was regarded as a farce, and compliance with its provisions was considered an insult to the throne.

Next morning, when he left to join his army, the bourgeois sections of the National Guard lined the streets. His carriage went past the Tuileries, and on account of this the news was spread everywhere that before finally leaving General Lafayette had made a last attempt to intimidate the Court. In this unending guerrilla war of the royalists against all the protectors of the detested Constitution, the Tuileries went so far as to support their most radical enemies, the republicans, in order to weaken the constitutional monarchists. Thus, when

Bailly came to the end of his mayoralty the crown spent a great deal of money to secure the election of the Girondist Pétion as mayor, for fear of the election of the "democrat" Lafayette. In the days of the sanguinary crisis, this choice delivered the king into the hands of his enemies.

Lafayette installed his headquarters at Metz, where he had begun his military career as the youngest of cavalry captains. His experience in America had made him familiar with the difficulties of the equipment of an army, and he had a strong suspicion of the sabotage in which the crown was indulging. His letters to Washington show that he was too conscientious an observer to be under any illusions:

The regular regiments are short of their complements. The volunteer battalions do very well; in general, the soldiers and non-commissioned officers of the army are patriots, but want discipline. A third part of the officers are good, another third gone, the remainder very ill-affected, and will soon, I hope, go out; they are tolerably well replaced. We want general officers, most of them being tories. I am going, and am the only one whose popularity can stand it, to establish, in spite of the clubs and jacobin clamors, a most severe discipline, and I think the army afterwards will do pretty well.

These "clamors," of which Lafayette, to his undoing, underestimated the importance, represented the first thunders of the great storm.

The hatred of his influential enemies, on the other hand, had its advantages for him. The Duc de Lauzun, who before the arrival of the handsome Count von Fersen was said to have been very dear to Marie Antoinette, spoke of Lafayette's military capacity with such contempt that the Court imagined that it was weakening the center army by entrusting its command to him.

The Comte de Narbonne promised Lafayette that he would double his effectives and summoned him to Paris in the middle of February, 1792, for a council of war, over which the king presided with his customary geniality. Louis XVI had without doubt been initiated into the mysteries of his wife's secret correspondence. Lafayette's ambition provided a trump card in the king's double game: he suggested that the general should go to the aid of the Belgians, who had revolted against their Austrian oppressors. Old Luckner remarked with a smile:

"Is not M. de Lafayette a specialist in the matter of revolutions?"

These plans and decisions had in reality only one purpose: to give the enemy time to complete their preparations. There were complaints of shortage of money and of the devalorization of the new paper money; every pretext was used to retard the equipment of the army and the increase of the effectives. Lafayette spent weeks in Paris in order to hasten the preparations, and Marie Antoinette steadily undid his work with the patience of Penelope and with disastrous intrepidity.

But it seemed as if Destiny itself was infected with the virus of democracy. The queen suffered heavy blows. On the 1st of March, 1792, she lost her brother Leopold, on whom she had counted most. This most gifted of all the sons of the prudish Maria Theresa died suddenly from the excessive use of a drug to revive his virility. He was found dead on the floor, with the empty flask in his hand, in front of an opened secret cupboard full of women's silk and lace underclothing.

A few weeks after this irreparable loss, Gustave III was assassinated at a masked ball in Stockholm. The fall of these two main pillars of her vengeance should have brought the queen at last to more prudent courses; instead of this, she became still more impatient in urging her husband into fresh indiscretions; meanwhile the émigrés gathered along the frontier like hungry hyenas. Marie Antoinette could no longer show herself at an open window; if she did she was loaded with abuse and threatened with death by the crowds outside the palace.

Lafayette was almost as much out of favor. Long after he had returned to his headquarters rumors were still going round Paris that he was hiding in the palace, with the intention of finally drowning the new liberties in the blood of the Parisians. All possible means were employed by the radical leaders in order to discredit with his remaining followers the one man the radicals had still to fear, since he commanded a strong army. Thus Robespierre demanded that Lafayette's bust should be removed from the hall of the Hôtel de Ville, its presence there being an insult to the memory of the good citizens whom he had had massacred on the Champ de Mars. Three days later Lafayette's own removal was demanded on the ground that the protection of France must not remain in the hands of a man who was betraying the people and was in the king's pay.

Meanwhile Lafayette was suspected by the royalists of aiming at a dictatorship. He no longer had in any camp a defender who would venture to compromise himself on his behalf.

At first, for all that, there was a fever of enthusiasm in all the country which Lafayette was the very man to utilize. His orders to his troops struck for the first time the new note which later was to win the soldiers' hearts for Bonaparte. His form of address, "Soldats de la Liberté," itself sounded like a trumpeting of the new era. Discipline and order were no longer maintained by the degrading fear of "running the gauntlet"; the "soldiers of Liberty" fought for their new right to become officers, generals, marshals, and the fear of once more being burdened by the old salt taxes and tithes and corvées impelled to the colors an inexhaustible supply of recruits without need for recruiting sergeants or gratuities.

Lafayette's army began the war with small successes. His troops had unbounded confidence in their leader, who had learned in America how to treat "citizen soldiers." But the events in the interior were too disturbing to permit the general to push far beyond the frontier. He knew the Parisians and the queen well enough to fear already for the life of the sovereigns, and regarded it as his duty to protect the throne against the people and the people against its own fury. A violent outbreak would not only cost the lives of the king and queen but would compromise the Revolution. All the opponents of a constitutional régime would triumphantly make use of this new evidence of the unwisdom of the liberation of the peoples.

On June 20, 1792, the Tuileries were invaded by an enormous crowd. It was no more than a sort of dress rehearsal of the decisive blow. It passed without effusion of blood; but the king had to remain for hours in the embrasure of a window; a red cap was put on his head, and he was made to drink the nation's health out of the half-emptied bottle of some loafer. Only his self-restraint saved the king and his family from death. The invasion lasted five hours. Tens of thousands of people strolled through the king's palace without Pétion, the chief magistrate of the city, deigning to summon the National Guard to protect the sovereign, or the Assembly troubling to interrupt its labors at the news that the head of the nation was in peril. Only when all was over did the mayor arrive at the palace and express his satisfaction that the crowd had refrained from abusing its strength by going to extremes.

"Taisez-vous!" shouted the king furiously. *"Allez-vous-en!"* ("Shut up! Get out!")

But his master's wrath no longer frightened Pétion. The experiment had shown that any serious thrust would overturn the tottering throne. It was possible now to go quietly ahead with the preparation for the decisive attack!

How thoroughly Lafayette had realized the danger in spite of his distance from the scene is shown by the threatening letter he sent from his camp at Maubeuge, four days before the invasion of the Tuileries, to the president of the Legislative Assembly. The success of that incursion made the letter into a boomerang. An army leader who sends threatening letters from his headquarters to the representatives of the people is turning against the power it is his duty to protect. From this commination to an armed march on Paris at the head of his army would be but a step! Had not Marat always prophesied that Lafayette intended to make himself Dictator?

But Lafayette had no intention yet of marching his troops against the capital. When the news reached him of the "mass visit" to the Tuileries he went to Paris *alone*. He put up secretly with his friend the Comte de la Rochefoucauld, in order to obtain exact information before definitely intervening.

It seems amazing that such unheard-of audacity had no fatal result! The unexpected appearance of the army commander in the Legislative Assembly was more than an impulsive action, it was almost an attempt at suicide. The few supporters who remained loyal to him had tried to make out that his letter was a forgery and the work of an enemy of his. And now the writer himself stood there and protested against the suspicion of not being its author!

How he would have blanched, this knight without fear and without reproach, if a ghostly hand could have held before his eyes the evidence which now justifies the worst "slanders" of

Danton, Desmoulins, Marat, Pétion, and Brissot—the cipher letters from the queen which now rest in the archives! His happy ignorance of the truth gave him confidence to withstand every onslaught.

"Has the enemy been chased away from our frontiers, since the general who is supposed to be facing them can appear in our midst?" asked the most moderate of his opponents, and the extreme Left wing demanded the immediate arrest of this army leader who was spending his time in Paris teaching the legislators instead of doing his duty at the front. His boldest and most faithful supporter did not venture farther than to beg the House to judge the first and most famous of the protagonists of Liberty "more leniently" than an ordinary offender.

Immediately after this slap in the face, Lafayette left Parliament to go to the Tuileries. Only there did he disclose the real purpose of his visit to Paris. He put before the king a plan of flight which might well have been devised by his good cousin Bouillé himself. The Constitution restricted the monarch's freedom of movement to a defined area round Paris. On the border of this, but still within it, lay Compiègne, so that the royal family could undertake an excursion there without special authority. Lafayette would bring the best of his troops to the neighborhood, and so would liberate the sovereign without any risk. Once delivered from his situation of constraint, the king should order the immediate retirement of the enemy armies and his émigré subjects and should confirm his voluntary acceptance of the Constitution.

With his usual indecision and lack of straightforwardness, Louis XVI asked for time to consider the plan; and Marie Antoinette helped him to put off Lafayette with various pretexts. The queen was determined to overthrow the Constitution with foreign aid and to inflict due punishment on the author of all her troubles. She had no intention of foregoing her revenge. In vain did Mme Elisabeth, the king's sister, try to win over her brother to the plan: the queen declared that she would "rather die than be saved by Lafayette."

Lafayette himself understood the reason for hesitation; but he was better able to appreciate the danger than the Court in its isolation from the people. He knew there was no time to be lost and felt that he could not abandon the king and queen to their fate. He still had the support of part of the National Guard. When he left the palace the news of his arrival had spread and some loyal companies from the richer districts of the city accompanied him to his house.

In order to count his strength he ordered a review for the following day in front of the Tuileries, in the mad hope of organizing with a few thousand brave helpers the forcible rescue of the royal family. Instead of the few thousands, less than two hundred men answered his summons. He refused to believe in such cowardice, assumed that twenty-four hours' notice had been too little, and put off his departure until the morrow.

Concealed in the house of friends, he heard through its windows the growing volume of shouts from the masses who called for his head. Next morning no more than forty of his faithful followers ventured to present themselves. So he left Paris, defeated and broken. He was not to see the city again for many years. He retired, discouraged, behind the protecting cordon of his troops. Seven weeks had still to pass before he shook the dust of his country from his soles, but his departure from Paris on June 30, 1792, was already the beginning of his flight.

Three days later, in Parliament, Vergniaud, the Cicero of the Girondins, the greatest orator of the Revolution, rose to deliver the funeral oration over the grave, already yawning, of the monarchy. His acid and trenchant sarcasm pitilessly tore the mask off the face of Louis XVI:

"The king says: 'I have obeyed the Constitution, I have sent forces against the approaching enemy. It is true that these forces are too weak; but the Constitution does not lay down the strength of the armies that I should put in the field. It is true that I have been too dilatory in assembling them; but the Constitution does not define the date by which I ought to assemble them. It is true that they have not had the support of reserve columns; but the Constitution does not require me to form reserve columns. It is true that when the generals were advancing unresisted on enemy territory I ordered them to retire; but the Constitution does not require me to win victories. It is true that my ministers have deceived the National Assembly concerning the strength and disposition of the troops and their provisioning; but the Constitution gives me the right to choose my ministers;

nowhere does it lay down that I should place my confidence in patriots and get rid of counter-revolutionaries. To sum up, it is true that the counter-revolution is in progress, that despotism is about to replace its iron sceptre in my hands, that I shall crush you, that you are going to grovel, that I shall punish you for having had the insolence to want to be free; but all this is being done constitutionally.' "

These few phrases from the orator's smashing indictment should have reminded Lafayette that he had often made the same charges of reinforcements promised but not sent, of inadequate supplies of arms and equipment, of secret wrecking at Court. But his own feelings had been roused; when three representatives of the legislature arrived at headquarters to interrogate him in the name of the Assembly, he arrested them without ceremony and lodged them in the neighboring prison at Sedan. In this treatment of the delegates of a body which had lawful authority over him, he denied for the first time his own superstitious respect for all democratic institutions, and he would have been obliged to flee from France even if the storming of the Tuileries and the arrest of the king on the 10th of August, 1792, had not sealed his fate.

He made one more effort in a visit to the headquarters of old Marshal Luckner, but without result. His only consolation in his flight was that, in spite of his personal unsuccess, he was leaving behind him a new France. For all the "soldiers of Liberty" whom he had himself taught to fight for law and justice, not against peoples but against tyrants, old Luckner's ideas represented a dead past. The Alsatian's address, in his quaint French, to his soldiers was a pretty legacy from the epoch of the mercenaries who sold their skins in the best market, equally ready to spill their blood in the cause of justice or injustice. He said, in effect:

"Officers, N.C.O.s, and men, a creat misfortune has come ofer Paris. I don't care a fic for the enemy in front of us, but I do for the enemy behint me. When you ket your pay put it in your pocket; that's all I care; you will not leafe me. Nor will I leafe you."

This was not to Lafayette's taste. He went back to his headquarters, too faithful to his past to use his influence with his soldiers. He had tried everything he could in the defence of the Constitution; often enough he had risked his life in its

making. Called to account now in the name of a legally elected
authority, he had no choice left but to flee the country.

All his aides-de-camp and friends fled with him, the Comte
de Lameth, the two Latour-Maubourgs, father and son, the
Romeuf brothers, twenty of the best officers of his staff, most
of them old comrades of the war in America and colleagues
in the building of the constitutional monarchy which was col-
lapsing behind them. The only one among the party who was
not voluntarily leaving the country was Lafayette. The Assembly had proscribed him as a traitor and set a price on his head,
and it was necessary for him to cross the frontier before his
successor, General Dumouriez, reached his headquarters to
send him in custody to Paris.

On August 19, 1792, he informed his troops of the capture
of the Tuileries and the king's arrest and took upon himself
the whole responsibility for the incarceration of the Paris
deputies in order to protect the Sedan municipal council. Then,
just before his thirty-fifth birthday, he disappeared from the
scene, struck out of the cast just at the moment when he
imagined that his time had come to play the leading part in
historic events which would decide the future of his country.

It was hard, it was painful for this passionately earnest
builder of the new monarchy to abandon his work, his homeland and his family! Mercifully he could not yet know how far
he was to fall, or the sufferings that were in store for him and
the perils for his wife. On his arrival in Belgium he hastened
to reassure her as to his safety. His letter to her is the finest
epitaph on a youth rich in achievement:

As for me, my destruction has long been decreed. With more ambition than moral sense, I could have had a very different existence;
but there will never be anything in common between me and crime.
I have maintained to the last the Constitution to which I swore. You
know, my dear heart, that my feelings would have been in favour of
the Republic if my reason had not spoken in favour of monarchy and
the will of the community had not made the defence of the constitutional king a duty. And so I have become the target for universal
attack from both sides.

The mathematical demonstration of the impossibility of effectively
opposing the crime, and the fact that I was the object of a further
crime, have forced me to withdraw from a struggle in which it was

clear to me that I should have died to no purpose. I do not know at what point my progress might be retarded, but I am going to England, and want my whole family to join me there. I know that families of émigrés are being prevented from leaving, but this means those of the émigrés who are fighting their country; and, Great God! where is the monster who could dare to suppose that I am one of these? Both the Austrian and the Jacobin postal services will read the letters I write; I do not mind that, provided that they reach you. I have never had a single sentiment that needed hiding.

I make no apology either to my children or to you for having ruined my family; not one among you would have desired to owe his fortune to conduct contrary to my conscience. Come and join me in England; let us settle in America; there we shall find the freedom that no longer exists in France; and my affection will try to compensate you for all the joys you have lost. Adieu, my dear heart.

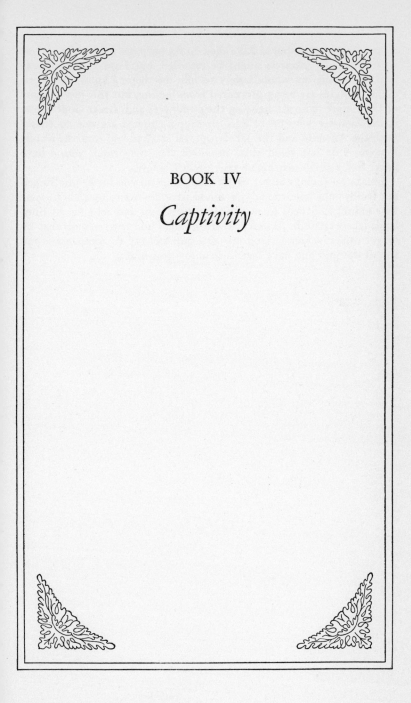

BOOK IV

Captivity

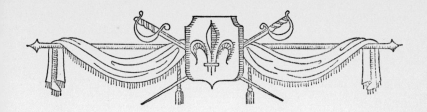

I. INTO THE TRAP

NINE DAYS after the fall of the Tuileries and the arrest of the royal family, Lafayette crossed the frontier with twenty-two officers who had followed him. Once arrived on neutral Belgian soil he imagined himself to be safe from pursuit, but that did not make it easier to leave his homeland.

He had no fear for his security; who was likely to prevent him from returning to America, of which he had been made a citizen? Merely as a precaution, a safeguard against any excess of zeal on the part of the Austrian patrols, he sent the Comte de Latour-Maubourg to the commanding officer of the nearest post of any importance, to ask for a safe conduct.

Officers of the royal French army, driven out by the Paris mob government? The Austrian count, full of sympathy, picked up his pen—and then suddenly dropped it. What was that? Lafayette? The notorious revolutionary ringleader? The man who had put his king under lock and key, who had compelled the daughter of Maria Theresa to go to bed in the presence of common soldiers and to expose her royal limbs to their lascivious gaze?

As happy and excited as if he had just won a battle, the Austrian general sent urgent orders in the night for this unhoped-for prize to be conveyed to Namur under a strong escort. Nobody troubled about the protest signed by the twenty-three prisoners. What naïveté, this appeal to international usage! Cashiered and outlawed by the so-called new government of France, the prisoners were no longer officers of the enemy army; the Archduke of Sachsen-Teschen, uncle of the emperor and commander-in-chief of the Austrian troops, readily agreed to this contention of theirs. But it would be much too easy a way for malefactors to escape from their just punishment if all they needed to do to wipe out the long list of their crimes was to leave their country.

With his pockets still full, Lafayette had no difficulty in finding a messenger; but he did not venture to write to his wife. He wrote to the Princess d'Hénin, who had made good her escape to London, confidently informing her that his family would soon be in England. And he wrote proudly to his old aunt at Chavaniac:

My reverses have not changed my principles, or my sentiments, or my language. I remain here what I have always been throughout my life. My spirit, I must avow, is delivered over to profound depression, but my conscience is clear and tranquil, and I doubt whether the leaders of the different factions who have torn me to pieces can say as much.

What simplicity! What astonishing lack of knowledge of men! Lafayette at thirty-five still believed in a "better self," coming at night like a ghost to disturb the conscience of his adversaries and destroy their rest.

In the camp of the émigrés there was feasting to celebrate this capture, and glasses were emptied to the health of the executioner who would send Lafayette's black soul to hell. Only the Duc de Lambesc-Lorraine had the courage to pay a visit to the captive in the interest of the good cause. But instead of the information for which he had come on the strength and disposition of the French troops, all he received from Lafayette was some disagreeable truths about the vast difference between a man proscribed for political reasons and a traitor at war with his country. The sympathetic commandant at Namur, who tried in his report to Vienna to minimize Lafayette's "complicity" in the French Revolution, found this incorrigible rebel aghast at the idea. He had to draw up a new report; the prisoner would not permit any watering down of his "meritorious services" to his nation. The archduke demanded that the French army funds should be handed over, and had to pocket this answer:

"From this request I can only infer that in my place His Imperial Highness would have run off with the money of the state."

This provocative tone did not improve matters. Frederick the Great's half-humorous prophecy was very nearly fulfilled: Lafayette was within a little of being hanged for his opinions under Frederick's successor. The émigrés pestered the coalition leaders to execute him. He was well aware of his danger, as is shown by the farewell letter, one might almost say the last testament, which he smuggled into the pocket of his faithful Romeuf at the moment of their parting:

I fully expected that if I fell into the hands of the despotic governments they would wreak vengeance on me for all the injury I have done to them. But, after defending the free and national Constitution of my country to the last moment against the factious, I have abandoned myself to my fate, feeling that it would be better to perish at the hand of the tyrants than by the mistaken hands of my fellow-citizens. It was important, above all, to prevent the people's cause from being injured by a great example of ingratitude! They may do what they will; the truths I have spoken and my labours in two worlds are not lost. Aristocracy and despotism are mortally wounded, and my blood, crying for vengeance, will bring liberty new defenders.

But it was just this satisfaction that the allied sovereigns had no desire to give Lafayette: they did not want to nourish dangerous germs with the blood of a martyr. Emperor Francis of Austria had the prisoners divided into three groups. Those who had not served in the National Guard were set free, only being banished, as a safeguard, from all states under the Austrian crown. The second group were to expiate in Belgian fortresses their participation in the Rovolution; but they had to be released prematurely and to flee before the victorious advance of the French troops.

Lafayette, Puzy, Lameth, and the elder Latour-Maubourg were incarcerated as revolutionaries. The inconsistency of this when they were actually in flight from a revolution which had outlawed them was not allowed to weigh in their favor in the slightest. The archduke replied to their protest against the illegality of their imprisonment with ironic courtesy:

I should have regarded it as a high honour to fight against an army commanded by General Lafayette, if he had owed his appointment to the king. But since, as head of the French insurrection, he has been forced to leave his country by the very people whom he had taught to revolt, and has fallen into the hands of the allied powers, he will be kept in custody until his sovereign, in clemency or justice, has decided his fate.

As though they were trustees for valuables placed in their charge, their majesties of Prussia and Austria carefully deposited the four Frenchmen in the casemates of their fortresses until the moment when the legal owner should claim them. Lafayette could not even take with him into the gloom of his dank cell the one consolation of all prisoners, hope, for his liberation would mean the defeat of liberty and the restoration of tyranny.

The great gate of the citadel of Wesel closed behind him; the world disappeared. The guards did their duties in silence, as in a Trappist monastery. All his questions remained unanswered; he was not allowed to write or receive a single letter. He petitioned the king at least to allow him to obtain information as to his family's welfare; in reply he was told that his situation might be alleviated if he would give information about the strength, disposition, and guns of the French army and the defences of the forts on the frontier.

"Tell your king," Lafayette replied, "that he is supremely impertinent in making such a proposal to me."

At this the lid of the coffin was screwed down over the living corpse. Watched day and night by a sentry, and so rigidly isolated from his friends that he did not even know whether they were in the same prison, Lafayette had for months no other company than his anxieties over the fate of his family. But this intended aggravation of his punishment was in reality merciful; for how could he have endured his impotence if he had known of the massacres in the prisons of Paris, of the assassination of his relative and best friend La Rochefoucauld and of his wife's arrest!

II. MADAME DE LAFAYETTE

PUBLIC OPINION was aroused in America and England. Washington and the diplomatic representatives of the United States in Europe left no stone unturned to secure Lafayette's liberation. But it was not the American citizen but the rebellious subject of the King of France who had fallen into the hands of the allies, and the American Minister at The Hague was unable even to discover in which of the Prussian fortresses Lafayette was imprisoned. He wrote to Gouverneur Morris in December, 1792:

The most impenetrable secrecy has been observed with respect to him and his fellow sufferers. It is certain that he is the individual, of all France, that the Austrians and Prussians hate the most cordially. The desire of revenge, and determination to punish, made them commit the most flagrant act of injustice, and the most shameful violation of the *droit des gens*. They are probably sensible of it, and therefore wish to smother the whole business, and the victims also.

At bottom it was neither the truth nor their captives that the Courts of Berlin and Vienna wanted to stifle. Their real motive was not the desire for vengeance but the fear that the epidemic of Liberty might spread into their own countries.

No attempt has been made here to conceal Lafayette's weaknesses under the theatrical cloak of a heroic stage figure of history. His failure to comprehend the needs of the starving masses, his sternness toward the poor whose stomachs could not be filled by "political equality," made it easy for his opponents to discredit him. The only one who really understood him was his wife, who, though so often abandoned, neglected, and relegated to a secondary place, never ceased to revere and idolize him. With the indomitable pride she had learned from him, she continued to declare her admiration for the proscribed man—a dangerous admiration, for the executioner was sent to destroy Lafayette's bust in front of the Hôtel de Ville, and the Paris house of the man who had had the Bastille destroyed would have been razed to the ground in its turn and replaced by a column recalling the traitor's disgrace, were it not for the cupidity of the speculators who profited by its preservation.

But the more viciously his victorious opponents defiled the memory of the man who was now coffined alive in the casemates of despotism, the more openly Mme de Lafayette took pride in bearing his outlawed name. His enemies might imprison her, might orphan her children, the executioner might take her life, but she would never deny her pride and happiness in her twenty years as Lafayette's wife. Wives of émigrés left behind in France obtained divorces from their husbands in order to preserve their properties from confiscation. This tender and fragile mother of three children, thrown unprotected into the whirlpool of raging passions, never spoke or wrote of herself otherwise than as *"La femme Lafayette"* or *"La citoyenne Lafayette,"* as if she were totally unaware that the designation *"Fayettiste"* in a charge sheet was sufficient in itself to bring a sentence of death.

Christmas week, so consistently the period of critical events in Lafayette's life, also marked a turning point in his wife's destiny. Shortly after his flight she had been imprisoned in the principal town of her department; on December 24, 1792, she was released on parole to return to her children at Chavaniac. A week later, on December 31, six months after his arrest, Lafayette was transferred from the fortress of Wesel to that of Magdeburg.

For four thousand endless hours he had been without news of all whom he loved. Too proud to allow himself to be broken by the exaggerated harshness of his jailers in their servility towards their masters, he had braved with a show of indifference even this worst of his tortures. Still more admirable and almost superhuman was his wife's steady maintenance of the part which she regarded it as a duty to her name to play. It was only with a great deal of effort that influential helpers in every camp had secured her release in order to enable her to look after her children. The provincial authorities, fearing for their own heads if they failed to deliver this precious pledge on demand to Paris, stationed National Guards as sentries in the gatekeeper's house of the Château de Chavaniac.

"I declare," proudly said Mme de Lafayette, "that I do not regard myself as bound by my parole if these guards are left at my gate. Make your choice between the two sureties. I will not have my parole reinforced by bayonets."

III.   PLAYING WITH DEATH

THE MOST ABSURD TRAIT of the régime of the Terror was its cult of antiquity. Every unemployed wigmaker changed his name from Jim or John to Brutus or Cato; the heroics of the stage were transferred to everyday life. Camille Desmoulins himself, the satirist with the flair of a hound for the weaknesses of humanity, and the sure hand of a hired bravo as he impaled them on the point of his pen, called his little son Horace. For all his clearsightedness, it escaped his notice that it was the astonishing intrepidity of the victims of the Terror that provoked this caricature of the heroic style of the ancients.

The arrogant contempt of death shown by the *ci-devant* aristocrats undoubtedly bore some of the responsibility for the inhumanity of those bloodthirsty years. Men and women, believers and unbelievers, mounted the scaffold as though it were a stage, and the spectators, who were not evil at bottom, watched without emotion the cruel scenes which the victims themselves reduced to theatricality. Mme Roland gave up her place to the next victim in order to shorten his sufferings; Danton, before allowing himself to be bound on the plank beneath the guillotine, said to the executioner:

"You must show my head to the people, it is worth it."

The twenty-one martyrs of the Gironde sang the Marseillaise in chorus; the fall of the knife for the twenty-first time cut short the last voice in the middle of a word.

This reduction of death to banality made the small man who trembled at the foot of the scaffold play Mucius Scaevola himself, and show a stony indifference, in order not to be outdone by the victims. When the Dubarry struggled for minutes with the executioner's men who were binding her, and when she cried out, as she lay actually under the knife, *"Encore un moment, monsieur le bourreau!"* ("Do wait a minute, Mr Executioner!") the insensible habitués of these daily executions separated in silence, ashamed.

It was not heroism but pride and contempt that at the moment of death spat in the face of the people: "In spite of this I am still your master!" The true heroes were those who suffered modestly and in silence, repenting nothing but hating no one. Even if there had been nothing else to bring forward in Lafayette's favor than the admirable constancy shown alike by his wife and himself, in their conviction that none of the atrocities committed by the liberated masses could excuse the sufferings that had been imposed on them for centuries—this unshaken impartiality in the midst of misfortune would alone suffice to keep his memory bright.

Lafayette had been incarcerated at Wesel at the moment of his wife's arrest; he was transferred to Magdeburg at the moment of her release. Until the 18th of March, 1793, he remained without news in this new tomb. He was not even allowed the usual exercise in the prison yard. Hours and days, weeks and months went by in murderous monotony, sapping his life, until the day when at last some good soul, nobody knows who, risked his freedom and his life by smuggling out of the fortress a letter from the victim.

This first letter showed that not all the stone walls, the bolts and bars and the ramparts of tyranny, are powerful enough to shut out human sympathy. Lafayette's message, addressed to the Princess d'Hénin, reveals a knowledge of events of which he could have learned only from the whispers of some sympathetic officer who could speak French. He knew of the victory of the French at Valmy and spoke with deep emotion of the death of Louis XVI, which had compromised the future of liberty and stained it with blood.

His only fear was for the safety of the postilion who was braving the vigilance of the king's myrmidons and risking "his property, his freedom, and his life," in the secret transmission of the message. How unbroken was his own spirit was shown by his ironic comments on the servile zeal of the commandant of the fortress in carrying out his orders. He assumed that his wife and children were in England and begged for news of their condition.

Only during the transfer to Magdeburg had it been impossible to prevent the companions in misfortune from meeting again. The stern warders did not suspect that this fugitive meeting was an added trial, since each of the prisoners was able to infer from the aspect of the others how greatly his own frame had suffered.

The malice of chance played a further unkind trick on the leader of this little group. By a strange coincidence the two brothers of Louis XVI, the Comte d'Artois and the Comte de Provence, passed through Ham on that same day and dined in the same room of the hotel in which the prisoners were taking their meal. It might have been imagined to be an arranged meeting: princes and prisoners were separated only by a few tables. But what a satisfaction for the princes to watch Lafayette, ill clothed, with features of the glassy pallor of some cell plant, eating, like the criminal they considered him, under the menace of loaded pistols!

Christmas week once more brought its event. Lafayette had been consigned to Magdeburg at the beginning of 1793; just at the end of that year he was transferred to the fortress of Neisse. The happiness of being no longer cast out of life, of being reunited with the outer world by the thin thread of occasional news, had braced his powers of resistance. With the transfer to Neisse this precarious bond threatened to break, but the rare news that continued to trickle in showed that he still had faithful friends. Lafayette was supported by the consciousness that he had defenders who were unceasingly pounding on the heavy iron doors of his prison.

Not one of the twelve letters that found their way out of his new cell contains a single sentence that he could not have written in freedom in his Paris home. Even in prison he was concerned for the fate of the Negroes on his plantations in Cayenne; he devoted part of his precious sheet of paper to asking the Princess d'Hénin to remind Mme de Lafayette not to sell the plantation without first emancipating the Negroes.

IV. THE HEROINE OF CHAVANIAC

WHEN THIS REQUEST reached Mme de Lafayette she had already long sold the plantation; but she had first released the Negroes. She knew every wish and every thought of the man in whom all her life and love centered. The Princess d'Hénin in her letters continually scolded Lafayette for his proud and provocative attitude, which could only damage him. Meanwhile his delicate wife, abandoned, persecuted, threatened with the guillotine, made a point of replying to her husband's accusers and enemies with the same spirit, ready to mount the scaffold before she would show herself unworthy of the man whose pride was also her pride.

Shy when a child, brought up in seclusion from the world, prematurely arrived at motherhood, Citizeness Lafayette had grown in stature in her husband's company. As a wife she might well have detested the ideas which for twenty years had robbed her of her husband's society. But her love had inspired her with absolute faith in him. The ideals which had drawn him away from her side when she was expecting her first child had become her own ideals. He might make mistakes or be misled, but she alone among his contemporaries fully realized the integrity and the stanchness that made him adhere as unshakably to his convictions at the summit of success as in the depths of misfortune.

Fourteen months passed before Mme de Lafayette saw her husband's writing or was able to give him the consolation of a single line from herself. She was enabled by Brissot's intervention to stay a year at Chavaniac with her children; she devoted the year to the struggle for her husband's liberation. Instead of remaining quiet, so that she might be forgotten in Paris, she moved heaven and earth to secure permission to follow him and share his fate. She wrote to the Duke of Brunswick, to the King of Prussia, and to Washington. She defended her husband from every accusation with a fanatical energy which impressed even men like Gouverneur Morris who had had no love for Lafayette. Morris and others were touched and influenced by the magnificent courage of this frail little woman.

The inexhaustible natural wealth of the United States and their rapidly growing requirements and purchasing power had given their diplomatic representatives great influence in Europe. The most retrograde governments found themselves compelled to overlook the objectionable constitutional forms and the dangerous principles of so rich a customer, and their competition wrung concessions from them. Yet Washington himself wrote in vain to demand Lafayette's liberation; all the urgency of his ministers secured no more, after eighteen months, than permission for the prisoner to write a single letter and to receive one letter in reply. This needless cruelty, through which the prisoner and his innocent family were punished by being left for a year and a half in ignorance of one another's fate, was characteristic of the rancorousness of the "justice" of the period. For a year and a half Lafayette and his friends were incarcerated alongside one another without any of them knowing anything about the others. Their sense of entire abandonment must not be allowed to be mitigated by the sight of a familiar face.

Even this concession of a single exchange of letters was reduced virtually to nothing by the censorship of the commandant of the fortress. The letters gave no more information than that the two parties were still alive, and even that might have been no longer true when the single letter in either direction reached its addressee through a long succession of administrative officials. Lafayette had good reason for writing, as he did, in one of his secret messages to the Princess d'Hénin, that his crowned jailers were doing their best to make arbitrary rule still more odious to him. The man who had had the Bastille razed to the ground was now himself suffering a belated course of oppression.

On December 30, 1793, the fortress of Magdeburg received orders to transfer Latour-Maubourg to Glatz and Lafayette to Neisse. At the same time the order went from Paris to the authorities of Brioude to proceed immediately to the arrest of Citoyenne Lafayette. In the course of the first week of January, 1794, the husband was sent to Neisse as a dangerous agitator, while his wife was sent as a counterrevolutionary into a prison of the Republic. Her children were torn from her, and she would have had to make the journey in a prison cart if the curé of the village had not collected together the modest jewels of the whole of the domestic staff in order to pay the cost of a post chaise. So husband and wife both went off to new destinies. Lafayette, full of confidence, little dreamed that every turn of the wheel of his conveyance corresponded to one of his wife's that was taking her nearer to the guillotine.

V. THE MAFIA OF HUMANITY

THE STRONG FORTRESS of Neisse lies at no great distance from the Polish frontier—sufficient ground for Lafayette's unshakable optimism to elaborate the boldest plans of escape. Before his transfer robbed him of his secret courier he wrote a hasty letter to the King of Poland asking for protection, and sent to all his aides-de-camp and officers a circular letter asking them to go to Poland in order to establish liaison with Neisse from that neutral ground. He wrote a letter full of confidence to Princess d'Hénin, telling her that he had had the autobiography of Baron Trenck smuggled into his cell and was studying it with interest for its story of how the unfortunate baron, riveted, by the orders of Frederick II, by a triple chain round his body and limbs to the granite walls of an underground dungeon, succeeded in thirteen years in wearing through his chains and digging a way to escape.

The thing he did not know was that Baron Trenck, after expending first seven and then thirteen years on his two escapes from the iron grip of Frederick the "Great," had fallen into the clutches of Robespierre, who on the eve of his own fall and death had the baron guillotined as a suspected foreigner. Lafayette only learned the full story of this sanguinary tyranny in the name of liberty when he had at least no longer any need to tremble for the fate of his wife.

While he sank at Neisse into a new tomb, to be heard of no more for months, there rose over France the foul vapors of the Terror of 1794.

Chavaniac was sold as a national possession. Only with difficulty was as much as the bed of Lafayette's eighty-year-old aunt bought back. His three young children would have been without a roof, were it not that in the whole region there was not a peasant family who would not contend for the honor of sheltering them. Thanks to her own goodness, Mme de Lafayette had no need to fear for her children. Her faithful chaplain was even able now and then to take his three charges beneath the window of their captive mother, until the guillotine made room for her in one of the crowded Paris prisons.

Lafayette once more found secret allies ready to act as his messengers, in spite of the enormous risks. They served him at their own expense, out of loyalty and admiration. The American minister procured money for him, in the name of the country of his adoption, but he could dispose of it only under supervision.

No violence was able to suppress the Samaritan mafia of humanity which stood at the service of the victims of wrong alike at Magdeburg and Neisse, in Paris, and everywhere. As compatriots hurry indifferently past one another in their homeland but abroad fraternize at once and hold together, so oppression strengthens the solidarity between all decent people. Wherever there was freedom of opinion, newspaper articles and parliamentary orators hammered on the doors alike of the Prussian fortress and of the Paris revolutionary tribunal. However severe the supervision might be at Neisse, revolting details of Lafayette's treatment got abroad, and gradually the King of Prussia tired of being denounced all over the world as the jailer of an innocent man. The humiliating retreat from France after the battle of Valmy had entirely destroyed his sympathy for the émigrés. He had been assured that they would be received with open arms as saviors of the country; instead of this, his uncle's "invincible" troops had had to give way before the despised tatterdemalions of the Revolution.

The protocol of the mutual engagements between the allied sovereigns declared that the existence of the Marquis de Lafayette (his existence, not his liberty!) was incompatible with the safety of the European governments. But if his imprisonment was to continue until his physical and mental sufferings had completely broken him and made an end of the undesired existence, was it not more fitting that the Emperor of Austria, who had to avenge a sister and a brother-in-law on the prisoner, should take over the rôle of executioner?

Luchesini, the Prussian minister, put pressure for a long time on Baron Thugut in Vienna to get his royal and imperial sovereign to take charge of the prisoner. But the Austrian minister, who had recently been ennobled for his services, was not prevented by that fact from seeing farther and more clearly than the nobility of the Court, with their ties of relationship with the émigrés. He put off the acceptance of the prisoner as long as he could. Why should he burden his master with the unpopular rôle of jailer? Not that he had any reason to fear that Austria was unequal to the task. The Habsburg monarchy enjoyed a worldwide reputation for the perfection of its art in the silencing of rebellious subjects. But this Marquis de Lafayette was a special case. His unexampled popularity in America made it impossible to consign him to oblivion, and the Whigs in the English Parliament knew how to represent him as a martyr who had been outlawed for his fidelity to his king and was expiating the sins of his adversaries.

As time went on Lafayette grew more and more indignant at the injustice of representing him as responsible for the fall of Louis XVI and Marie Antoinette. He was too proud to defend himself before his jailers, who were not called upon to judge of his actions, but he wrote in a secret letter to Princess d'Hénin:

Rather than remain silent in the face of crime, than connive at injustice, I, who had no royalist superstitions, and who had been deceived again and again by the Court, a convinced democrat, perhaps too much so, rejected nevertheless not only offers that had no charms at all for me, but the immense perspective of glory for which I had been working for sixteen years and of which I imagined myself to be assured. I abandoned my family and friends and mother country, and sacrificed the only possession I valued, my popularity. Could I not have excused myself on the score of the needs of the defence of the country, and the desire to make an end of disorders? And would not success have absolved me from all blame, except that of my own conscience? No, my dear Princess, in disdaining the rôle of usurper, in order to remain faithful to liberty and virtue, I have won the right, during the remainder of a life that my present régime is greatly shortening, to continue not to flatter either the men that I despise, or the vices that I hate.

This explosion shows the injustice of those historians who have represented Lafayette as a man of missed opportunities. At the time when these bitter words were flowing from the toothpick which had to serve Lafayette as his pen, the young artillery officer Napoleon Bonaparte was playing the wild revolutionary, and outdoing any courtier of the days of the Roi Soleil in his efforts to flatter the younger Robespierre. Clearly Lafayette was well aware that the part of a "great usurper" was to be had for the taking! Far from missing the opportunity, he saw it and refused it. Rather than destroy as a "great usurper" every liberty that had been won, he took the course that led to years of captivity.

VI. OLMÜTZ AND PARIS

THE LETTERS smuggled into Lafayette's cell deliberately left
him in ignorance of his wife's fate. He imagined her to be in
freedom with her children, and however evil were the Austrians' intentions with regard to him, the hermetical confinement he was to suffer at Olmütz did him very great service in
saving him from a worse torment, that of asking himself day
by day whether his wife still lived.

A few days before he was taken to Austria, he learned that
he had been the subject of a great oratorical duel in the House
of Commons, and this evidence that he was not forgotten
electrified his failing physical powers. At once he forgot the
sense of suffocation that had been torturing him, he complained no longer, his grave illness disappeared, and the specter
of death, which had already seemed to be approaching through
the bars of his window, was banished by joy. With an astonishing mental activity he considered the most effective opportunities, distributed rôles and urged a simultaneous attack wherever
public opinion could be appealed to. But this appeal "to my
friends" was dictated once more by the false hypothesis that
his adversaries would think just as he would have done in their
place. Thus he attributed to the Court of Vienna a sense of
honor which it lacked, and confidently assumed that the good
Emperor Francis would be glad to throw on Prussia all the
odium of his illegal arrest. He needed only to order Lafayette's
release, and Berlin would bear alone the moral responsibility
for the ill-treatment he had suffered. Consequently, the protests should be redoubled in Parliament and press in England
and America on the occasion of his transfer to Austria.

This naïve idealization was prompted by the visit Lafayette
had once made to the Court of Vienna. In Austria they would
have better taste than the "dirty old corporal" of Potsdam!
But while the Austrians had turned a deaf ear to the subversive
ideas of this member of the Noailles family so long as he was
in favor, now that he was publicly compromised they turned a
blind eye to his slow death in the emperor's prisons.

There were, indeed, capital differences between the methods

of Berlin and Vienna. The prisoner made their acquaintance at the very frontier, and he was to have ample opportunity of learning by bitter experience in the fortress of Olmütz the superior efficiency of the Austrian prison officials. But the actual transport was a well of fresh strength; it may have saved Lafayette's life.

The journey began on May 17, 1794, and the elaborate precautions, the ceremony of transfer, and the short halt at Brünn gave the unfortunate prisoners time to refresh their faint memories of the outer world. Their outlook had been bounded for many months by the bare slope of the prison rampart; now they could look into the distance, feast on the fresh colors of the spring scene, and store up impressions of green fields and blue skies until the moment when the heavy iron gates of Olmütz closed behind them.

For Lafayette the new régime was a cruelty mixed with mercy, for with the spring a murderous fury took possession of Paris. From every corner of the country there was carted to the capital the "material" for the revolutionary tribunal and the guillotine. As the French prisoners were being transported stage by stage to their Austrian prison, Mme de Lafayette was being conveyed from Brioude to one town prison after another on the way to the great antechamber of death in Paris.

The growing procession of carts, more and more crowded as they neared the capital, took longer to reach their destination than the little Austrian convoy. Mme de Lafayette only reached the end of her journey on the evening of June 1, 1794, the eve of the festival of the Supreme Being, which was officially to restore in France the reign of God, in collaboration with Robespierre. For this period of twenty-four hours, the climax of his period of rule, Robespierre suspended the working of the guillotine. Thereafter, with the coming into operation of a law suppressing the examination of witnesses and the defence of prisoners, the guillotine worked at maximum pressure, with fifty to seventy executions every day, until with the beheading of Robespierre himself this period of mass murder was brought to an end.

Mme de Lafayette was placed in the prison known as "Petite

Force," and was transferred a few weeks later, by the irony of fate, to the very Collège du Plessis in which the young Lafayette had dreamed his first confused dreams of the liberation of the people. In one of the dormitories of this former college, now transformed into a supplementary prison, perhaps on the very spot where her husband's bed once stood, poor Mme de Lafayette passed sleepless nights, tortured with anxiety about her loved husband, her children, and every member of her family.

Her mother, her grandmother and one of her sisters were already awaiting their turn before the tribunal whose next-door neighbor was the executioner. A faithful servant passed each evening beneath Mme de Lafayette's window to let her know by an agreed sign whether these three dear ones still lived.

So the bright summer days passed, until the end of July, 1794.

The Habsburg empire, a conglomeration of rival nations forcibly held together under one rule, was maintained only by the continuance of force. It was the greatest of schools for spies and jailers. In the eyes of such a régime, sympathy or readiness to do anything for political prisoners would be a moral leprosy. Consequently, during their severe imprisonment at Olmütz there was not a single "traitor" who could venture to smuggle in or out so much as a short note for the prisoners.

Prussian accounting had at least enabled the American diplomats to discover where the prisoners were from their receipts for money sent to them. The Austrians grinned at such bungling. All the faithful helpers in the world failed to discover into which of the many imperial and royal state prisons Lafayette had disappeared.

So, far from one another, husband and wife languished, waited for by death, the wife proscribed in the name of the Revolution, the husband in the name of absolutism, as though history had chosen them to illustrate the old truth that everywhere and at all times opposition to the powers that be is accounted a crime. Whether the sheep goes upstream or downstream to drink, the state, like the wolf in the fable, devours it.

VII.　FOUR WOMEN IN THE STORM

THE MAIN DRAIN of the fortress, an open channel, passed under
Lafayette's window; he crouched in his cell in a pestilential
atmosphere, compelled to fish with his fingers in dirty vessels
for the unappetizing food served up to him, since a fork would
have enabled him to cheat justice by killing himself.

The French tyranny, in its inexperience, was guided by
Barrère's principle: *"Il n'y a que les morts qui ne reviennent
pas"* ("Only the dead are safely out of the way"). For hundreds of years the house of Habsburg had had no fear of the
nibbling of the worms it permitted to live in its dungeons.

For weeks Mme de Lafayette had had the knife hanging over
her every day until the official who came every evening to call
out the names of the "accused" unfolded and read out his list.
The machine of the philanthropic Dr Guillotin was merciful;
it reduced nature's tortures to the duration of a flash of lightning. The only hardship was this bureaucracy which, in spite
of all the "simplification" of court procedure, compelled its
victims to wait so long in the abattoirs. Poor Fouquier-Tinville,
so defamed on account of his post of public prosecutor to the
Revolutionary Tribunal, was not paid enough to enable him
to buy shoes for his big family without running into debt.
He could easily have earned a fortune by saving a single head,
but it would have been at the risk of his own, and he was too
fond of his wife and children to incur the risk. Yet he had little
opportunity of seeing them. At midday he hurriedly ate a sand-
wich; he rarely got home from the Comité de Salut Public
before midnight, and at 8 A.M. he had to be back among his
documents—and all this for starvation wages, and not even a
pension at the end of it!

"In heaven's name," he wrote from his prison cell, before
paying with his life for his obedience to his superiors, "in
heaven's name, take care of my wife and children!"

On July 22, 1794, the 4th Thermidor under the new Republican calendar, only four days before Robespierre's fall and the
end of the Terror, there came among the stream of documents
that poured unendingly on to Fouquier-Tinville's desk the
charge sheets of the eighty-year-old Maréchale de Noailles, the

Duchesse d'Ayen-Noailles and the duchess's daughter. Mme de Lafayette's grandmother, mother and sister appeared before the tribunal. For a long time there had been no words wasted over much less clear cases. The jury nodded three times— "Guilty." On that same afternoon, grandmother, mother and child went together in the same tumbril and were executed, simply because their papers had not waited four more days.

As though the elements themselves revolted against this unnatural companionship of three generations in death, the clouds burst over Paris, and the carts rolled on toward the scaffold amid livid lightning and crashing thunder. The octogenarian marshal's wife, with her hands bound behind her, could not keep on her feet in the rocking tumbril, which was nearly blown over by the violence of the storm; daughter and granddaughter had to keep her between them to prevent her from falling. The wind blew off the old lady's bonnet. The executioner had cut off the hair at the back of her head, but in front the snow-white locks were tossed in the wind above her furrowed brow, as though in wild protest. It was as if an angry hand had plunged down from heaven to expose this crime against old age.

The Duchesse d'Ayen-Noailles, Lafayette's mother-in-law, stood up to her ankles in blood as she came onto the scaffold after her mother and daughter: their blood had flooded its boards. She had seen her mother and daughter beheaded, and now saw their heads beneath her in the basket of the guillotine before the plunge of the knife made an end of this horror.

This triple loss, with the frightful spectacle it evoked, was too much for the frail prisoner in the Collège du Plessis, parted from all those whom she loved and compelled to bear her dreadful burden of grief alone and unsupported. Her resistance was broken. Marked down herself for the same end, she bade farewell to the dear ones she had to leave behind. The letter she entrusted to her faithful old servant was an agonized prayer. After every few phrases there came the pathetic entreaty:

"Ayez pitié de moi, O mon Dieu!"

And her prayer was answered! From the very edge of the grave, from the foot of the scaffold, a miracle restored her to life, to freedom, to her children, her husband, and the happiness of which she had no longer dared to dream.

The Comité de Salut Public was ostracized by the governments of Europe as a thing of ill fame. Even the diplomatic representatives of states which were not at war with France objected to staying in the Paris of the Terror, where a whole quarter was filled with a pestilential odor of blood. Morris, the American minister, was almost the only one who remained at his post. And France, with her trade destroyed by war and by currency depreciation, could not afford to alienate her last customer.

But in America—and Gouverneur Morris was able to say so of his own knowledge—every man was with his whole heart a "Fayettist." To execute the wife of the idolized hero while he himself was suffering in the prisons of despotism for his republican ideals—that would be more than public opinion in America would stand. In consideration of her husband's popularity in the United States, the Committee of Public Safety buried the charge sheet of Citizeness Lafayette at the bottom of the daily growing pile of dossiers.

And so the poor little woman, whom her husband in his obsession with the cause of Liberty had allowed to face her first confinement alone, was saved by that very act. More than twenty years later Destiny replied from across the ocean to his naïve question *"Cui bono?"*—"who gains?"—

"You and yours!"

VIII. JUSTUS ERICH BOLLMANN

FOR SOME THREE MONTHS Lafayette had been languishing in one of the many political prisons in Austria, no one knew where. Nobody, it was stated, but the commandant of the fortress of Olmütz knew the names of the three foreigners in his charge. On the cards hung outside their heavily barred and bolted cell doors was written "French internee No.——." In the lists of prisoners and the account books they were represented only by their numbers.

This total disappearance was a serious check to the campaign on behalf of Lafayette. General Washington had received no reply whatever to his letters to the kings of Europe, and as

head of the state he owed it to his country's dignity to leave
it now to his diplomats to do what they could for his friend
and his family. The enthusiastic leaders of the English Whigs
were silenced by the ironic allusions of Pitt and Burke to the
sanguinary harvest of Lafayette's sowing. Only money was
available in ample quantity if anyone would make the attempt
at Lafayette's forcible rescue.

Famous men whose names were a household word in all Europe, diplomats restricted by the obligations of their profession, rich persons devoting their money to his cause, and
high-born friends of his, were not in a position themselves to
undertake this dangerous adventure. A young and unknown
man, enthusiastic and devoted enough not to be deterred by
the serious consequences of failure, was needed as their instrument.

Chance had brought Mme de Staël into touch with an
intrepid young German just at the moment when she urgently
needed a helper of his caliber. She sought and succeeded in enlisting the proved courage of this adventurous enthusiast for
liberty.

This young Hanoverian, Justus Erich Bollmann, was the son
of an honest and fairly prosperous merchant, and was a dare-
devil out for adventure. He was the eldest of no less than
seven brothers. After studying at various German universities
he had managed somehow to get a degree of Doctor of Medicine. A bachelor uncle who had made a substantial fortune in
London promised to look after him and sent for him to Paris,
where the young doctor was to perfect himself in French and
in obstetrics, before establishing himself in London with his
uncle's help.

The uncle, miserly and authoritarian, exacted from his
nephew in return for a minimum of support the obedience of
a bond slave. The nephew, however, had already absorbed the
ideas of democracy that were secretly germinating in the small
German universities; he arrived in Paris just in time to witness
the awakening of the French nation out of its centuries of
serfdom. He was much less attracted by the operating theater
and the medical libraries than by the meetings and the salons
of revolutionary enthusiasts, and instead of perfecting himself
in his profession he devoted himself to the intellectual ac-

couchement of the French nation. In this romantic young German's heart Lafayette won the place of a sainted leader. As a foreigner and a medical man, full of fiery eloquence and pugnacity, he found a friendly welcome in all the advanced society in Paris, and was equally at home in the radical circle of Pétion's friends and among the wits of Mme de Staël's salon.

The storming of the Tuileries on August 10, 1792, brought all Louis's ministers into peril. Woe to those who failed to evade arrest! They perished in the September massacre. Mme de Staël saw the danger approaching and trembled for the life of her adored Narbonne. Her husband, generally so accommodating, was unwilling to risk his position as minister by providing a Swedish passport for a French friend of the family. The young Hanoverian doctor—a Hanoverian at that time counted as a sort of German-speaking Englishman—found the daughter of the famous Jacques Necker on her knees before him. Through his connections with the Hôtel de Ville he secured two passports for England, and delivered the Comte de Narbonne safely in London.

But, abandoned by his uncle and suddenly cut off from his little practice in Paris, Bollmann was driven to have recourse to Mme de Staël's and Narbonne's "eternal" gratitude; thus he found himself, much against his will, closely associated with those of the high nobility of Paris who had taken refuge in London. His medical career was ended; he could not return to France; and he thoroughly disliked his enforced idleness among a society with which he was entirely out of sympathy. He hated the Jacobins because they were bringing into disrepute the high ideal of liberty; but he was no less disgusted by the reactionary talk of the rich and high-born idlers around him. Thus, when the mission was offered to him of rescuing the martyr from the tyrant's clutches, he accepted it with the utmost enthusiasm.

Furnished with money and credentials by the American diplomats, and supported by Princess d'Hénin, Lally-Tolendal, and Mme de Staël, he made his first efforts in Berlin; but with no success. In vain did he recall Lafayette's services to the French court; the Prussian minister saw in the journey to Paris and the attack on the Jacobins after the mob invasion of the Tuileries only a subtle maneuver of a Cromwell out to conquer power for himself. In any case, he contended, the King of Prussia had no competence in the matter. He was only a trustee for the allied monarchs, and without their consent could take no step in regard to the prisoner entrusted to him. Only after peace had been concluded would it be possible for the rightful sovereign of France to determine the fate of the accused man, in accordance with his own judgment.

The failure of every effort to secure an amnesty left no other course open than to attempt to rescue by force. But at the moment when young Bollmann was about to set to work at Neisse, Lafayette was transferred to an Austrian prison, nobody knew which.

IX. BOLLMANN AT WORK

No SHERLOCK HOLMES of our own day could have gone to work more cautiously or more ably than the young German doctor. He prudently made no attempt to follow the traces of the convoy. He made a random journey to Brünn; then he returned to Germany. Something determined him to try Olmütz; but he allowed some time to pass before going there. When he went he stayed only a few days; a longer visit might arouse the suspicion of the fortress spies. He put up at the best hotel in Olmütz posing as a distinguished scientist on his way to Vienna.

Now it was that Lafayette had his reward for fighting as a volunteer, at his own expense, for American independence. The ample resources with which now, in recognition of that service, Bollmann had been provided for his attempt at rescue, enabled him to live in such style that he was invited to a meal in the official residence of the commandant of the fortress. There he made, as Americans now say, "contacts."

He was still further helped by the traditional shortsighted-ness of despotisms. For the very fact that in the fortress there were some French political prisoners of whom nobody, it was stated, but the commandant was allowed to know the names, was a sensational circumstance that aroused the keenest interest among the population of the little town. The grocer at the corner shop, who had never heard of Lafayette, was bursting

to tell all he knew about one of the mysterious prisoners. Bollmann then went on happily to Vienna.

When the rich scientist next came to Olmütz, he suddenly
fell ill. Could the medical officer of the fortress come to see
him? His friends in Vienna had spoken of this officer in the
warmest terms.

Very soon Bollmann had tripped up his colleague. The distinguished scientist had seen so much of the medical world,
and had studied under so many eminent professors, that he
was able to engage his visitor in a fascinating conversation. In
the midst of it he broke off to ask:

"By the way, how is Lafayette?"

He did it so simply and casually that his victim blanched
and stammered:

"B-but how did you know?"

The secret was out.

That was the first step gained. But Bollmann did not want
to leave Olmütz until he had let Lafayette know that efforts
were being made to rescue him. He was determined to send
a ray of light at once into the blackness of that prisoner's
despair. It flattered the vanity of this medical officer, vege-
tating in his prison post at Olmütz, to learn that his distinguished patient and colleague would like to inspect his
hospital.

After the visit Bollmann took his leave and entered his
coach. The magnificence of the great man's surroundings had
quite overcome the poor army surgeon, and the servility well
drilled into him by his official career did disservice for once
to Authority. Dr Haberlein allowed his distinguished colleague to slip a visiting card into his hand and promised to
give it to Lafayette; it had on it only the names of the émigré
nobles Bollmann remembered meeting in London.

"When he learns that so many of his best friends are still
alive, the news will do him more good than all your medicine,"
said the departing foreigner, appealing to Haberlein's medical
conscience. Just before driving off he asked his colleague to
tell Lafayette that his good friend the Comte de Narbonne
had been in grave danger and had been saved by Dr Bollmann,
who did not want to pass through Olmütz without conveying
the count's kind remembrances to M. le Marquis.

"Grave danger—saved" sounded entirely unsuspicious in a message from a physician, and it is easy to believe the repentant staff-surgeon's subsequent declaration that he had been an entirely unconscious instrument in Dr Bollmann's hands. How could he dream that anyone would have so desperate an idea as to try to get a prisoner out of an imperial fortress with its whole army of guards and sentries!

The admirably kept archives of the Vienna police, with the record of all the hearings, enable the share of each of the conspirators to be assessed from his own statements. The only thing missing—a strange omission in the otherwise exhaustively complete material—is the sheet of directions given in his own hand by the good Emperor Francis; this may explain the very contradictory tales of Lafayette's treatment in the prison at Olmütz. According to some accounts the emperor provided amply for all the prisoner's needs; but though there is repeated mention of instructions in the emperor's own hand to the commandant of the fortress, there is no trace of the document itself.

It is very possible that the accounts supplied to foreign papers deliberately exaggerated Lafayette's privations and sufferings in order to excite public sympathy. On the other hand, the regulations posted up on the walls of the prison corridors to remind officers and soldiers of their duties are sufficient refutation of the idyllic pictures of Lafayette's prison life painted by the Austrian authorities:

In the first place it must constantly be borne in mind that when anyone is sent to a state prison the purpose is that so dangerous a person should be made to disappear completely from the world, only his life being preserved, and that he may thus no longer exist but fall into oblivion. To this end it is also necessary that no answer shall be given to his questions about events . . .

—and so on.

Whatever may have been Lafayette's actual situation, this extract from the regulations is sufficient to account for the joy of this prisoner "no longer existing" when he received the list of friends who were still thinking of him in distant London. Lafayette understood, of course, at once that the sender of the message, who had already rescued Narbonne, was now working at Lafayette's rescue; and Bollmann's prognosis proved correct: neither powder nor potion could so have revived the sufferer as the daily hope he now had of receiving further news.

He must have found it a terribly long wait, for Bollmann now went back to Vienna, where, in order to remove all suspicion, he showed the liveliest interest in the hospitals and kept in busy communication with the leading physicians. Great was the indignation of the Olmütz military authorities, later on, at the way the Viennese police had permitted "men of so dangerous a type to proceed undisturbed with their criminal preparations." Bollmann procured from various districts of the city, separated from one another as far as possible, strong saws, files of English steel, pickaxes and ropes, taking care to let a week or two pass after each purchase, lest any spies in his hotel should become curious. Not until after three months did he return to Olmütz with his secret store of implements.

He now faced the most difficult part of his task; he had to win the coöperation of the poor doctor—a government official and, moreover, the father of a family—in the dangerous enterprise, which was to bring the unfortunate man to ruin. How Bollmann did it Haberlein himself was unable to say when he faced his judges. The staff surgeon was called again to the bedside of his sick colleague, in the principal hotel in the town. He was himself a man whose independence of spirit had been destroyed by the combined workings of military discipline and petty domestic cares; and he was overcome by the magnificent style of living, the wide range of knowledge, and the dominating self-assurance of this traveled cosmopolitan, rich and independent, who could command almost anything. In violation of the strict rules, he smuggled a letter into Lafayette's cell. The letter was unsealed and was confined to news of his relatives and friends. The prisoner was asked in it to read it with "the same warmth" as the messages he used to receive at Neisse and Magdeburg from Princess d'Hénin, but Dr Haberlein saw nothing suspicious in that. Never would he have consented to take the message if he had known that on the back of the sheet there were secret communications written with lemon juice. Warmed over the flame of the prisoner's candle, the sheet revealed quite a different message from the open one.

Having sinned once, the unfortunate staff surgeon could say nothing when at his next visit Lafayette quietly dropped an English novel into his bag of instruments. A message was written in the margins of the book. It began merely with a few words of thanks, but Bollmann was sharp enough to examine the margins further until the warmed pages revealed a complete plan of escape devised by Lafayette. To the misfortune of all three men, Bollmann allowed himself to be led astray by his admiration for his hero; for it is probable that by sawing through bars and bribing sentries better results would have been obtained than by Lafayette's wild plan, which took no account either of the circumstances of the little town or of the character of its people.

X. ON THE WRONG TRACK

SICK PRISONERS were permitted, on medical orders, to take exercise outside the fortress under military surveillance "in order to restore their health." Lafayette was allowed this privilege, and he built on it his plan of escape. The plan thus had the fundamental defect that flight must be attempted in broad daylight. Lafayette wrote that on these excursions his coachman was unable to leave the horses. He would therefore call a halt on several consecutive days at the same spot, and there he would walk with his guard along a certain narrow pathway as far as a group of trees in which Bollmann could conceal himself with two saddled horses. Before the guard, taken by surprise, recovered and reached the coach, the two horsemen could be out of sight. Bollmann could easily have demonstrated to Haberlein in a few words the many objections and weak points in this risky plan, but he made no attempt at all to gainsay the great Lafayette. It is true that there were limits to what he could ask of the unconscious messenger. Haberlein would only consent to convey one more letter with its visible and invisible contents; thus there was no possibility of any long discussion of what could be done.

The very idea that it could be possible in the little town of

Olmütz to buy two suitable mounts betrayed Lafayette's entire ignorance of the locality and should have made Bollmann doubtful. But instead of raising objections he went back at once to Vienna, promising to return as soon as he could. A month passed before his return—a long trial for Lafayette's nerves. He would have become ill with impatience had not a bribed official brought him books from a lending library. Fortunately the many locks and bars gave the prisoner ample time to hide everything before his door opened.

Bollmann well understood the feverish expectation that must be consuming Lafayette; but he was too prudent to hurry over his necessary purchases; he was constantly on his guard against the notorious police spies of Vienna. But in spite of his circumspection he built so confidently on his knowledge of men that one day, in a restaurant frequented by medical men, he talked about Lafayette with a chance neighbor at table, a young American studying medicine at the University of Vienna. This young man was no other than the little son of Major Huger, whose cheek Lafayette had patted on the morning of his first day in America.

Young Huger, indignant at the infamous treatment of the hero who had shed his blood for the liberation of America, at once declared himself ready to join in the effort to rescue him. On November 2, 1794, he left Vienna with Bollmann, in the distinguished scientist's coach, ostensibly to return with him to England.

With them were the two saddled horses, one with a pillion. The groom they had engaged was made to ride sometimes on the coachman's seat and sometimes on one or other of the saddle horses, so that he should not be surprised at any whims of his masters. The two friends spoke entirely in English. They agreed that at the critical moment they would have no other thought than for Lafayette's escape, without consideration for their own or one another's fate; they were ready to face the consequences of their action, whatever they might be, so long as their hero was saved.

Once more, absolutely for the last time, poor Major Haberlein conveyed a note to Lafayette—a little farewell letter containing imaginary and perfectly innocent news. The invisible writing on the back informed Lafayette that on his next two days for exercise, the 6th and 8th of November, everything would be ready for his flight and that it was inadvisable to put off the attempt any longer. The new commandant of the fortress, Count Arco, had his eyes all round him, and the two strangers in Olmütz would be in danger of attracting his suspicion, all the more since he hated the French "rebels" with all the venom of his limited intelligence. Even before all the trouble over the attempted escape, which might have excused his boorishness, he told the defenceless prisoner that it would give him the greatest of pleasure to see him swinging on the gallows that stood always ready in the prison courtyard.

XI. THE FLIGHT

ON THE MORNING of the 8th of November Bollmann sent the groom and the carriage ahead of him to Hof, on the Prussian frontier. The groom was to harness fresh horses there and to be ready to continue the journey at 4 P.M. The two mounts were already saddled, and Huger, ready to start, walked up and down in front of the Golden Swan, keeping a watch on the distant gates of the fortress. Shortly after two o'clock the gates opened to let out Lafayette's coach.

A few minutes later Bollmann and Huger left the inn. They remained at a considerable distance behind the coach, since the sentries on the ramparts had a view of the road. They had divided their considerable stock of ready money into three equal parts, and each carried half of Lafayette's third in a separate purse, so that at the worst the fugitive should have half of his money to travel with.

The carriage hired by the military authorities for the prisoners' drives belonged to an Olmütz baker, who also supplied the coachman. Thus the responsibility for the prisoner rested entirely with the two guards who accompanied him. Defence against any attack rested mainly with the staff sergeant, who sat next the prisoner in the carriage and was not to leave his side for a moment during his exercise. The other guard, a private, stood at the back of the carriage and was to support his superior in case of need; but as a rule he remained by the carriage, and had a drink with the coachman at the prisoner's expense while the prisoner and the sergeant walked across the fields. Coachman and guard awaited the other two where the footpath rejoined the main road, and then the party returned to the fortress.

On this day everything went according to program up to the moment when the carriage with the coachman and guard were out of sight and Lafayette and the sergeant had completed about half their journey. Thus Lafayette's sole escort, armed only with his sword, would have to deal with two men on horseback, with loaded pistols, as well as the unarmed prisoner. Was it not reasonable to suppose, as Lafayette had written in his detailed letter to Bollmann, that the plan could not possibly fail?

Lafayette added one more precaution. Arm in arm with the sergeant, he engaged him in a lively discussion, and partly unsheathed his sword to test it as an expert. Thus he had its hilt in his hand at the moment when Bollmann and Huger burst upon them, one on each side of the sergeant, to whom they shouted: "Hand over the prisoner!"

Disarmed, since Lafayette would not let go the sword, and faced by two horsemen with pistols leveled at him, the sergeant would have had no alternative but to capitulate, if Lafayette had not forgotten to take account of an essential factor, altogether beyond the cognizance of the high-born *grand seigneur*, but keenly present to the mind of the noncommissioned officer.

In a letter which Lafayette had dropped unnoticed out of the carriage during Bollmann's second visit to Olmütz he had written:

The staff-sergeant is a cowardly and avaricious wretch. He can probably be bribed, but is such a coward that he would rather take a small sum without running any risk than a large one involving risk. I undertake to give the cowardly little sergeant such a fright with his own sword that I can mount horse without the slightest difficulty.

This was characteristic of Lafayette's disastrous misjudgment of the ordinary man, who in reality acquires the strength of a giant the moment he is threatened with the loss of his one possession, his job. The poor Austrian jailer was not one of Lafayette's National Guards; stupid and cowardly as he might be, he had learned from his superiors one terrible lesson, that punishment accumulates like an avalanche as it descends upon the lowest of a hierarchy. Count Arco, commandant of the fortress, would be reprimanded if the prisoner escaped, and the officer on duty might be placed under domiciliary arrest for a few days, but the plain soldier would suffer destruction! He would be thrown on the street with his wife and children. Thus the instinct of self-preservation turned the "cowardly wretch" into a hero, despair giving him a courage surpassing that of all his superiors in their gold lace.

So it was that the Olmütz sergeant offered an unexpected resistance. He clutched his prisoner, the nameless human number in his charge, with such energy that Bollmann vainly tried to get Lafayette free; the sergeant brought his two opponents to the ground with him, so that Huger also had to dismount and apply his skill as a boxer.

The peasants working in the fields around phlegmatically watched the unequal struggle. To prevent the sergeant's shouts for help from reaching the private and the coachman, Lafayette tried to stuff Bollmann's handkerchief into the man's mouth, and received such a bite on the fingers that he was forced to let the man go. The powerful young Huger finally succeeded in wresting Lafayette free, and with his big leather riding glove he gagged the guard, but one of the horses took fright at the glistening of the sword, broke away and galloped off.

Lafayette was not easily to be persuaded to jump onto the remaining horse and leave his rescuers still fighting. But Huger put his purse in his hand and implored him not to delay and so make useless the sacrifices they had made. Thus Lafayette mounted, unfortunately on the horse with the pillion saddle.

What followed amounted to tragi-comedy. One of the peasants brought back the second horse; meanwhile the sergeant had run away to fetch the guard and coachman. Huger and Bollmann tried to mount, but the horse was not used to two riders and refused to carry them. Huger was the first in the saddle; his German friend, heavier and more bony, got up behind him, but at once he was thrown off. Bollmann was too much hurt to make a second attempt. Only with the help of a peasant did Huger succeed in lifting his friend into the saddle.

but when he tried to mount behind him he had no better success; finally they found themselves both on the ground, and the horse had to be caught again.

Huger then decided to make the necessary sacrifice. He recalled to Bollmann the agreement they had made and persuaded him to go alone after Lafayette.

"I can't speak German; you will be more useful to the general than I can be. I shall manage to get away somehow."

The young American knew that he could not possibly escape; his ignorance of the language would betray him everywhere. But the one thing was to save Lafayette. The two friends imagined him to be on his way to Hof, where he would be able to start towards Breslau in Bollmann's carriage, and then, turning out of the road at night, reach the country house of a friend in the plot and remain concealed there for some time.

Bollmann, heavy-hearted, rode away; Huger set off across the fields to try to reach the Prussian frontier. Limping, spattered with blood, and ignorant of the way, he was soon caught by peasants who had gone in search of him out of sympathy for the lamenting sergeant. With his hands cut by the blade of his own sword, his mouth flayed by the attempt at gagging him, the unfortunate "coward" limped along the road, crying bitterly, his face swollen and disfigured by Huger's blows. The American was put in irons and handed over like a common criminal to the police at Olmütz.

Lafayette, meanwhile, had ridden off—at random. He had no idea that there was such a place as Hof in the neighborhood and had understood Bollmann's cry of "Get to Hof" as "Get off." He rode on until he reached a village. There, in broken German, he asked the way to the Prussian frontier. His bitten fingers were still bleeding, his clothes were stained by blood from the sergeant's cut hands and he had all the appearance of a fugitive bandit. No wonder he aroused the suspicion of the village mayor. In vain did he offer a thousand and then two thousand crowns for a guide and a fresh horse. The mayor took him into his best room, kept him waiting there for the promised horse—and sent a message to the authorities.

On the afternoon of November 9, twenty-four hours after the sensational attempt at rescue, Count Arco was able to report to his superiors at Troppau that the French prisoner who ran away the day before had been brought back to the fortress. One of the accomplices, who claimed to be an American, was in custody. Search was being made for the other.

His Excellency Field Marshal the Marquis di Bolla, *statthalter* (governor) of Moravia, sent out a large force in pursuit of the wanted man. An express messenger was also sent from the *statthalter's* office to the Prussian frontier authorities with a warrant of arrest, accompanied by a courteous request for energetic assistance in the pursuit; all expenses incurred would be reimbursed by the Imperial and Royal Treasury.

XII. THE COURT OF JUSTICE

IN SPITE OF ALL, Bollmann succeeded in keeping out of his Austrian pursuers' hands for nineteen days, until November 27. The carriage was waiting at Hof as he had ordered; he could have raced through Prussia and have embarked at Altona for England; the long formalities of extradition applications assured him an ample start. He let it go unused, hoping to find Lafayette somewhere. He spent a whole week exploring the Prussian-Austrian frontier. Finally his questions about the French fugitive, and the warrant which in the meantime had been issued, led to his arrest by the Prussian military authorities on November 16, 1794.

In their malicious pleasure over the neighbor country's troubles and their respect for Bollmann's exploit, the Prussian authorities treated him with indulgence. As a political prisoner on parole he was able to go where he liked all day long, and the secret sympathies of the German bourgeoisie for democratic principles found expression in endless invitations and banquets and compliments. Only when he had been conveyed by a Prussian patrol to the frontier and handed over to the Austrian hussars did Bollmann discover the full heinousness of his offence. He was put into irons and thrown into a criminal's cell as though he had been guilty of housebreaking. In chains in an underground dungeon, fed on bread and water, he remained for two months under the ordeal of examination.

But this unsuccessful attempt at rescue had had one important result: all the world now knew where Lafayette was.

Baron Thugut was exasperated to find a campaign launched against Austria in every country where the press was free. It is instructive to study in the archives of the Vienna police the documents in this case of a century and a half ago. The signatures themselves give a picture of the empire. As already mentioned, the commandant, Count Arco, was under the orders of the Marquis von Bolla. The minutes of the hearings are signed by Colonel di Verga, and the very peasants who assisted in the arrest of Lafayette bore Czech names; their patron saint was St Nepomuk. The bundle of records of the investigation is a sample of the Austrian babel.

Good Emperor Francis in Vienna was speechless with indignation at the scandalous negligence shown by his prison authorities. That it should be possible for so complicated a crime to be organized and carried out undisturbed under their very eyes, compromised his empire before all the world; it would ruin the good reputation of the Austrian jails! The first official news from the *statthalter* to the emperor's privy secretariat bears the sarcastic marginal note in His Majesty's own hand: *"Zur angenehmen Kenntnisnahme"* ("Please note—a pretty story").

The painful task of investigating this unexampled outrage occupied nearly six months. In the end the innocent parties who had the misfortune to be Austrian subjects were punished more severely than the guilty foreigners. Not that the report of the conditions of Lafayette's imprisonment, conditions which were illegal and dangerous to his health, would make the slightest impression on the imperial authorities.

To read the reports and covering letters to the privy office is to be reminded of the cringing of dogs who know they have done wrong. All the more striking, alongside this excess of humble "devotion," is the boldness and outspokenness of the three accused prisoners. Even the tribunal was unable entirely to resist the influence of their courageous stand.

Bollmann and Huger were kept in irons for no less than three months. It was assumed that they were agents of a vast conspiracy with ramifications extending throughout the country. The examining judge pounced on the thread supplied by Bollmann's relations with Count Salm and the Polish Count Mitrowsky in Vienna, both notorious freemasons. In the end

the attempt to reconstruct the course of a vast conspiracy had
to be abandoned, and the examining judge became human and
almost benevolent when the case dwindled to one of an adventure of two devoted hotheads. Whether the two counts,
who were friends of Mme de Staël, exerted their influence in
aid of Bollmann has remained their secret.

Freed from their chains and decently treated, the two
friends exerted themselves to exonerate one another, and the
judge was put to it to contest the claim of each of them to
bear the whole guilt. Bollmann declared that he put pressure
on Huger to involve him in the crime by invoking America's
indebtedness to Lafayette; Huger retorted that he needed no
pressure: he had jumped at the opportunity of helping the
moment he learned from a casual remark of Bollmann's where
Lafayette was. As to poor Major Haberlein, Bollmann and
Huger vainly protested that he had had nothing to do with the
affair: the staff surgeon in his distress had already made a full
confession.

At the very first interrogation, immediately after his arrest,
when he was still breathless and exhausted, young Huger
bravely stood up for himself. Threatened with the gallows by
Count Arco, loaded with chains, and continually bullied and
abused as the worst of criminals, he found words in his defence which it is impossible to read without emotion in these
old records, in their fading ink of a century and a half ago:

I had decided to go back peacefully to my distant homeland, when
an unexpected opportunity came to me of doing a service to the man
who had done so much for the liberation of my country, who had
helped it to win the independence I enjoy at home. I had no desire to
do any injury to anyone; my desire was to restore an unhappy man
to liberty and to his friends. My conscience is clear and I cannot
regret my intention. At twenty-one years of age one is influenced
more strongly by passion than by reason. If among the gentlemen
who are to pronounce judgment on me there are fathers, I ask them
to think of their sons, and to reflect that I had to decide entirely for
myself and had no one to advise me.

Dr Bollmann, more than ten years older than his young
comrade, was an experienced revolutionary and took up an entirely different attitude. When at the moment of his reception

in Austria he was stripped naked and searched and then put in chains, he shouted in a menacing tone: "The whole world will learn of this treatment." His admissions to the examining judge have the air of a propaganda speech in praise of Lafayette; he pilloried the hero's jailers instead of answering the charge against himself:

"If Lafayette is a criminal, then I am too: if he is a dangerous man, then I must be too, for I accept his principles as mine."

He reminded his judges of Lafayette's intervention on behalf of his king on October 5 and 6, 1792, and of his return from headquarters to Paris in order to defend his sovereign, and so demonstrated on the strength of "historic facts" that the crime was Lafayette's incarceration at Olmütz and not the attempt to free him.

In spite of this challenging attitude, and of the venom of the subordinate officials involved in the affair, the Vienna government showed surprising indulgence. Thugut was too wise a minister to furnish the cause of freedom with fresh martyrs. Bollmann and Huger were sentenced to a further month of imprisonment in irons, and the treasury not only confiscated their money but sold their carriage and horses by auction, to cover the expense of their trial and imprisonment.

Lafayette suffered no other punishment than the loss of the privilege of his exercise outside the prison walls. The military court also sentenced him to three months in irons, but the court's decision bears this note in Emperor Francis's writing:

Fetters are to be dispensed with.

Lafayette was not a prisoner of war on parole; his attempt at escape was not therefore a punishable act; the only offence was disarming and assaulting a guard.

It was the poor sergeant who came off worst. His leg had been kicked by Bollmann's horse, his hands cut by his own sword, he had been knocked out by Huger. All this went for nothing, and it went for nothing even that he had belied Lafayette's poor opinion of his kind and had fought like a lion to prevent his prisoner from escaping. Penalties, like taxation, obey the law of gravity. As they go down they acquire momentum, and they fall with the maximum of force on the lowest and weakest shoulders. He was reduced to the ranks; and he and the staff surgeon, both reduced to penury, remained the only victims of the adventure. Bollmann and Huger were released at the beginning of August, 1795, less than a year after their "offence." On their way through Germany they were fêted everywhere as heroes. They went on to England and embarked together for America.

Huger, on his arrival in his own country, became almost a national figure. Poor Bollmann, however, in spite of his considerable medical qualifications, his literary talent, and his energy, gradually fell a victim to his fever for enterprise. Instead of devoting himself to his profession, he plunged into all sorts of speculations, went restlessly to and fro across the ocean, and ultimately died in oblivion. Lafayette and his wife had joined in giving him a life pension, but this had to be capitalized to pay his debts. He drifted like an uprooted tree, unsettled for the rest of his life by the two adventurous exploits of his youth.

Lafayette had to pay dearly for Bollmann's enterprise, which had been so generously financed from America. The prisoner was entirely deprived of fresh air and sun, robbed of his one distraction, reading, and kept without news of the fate of his family or of anything that occurred in the world. He might well have succumbed to this systematic undermining of his health by dismal monotony and insanitary conditions. For a full year, from the attempt at escape in November, 1794, until the middle of November, 1795, nothing happened. Nothing new to think of trickled into his cell; continually his tired brain was tortured by the same uncertainties, hopes, questions, memories; and what is the physical exhaustion of a slave at the treadmill compared with the mental torture of these eternally circling thoughts! The time came when the prisoner longed for death.

What a miracle, what indescribable happiness for this dying man when the hated iron door clanked and opened to reveal, instead of the dirty guard, Mme de Lafayette and her two daughters! This dream, which did not dissolve but brought his dear ones in flesh and blood into his open arms—what a task for heart and brain, to cope with such joy!

The journey that led from the antechamber of the guillotine to the cell in the fortress of Olmütz was long and difficult enough to call for a full description.

XIII. THE FLIGHT TO PRISON

IT WAS NOT because Robespierre, that cold-blooded, pedantic provincial lawyer, was defeated by jealous colleagues and a few villains in the Convention, that the Terror came suddenly to an end with his death. The fear of death was simply acting in a different way: it now drove great and small to serve those whose favor kept the executioner at a distance. The bloodhounds who but the day before had hunted for new game to feed the guillotine were now turned into compassionate animals welling over with pity and crying for the liberation of the innocent—because cruelty, up to now a virtue, had become a crime once more.

So on the 10th Thermidor, July 28, 1794, all the prisons began to empty. Orders for release fell like snowflakes over Paris. The first served were the lady friends of the influential: Barras brought out of prison the pretty creole Josephine Beauharnais; Tallien in person restored to freedom his Theresa Cabarrus. The expensive, abandoned amusement centers of the Palais Royal—now the Palais Égalité—filled up again with carousing couples, like the streets after a storm. Hurrah! Now that Robespierre was got rid of there was no more need to play the Spartan!

Who, amid the pleasure-seeking crowd of rich contractors and their venal protectors, would trouble about the quiet, melancholy woman prisoner who bore the compromising name of Lafayette? The new rulers feared nothing so much as responsibility. Their extravagance and their manner of living did not leave them a clear enough conscience to permit them to run any political risks. Now that by a miracle she had escaped the executioner, now that her life was in no danger, Mme Lafayette might thank God that she still lived to be a prisoner!

Commissaries of the Convention went through the prisons. Victims who had been robbed of their freedom by the *loi des suspects* streamed out of their cells like miners coming from the pit at a change of shift. Men and women who had long believed themselves to be lost, and had abandoned every moral principle in the antechamber of death, now plunged into the gay life: the most aristocratic ladies of the *ancien régime* engaged in rivalry with the beauties of the Palais Égalité!

What could there be in common between this company and Lafayette's faithful Penelope, mourning her dead and tortured with anxiety about her husband? The Terror had brought degradation. The Abbé Sieyès, honored as "the thinker" of the Revolution, had seemed destined to become its moral leader when he published his famous pamphlet, "What is the Third Estate?" One of the captives returning home asked him what he had done in all the years of Jacobin rule; he replied cynically: *"J'ai vécu!"* ("I have kept alive!") Mme de Lafayette, one of the few women who sacrificed nothing of their dignity in captivity and were true to themselves in face of the peril of death, remained in the prison weeks and months, nearly six months, after the general delivery. Gouverneur Morris had been able to use his influence as American minister to save her from execution, but found it much more difficult to secure her liberation. Morris's successor, Monroe, who was to be made famous as President by his "Doctrine," worked equally hard to free her. Human lives were cheap, but freedom was the most expensive of luxuries in this republic out of joint.

Prison discharges were dealt with by Legendre, a member of the Convention, and he well knew the danger of intervening on behalf of persons out of favor. He was a prosperous master butcher who had been elected a captain of the National Guard and had become one of Danton's closest intimates. After the night during which Danton and his followers were arrested, Legendre was the only one who dared to speak a word on behalf of his friend. One word from Robespierre sufficed then to silence him; he turned deathly pale and fled; he had heard the hissing of the knife. The moral cowardice of this robust butcher who had marched intrepidly at the head of the assailants of the Bastille, is eloquent evidence of the demoralizing effect of the Terror. This same Legendre had charged against the Girondins like a bull and threatened to throw Vergniaud, the most eloquent of their leaders, off the platform; Vergniaud promptly retorted:

"Have it decreed that I am an ox, and then you can slaughter me!"

But this erstwhile swashbuckler had been so daunted by Robespierre's sinister croaking tones that he could no longer straighten the back he had bent in humble subservience. Long after the man he had feared had been thrown into the common grave, Legendre's blood still ran cold with fright. Monroe applied to him time after time, for six months, in vain. To put his name at the bottom of a sheet which had at the top the dangerous name of Lafayette was more than Legendre could bring himself to venture. There might be a new change of régime, and one of his enemies might fish this compromising document out of the archives!

The year 1794 came to its end; not until the 22d of January, 1795, was Mme de Lafayette at last brought away from the echoing corridors and empty dormitories of the former boys' college that had been her prison.

Her first visit was to Monroe. She thanked him for all his efforts, but came above all as a petitioner: she wanted him to help her to join her husband in the prison at Olmütz. She begged Monroe to complete his work of mercy by providing her with an American passport. Was not her husband an American citizen by adoption?

She sent her only son with his tutor to America, and begged his famous godfather to bring him up to be a good citizen of the United States. She added the pathetic request:

Mon voeu est, que mon fils mène une vie très obscure en Amérique" ("It is my deep desire that my son should live a very obscure life in America").

She knew from her husband's experience how dearly it is possible to pay for popularity. Her son should at least be spared the consequences of his doubly famous name—Georges Washington Lafayette!

She took her son and his tutor on board, said good-bye to the boy, and smothered her grief at the parting in her thankfulness to her husband, who had won by his own sacrifices a safe asylum across the ocean.

Her return to Chavaniac brought an unexpected joy. She found her daughters living with the old aunt in the château, which the Duchesse de Grammont had bought back by selling her jewels. The vultures who had exploited the sale of the confiscated properties had parceled out the cheaply bought estates in order to enrich themselves out of the peasants' land hunger. As for the old seignorial residences with their luxurious appointments, only a few contractors who had grown rich out of army supplies were interested in them. There were too many feudal castles, and in most cases their new owners were glad enough to get rid of them—of course, at the customary enormous profit.

So the duchess, Mme de Lafayette's favorite sister, had ruined herself for Chavaniac. The Grammonts had become too poor to hire a post chaise and came on foot to bid farewell to Mme de Lafayette before she started her journey with her children to Austria. The duke and duchess walked half across France, from Franche-Comté to Auvergne, leading a horse that bore their three little children slung in baskets. The little caravan hid in the woods, like vagabonds afraid of the police, if they heard a carriage approaching. It was wiser for *ci-devants* to avoid meeting anybody.

Mme de Lafayette made her sister's homeward journey easier.

Once she had returned to a normal daily life she concerned herself with its needs; she defended the interests of her husband and children with the sober energy of a conscientious administrator. The buyers of "national properties" were too numerous to be disturbed; even the Bourbons on their return did not venture to disturb this wasps' nest for "their faithful nobles." On the other hand, soon after Robespierre's fall the government decided to return to the legal heirs the still unsold properties of the guillotined, and Mme de Lafayette made the journey alone to Paris, mobilized all her connections and shrank from no journey to the provincial authorities until she had regained possession of her family's legal property.

Conscientiously she made provision for all her relatives. Her most precious possessions, the gifts that had come from America in honor of her husband, she buried in the park. A good many of them she never found again. Only the golden hilt of the sword of honor withstood corrosion during its long burial. At a later date admirers of the general had a new blade forged out of heavy bolts from the Bastille. Finally Mme de Lafayette provided money for her old servants and maids; and then, on September 5, 1795, she went with her two daughters on board an American ship.

More than twelve months had passed since the end of the Terror, and nearly nine months since her own liberation, when she watched Dunkerque harbor and the shores of her homeland disappear below the horizon. All she knew of her husband was that in November of the preceding year he had been recaptured by the Austrians and was in one of the imperial prisons, probably still at Olmütz. Her ship sailed for Altona; once landed on the free soil of the old Hansa city she intended to use every possible means for reaching her husband!

After more than twenty years of marriage, she still clung to her husband with all the fervor of a young bride; and the long uncertainty about his fate consumed her like a malady. She did not remain at Altona a day longer than was necessary for obtaining her American passport, which was made out in the name of Motier. Wherever there was a diplomatic representative of the United States her name worked magically. All the resources of a grateful nation were at her disposal.

She could have left her two little daughters at Altona. Her sister, Mme de Montagu, had fled in good time with her aunt, the Comtesse de Tessé. The countess had a small property in the neighborhood of Hamburg; there the two ladies had found shelter from the storm, and the two children would have been in good hands with their aunt and great-aunt. But Mme de Lafayette unhesitatingly risked their youth and health in the hope of being able to take them with her into prison in order to brighten their father's dismal existence.

Thanks to her American passport, Mme de Lafayette entered Austria without hindrance and reached Vienna, to the rage of Baron Thugut, who would have been only too glad to be rid of all the French, the Olmütz prisoners included. The importunity of the émigrés, who presented their misfortune as though it were a bill of exchange to be cashed, was becoming frankly insupportable.

Mme de Lafayette was thus unable to secure an audience with the emperor through Baron Thugut. But she secured the help of Prince Rosenberg, a sworn enemy of the baron, and with his aid obtained an audience behind the baron's back.

The good Emperor Francis told her that it was impossible for him to set her husband free: he was bound by the common decision of the allied monarchs. But he graciously permitted her to proceed to Olmütz and to take up her quarters there with her two daughters.

"You are quite right," said the good Emperor Francis, nodding in approval. "In your place I should have done just as you are doing."

He had much too many papers to read and sign to be able to remember the instructions he had given for the treatment of the three French prisoners! He assured Mme de Lafayette that she would find her husband well looked after under Count Arco's care; the count was "a charming man!"

Is there, perhaps, some connection between this imperial failure of memory and the disappearance of just one document from the big file, the document containing the emperor's instructions as to the treatment of the prisoners? It would, in any case, have been well to do away also with document No. 1 in the file dealing with the attempt at escape, or, at all events, to cut off its margin, with these instructions on it:

Since this incident confirms once more that these prisoners of the state are only thinking of cunning and deceitful ways of misusing their good treatment, the action taken in putting an end to the liberties they had been accorded for their health is entirely justified.
FRANCIS.

Baron Thugut, less forgetful and more cautious than his imperial master, was unable to refrain from showing his annoyance at the permission so unscrupulously secured behind his back. He knew very well that military prisons had no suitable living and reception rooms for ladies of the high aristocracy, and he would never have become a baron and the prime minister of the monarchy if he had not had sufficient intelligence to be able to foresee the results of this act of grace. To apply the regulations for prisoners to their wives and daughters would be a barbarity which would supply precious material for the agitation carried on in the countries with a free press, and by the Whigs in the English parliament. By sharing her husband's fate the cunning little woman had attracted the attention of the whole world to him.

The minister of war, Count Ferrari, expressly warned Mme de Lafayette in handing her the unusual permit:

"I regard it as my duty to ask you once more to reflect upon your decision. I must warn you that you will be accommodated in very bad conditions, and that the regulations to which you will have to submit will have very grave inconveniences for you and your daughters."

But what could words do to influence a woman who was waiting to see once more the man she loved, after four years of separation? If Count Ferrari had depicted the inferno of the Austrian military prisons with all the genius of the author of the *Divina Commedia*, it would have availed nothing; the more horrifying his picture of the fate of the prisoners, the more impatiently would Mme de Lafayette have insisted on being allowed to share her husband's sufferings.

That same evening she left Vienna; and when at last, at the end of two days' journey, she saw the church towers of Olmütz on the horizon, tears of joy filled her eyes, and an old canticle came to her lips, a thanksgiving to the Lord, who had restored her to the arms of her husband.

XIV. THE MARTYRS OF OLMÜTZ

MORE THAN A THOUSAND DAYS had trickled, hour by hour, minute by minute, like a corrosive acid over the body and soul of the prisoner. The new medical officer was not allowed to exchange a word with his dangerous patient when, under the supervision of the officer on guard, he renewed the bandage on the finger the staff sergeant had bitten. During eleven months the prisoner lay like a stone at the bottom of a well. No word came through the grating of his cell door save an occasional command in an ill-understood language. The dirty Bohemian soldier in charge of him, warned by the fate of his predecessors, withdrew hurriedly and nervously from the cell as soon as he had placed on the table, or removed, the uncleaned vessels that contained the revolting food provided. No book, no printed sheet helped the unfortunate captive through the long days, no word of news from outside came to bring relief from gnawing anxieties.

What a change with his wife there, what a magical change!

The hours of the first week flew by like an instantaneous dream, the minutes were too short for their happiness to be consciously grasped. But gradually his savior found that she had overestimated her strength and that the sufferings she had tried to relieve were undermining her own health.

Three times a day, at meal times, the family were able to meet in Mme de Lafayette's cell; her two daughters remained with her from midday until eight in the evening; then the guards arrived with a rattle of arms, and the two young girls went back to their own cell, conducted by soldiers with fixed bayonets, to sleep in the bed they shared. At nine o'clock the sergeant took the candles from all the cells, and the commandant took the keys to his house at the far end of the town. Fire might break out, one of the four prisoners might be at the point of death, but until the next morning the bunch of keys remained under Count Arco's pillow. It would have been easier to persuade the prison staff to trample on the Host than to commit the outrage of disturbing the commandant's rest for the sake of these mad Frenchwomen who had voluntarily come under lock and key in a military prison.

All Thugut's apprehensions were fulfilled. Mme de Lafayette wanted to let the good Emperor Francis know—she imagined it would surprise him!—that her husband was actually being treated under prison rules, and that Count Arco was by no means the "charming" cavalier she had been led to suppose. Since the failure of the attempt at flight, Lafayette had suffered from attacks of high fever; he had only two shirts, both in rags. His daughter made him a pair of slippers out of bits of cloth. The parsimonious meals had no other purpose than to prevent the prisoners from escaping from their punishment through death; and they were not suitable for any but men in full health. Mme de Lafayette had already been weakened by her imprisonment in France and by the sufferings of the past years; she fell sick of scurvy. She bombarded Count Arco with complaints which the charming man did not deign to honor with a word of reply.

The good Emperor Francis had given orders that any serious complaints should be communicated direct to him. But how could correspondence of this sort be reconciled with the absolute isolation from the outer world imposed by the regulations? The lady had been warned that a military prison was not a health resort.

One of the girls fell ill and was confined to her bed with an infectious malady; the commandant saw no necessity for providing a second bed for her sister. The only correspondence he permitted was the signature for the remittances made by the American Consulate through a Moravian bank. It was only right that these voluntary prisoners should pay the cost of their maintenance. If the payment was out of all relation to the quality of the food, at all events it covered the cost of the service. Routine could not be interfered with if a marquise with her two daughters chose to take up her lodgings in the military prison of Olmütz.

This shameful situation lasted nine months. Count Arco refused to be seen. The ladies must eat with their fingers; forks were against the regulations. In vain did they ask for permission to go to Mass on Sundays; even the request, which indeed seems a modest one, to be attended on by a soldier's wife instead of the dirty Bohemian guard, was refused.

Only once did Mme de Lafayette insist so energetically on her rights that the commandant no longer had the courage to disavow the emperor's promise. He transmitted her application, in view of the state of her health, for permission to consult Viennese physicians and to be allowed to go to a Vienna hospital until she had recovered from scurvy. The sick woman might have died many times over before the reply came, months later. The good Emperor Francis granted permission for the invalid to leave the prison but only on condition that she did not return there.

Mme de Lafayette lost no time in replying. She owed it to her family, she wrote, to do all she could to get well again, but if her recovery must be at the cost of living once more without news of her husband, that was too heavy a price to pay.

However much my state of health may grow worse and whatever the disadvantages of the stay here for my daughters, all three of us will continue, with deep gratitude, to profit by the great goodness of Your Imperial Majesty in permitting us to share the imprisonment in every prescribed detail.

XV. PUBLIC OPINION INTERVENES

THE PRISONERS were under an illusion if they imagined that the irony of this reply would be realized by the good Emperor Francis in Vienna. On the other hand, the harshness of their treatment only increased the sympathy extended to the victims. From May, 1796, strangely precise reports of the treatment of the "martyrs of Olmütz" began to appear in the foreign newspapers, without its ever being discovered through what channel the reports were reaching the press. Count Arco raged through his realm with all the fury of a typhoon—in vain! Every detail of his "shameful" treatment of the prisoners was published to all the readers of the two hemispheres; exact bulletins of the state of health of all four of the prisoners appeared; and an unexampled campaign was started. Such were the thanks the good Emperor Francis received for his great favor.

The names of the heroes who undertook the perilous service of secretly carrying news from the prison are unknown, for the Austria of the Metternich system outlived all those who took part in the drama. We only know from Mme de Lafayette's letters to Mme de Tessé that these secret helpers had long been waiting for the opportunity to prove their devotion. Subsequent allusions reveal that young students carried the letters over the frontier on their own persons in order to post them in Prussia.

When it was learned that Count Arco had refused a separate bed to the sick girl and so exposed her sister to infection, and that Mme de Lafayette had been given the choice between suffering unattended from scurvy or never again seeing her husband, indignation flamed up everywhere, and all friends and relations of the victims made desperate efforts to help them. In spite of his experience with the King of Prussia, Washington addressed a personal letter to the emperor; but the emperor saw no reason to reply to a letter from a president who was himself a rebel, the standard bearer of the abominable theory of "the rights of the people."

But silence was not enough. The imperial government, even the exalted person of His Imperial and Royal Majesty, was being continually held up to dishonor by the English news-papers; it was necessary to proceed to a counter attack. A vast sum of money was thrown away in the vain attempt to dis-cover who it was that was incessantly denouncing Lafayette's "executioners," under the pseudonym of Eleuthère, in the columns of the *Morning Chronicle*. The foremost detectives presented heavy bills for expenses, in sterling, to the Austrian ambassador in London, without ever being able to trace the authorship of the sensational articles.

The man would have been allowed to bark his worst, had he not been able to give such precise details. He related how sol-diers under punishment were whipped beneath Mme de Lafayette's window, how her husband's cell overlooked an open cesspool, the exhalations from which poisoned the air he was breathing—intimate details which could only have been revealed either by the prisoners themselves or by a member of the prison staff! The odious "freedom of speech" customary in the English Parliament was practiced with enthusiasm. The whole phalanx of the Whig orators attacked Pitt at Austria's expense. General FitzPatrick, a friend of the Lord Cornwallis whom Lafayette had defeated in America, came to the aid of Charles James Fox, and the whole world, with its lust for the sensational, was fired by the passionate eloquence of the at-tack, and deaf to the sarcastic replies from the Tories.

Even among the French émigrés, in the immediate entourage of the princes, a royalist of unsullied reputation came forward to demonstrate Lafayette's innocence. The Comte de Lally Tolendal addressed a petition to the crowned "trustee," in which the martyr of Olmütz was represented as actually the most courageous of defenders of the assassinated sovereigns:

It was through trying to save Louis XVI that M. de Lafayette came to disaster. He was offered the highest place in the Republic; he re-fused it! These facts are mathematically proved. I cannot be sus-pected of partizanship; for two whole years I broke off all relations with the man for whom I am now interceding. Those people who credit M. de Lafayette with responsibility or even partial responsibil-ity for the French Revolution are the victims of entirely mistaken conceptions. He played an important part in it, but he was not its author; he had no part in any of its evils, and the only good things done were his own work.

Nobody has summed up Lafayette's rôle better than in those last lines. But though his defenders spoke with the tongues of men and angels they could do nothing: vengeance has deaf ears. In Parliament Lord Wyndham revealed in two short sentences the hardness of heart and the pitilessness of the people who recognize the justice only of those institutions which serve their interests:

Those who start revolutions will always be, in my eyes, the object of an irresistible reprobation. I take delight in seeing them drink to the dregs the cup of bitterness that they have prepared for others.

Thus there came no change in the fate of the prisoners. The two years Mme de Lafayette passed in the prison cells of Olmütz robbed her of ten years of life. But with the breaking of the silence that had towered over them like a wall of steel, the most effective instrument of torture had been robbed of its terrors. Husband and wife now corresponded with their friends and relations; the echo of public opinion reached them, kept hope alive, and strengthened their souls. Only their bodies were still delivered over to the tortures, and the polluted food and pestilential atmosphere destroyed the frail health of the poor woman who had entered into this voluntary martyrdom.

Perhaps her greatest solace was the ability to bring to completion a task she had set herself. She wrote a biography of her mother, *La Vie de la duchesse d'Ayen,* on the margins of Buffon's *Natural History.* It is a touching picture of devotion, the raising of this monument of filial piety, in her prison cell, by this woman of heroic abnegation, enduring the horrible sores of scurvy in her mouth, her chest suffering from the pestilential prison atmosphere, her life fading away at her husband's side, because she would rather have it so than save herself by leaving him.

Gouverneur Morris was the first to succeed in making a small breach in the sacrosanct ramparts of "reasons of state." Monroe had taken his place in France as minister, but Morris remained in Europe as a sort of cross between a commercial attaché and a commercial traveler. He came to Vienna in October, 1796, to hand to the only survivor of the royal family a sum of money which Louis XVI had secretly entrusted to him. Marie Antoinette's daughter, exchanged against three captive members of the Convention, was staying for a short time with her uncle, the emperor, in Vienna. The sum Morris brought—a hundred thousand francs—was not a royal fortune, but Morris's arrival was a sensational event for the poor émigrés, who not so long before used to receive him in their luxurious homes in Paris.

Morris had never felt sympathetic toward Lafayette personally; he makes no secret in his memoirs of his dislike of him. But the state of health of Mme de Lafayette aroused universal concern. Mme de Staël wrote to Morris from Switzerland, where she was staying with her father, Jacques Necker:

> Open M. de Lafayette's prison! You have already saved his wife; save his whole family! Pay your country's debt! What greater service is it possible to perform to one's country than to pay its debts of gratitude? Has ever a more flagrant injustice aroused the sympathy of all Europe?

There was no need to put any pressure on Morris, for he knew the feelings of the head of his country for Lafayette; and the émigrés by their hostility helped him to forget his own. When he heard these people, after Lafayette had already suffered four years of imprisonment, still expressing the hope of seeing him hang, when a certain M. de la Vaupillière charged the "hero of two worlds" with cowardice, Morris lost patience; for all that he had not the slightest sympathy with revolutionary ideas, he wrote:

> Really, the self-assertiveness and the ridiculous pretensions of these gentlemen, most of whom have no other title to public esteem than the name and the glory of their ancestors, almost tempt me to forget the crimes of the French Revolution. Often their intolerant character and their bloodthirsty vengefulness have made me feel that there is truth in the assertion that only the ultimate issue will determine on which side were the criminals and on which side the victims.

There was only one man of great influence who would really have been glad to do what Morris wanted—Baron Thugut. In a confidential letter to his best friend he wrote:

> I should thank God if I could be rid of the whole caravan!

But to the foreigner who presented himself with a whole arsenal of letters full of indignation against the Vienna government Thugut adopted a different tone. He professed indignation at Mme de Lafayette's "ingratitude" in giving His Imperial Majesty no better return for his clemency than to smuggle abroad complaints of her treatment. Was it likely that the military prisons even in America would be organized to receive high-born ladies? As to the protests in the English Parliament, why did not His Excellency Mr Pitt announce his readiness to take over the responsibility for the custody of the prisoners? His offer would be most gratefully accepted by the imperial government.

XVI.   DANCE OF THE DIPLOMATS

IF THE POURPARLERS had continued in this tone, Mme de Lafayette would have run a grave risk, as she wrote in one of her letters to her sister, of "going from the casemates straight to Olmütz cemetery." The guns spoke with more effect, in a language the monarchs understood. The fall of Milan and later of Mantua made more impression than all the protests from the conscience of the world. The oldest names of France lost their brilliance at the Court of Vienna when the sword of Bonaparte, the twenty-eight-year-old Corsican, was thrust almost as far as the capital of the empire. After Arcole and Rivoli, in the spring of 1797, the good Emperor Francis began to remember that Mme de Lafayette was not entirely satisfied with her treatment at Olmütz and that she had been complaining of her health—some eighteen months ago! The Marquis de Chasteler, who himself had drawn up in Belgium the first report of the arrest and examination of the prisoners— five years earlier—was now instructed to see what substance there might be in their complaints and what could discreetly be done to dispose finally of this awkward affair.

The Marquis de Chasteler spoke and wrote six European languages; and he really had the qualities that had so imaginatively been attributed to Count Arco! It was not his fault that the matter continued to drag and that Lafayette still had to wait for release until after his fortieth birthday, in September, 1797.

His liberation took place after a very complicated political country dance, an interplay of personalities which carries us behind the scenes of Napoleon's career. As gamblers try to bluff their opponents by an affectation of indifference, so the Directory, Bonaparte, and the Austrian government played from Paris, Leoben and Vienna a subtle game which can only be understood if one has a view of all the hands. The Marquis de Chasteler would have had an easy task if the prisoners had not themselves put obstacles in the way. In his eyes their complaints were unfounded. Mme de Lafayette called it "inhuman cruelty" to leave her without news of her son; but this was entirely in accordance with regulations! As for the notions of cleanliness of a daughter of the house of Noailles, it was not reasonable to ask the commandant of the fortress to take account of them. The marquis's mission came to grief over minor points like this, on which Lafayette considered it his duty to his historic rôle to insist.

Emperor Francis demanded that the prisoners should give him their word of honor not to return to Austria without his express permission. He wanted to be able to sleep peacefully in his capital, free from apprehension of the noxious influence of rebellious cranks on his subjects. Lafayette must promise to embark at once for America.

After three years of enforced sojourn in Austria the prisoner can certainly have had no urgent desire to remain or return there; and was it not his own intention at the time of his original arrest to sail for America? But five years in prison had only stiffened his adherence to his principles:

The Emperor had me arrested on neutral soil, in contravention of international law; I owe him no account of my further plans and intentions; I decline to enter into any undertakings towards him which might give colour to the claim that he has any right of disposal of my person.

This obstinacy at the expense of his sick wife, whom every delay brought nearer to the grave, aroused indignation in Vienna. But Mme de Lafayette herself urged her husband to make no concession unworthy of his dignity. The Marquis de Chasteler, thus driven into a tight place, threw down his cards; he dropped the demand for immediate embarkation for America but declared that the views and principles of M. de Lafayette were incompatible with peace and order in the Austrian monarchy; on this account it was impossible for his imperial master to restore M. de Lafayette to liberty until he had in his hands a declaration from the prisoner that he would not again enter any of the territories of the house of Habsburg.

At bottom all this was equally unnecessary on both sides. The two parties might well have tacitly assumed that they would never be brought together by any irresistible desire to see one another again. But Lafayette at forty could not deny the whole of his past life. The protection of the weaker against arbitrary treatment by the stronger had been the purpose for which he had always fought. The hand that had written the school essay about the proud steed throwing his rider, refused to sign any undertaking wrung from him by taking advantage of his situation, and the poor Marquis de Chasteler had to employ all his eloquence to arrive at a compromise.

Lafayette declared, to begin with, that he could do nothing without the assent of his brother officers. So it was that at seven o'clock in the morning of July 25, 1797, the three companions in misfortune—Lafayette, Latour-Maubourg and Bureaux de Pusy—who had suffered so many years of solitude under the same roof, saw one another again for the first time since their transfer to Olmütz. M. de Chasteler wrote to the emperor that he allowed them a short time together to open their hearts to one another. Their joy cannot have been unalloyed with bitterness against their jailers. Who does not know the pain of discovering after long separation the havoc wrought by time in the friend's face? Two years without sun and air, delivered up to the stress and strain of their own thoughts, chained to solitude as Prometheus to his rock, and torn by the talons of hope and fear!

It was easy for Chasteler, well cared for and secure in his high station, to find fault with the obstinacy of these three haggard prisoners, literally in rags, and to charge them with uncalled-for hair-splitting. The declaration Lafayette delivered to his negotiator revealed his anger at the treatment his wife and his friends had had to endure. The prisoners declined to contradict, as the emperor wished, the "atrocity stories" that had been spread through Europe about the treatment they had

suffered at the hands of the Vienna government. His Majesty
had only to read again the instructions, written in his own
hand, which he had been pleased to send to the commandant
of the fortress. As for contraband traffic in the new political
ideas, the three signatories gladly undertook to avoid the
countries under His Majesty's rule—subject to one reservation: "Saving the rights of their country over their persons."

The only purpose of this qualification was to prevent the
three French officers from finding their consciences confronted
with a conflict of obligations in the event of a war; but with
Bonaparte only three days' march from Vienna it had a provocative air! The timid emperor saw also a further possibility:
the government of their rebel state might take advantage of
their subtle reservation to entrust them with the propaganda
of its abominable ideas in Austria. In any case, prisoners imposing conditions—who had ever heard of such a thing! They
could remain where they were.

The difficulty was that Bonaparte had been instructed by his
government to include in the peace conditions the liberation of
the martyrs of Olmütz. On August 1, 1797, the "citizen
general" was instructed to insist on the liberation which had
been repeatedly demanded:

> With reference to the new demands addressed to the Directory,
> Citizen General, concerning the Olmütz prisoners, the Directory re-
> minds you of the desire it has expressed to you of seeing an end of
> their captivity. It does not doubt that you will share its interest in
> their misfortune.
>
> CARNOT,
> *Executive President of the Directory.*

The Directory might well have had its doubts. The young
conqueror showed little inclination to trouble about what his
government wanted. His triumphal progress through Italy and
to the very gates of Vienna had turned his head, and the
Parisians too were beginning to forget that the revolutionary
armies had set out to defend the freedom of France and to
bring freedom to the oppressed, not to conquer nations and
annex territories. Lafayette, the first prophet of the rights of
man, with his incorrigible fanaticism for those obsolescent
principles and with the halo of his five years' martyrdom

round his head, might easily become a nuisance to Bonaparte in France. The man who had refused to accept the command of the National Guard of the whole country, on the ground that the concentration of too much power in one man's hands held dangers for freedom, that it might bring the military domination of a Cromwell—no! Bonaparte had no use for such dreamers.

But the time had not yet come for open insubordination, for driving the "lawyers" out of Paris. The victorious general therefore energetically demanded the liberation of the prisoners of Olmütz. But at the same time he sent General Clarke to Vienna with secret instructions to modify the demand. Let the prisoners be released, but only on condition that they did not return to France.

The imperial government did not waste an instant over the question whether Bonaparte, the army commander, was entitled to impose these secret conditions. But while it would have been delighted to dispatch the mischief maker to America, it must save its face before the world and could not let it be said that it had had to obey the dictate of the youthful general and his army of rebels. Lafayette, meanwhile, had become ironic: it was a high honor to him, he said, that His Majesty was treating with him as between one power and another, but he could not admit that the emperor had any right of disposal of his person. It was a complicated situation; and time was pressing, if the Court was not to have to flee from Vienna.

A pretty solution of the dilemma was finally devised; it was the work of Lafayette's faithful aide-de-camp, Romeuf, who had persuaded Bonaparte to give him leave to proceed to Vienna in order to hasten the liberation of his general. From there, furnished with a safe conduct by Thugut, he went on to Hamburg and there found Parish, ex-American consul general, who had furnished Mme de Lafayette with her American passport, and whom he now persuaded to play his part in a farce which would satisfy everybody.

Vienna was in the greatest hurry to be duped. Its representative at Hamburg affected to be unaware that Mr Parish was no longer consul general; and Baron Thugut contented himself with the retired official's assurance that he would "do all

he could" to ship Lafayette to America. As he could do
nothing, the promise was easily made. He wrote to Vienna that
an American ship had just dropped anchor in the harbor of
Altona. American ships were doing so almost every day; but
so great was the goodwill of the Austrian government that it
took this information as amounting to the assurance it required; and so, on September 19, 1797, the gates of the
fortress of Olmütz opened to let out the prisoners, and at last
Baron Thugut was rid of "the whole caravan."

The state of health, or rather of sickness, of Mme de Lafayette compelled them to travel slowly, by short stages. This
was a piece of good fortune for Lafayette. It enabled him to
see as he crossed the German-speaking territories how deeply
the principles for which he had so struggled had become im-
planted in men's hearts. The liberated prisoners were fêted
like conquerors; the students of Heidelberg organized a torchlight procession in their honor; Lafayette was able to nurse
the illusion that he was returning to the great stage of history.

In Hamburg Gouverneur Morris and the Austrian minister
awaited the arrival of the "convoy of prisoners" at the house
of ex-Consul General Parish. Here the formality of taking
over the famous prisoner was duly carried out on October 4,
1797. Morris, as a participant, described the ceremony in his
diary as "very worthy." It was—worthy of an operetta. The
prescribed American merchantman was lying in the port, ready
to carry the prisoner away to the New World—if he wanted
to go. Lafayette even went on board. The captain gave a banquet in his honor. And then the three heroes of Liberty went
back on shore to their hotel, where they were the guests of
the United States.

XVII.   RETURN TO LIFE

ALL OVER EUROPE, and still more in the New World, the liberation of the martyrs was the sensation of the day. Mme de Lafayette's illness aroused universal sympathy, and the story of
this woman who passed from Robespierre's prisons to the casemates of despotism, and who had braved death rather than
leave her husband to suffer alone, became the subject of emo-
tional romances celebrating her as a modern Alcestis—until

the day when the reading public passed on to its next sensation. For in life, too, the interest is exhausted when the happy end is reached.

The memoirs of famous prisoners tell us that their long confinement in the narrow space of their cell leaves them the victims of agoraphobia, a dread of open spaces. The streets and squares seem too vast; their gaze, accustomed to their four narrow walls, wanders distressingly in the infinity of space. Freedom flaps too loosely about them, like the rags on their emaciated bodies.

Lafayette's experience was the contrary of this. He could not adjust himself to a changed world which had become too narrow and confined for him. The France of the Directory, peopled by a race of dwarfs, of men without faith or enthusiasm, and saved from exploitation by aristocrats only to be exploited anew by pushing parvenus, had no attraction for him. The name of Lafayette flamed up for a last moment, like the wick of a burned-out candle, while its bearer journeyed from Olmütz to Hamburg amid the echo of the clanking of his broken chains; then darkness fell around him. This man of only forty years of age, who had fought for freedom in two hemispheres, devoting to the cause a large part of his fortune and sacrificing the five best years of his life, was now overshadowed by the great Corsican conqueror. General at twenty, world-famous hero at twenty-four, Lafayette had become in his ripe manhood a man without a country, without a roof over his head, forgotten and impoverished. He was not even spared anxiety for his daily bread.

The Jacobin régime had collapsed; France was a free republic. Lafayette found himself fully in sympathy with the new Constitution of the year III, drawn up by the Convention and based entirely on the principle of the sovereignty of the people. He could thus return to his country, although his name had not yet been struck off the list of émigrés. The fact that he was an outlaw would not deter him for a single day from returning; had not the Directory intervened to secure his liberation? The men who had outlawed him had been guillotined, or were crouching in anxious obscurity. The hero of the Fédération had been as completely forgotten as the author of the "massacre" on the Champ de Mars; and the man who had been the most fêted and the most hated of all could have returned home unnoticed.

Unfortunately, in the new and narrowed world, ruled by greed and vanity, the prisoner of Olmütz stumbled in all directions like a child learning to walk. The day after his arrival in Hamburg the French consul called on him; and with his old frankness Lafayette threw at the head of this representative of the government reproaches and complaints which were faithfully reported to Paris. At the moment of his liberation the republican Directors had driven out or actually deported two of their colleagues and certain deputies, with royalist sympathies, and this arbitrary action aroused Lafayette's disapproval, like every act of oppression. He had no knowledge of the intentions of the victims, who might have employed the very methods from which they were suffering in order to overthrow the republic and restore the monarchy; but this "theorist," who had only just come out of prison, roundly condemned the undemocratic proceedings of the Directory, and in doing so infallibly condemned himself to fresh exile.

"Venez en France!" wrote Mme de Staël enthusiastically to him; but Talleyrand, the friend for whom she had won the portfolio of Foreign Affairs, the same Talleyrand who as Bishop of Autun had administered the constitutional oath to Louis XVI, had other views. He had this troublesome crank warned by the Consul at Altona that he would be running a risk in returning to France. Lafayette was still *de jure* an outlaw. Barras, more out of indolence than good-nature, had not put into application the decrees against Lafayette; but the report from the Hamburg consul general reminded him of them; he preferred praise to criticism and took advantage of the exclusion of Lafayette from France to sell by auction the last of the proscribed man's properties in Brittany. General Bonaparte might have spared himself the trouble of his intrigues in Vienna. Nobody could improve on the obstacles General Lafayette put in his own path by his passion for speaking his mind without fear or favor.

Fortunately the Comtesse de Tessé was in love with her illustrious nephew, whose views—alone among the whole of his wide circle of relations—she entirely shared. She was proud and glad to be able to give shelter to "the whole caravan." Her

property was close to Hamburg, on the neutral soil of Danish
Holstein; Lafayette and Latour-Maubourg and their families
were safe there.

Mme de Montagu had taken refuge with Aunt Tessé. On
the day of the arrival of the "caravan" she hurried to meet
her beloved sister, beside herself with joy. As the horn of the
German postilion announced the approach of these dear ones,
whom she had had little hope of ever seeing again, she jumped
into a decrepit old fishing boat and prevailed on old M. de
Mun, who had just come on a visit, to row across with her to
the posting station; and there she embraced her sister and
nieces and brother-in-law, one after the other, again and again,
between laughing and crying.

The little house could hardly hold so many people; but
times had changed; these families, which formerly had had
more millions than they now had members, were happy to
have a roof over their heads, and the wit and vivacity of their
hostess kept them all in good spirits.

Lafayette's first care was to send his thanks to all his defenders, friends and helpers, from General Washington to
young Huger, from Charles James Fox to General Bonaparte.
The three liberated men sent a joint letter of thanks to the
conqueror of Italy, not yet thirty years old, whose star now
shone brighter even than the name of the "hero of two
worlds" had done in the past. This first letter already reveals
to anyone with a sensitive ear a vague disquiet, if not actual
mistrust, in Lafayette. Not that he had yet learned of Napoleon's double game at Vienna. But the two men differed too
greatly to be able to trust one another. Lafayette, a multi-
millionaire at fourteen, at seventeen the husband of a Noailles,
sacrificed fortune and fame, popularity and freedom, to his
altruistic longing for a free and happier world. When the
Austrians entitled him "marquis" in the Olmütz documents,
Lafayette struck out the "obsolete" description, putting in its
place the word "general," and gave some annoyance by dryly
remarking that he had given up the use of his inherited title
since he had succeeded in gaining by his own efforts the rank
of a general.

Unlike him, Bonaparte, the second son in the large family
of a Corsican lawyer, who had deserted the Corsican patriot

Paoli for the French oppressor in order to gain a small post with which to support his family, had learned one thing above all from his father and from the penury of his youth—that anyone who wants to get on in the world must climb the shoulders of others. Young Lieutenant Bonaparte cast hungry glances over the barrier that shut him off from all the joys of wealth and power. He toadied to the younger Robespierre and played the Jacobin until the 9th Thermidor. He was bitterly envious at his brother's marriage with the daughter of a prosperous provincial shopkeeper and did his utmost to win the favor of his young sister-in-law; but she preferred Bernadotte (who later was to become King of Sweden). He next tried his fortune with a fashionable actress, twice his age, who owned several theaters. Finally he relieved his patron Barras of Josephine, the beautiful Creole, in consideration of his appointment as commander-in-chief of the Italian army. Rich army contractors lent him money with which to open his campaign; he promised to repay them with big orders. Too late they discovered to their astonishment how this unprepossessing little officer could shake off friends who were no longer of use to him.

"What are a hundred thousand human lives for a man like me?" he asked disdainfully when he had advanced from Bonaparte to Napoleon. Later still, on the isolated rock in the ocean on which he had been confined like a dangerous wild beast, his regrets were not for the three million Frenchmen he had uselessly sacrificed, not for the frozen corpses on the banks of the Beresina; a worse trouble than all this was that his guard only called him General Bonaparte! He had insisted on his own brothers, even if they were alone with him in the Tuileries, making the prescribed obeisances and duly addressing him as "Sire."

How could these two men, of such fundamentally different character, ever work together? To one of them men were only a means and his own advantage was the end, for which he was ready to sacrifice any of his fellow men without a qualm; the other had sacrificed his own fortune for the independence and the well-being of oppressed peoples and would willingly have sacrificed his life for them. And it was soon evident that Lafayette, on his emergence from prison at forty years of age, was the same Lafayette who had sailed for America at twenty. "He was so little changed that it made one feel young again to listen to him," wrote Mme de Montagu to Mme de Grammont.

"In talking with him," she added, "I avoid as far as possible any reference to the Revolution—I am afraid of exploding and wounding him. Have patience and avoid all discussions—that is my rule." The memory of a mother, a grandmother, and a sister brought to the scaffold made it more than Mme de Montagu could endure to hear the principles of the Revolution still defended. The stain of the Terror blinded her, as so many, to all the gains and achievements of the Revolution; whereas Lafayette, as she writes, "still dreams of the Declaration of the Rights of Man and of the dawn of the Revolution. The rest, for him, is merely a mischance, deplorable, no doubt, but of no more significance than a shipwreck, which does not prevent men from continuing to sail the seas."

Was it the eternal debates at table and his sister-in-law's susceptibilities, or was it the lack of room, that decided Lafayette to find a home of his own? After a few weeks he rented a very modest estate at Lemkulen, not far from Mme de Tessé's home; here he was able to receive his friends, until his wife's health should permit the whole family to sail for America.

But during the five and a half years Lafayette had spent in prison there had been a good deal of change in the New World also. Without waiting to be asked, Washington sent his godson straight back to Europe the moment he received the news of the impending liberation of the boy's parents. The letter he gave the young man for his father said that George was not to be prevented from setting off; and after mentioning, as a matter of course, that General and Mrs Washington would be delighted to receive the whole family at Mount Vernon, it added:

You may be assured that yourself never stood higher in the affections of the people of this country, than at the present moment. . . . If inclination or events should induce you or any of them [Lafayette's family] to visit America, no person in it would receive you with more cordiality and affection than Mrs Washington and myself.

It was quite true that Lafayette's popularity had grown through his martyrdom. But feeling was very strained between France and the United States, and it would have been difficult for the President to give official hospitality to French friends. He had sent the young Lafayette to the University of New York, and now he sent him hurriedly back to his father because war between the two republics was dangerously close. French privateers were confiscating American cargoes consigned to England, regardless of the serious commercial loss to the United States. The Americans were conscious of their debt of gratitude for French help under the Monarchy, but were not inclined to allow the Republic to exact a return in the form of this pillage, and the continual friction that resulted became so burdensome to Washington that he finally resigned from office, declining the supreme honor of a third presidency in spite of the law specially enacted to permit it in his case.

Lafayette tried to intervene as a peacemaker between his two homelands: the result brought home to him how mercilessly time had thrust him out of public life. He felt paralyzed in the best years of his manhood and wrote sadly to Washington:

If I had not been outlawed the mistakes of enemies and the chances of time would have placed in my hands a success far more outstanding and much less meritorious than my campaign against Lord Cornwallis. But now I no longer have any military ambition, and I am equally unfitted to be a statesman or an orator.

XVIII. THE GUARDIAN ANGEL

IT IS AN ANCIENT BELIEF that one person's happiness has to be paid for by another's misfortune—a cynical half truth, serving generally to excuse ruthless selfishness. But in Mme de Lafayette's case it is true that the happiest ten years of her life were paid for by her husband's premature exclusion from public work. He had been driven off the stage at forty by Bonaparte's success; now at last he belonged to her. They had scarcely been married when she had to give way before glory and freedom and yet other rivals; she passed years in daily uncertainty whether he might not be brought back home streaming with blood, perhaps dead. At last, at the heavy price of her health, she had bought the quiet life with him for which she had longed. Their silver wedding brought their first real married life.

The arrival of their son from America heralded the beginning of this period of peaceful family life. Soon afterwards the elder daughter became engaged to the younger Comte de Latour-Maubourg, a relative of her father's companion in misfortune at Olmütz. Mme de Lafayette, still confined to her bed by scurvy, was unable to direct the preparations for the wedding, and the family therefore returned for a short time to Mme de Tessé's house. The good aunt threw up her hands and declared that such a marriage had never been known since the days of Adam and Eve. The young couple had scarcely anything in the world beyond the clothes they wore. *"On ne se marie pas comme cela!"*

Everybody agreed with her, except Lafayette, who declared the match *"avantageux."* But he was himself blind to all the discomforts of lack of money, content with the barest everyday necessities, as though he were camping once more in the virgin forests of the New World.

Was he really as happy and contented as he appeared to the wedding guests, and, above all, to his poor wife, who had been used to looking after her family but now had to be tended by others? Thanks to his activity and his youthful temperament he did not suffer excessively. He corresponded with his friends and partisans and admirers, and his world-wide sympathies helped him to reconcile himself to facts. Rarely did a complaint slip from his pen. He would have given worlds, he writes to Romeuf, to be able to contribute further to the work of the Revolution "to render to my country the sort of service for which I seem particularly fitted, even if I had to die an hour later."

His wife, who knew him through and through, was troubled at the spectacle of this man, who had lived to be so acclaimed, now unoccupied and forgotten by the world like the portrait of a victorious general removed from its gold frame and covered with dust and cobwebs. With the ulcers on her frail body still incompletely healed, she set out bravely for France to claim the family property of her mother and grandmother on behalf of her sisters and herself. With the same tenacity with which she had endured sickness in prison for her husband's sake, she set out now to free him from poverty. Nobody knew better than she that his money was at the service of everybody who came to him for help. It was enough to pronounce the word "Liberty" to take the very bread from his mouth. But it was just the open-handed *grand seigneur* that she had always loved in him. It was terrible to her to see closed, against his whole nature, that hand made for careless prodigality. She set out to prepare a new frame worthy of her ikon: it would be a small frame, but of gold. In August, 1798, she left Lafayette with her aunt Tessé and plunged bravely into the haggling, so foreign to her, with lawyers and public authorities and even with her own relatives; for need has given strange lessons to many a despiser of money.

While his wife was in Paris Lafayette, overcome with homesickness, swallowed his pride and sent a petition to the Directory. His two friends, he wrote, had had to flee from France entirely through his fault; he asked permission for them, and also, incidentally, for himself, to return. Mme de Lafayette, with her three children, personally presented this petition. But it was refused; all that she was granted was a passport for herself. She could cross the frontier at any time, as often as she wished. As for the exile, the Directory considered that "the time has not yet come for considering his case."

The decision is not surprising. The Directory had only just unburdened themselves of Bonaparte, the would-be dictator, by sending him on an expedition to the Near East. They had had to procure a fleet of warships and transports, a splendidly equipped army, and several million francs in gold. It had not been too high a price for getting rid of that dangerous man. But, with the autocrat only just gone, they had no desire to see the dreamer return to France to create fresh unrest with his Utopias.

Nevertheless, the passport made it possible for Mme de Lafayette to take her son back to his father and to instal the two at a spot nearer the French frontier, outside Utrecht. Lafayette wrote with childish glee to all his friends that once more he was on "republican" soil. He remained there with his son for a whole year. The Comtesse de Tessé, who paid them a visit to see how they were getting on, sent a horrified description of their condition. She had to go to Utrecht to buy them plates and knives and forks. Mme de Montagu, Mme de Lafayette's sister, added her testimony that it was impossible to stay with them for more than a few days, because they all went hungry to bed every night. Only the host himself was unable to see that anything was lacking. Not a day passed but he was visited by old friends. Officers of the Dutch and the French army accounted it an honor to sit and starve at Lafayette's table.

He found compensation for everything in the great moment when he first saw French troops marching past once more. Who was it that had given the National Guard the red, white and blue of their *tricolore,* and predicted to the councilors of Paris: *"Elle fera le tour du monde"* ("It will go round the world")? Now the little cockade had grown into a flag; it had ousted the lily banner of the Bourbons after four centuries; it had floated above the Pyramids and from the *campanili* of Italy; it had put to flight the flag of the Habsburgs and the orange-colored banner of the Stadhouder of the Netherlands; it hastened to the aid of every oppressed nation. Him they might banish like a leper, but the three colors which he had prophetically joined would preserve his memory forever, together with those "Rights of Man" which, though they might be torn up today, would be reconquered tomorrow and could never again fall entirely into oblivion. Men might be dull and thankless, might still be ready to serve anyone who would give them their daily crust of bread in return for the yoke he imposed on them; they nevertheless possessed now and for all time the new doctrine, ineradicably impressed on heart and brain, that all are born free and equal. Intoxicated with words of hatred and vengeance, or with insane megalomania, whole nations might ignore or deny that sacred doctrine. When they came to themselves, the fragments of the broken law would come together again, and the slaves of the day before would again give their last drop of blood for the inalienable rights which that *très haut et très puissant seigneur,* Monseigneur Marie Joseph Paul Yves Roch Gilbert du Motier, Marquis de Lafayette, Baron de Vissac, Seigneur of Saint-Romain and many other places, had brought for the first time from the New World for his enslaved fellow men.

And yet this flag, of which he was so proud and so justly proud, was a danger to Lafayette. His son enlisted as a simple grenadier in the Dutch army, which with the aid of the French ultimately defeated the troops of the Duke of York.

But if the Stadhouder's party had won the upper hand
Lafayette would have had to flee again and would once more
have been separated from his wife. Mme de Lafayette trembled
for the happiness she had so dearly bought. But danger came,
after all, not from the north but from the south. The Duke
of York had to retreat with his army; but on the other hand
Bonaparte, who had been imagined to be tied to Egypt by his
responsibilities as commander-in-chief, unexpectedly returned
to Paris.

Like the diviner who is able to sense hidden waters,
Lafayette, usually so credulous and confiding, this time per-
ceived with a sure instinct the sprouting germ of tyranny.
On October 17, 1799, before anybody else dreamed that a
general of the Republic could venture to abandon the army
under his command without at once being arrested and shot as
a deserter, Lafayette wrote to his friend Latour-Maubourg:
"As for Bonaparte, he may become the master of France. His
halo of glory gives him immense advantages."

The exile allowed himself, nevertheless, to be persuaded by
his wife to send her a letter of greeting for the "master" of
the morrow, thanking him as his "liberator." Mme de Lafayette
had just time to get the letter into Bonaparte's hands. Ten
days after its dispatch to his wife, Lafayette saw his faithful
Romeuf dismount at his gate. Romeuf brought the news of the
Coup d'État, and a French passport in a false name. "Now or
never!" wrote Mme de Lafayette. The moment had come for
returning to France, regardless of all the decrees of past governments. She knew that her husband would not hesitate. And
so Lafayette returned in his ripe years to his homeland,
smuggled in as in his youth, disguised as a courier, he had
smuggled himself out.

"May God preserve Gil from ever climbing again upon the
stage of public life! He would be ready at once to squander
his fortune again for his old ideals, and not only his own fortune!" So, at the time when they were living together in
Mme de Tessé's house, Mme de Montagu had written to her
sister. God might not have preserved him from it, but
Napoleon took care to. So long as he was on the stage he never
allowed Lafayette to approach it; this hot-headed "ideologue,"
this "simpleton," was never allowed the smallest part, even as

a "super," in the spectacular drama which for sixteen years turned all Europe into a battlefield.

When General Brune brought the First Consul Lafayette's letter announcing his return to France, the windows of Malmaison shook with Bonaparte's fury. On his instructions Talleyrand and Sieyès put strong pressure on Lafayette and threatened him with the wrath of the *"maître de la France,"* as Napoleon now was indeed; but Lafayette was determined to go to prison rather than leave the country again, and in the end Bonaparte gave him permission to remain, so long as he held entirely aloof from public life. He must undertake to live in complete retirement on his estates.

Mme de Lafayette thus found her husband relegated by Napoleon to the domain she had recovered for him out of their inheritance, to conceal for him the emptiness of his days. And Lafayette did really discover in himself a gift for farming. Since his release from Olmütz it had been a favorite jest of his that it was a pity that the dollar he was just spending was not the first of the price of a farm in America. Mme de Lafayette had therefore claimed for herself out of her family's property the estate of La Grange and had energetically brought it so far out of the state of dilapidation in which she found it that her husband, faced with this beginning, felt himself challenged to carry it to further success.

What patience, what care this wife had expended, what sacrifices she had made for the reward of the seven years that remained to her, in peaceful seclusion, by the side of her husband! For these last seven years of her life she had him entirely to herself. The iron hand of Napoleon clanged the gates of La Grange behind Lafayette the general and politician and locked and bolted them so securely that Mme de Lafayette had no need to fear for her quiet happiness.

The domain prospered, the produce grew year by year; but the mouths to be fed grew in number also. The second daughter married the Comte de Lasteyrie, after almost becoming the wife of Lucien Bonaparte. Then the son brought home a young wife. Grandchildren came on the scene. The only interruption in the peaceful regularity of this existence came with an accident to Lafayette, a fracture of the thigh. With his enthusiasm for every advance of science, he bore like a hero the tortures of a new apparatus for keeping the limb extended, of which he was the first to undergo an experimental test. He had the double satisfaction of making a complete recovery and of demonstrating the merits of the new invention, for the benefit of future sufferers.

How glad they would all have been to see a few more years of this peaceful happiness granted to the wife and mother who, at last freed from all cares and anxieties, was now able to enjoy the *"vie obscure"* she had asked Washington to assure for her son! But the years in the suffocating atmosphere of the prison cell at Olmütz, shut out from sunlight and fresh air, exacted payment with usurious interest.

When death stood by her bedside her pious spirit was troubled by fears for her husband's soul. She took his hand between her transparent fingers and asked anxiously:

"Vous n'êtes pas chrétien?"

Was he a Christian? He could not answer. Fearing that she had wounded him through her indiscretion, she lightly turned the question aside:

"I know what you are—you are a Fayettist!"

Entering into the joke, he asked her whether she was not herself a bit of a Fayettist. She replied with fervor, struggling to find her breath:

"Ah oui, de toute mon âme! Je sens que je donnerais ma vie pour cette secte-là!"

Death itself obeyed the strange law which had ruled Lafayette's whole existence. It was on Christmas Eve, 1807, that his faithful wife breathed her last, twenty-nine years to the day and hour after she had given birth to their son—the son whom she had left to remain at his side and care for him with her own devotion, as though she could not rest in her grave without the knowledge that her husband was in good hands.

A few weeks later he wrote a long letter to the elder Latour-Maubourg, his loyal friend and fellow sufferer in captivity, who was now living in America. The letter is a lament for the dead and a tender tribute to her memory:

I have not written to you, my dear friend, from the depths of the abyss of misery into which I have been plunged. I was very near doing so, when I sent you the last proofs of her friendship for you, and of her confidence in your feelings for her. Until now you have found me stronger than the vicissitudes in the midst of which I have often imagined myself unhappy. Today circumstance is stronger than I. I shall never recover from it.

During thirty-four years her tenderness, her goodness, the elevation, the delicacy, the generosity of her spirit charmed, adorned, honoured my life; I felt so used to all that she was to me that I did not distinguish her from my own existence. She was fourteen years old and I sixteen when her heart became absorbed in everything that could interest me. I thought that I loved her well, and that I had need of her, but it is only now when I have lost her that I am able to distinguish all that remains of me for the rest of my life—a life which had seemed to me to be given over to so many distractions, but in which there is no longer any possible happiness or comfort. . . .

The day she received the sacraments, she took pleasure in seeing me stay. After that she fell into a constant delirium, the most extraordinary and the most touching ever seen. Imagine, my dear friend, a brain entirely deranged, supposing itself in Egypt, in Syria, in the midst of events of the reign of Athalie, which Célestine's lessons had impressed on her imagination, mixing up all the ideas which had no hold on her heart; and finally the most constant delirium, and at the same time an unfailing sweetness and that kindness which sought always to say something pleasant; that thankfulness for all the care taken for her, that fear of tiring others, that need of being useful to them, all those feelings, all that goodness that would have been in her had she been entirely conscious . . .

"*Que j'ai été heureuse*," she said on the day of her death; "*quelle part d'être votre femme!*" And when I spoke of my love, she replied, in so touching a voice, "*C'est vrai! quoi, c'est vrai! Que vous êtes bon! Répétez encore. Cela fait tant de plaisir à entendre!* . . . If you do not find yourself loved enough," she said, "lay it at God's feet, He gave me no more faculty than that. I love you," she said in the midst of her delirium, "*chrétiennement, mondainement, passionnément.*"

Sometimes we heard her praying as she lay there. She asked her daughters to read her the prayers of the Mass, and noticed where anything was passed over so as not to tire her. In the last nights there was something celestial in the way she recited twice over, in a loud voice, a canticle of Tobias, the same one which she had recited to her daughters when they saw the spires of Olmütz. . . .

One day I spoke to her of her angelic sweetness. "It is true," she said, "God made me sweet, but it is not like your gentleness; I do not aspire to that; you are so strong and at the same time so gentle; you look out from such a height! But I agree that I am sweet, and you are so good to me!" "It is you who are good," I replied, "and generous *par excellence*. Do you remember my first departure for America? Everybody was upbraiding me; you hid your tears at M. de Ségur's wedding. You did not want to show your grief, for fear that I should be blamed." "*C'est vrai*," she said to me, "it was rather nice behaviour for a child, but how good of you to remember it all this time."

It is a solace to me to repeat to myself with you everything that recalls how tender and happy she was. *Mon Dieu!* how happy she would have been, this winter! The three families reunited, the war over for Georges, Virginie with her baby, and I might add, after my sickness, when our fears redoubled our tenderness! Was she not full of goodness lately in interesting herself in my little pleasures at La Grange, in my farm, in the things she remembered. "*Mon Dieu, mon Dieu*," she exclaimed one day, "another six poor years of La Grange!" . . .

You know as I do all that she was, all that she did during the Revolution. It is not for having come to Olmütz that I want to praise her here, but for having remained in France until she had done all she could to assure the well-being of my aunt and to meet the claims of my creditors; for having had the courage to send George to America.

What noble *imprudence de cœur* to remain the only woman in France compromised by her name and steadily to refuse to abandon it. Every one of her petitions or declarations began always with the words "*La femme Lafayette*." Never did she allow a word against me without protest, even when she was under the shadow of the scaffold, never did she let an opportunity pass of avowing my principles, or avow them without taking pride in the avowal and adding that she had them from me. . . .

My letter would never be finished, my dear friend, if I allowed myself to yield to the feelings that dictate it. I embrace you in her name, in my own, in the name of all that you have been for me all the time we have known one another.

Adieu, my dear friend.

XIX. SKIRMISH WITH NAPOLEON

THE YEAR that robbed Lafayette of his wife brought Napoleon the victories of Eylau and Friedland. As ally and friend of the Czar, and with one hand stretched out toward Spain, the only country on the Continent that he had not brought to its knees, Napoleon was able to decorate the Christmas tree at the palace of the Tuileries with new crowns, big and little, for his faithful followers.

In his omnipotence he cut up Europe as a child may cut up a map. Duchies and provinces fell off one by one for his marshals and ministers. For his youngest brother he stuck together the kingdom of Westphalia. Only his sister Caroline had to wait until the following year, when her brother Joseph went on to Madrid, leaving the throne of Naples for her husband, Murat the innkeeper's son.

In this limitless empire there were castles and domains, palaces and estates and fortunes for all who served their leader well. What the masses needed was bread and a master whom they feared and who did their thinking for them. "Liberty," that imposture of ambitious lawyers or pet subject for the superficial chatter of "simpletons" and "ideologues," belonged only to the man of power. The crowd was always ready to give passive obedience to anyone who assured it its daily bread, its profits and its distinctions. Hunger, vanity, cupidity, these were the motive forces of mankind!

It was on the basis of these principles that the vertiginous tower of the Napoleonic empire was built. Too late did its architect discover his error. "I have made you all too rich," he said bitterly to his marshals when they impatiently urged him to abdicate—"you want to live in your palaces instead of sleeping under tents." He spoke the truth. Those who have much to lose do not willingly stake their all on a single card. But was it not the leader himself who had placed his trust in the sort of "fidelity" that has to be well rewarded? Now that he had nothing more to give, he was suddenly appealing to sentiments in which he had never placed faith.

The Marquis de Lafayette, who despised all that is venal, who sacrificed wealth and career and popularity for "humanity," could be nothing else but an imbecile in the eyes of Napoleon, the egoist and megalomaniac who did not scruple to sacrifice whole nations to his own exaltation, and for whom men were but instruments. If at first the prisoner of Olmütz continued to speak with admiration of his liberator, it was the admiration of the French officer, the victor over Cornwallis, who could not but watch with pride the triumphs of the national army he had himself created.

For Lafayette, who could make no compromise with his conscience, it was a fortunate thing that he returned to his country as a private individual with no political responsibilities. The decree which had outlawed him and set a price upon his head was still in force. He had no rights of citizenship and could not vote either for or against the government. It was possible for him to rejoice in the French successes in the theater of war without entering into discussions of the home policy of the First Consul. He was free of all responsibility, and was ready to confine his attention to his own estate.

It was on these conditions alone that the First Consul had tolerated his return. But Napoleon did not entirely trust this settlement; care had to be taken that this man with his dangerous ideas, this potential center of infection, should remain in isolation. Not even the name of the "simpleton" must be allowed to remind the Parisians of their past stupidities and disturb the process of their recovery. A few weeks after Lafayette's return home General Washington died—nearly seventeen years after the melancholy parting from his young friend whom, as he had then feared, he was never to see again. The Consul decreed a solemn memorial ceremony in honor of the first Republican President of the new era; but the name inseparably bound up with Washington's must not be allowed to be heard during the ceremony. Bonaparte sent for the orator who was to deliver the speech in Washington's memory and strictly forbade him to make any mention of Lafayette. The American guests looked in vain around the crowded audience in the Invalides for the man who had been nearest to Washington's heart. Even that was not enough for Bonaparte. When some eager tale-bearer revealed that Georges Lafayette had been standing behind one of the pillars to listen to the eulogy of his godfather, there was a tempest in the Tuileries. Not until after his victory at Marengo did the First Consul feel sufficiently secure in the saddle to have no more fear of the impoverished and almost bankrupt farmer of La Grange. He knew that Lafayette was besieged by a swarm of creditors; and a man in the grip of financial embarrassment was not a dangerous rival in Napoleon's eyes.

Thus there came a rapprochement between the two men. Lafayette himself says in his *Mémoires* that after the first "audience," at which Latour-Maubourg had accompanied him, he came away from the Tuileries fascinated. Later on he again writes with enthusiasm of his meetings with Bonaparte. Every man is inclined to admire in other men the qualities most foreign to his own. Napoleon, the poor lawyer's son, was impressed by the self-assurance of the *grand seigneur* who had lost the whole of his fortune but could display the same ease of manner as if he were still wealthy and powerful; Lafayette admired the "self-made man" who with no advantage of birth had risen so high entirely by his own strength. In his incorrigible trustfulness he only discovered when the bill was presented that every smile of Bonaparte's was carefully calculated.

Shortly after his first visit to the Tuileries, Lafayette met in Talleyrand's antechamber a gentleman whose features struck him by their close resemblance to the First Consul's. This was Joseph Bonaparte, a man of liberal views which brought him closer to the apostle of the Rights of Man than to his younger brother, the Dictator. He invited Lafayette to a *fête champêtre*, a garden party at his country seat, and here the First Consul took the opportunity of a confidential talk with the "enemy of tyrants." He drew Lafayette into a recess and entered into a conversation with him much in the way of a cat playing with a mouse.

He asked Lafayette what he thought of the new consular Constitution. Lafayette made no secret of his view that the powers of the government were too extensive. Bonaparte replied, laughing:

"What would you have me do? Sieyès had put nothing but shadows into his draft Constitution—the shadow of a legislative power, the shadow of a judiciary, the shadow of an executive. There had to be substance somewhere. *Ma foi!* I put it in."

There seldom failed to be a theoretical skirmish of this sort between the two when they met, but the Dictator, little inclined as he generally was to put up with any criticism, never let it come to a breach between them. He said once to his intimate collaborator Berthier, with the melancholy that sometimes overcame him:

"Lafayette has the talent of making friends. Even now, when

he has lost his game! If tomorrow I were in his position, who would remain true to me, except my wife? Perhaps my brother Joseph?"

This passing mood betrays a little enviousness on this despiser of his fellow men. Napoleon, surrounded by lackeys paid to be loyal, still felt at the bottom of his heart a desire to escape at times from the flattery and cupidity that eternally surrounded him. He would have been glad to find himself mistaken in his estimate of humanity, but his entourage only confirmed it and deepened his contempt. That was why he did his utmost to save from death the young Vienna student who tried to assassinate him. This man, who planned his battlefields without troubling about the lives they would cost, only reluctantly sacrificed the assailant who refused to accept his amnesty. He would haggle over the cost of his white buckskin waistcoats; but the men he needed he paid to excess; for that very reason he had a great liking for any men who were not simply out for what they could get.

Napoleon was so well served by Fouché, his minister of police, it was a pity he did not have copies supplied to him of Lafayette's letters. He would have found a good deal in them to interest him and even to flatter him. Thus there is this passage in a letter to a friend on the Napoleonic tyranny:

I must confess that the person of the oppressor seems much less repulsive to me than the unconditional submission of his servants. How can he fail to despise men, when he sees them continually crawling at his feet?

It must have been partly a surfeit of flattery and the attractiveness of a man of integrity that kept alive Napoleon's interest in Lafayette at a time when he was much too secure in his power to need to fear the small farmer of La Grange. But just as a child cannot rest until he has taken his toy entirely to bits, Napoleon was driven by curiosity at Lafayette's unintelligible indifference to wealth and power. Lafayette was struggling amid serious financial embarrassment, and Napoleon tried every possible means of tempting him—but in vain. It will be remembered that Lafayette was in the act of restoring Chavaniac when he was recalled to active service in the field. One of the last letters that reached him before he fled from France was a statement from the artist who had decorated the interior with a fresco portrait of Washington and a picture of the battle of the Brandywine. To save her husband's reputation from any sort of stain, Mme de Lafayette had paid for the restoration and met every bill. Only when she had been imprisoned and had to turn in every direction to make sure of her children's subsistence did she beg Gouverneur Morris to procure her a loan from America. Morris offered her a hundred thousand livres in assignats out of his own pocket, and in her extremity she accepted it.

After the long imprisonment and the exile that had followed it, Lafayette returned to France so poor that he could not afford a second plow and had to content himself with tilling only half his land. Nevertheless, with his wife's help, he succeeded in paying all his French creditors by annual instalments. Only Morris's big claim was a terrible worry to them. At the time of the loan the French armies were victorious everywhere, and the assignats stood at par. Since then they had depreciated until they had scarcely one per cent of their purchasing power left, and the family's whole fortune would no longer have sufficed to repay the debt at its original value in American money. When passing through Hamburg, Mme de Lafayette had offered Morris some of the jewelry she had saved as security, and he had had the delicacy to refuse it. But since then Washington had died and Morris had retired; and his French agent pressed the debtors to repay the whole sum, regardless of the actual rate of exchange.

If the case had been taken into court, Morris would have received a hundred thousand francs in assignats, as that was the sum he lent. But in their conscientiousness the Lafayettes had made the greatest sacrifices in order to repay half the sum at its original value. More than that would have made their children and grandchildren penniless. Gouverneur Morris acidly remarked that he would rather do without the fifty thousand livres than have Lafayette's uneasy conscience.

What a humiliation to have to endure this! A letter to a friend revealed the wound:

You know how little I have cared for money all my life. Yet I could do with a little more just now.

There were plenty of veterans of the French Revolution and ex-generals of less importance than Lafayette who could not receive a letter until it had passed through Fouché's hands. Lafayette's incautiousness made their work easy for the spies who lurked everywhere. Bonaparte knew all about the money troubles at La Grange. He also knew all about Lafayette's views on dictatorship. On the morning of the Coup d'Etat the placards in the streets had proclaimed that the new government regarded as inviolable those very principles which Lafayette held to be sacred—the sovereignty of the people, parliamentary control, the freedom of the press, and so on. But since then it had become a punishable offence to make any reference to these promises. Bonaparte intended, like the Roi Soleil, to rule with the whip.

But if he was not keeping his promises, he preferred to give as little prominence as possible to the fact until prosperity had reconciled the bourgeoisie to the dictatorship. Consequently he was delighted to have Lafayette as a frequent visitor to the Tuileries. Nothing could do more to make the military dictatorship respectable than the apparent approval of the "hero of two worlds." Washington's comrade in arms and intimate friend, the protagonist in Europe of the Rights of Man, could never be on friendly terms with the consular régime if its head were a tyrant! To protest when Lafayette was content would be to be more Catholic than the Pope!

But this playacting, in which Bonaparte's southern temperament excelled, did not triumph for long over Lafayette's unshakable fidelity to his principles. In the end there came an irreconcilable breach between the two.

Until that moment came there was nothing that Napoleon left untried to win Lafayette over. No request from the outlawed "traitor" could be presented to Bonaparte without being at once granted. Lafayette was restored to his rank, with all the officers who left France with him; his general's pension of six thousand francs a year constituted an important item in the tiny budget of La Grange. His uncle and aunt Tessé were also allowed to return, and recovered those of their properties which had not been sold. Anyone who could get Lafayette to speak for him was struck off the list of émigrés. Bonaparte was, indeed, glad to add the bearers of great names of the old nobility to his following. He had the weakness of the parvenu for the old families he had looked up to in his youth—Ségur, La Rochefoucauld, Noailles—and was encouraged by his wife, with her royalist outlook, in showing favor to them; even as Empress of France, she felt flattered when the "good" old nobility came to her receptions in the Tuileries. As the daughter of a small port official in the Antilles she remained, like most women who have had a struggle to mount the social ladder, conservative to the marrow.

But this liking for the feudal nobility did not extend to Lafayette, with his evil reputation as a "rebel chief." In talking to him Bonaparte could not forget his revolutionary past, and Lafayette's insistence on his own views gradually began to exhaust the First Consul's stock of patience, never very large. His sallies grew more and more aggressive. On one occasion he said chaffingly to Lafayette:

"You must find the French greatly changed. Their old enthusiasm for liberty has cooled off considerably!"

Lafayette replied that the nation was all the more ripe for receiving its lost rights at the hands of the Consul. The Dictator, a little irritated, retorted:

"Your Parisians are sick of them. The shopkeepers have had enough of liberty!"

So their relations grew more and more strained.

Since Lafayette was indifferent to money, Bonaparte referred as often as he could to his services in securing his release from Olmütz. "What on earth had you done to the people?" he asked once. "It was no easy matter to get you out of their clutches." On another occasion, when the Comte de Provence had written to him to claim the throne of France as its legitimate heir, Napoleon took the opportunity to give Lafayette a transparent reminder of his indebtedness to him:

"God knows, these people hate me like the devil. But that is nothing to their ferocious vindictiveness against you. It was a hard task to overcome the opposition and intrigues at the Viennese Court and make them release you."

Lafayette had had every reason to know how implacably the émigrés hated him. The return of the Bourbons could only injure him; but that fact would not affect his attitude; he was convinced, however, that a restoration of the Bourbons would have even worse consequences for France than the tyranny of Bonaparte.

Had it not been for their mutual toleration on prudential grounds, the final breach would not have been so long in coming. It must be admitted that the autocrat's patience with his stiff-necked opponent deserves admiration. With his penetrating insight into human weaknesses, he knew exactly how to keep Lafayette on his side. Sometimes he would speak with derision of the Bourbon claims, sometimes he would declaim rhetorically:

"It would be a piece of infamous cowardice on my part to give back the power to them! If I whom the Revolution, whom you, whom all the patriots have placed where I stand, were to bring in these people, it would mean delivering you up to their vengeance!"

Fascinated by the fine manners of the *ancien régime,* Napoleon said to his intimates: *"Il n'y a que ces gens qui savent servir"* ("Those are the only people who know how to serve"). But with Lafayette he adopted another tone:

"What are you to do with these people? When I threw open the doors for their return to the army no one moved. But I no sooner open the door of my antechamber than they all come off their perch."

XX. IN DISGRACE

BUT IT WAS IMPOSSIBLE to go on taking all this trouble for nothing! Bonaparte was not accustomed to suing in vain. He instructed his minister of foreign affairs, Talleyrand, to send Lafayette to America as minister. His great popularity could be useful there to the French government.

If ever a proposal could have induced the champion of Liberty to give the support of his name to Bonaparte's tyrannical government, it would be this; the prospect of being able to live in his second and really republican homeland would have been the most likely of all to help him to forget his scruples of conscience. But in America of all places it would be impossible for him with loyalty to his principles to represent a government with no parliamentary control, no free press, and no freedom of opinion.

To avoid an open breach, Lafayette declined on the ground of his wife's ill-health, which made it impossible for her to travel. The pretext had some substance in it, since about the same time Jefferson had offered him the post of governor of the state of Louisiana, which had just joined the Union, and he had been obliged to decline this tempting invitation from his friend for the same reason.

But Consul Bonaparte would not have become Emperor Napoleon if he had allowed himself to be put off by pretexts. He knew perfectly well why Lafayette had refused: he would not represent an autocratic government. The warnings grew more and more pointed. When the English government sent Lord Cornwallis to Paris, Joseph Bonaparte invited the two ex-enemies to dinner. Memories of old times led to a discussion of the republican form of government in America—a delicate question! At their next meeting the First Consul said to Lafayette in a chaffing tone which had an undercurrent of menace:

"I must warn you that Lord Cornwallis declares that you are not yet cured."

Lafayette affected not to notice the underlying seriousness, and gladly seized the opportunity of frankly declaring his opinion. He replied with an air of astonishment:

"Cured? Of what? Of my love for freedom? What is there that could have cured me of that? The misdeeds of terrorists? The murders of my relatives in France, or my imprisonment at Olmütz? Every injustice has only increased my hatred of despotism and oppression."

That was not the tone to which the future emperor was accustomed. His face darkened:

"I must tell you frankly, General Lafayette, that you are too free with your criticisms of the acts of my government. You are lending the weight of your name to my enemies."

This reproof from the mouth of Bonaparte was a compliment, a tribute to the impoverished farmer who had as guests in his little home such men as Charles James Fox and who had friends and admirers all over the world. Who but Lafayette could have given Bonaparte the reply he did?

"What more can I do? I live in the country, in retirement, and avoid any sort of public pronouncement. But if anybody comes to me and asks me whether your arbitrary rule is compatible with my liberal ideas I can only give one answer—'No.' For after all, General, I am quite ready to be prudent, but not to be a renegade."

Bonaparte's eyes flashed:

"Whatever do you mean by 'arbitrary rule'? You cannot deny that in the state of things in which I found France I was forced to take exceptional measures."

It was a duel like that between Hamlet and Ophelia's brother. The buttons were off the foils, and the points were envenomed.

"I am not speaking of any particular period," said Lafayette, "or of emergency measures. What I complain of, and what distresses me, is the whole system—yes, General, the whole system."

The autocrat did not feel sufficiently sure of his self-control to continue the skirmish in person. He sent General Dumas, who had been a friend of Lafayette's since the days of the American war, to convey a final warning to La Grange. Dumas, as instructed, repeated to his friend Bonaparte's own words:

"Nobody likes to be regarded as a tyrant; General Lafayette seems to be calling me one."

This was enough for anyone who knew the character of the First Consul to make it plain that final disgrace was perilously near.

Yet Bonaparte made two more efforts at conciliation. The first was an offer, in his name, from Talleyrand of a senatorship—to the apostle of the sovereignty of the people! The Senate was, of course, recruited from among Bonaparte's most zealous partisans, and its function was to give his decrees the form of laws voted by Parliament. For Lafayette to accept this distinction would have been to deny his whole past. But to refuse it point-blank would be a declaration of war. He therefore made the excuse that he was too exhausted by all he had gone through to feel equal any longer to the exactions of public life: he was like a shipwrecked man who had at last been washed ashore and for the remainder of his days he had only one wish—to live in peace. The next time the two met—the last time for more than ten years—Bonaparte asked Lafayette whether he still felt "too old" for a seat in the Senate.

After that, with the plebiscite in regard to Bonaparte's life consulship, there came open war. On the voting list for his district Lafayette wrote "No," adding:

I cannot vote for a magistracy of this sort until sufficient guarantees of popular liberties have been provided. Then, and then only, I should vote for Napoleon Bonaparte.

But for his Corsican ancestry, Bonaparte need not have taken the slightest notice of the few thousand "Noes" in face of the immense majority of "Ayes." But he carefully examined every list in order to revenge himself. Rouget de l'Isle, the author of the Marseillaise, the stirring rhythms of which had so often led Bonaparte's soldiers to victory, paid for his vote by the loss of his army rank and pension, and after a long life of privation died in utter poverty. Lafayette had not contented himself with saying "No" and publicly giving his reason on the voting list; he had felt that he owed it to the man who had freed him from his captivity in Olmütz, and to his own fixed rule of candor and straightforwardness, to send Bonaparte a private letter in support of his attitude:

It is impossible that you, General, first among an order of men which, for the purpose of comparison and the assignment of relative place, must embrace all ages, should desire that so immense a Revolution, so many sanguinary victories, so much suffering and so many great deeds, should have no other result for the world and for you than to produce a despotic government. The French people have become too thoroughly familiar with their rights to have forgotten them beyond all recalling.

This was war! Every friend who came from abroad to visit Lafayette at La Grange strongly urged him not to remain within Napoleon's reach. The Corsican had not hesitated to arrest the Duc d'Enghien beyond the frontier and to drag him into France for execution; why should he hesitate to have Lafayette put against the nearest barrack wall and shot?

But the hope of seeing France freed some day from her chains, perhaps of taking a part once more in the struggle against oppression, prevented Lafayette from emigrating even after the death of his wife. In his dauntlessness he towered

challengingly over the crowd of bent heads; he was silent and
was far from Paris, but he was still a warning, not to be forgotten by Napoleon, that the love of liberty was not yet entirely stamped out in France.

Napoleon himself realized this, and would have been glad if
Lafayette had gone to America. He gave vent to his irritation
one day in front of the Council of State:

"Everybody in France has learnt better, only one man still
has not, Lafayette! He has never budged an inch. You see
him sitting quietly at home! But I tell you, he is ready to start
again at any moment."

How the emperor would have pounced if he had known that
Lafayette, but a few steps away from the assembled guests, in
the best policed state in the world, where all the walls had
ears, had not been afraid to discuss with General Moreau, in
a window recess, the possibility of a new coup d'état! The
peaceful farmer declared that both the partisans of the Bourbons and the Jacobins were better prepared for the sudden
fall or the death of Napoleon than the Republicans of 1789:
"We too should organize!"

That single phrase would have sufficed for Fouché and
the emperor to build up a charge of high treason ending in
a sentence of death. A ballroom is not the place for dangerous talk of that sort.

General Bernadotte had no more love for the tyrant than
Lafayette had, but he knew how to keep silent, until, after
Lafayette had broken his leg, he was alone with him in his
sick-room. His words were spoken half in jest, but it is significant of the widespread impatience to shake off an intolerable despotism when a general still serving in Napoleon's
army could allow himself to utter them:

"If we three, Moreau, you and I, were to fall from the clouds
into the Place Vendôme, with drawn swords, we might be a
little embarrassed at first at the sight of one another. But who
can say whether the result would not be a revolution?"

Jest or no jest, this remark shows how it was taken for
granted that Lafayette would be ready at any moment to do
his part in the struggle against Napoleon's oppression. What
others could guess was not likely to be any secret from the
ruler. He knew the names of all the people who went to see

the "veteran of Liberty" at La Grange. It was certainly imprudent of Mme de Staël, after she had been exiled by Napoleon, to send letters to the strictly watched house with such
phrases as this:

So long as you are alive, General, I do not entirely despair of mankind.

There are various forms of courage. Napoleon could ride
coolly through a rain of bullets; but when he was crossing the
south of France, escorted by officers of the Allies, in order to
embark for Elba, and found himself surrounded by a raging
populace shouting threats and hatred, he turned as white as a
sheet and changed into the uniform of an English officer. Lafayette could look that myriad-headed hydra in the face without shrinking, could wrest from it its half-dead victims, could
plunge alone into the midst of a murderous crowd like a lion
tamer into the cage. But the hardest of all tests is to endure
constant uncertainty. To know that a danger exists which at
any moment may spring out of the darkness, perhaps within
an hour, perhaps not for months to come, is a thing that demands nerves of steel. This uncertainty made some men come
forward during the Terror with charges against themselves,
preferring to throw away their lives rather than continue to
endure the torture of uncertainty. Lafayette lived for ten
years in this uncertainty at La Grange. Every carriage he
heard approaching might be bringing Fouché's myrmidons.
General Bernadotte, after his election as Crown Prince of
Sweden, paid a farewell visit to Lafayette. At one point in
their talk Bernadotte threw up his hands and exclaimed:
"Votre existence est un miracle!"
And a miracle it was indeed. What was to prevent the emperor, for whom a human life counted no more than a grain
of sand, from getting rid of this troublesome subject with the
aid of his obsequious courts of justice? It was certainly not
magnanimity, for he lost no opportunity of making Lafayette
suffer for his obduracy. For years he prevented the promotion
of young Lafayette, who, as a second lieutenant, was twice
wounded and recommended for distinction, which was refused
on each occasion. Each time promotion papers for the young

man reached his desk the emperor threw them aside. At a review he noticed the badges of a second lieutenant who seemed too old for his rank; when he learned the officer's name he said, shrugging his shoulders:

"*Ah, c'est son fils!*"

At last Georges Lafayette grew tired of being constantly passed over and sent in his resignation. Napoleon gave his permission, without a word of recognition of his services. The young officer returned home, to the joy of his poor mother, who had then but a year to live.

Napoleon himself was to pay dearly in the end for this petty vindictiveness. The army leaders had refused to let this brave young officer carry out the same junior duties year after year and had successively made him their aide-de-camp. So it happened that during a cavalry attack young Lafayette saved the life of Marshal Grouchy. But for the young officer's courage the marshal would have been trampled to death—and another marshal would have been in command of the reserve corps at Waterloo.

It was not out of magnanimity that the unscrupulous autocrat bore with Lafayette's quiet defiance; it was because he respected a force which all through his life he had refused to acknowledge. He knew very well that the "simpleton" would become more dangerous than ever if a martyrdom resuscitated his half-forgotten name. Lafayette's provocative intrepidity annoyed Napoleon, but this despiser of men knew too well the power of ideas—by which he himself had been helped into the saddle. When, on his return from Moscow, he learned of the unsuccessful coup d'état of General Malet, he ordered that Lafayette should be arrested on suspicion of complicity, but he hastily rescinded the order.

In the period of wild profit-seeking which the Empire had brought, the founder and first chief of the National Guard stood out like a living monument of the ragged citizen armies which had had no ambition for conquest or pillage, but only for the liberation of their oppressed neighbors. To touch that monument would be to outrage the memory of the young heroes whose lives had been thrown away for the ambitions of a single man and whose bodies now lay in graves scattered over half of the world.

It was a strange duel, silent but formidable, between the omnipotent emperor and the small landowner whom his faith made invincible! The victor of Friedland, Austerlitz, Wagram, who for fifteen years had stamped out all resistance, had to endure the insolent provocation of the "simpleton's" silent disapproval. Napoleon, who had not been born away from the everyday world, in a royal palace in which none knew the soul of the people, was well aware that violence can avail nothing against the spirit, which can create a thousand new followers for one who is lost. It was the spirit that had enabled him to play so long with crowns, and it was the spirit that destroyed his own crown the day he denied the idea which had made him great.

When the news of the battle of Leipzig reached the owner of La Grange, he had his carriage brought out—ready, as Napoleon had prophesied, "to start again"! The hope of restoring on the ruins of the falling tyranny the free France of his dreams brought back his youth. Enrolled by Liberty at twenty, he hastened to answer the call of his old flag at fifty-one.

BOOK V

Return to Public Life

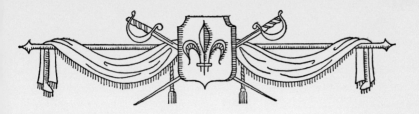

I. THE FALL OF NAPOLEON

EXPERIENCE HAD MADE Lafayette more modest in his expectations. He came from La Grange to Paris with fewer high hopes than in his youth. A good Constitution, a liberal franchise which would give every Frenchman capable of judgment his share of influence over legislation, and, as a basis of it all, the inviolability of the "Rights of Man"—given such a program, he would be contented with any form of government. Only the tyrant, who had reduced half of Europe to subjection and had harnessed the elemental force of the Revolution to his triumphal car, must go if France was to recover. As for the enemies who were marching on Paris from every direction, the nation had no need of the tyrant's help in disposing of them if the whole people once more sprang to arms. Lafayette's son and his younger son-in-law, the Comte de Lasteyrie, had enrolled at once in the National Guard. The younger Latour-Maubourg was serving at the front. Lafayette himself sought the honor of permission to serve as a simple grenadier if the enemy should really threaten Paris.

As always since he had strayed from the battlefields of the New World into the political labyrinth of the old one, Lafayette found himself as much of a stranger in his environment, in the capital of the tottering French empire, as if he had fallen from another planet. How could he make anything of the indescribable confusion everywhere? There were no flames to be seen, and yet there was the same chaos, as if everyone was

317

trying to save his possessions from a vast fire. Marshals and ministers, dukes and counts, Napoleon's own relatives among them—all who owed their fortunes to the empire were running to and fro like ants whose heap has been disturbed. For there was no sign yet of any port on the horizon. All were at sea on board a ship in distress; they could feel her tremors, but nobody could say whether the moment had come to abandon her or where to find safety for their possessions.

Napoleon seemed finished; but would the Emperor of Austria renounce the rights of his daughter and his grandson? If the cables were cut too soon there would be the risk of losing touch with the Regency; an open breach with the father might bring disgrace at the hands of his son. If only the intentions of the Allied sovereigns were known! Even Napoleon's defeat was not final. He had hastily collected a few corps and thrown himself against the enemy, sometimes in front, sometimes in the rear, and was so intimidating the victors that they were already considering marching into Belgium to escape from his formidable blows.

Where was the emperor? His own brother and wife had no definite knowledge! The roads leading to Paris were full of marching troops. A carriage inspected and passed by a Russian, Prussian, Austrian or English patrol might be held up five minutes later by some isolated detachment of Napoleon's troops, and any compromising document or incautious word might mean death.

"Fatherland?" "Tyrant?" "Liberty?" Everybody was full of fine phrases, but only children and simpletons could believe that it was really these abstractions that were at issue while princedoms and great fortunes, distinctions and dignities and high offices were at stake. Woe to those who came too late— and to those who came too soon! Every straw in the wind was watched, every rumor passed all round. Someone had seen Talleyrand smile; someone had had a few words with one of the empress's grooms, who had said that the Court was fleeing, or who had said that it was placing itself under the protection of the Emperor of Austria. Those who had been wildly cursing Napoleon began five minutes later to prostrate themselves before his dynasty—for another five minutes.

In the midst of these people at their wits' ends the naïve

Lafayette went from one to another like a man who has never had the key to the diplomats' cipher and reads their code words literally—"parliamentary government," "freedom of the press" and all the rest. Perhaps it was fortunate for him that at the height of the crisis he was called away to his aunt Tessé and her husband, who were both dying. He spent his days at their side, and after their death his sorrow took his thoughts away from patriotic cares. In his isolation from the council chambers of the great his worst apprehension, like that of the uninformed masses of the faubourgs, was that Paris might be occupied. The simple people who had nothing to lose and nothing to gain revolted against the disgrace of seeing foreign soldiers in Paris after they had spent twenty years in planting the tricolor in every capital of Europe. When the capitulation was signed and Russians, English, Prussians and Austrians marched into the capital, Lafayette shut himself in his room and wept.

He would have done better to stifle his grief. Behind his locked door he missed a lesson in politics which might have been of great value to him a year later, after Waterloo.

The story of Napoleon's abdication at Fontainebleau has been told only too often in all its moving detail, because his vertiginous fall has in itself a tragic quality which awakens compassion, apart from Napoleon's personal character and responsibility. If this aspect of all misfortune is left out of account, there is little grandeur about the closing chapter of Fontainebleau. It is true that Marshal Marmont committed base treachery when he signed the agreement with the Russians, in an inn at La Villette, to withdraw his troops. His action left the road to Paris exposed and left Fontainebleau also unprotected from the enemy. But was not Marmont one of Napoleon's creatures? He was not prepared to go on risking his duchy in Dalmatia and his accumulated millions with the stake of the great gambler, who had already tempted fate too long. Moreover, his treason spared Napoleon many humiliations, for his other Marshals, Masséna, Ney and the rest, had long been putting ruthless pressure on him to abdicate.

This baseness and ingratitude won universal sympathy for the fallen emperor; but perhaps unduly so, for was it not he himself who had set his collaborators an example in cupidity and egoism? Only one of his marshals, Macdonald, who was

partly of Scottish descent, had asked neither titles nor estates
from him; he did his duty as a soldier and was content with
his pay, and when misfortune came he remained loyal. Napoleon, touched, gave him his Egyptian sword of honor, embraced him, and said:

"Take it in memory of me; I have nothing else left to give."

The wave of cupidity that swamped the empire during the
last days of Napoleon's rule was the logical conclusion of the
fifteen years' carnival of greed and oppression, flattery and
unscrupulous self-seeking. Junior officers and men begged Marshal Marmont on their knees to permit them to defend Paris.
Tens of thousands of men wandered through the streets in a
frantic search for arms and leaders. Napoleon paid dearly now
for his mistrust of the common people and his aversion from
any restoration of the National Guard in its original form of
1789. All those whom he had enriched and made great were
now deserting him.

He had been lifted up by the tricolor and by the mass enthusiasm of the Revolution, which had sent him to Italy to
expel the Austrian tyranny. As a disciple of the new evangel
he had founded in Lombardy a realm of freedom and the rights
of man; but he had strangled the idea which had been the basis
of his strength. Of the pure flame which should have lightened
the darkness and brought warmth to the human race he had
made a furnace which had devoured a whole continent, until
the sea of flames at Moscow swallowed up all his conquests in
its turn.

Europe was like a ballroom after the dance, with day dawning over a floor strewn with streamers and trodden flowers,
the atmosphere close and heavy with the fumes of alcohol, a
thing no longer of gayety but of disgust. Like waiters disputing in the next room over tips and champagne bottles, monarchs and ministers were now haggling over their shares of
the yield of the great dance of death.

It was an entirely different picture that Lafayette saw
through the rose-colored spectacles of his unshakable faith in
a better future. Now that the autocrat had been vanquished,
the conquests of the Revolution which had been trodden underfoot must surely recover. Republic or monarchy, what did
it matter? Lafayette wanted to take things up from where

they had stood twenty-five years earlier, when he had had to yield to force. A new Constituent Assembly, a new Fédération, this seemed the only possible path.

II. THE RETURN OF THE BOURBONS

A RETURN of the Bourbons? He had no more thought of it than had the population of Paris or France. Who remembered any longer the two brothers of the guillotined king? They had been twenty-five years out of the country and had themselves given up all hope of regaining possession of their throne. Too often had a little ray of hope appeared, only to fade away again; too often had their impoverished suite had to retreat across Europe before the "usurper." Both princes had a strong distaste for any violent death. The crown might have tempted them, but the walls of Vincennes still bore too plainly the stain of the blood of the young Duc d'Enghien.

Thus the younger of the two brothers only ventured on French soil, with his two sons, when it was almost too late. Every attempt to reach the Allied monarchs failed. The Comte d'Artois, who now called himself "Monsieur," since his brother the Comte de Provence had begun to sign his promissory notes "Louis XVIII," drove cautiously to and fro in the rear of the foreign troops. An officer of the Austrian general staff politely explained to him that "With all respect for hereditary dynasties, I cannot forget that the Empress of France is my emperor's daughter." The Russian officers looked at one another in perplexity; they were inclined to regard this importunate gentleman as an impostor who wanted to make them believe a fairy story of a "legitimate" king of France.

Had France been less weakened by the frightful outpouring of blood in the Napoleonic Wars, she would scarcely have tolerated the intrusion of a dynasty that returned with the baggage wagons of the victorious enemy. The Bourbons bore this germ of destruction within them from the moment of the restoration. They had passed twenty-five years abroad in a sort of lethargy; now they claimed their throne-by-divine-right, and all their traditional rights and privileges, from the Holy Alliance in the spirit of the owner who recovers stolen property at the hands of the police. Their outlook was unchanged; their names alone had changed, and those only in accordance with tradition.

The three returning princes must be allowed the benefit of all these century-old traditions; otherwise their début would have an air of megalomania. Monsieur—the former Comte d'Artois—said in his first proclamation:

Frenchmen, the day of your deliverance is approaching; your king's brother has arrived among you. No more tyranny, no more war, no more conscription, no more exactions! At the word of your sovereign, of your father, may your troubles be effaced by hope, your errors by oblivion, your discussions by the union of which he wishes to be the pledge. He is burning to accomplish the promises he has solemnly made to you, and to signalize by his love and his beneficence the fortunate moment which gives him back his subjects, his children. Long live the King!

His elder son, the ill-fated Duc de Berry, was more concise:

I have come; I am in France! I have come to break your chains; I have come to unfurl the white flag, the spotless flag which your fathers followed with such transports. Rally round it, good Frenchmen! Let us all march together to overthrow tyranny!

Soldiers, I shall not be deceived in my hope; I am the son of your kings, and you are Frenchmen!

Such were the messages addressed on behalf of Louis XVIII to the people whom he had treated as enemies. The youngest of these three heralds of royalty, the Duc d'Angoulême, did not confine himself to words. By a roundabout route he succeeded in reaching Bordeaux, whose rich shippers and wine exporters had lost heavily through the Continental blockade and were therefore hot against Bonaparte. He hastened to offer this great port to the Duke of Wellington and to suggest that he should occupy Bordeaux with his troops! How the English were subsequently to be got out of Bordeaux, and what contributions the inhabitants would have to pay them, were questions about which this French prince did not trouble. After twenty-five years of Bohemian living at the expense of foreign courts he found France an appetizing morsel even without Bordeaux; a ticket of admission to the Tuileries was worth a town!

Lafayette learned of these instructive preparations only after the event, when the reinstatement of the Bourbons was already a settled matter. He had no reason to rejoice at the return of the men who had slandered him to all the sovereigns of Europe and had prevented his release from imprisonment as long as they could. But he clung to the hope he drew from the fall of the military dictatorship; he had too strong a belief in the nation's need of liberty to imagine that the old monarchy could be brought back; he did not realize that in its exhaustion the country asked only for repose.

Mme de Staël's courageous intervention on behalf of the prisoner of Olmütz had further strengthened the bonds of friendship between the Lafayettes and the Neckers. In her salon, the international meeting place of all who were eminent in the world of thought, Lafayette met Czar Alexander, who at that time held the fate of France in his hand. His daily meetings with such men as Benjamin Constant, Guizot, and Humboldt brought the grandson of Empress Catherine into sympathy with the idea of constitutional monarchy, and the most powerful of all autocrats became the protector of French "democracy."

The Czar showed himself delighted to make the acquaintance of the famous "veteran of Liberty." He drew Lafayette aside and described to him the furious resistance the Bourbons were offering to every demand for constitutional guarantees. They protested against the idea that the nation had recalled them! That would have involved a recognition of the right of the people to dispose of the throne. The king claimed to have returned not as successor of his executed brother but as uncle of the son of Louis XVI, who died in the Temple. He dated his reign from the death of that boy, whom the émigrés had regarded as Louis XVII, and issued his first decrees as belonging to the twentieth year after his accession. All that had happened in those twenty years, all the great French victories under the usurper, were null and void; French armies could only fight under the lilies of the Bourbons! The tricolor, the badge of rebellion, must disappear. These externals were of more importance in the eyes of the princes and the émigrés than the essential questions of the form of government. Louis XVIII was ready to give the French a Constitution "spontaneously," to grant a "charter" containing the democratic concessions the Czar wanted for France; he was ready to set limits to his own power and to set up a parliament, so long as he did it all autocratically, in accordance with the old formula—*"Car tel est mon plaisir."*

Lafayette had had experience enough in his own person of the limited and prejudiced outlook of the émigrés, but he refused to abandon hope: "their long years of misfortune must surely have taught them something." The remark startled the Czar into the phrase so often quoted:

"Taught the Bourbons? They have learnt nothing and forgotten nothing!—Only the Duke of Orleans," he added, "has liberal ideas; from all the rest you may expect the very worst."

Lafayette asked in astonishment why, in this case, the Czar had permitted the return of the dynasty. Alexander replied with a sigh that he had been so besieged by the royalists, so misled by false promises, and so tired out by their persistence, that in the end he had contented himself with their promise to grant a charter to the people, some sort of constitution, as "a voluntary gift to celebrate their happy advent."

This form of grant seemed to Lafayette to destroy the value of the "charter." To grant by royal favor rights which the nation had itself won long ago was a reactionary trick which justified all the Czar's apprehensions. Once the Allies had withdrawn their armies and the émigrés established themselves in power, what was to prevent them from sweeping away the last vestiges of the Revolution? Nothing would be easier than to enact new laws destroying the effect of the royal promises and restoring the old absolutism.

The first bitter compromise that Lafayette had to make was the removal of the tricolor from his cap. He had to destroy with his own hands his proudest work, and to put on the white cockade of the Bourbons. His respect for majority rule helped him to make this decision. Did he, perhaps, go too far? There were those who regretted that the prisoner of Olmütz, the seditious leader whom the Comte d'Artois had wanted to see hang, could bring himself to go to court. This attempt at reconciliation was misinterpreted; it was taken for the humiliating eagerness of a man who wanted to cover up his past.

But anyone who knows how greatly it is possible to be influenced by the memories of youth will not doubt for a moment the sincerity of the account given in the *Mémoires de ma main*. He had been born in the same year as the Comte d'Artois, and the two had learned horsemanship together in the royal riding school at Versailles; how could he now, at nearly sixty, remain indifferent at the sudden appearance of the count riding past him in the street? He describes in his memoirs how it took his breath away and made his heart beat fast.

But in their surprise at his visit to the Tuileries the king and Monsieur showed Lafayette no more than an embarrassed politeness. And the gross rudeness of the ultra-royalists saved him from any repetition of this misunderstood courtesy visit. He had lost three of his nearest relatives on the scaffold, had himself been banished and deprived of the whole of his property, and still the rancor of the émigrés was unappeased.

The king, when he was dauphin, had financed the publication of the most scurrilous pamphlets against Marie Antoinette; now he raised a monument to her as a martyr; and he found no praises too fulsome for his murdered brother. His courtesy to Lafayette at the Tuileries was due only to the presence of the Czar and to Lafayette's fame abroad. The Czar was not the only monarch to pay tribute to Lafayette. When the King of Prussia learned that young Latour-Maubourg, son-in-law of his old "guest" in the fortresses of Wesel, Magdeburg and Neisse, had been wounded and taken prisoner, he at once sent Alexander von Humboldt to Mme de Staël with reassuring news and gave orders for the wounded officer to be set free and handed over to his illustrious father-in-law.

This respect for his past protected Lafayette during the first years of Bourbon rule as it had under Napoleon's tyranny. But the zeal of the prefect and the open-handedness of the treasury succeeded in defeating the squire of La Grange in the first election. The "veteran of Liberty" was only able to observe from a distance the disastrous mistakes of the ruler, who allowed himself to be carried by the short-sighted vindictiveness of his entourage into a policy of extreme reaction.

There could be no question of depriving the countless peasants and small farmers of the little patches of land they had bought from the state and cultivated for a quarter of a century as their legal property. Such confiscation of hundreds of thousands of small properties for the benefit of a handful of feudal lords would have been suicidal. It was precisely the mass of ignorant country people who were the surest support of the throne, the bodyguard of the reaction, while the town bourgeoisie, oppressed by the new régime, had become a reservoir of discontent.

The disappointed émigrés would have been glad to revenge themselves on the ennobled commoners' sons who owed their titles and orders, their palaces and their wealth, to their own valor and not to that of their forefathers. But these dukes and counts, boycotted by the Faubourg Saint-Germain, retained their properties and their high commands. The lack of staff officers of unsullied past with war experience compelled the king to appoint the Napoleonic marshals to the important garrisons and military commands.

The only clear field for vindictiveness was furnished by the tens of thousands of commissioned and noncommissioned officers who had shed their blood as obscure heroes in so many battles for France. They were discharged and placed on half pay. Even the brave men of the Napoleonic guard were thrown on the street regardless of their services. When in anxiety for their bare existence they sent a petition to Court—"*Prenez nous, monseigneur, nous sommes des braves gens*"—they received the cool reply that the war was over and there was no more need of "*braves gens.*" With nothing to do, these soldiers in their shabby uniforms sat outside the cafés of their native towns surrounded by police spies.

Lafayette's letters to his friends in America betray his deep disappointment and his growing anxiety at the follies of the government. Soon he was unable to say which was most to be feared: the progress of the royalist reaction or the threatened return of the autocrat, whom the Court in its blindness was furnishing daily with new recruits.

Lafayette went to Paris in January, 1815. There, in Mme de Staël's salon, he met the Duke of Wellington, who had turned his back on the Congress of Vienna and its pretentious diplomats. The mistress of the house had invited the Duc de Riche-lieu, the prime minister, to meet the two, in the hope of effecting a rapprochement. But the gulf was less profound be-tween the ex-American general and the famous Englishman than between the two Frenchmen, one of whom had borne arms against his country with the émigrés and had served Rus-sian absolutism as Governor of Odessa. The Duc de Richelieu, compelled to meet the expense of the campaign and of the oc-cupation of Paris by bleeding the taxpayer, was sacrificing himself to his royal master by serving as scapegoat. France, downtrodden and despoiled, was wrongly throwing the whole blame upon the minister who was imposing the heavy taxation. A heavy, threatening atmosphere of discontent weighed on the country. Lafayette returned to La Grange still more depressed.

III. THE HUNDRED DAYS

LAFAYETTE was not the man to pay much heed to attacks on him. He had set out for the first time to reply to a pamphlet which charged him with having himself organized the flight to Varennes, in order to hasten Louis XVI's fall, when the pen was struck out of his hand by the news of Napoleon's landing.

The flight of the Bourbons was no surprise to him: it was the logical consequence of their follies. But, badly as he had been treated at Court, and little as the régime now again overthrown had been to his taste, he was entirely uninfected by the new enthusiasm for the autocrat. He knew Napoleon too well to believe him converted to democratic principles. Not until Joseph Bonaparte sent an express messenger to summon him to Paris did Lafayette reluctantly leave home for the capi-tal, which he found in transports of enthusiasm for the re-turned leader.

His distrust remained unconquerable, even after the em-peror had had an amendment to the Constitution drawn up by Benjamin Constant, under which he agreed—much as he loathed the idea—to parliamentary control of his govern-ment. Lafayette knew well enough that, once the emperor had crushed the "Holy Alliance" of the enemy, the wolf would throw off the sheep's clothing. But this very expectation made him secure a seat in the new Chamber of Deputies, the Parlia-

ment of the Hundred Days—in which his son sat beside him
for the first time. It was necessary to keep a careful watch on
the autocrat's claws. They were drawn in at present; but every
vote might become of critical importance in the struggle that
would inevitably come against Napoleon's paid retainers, who
were ready to sacrifice all the rights of the nation at their
master's command.

It must have been a trial to Napoleon to have to show politeness to the "ideologist" at the opening of the new Parliament.

"It is a dozen years since I had the pleasure of seeing you,"
he remarked.

"Just a dozen years, sire."

The quiet reply did not make it easy for the emperor to
continue the conversation.

"You are looking younger. The country air has done you
good."

Was Napoleon, who had so entirely unlearned the art of
flattery, trying it now on his adversary? Lafayette's reply was
almost impolite in its brevity:

"Yes, sire, it has done me a lot of good."

If the tone was cool, it was that of the sentinel of 1789 who
held the breach when the foreign mercenaries were posted
around the National Assembly. Courtesies could be exchanged
when the fighting was over! As then he had used the last hours
of freedom to promulgate the Declaration of the Rights of
Man, so now he wanted to utilize all the available time, perhaps
short, to secure the nation's liberties and to lay a firm foundation for the edifice of the future, whoever might come next,
whether Napoleon or the Bourbons.

Then came Waterloo. What next happened in Paris confirmed all his fears more quickly than he had expected.
Scarcely had Napoleon arrived at the Elysée when he began
to demand unlimited authority: without it, he contended, he
could not repel the superior forces of the enemy. That very
night Fouché, Minister of Police (who had become duke of
Otranto), went in haste to Lafayette to tell him that the
emperor was planning the dissolution of the Chamber and the
"temporary" creation of a military dictatorship. Was Fouché
speaking the truth, or was he merely out to bring Lafayette

into action? At a later date Napoleon denied having intended to dissolve Parliament.

In any case, Fouché gained his object. The next morning found the two irreconcilable antagonists at odds. Lafayette impatiently urged the President of the Chamber to open the sitting. A low murmur ran along the rows of seats as he ascended the rostrum. The Don Quixote of liberty had again swung into the saddle and was charging headlong at the tyrant.

But was the tyrant yet stretched defenceless on the ground? All the well-fed Sanchos in the assembly were nervously putting their heads together, concerned for nothing but their own creature comforts. All that was known in Paris was that the emperor had lost a battle; and the city was still full of soldiers obedient to his orders. A wave of his hand and any indiscreet babbler would face a firing party! Only the orator seemed to be unaware of the peril:

"The time has come to rally to the tricolor, the standard of 1789, of liberty, equality, and public order; it is this alone that it is our duty to defend, against encroachments from abroad and against infringements at home!"

Such was the appeal launched over these bent heads by the voice which Lafayette himself called that of a veteran of Liberty: the old friends of the people, he said, might perhaps still recognize it.

Regardless of Napoleon, and without a soldier at his own back, he proposed that the Chamber should be declared to be in permanent session. Whoever might attempt to disperse the representatives of the nation by force should be shot at once for high treason! Not content with this plain allusion to the emperor, he added a demand for a body of troops for the protection of the Chamber:

"The Minister of the Interior is invited to assemble the general staff, commandants, and majors of the Paris National Guard, to advise as to the means of arming and bringing to the maximum strength this citizen guard, whose patriotism and zeal, tested twenty-six years ago, offer a sure guarantee of the liberty, the property, and the tranquillity of the capital, and the inviolability of the representatives of the nation."

The effect of this determined speech was astonishing. After twenty-four hours of the indecision of a herd of sheep without a bellwether, the majority of the House greeted the bold proposals with storms of applause. *"Aux voix! Aux voix!"* ("Vote, vote!") was shouted on all sides. Napoleon's minions and his brothers turned pale but did not venture on an amendment. The resolutions were adopted unanimously, with a few abstentions, and were promulgated by placard throughout Paris.

At once Napoleon found himself in something like isolation. He had to choose between giving in to Parliament and causing a civil war inside the city, which might at any hour be occupied by the enemy. He raged when the Chamber's rebellious resolutions were laid before him, but he did not venture on any strong measures; he seemed prostrated by his defeat. He had lost his confidence in his star, and with it his energy. Benjamin Constant relates that the emperor followed the discussions with indifference, as though he were no longer concerned.

Fouché, on the contrary, went to work with the utmost energy. His own power was at stake, and the seventeen millions he had amassed while minister of police. His only serious rival, Prince Talleyrand-Périgord, was at the Congress of Vienna, busy selling his vote to the highest bidder without much care for Louis XVIII's interests, when the news of Napoleon's landing dispersed the Congress and left it to the generals to speak the next word. The absence of his formidable rival assured Fouché the opportunity of regulating his account with the Bourbons.

The bill against him was a heavy one. The Duc d'Otranto, when he was merely Fouché, member of the Convention, had had royalist nobles shot in batches because the guillotine worked too slowly for him. Still worse, he had voted for the execution of King "Louis the Last." Nothing of less value than the crown of France could be offered in settlement of such debts. Louis XVIII would not search too closely for bloodstains on the hands that gave him back his kingdom.

In any event it was safer to push forward the enthusiastic Lafayette. It was only necessary to feed him with the old slogans, "sovereignty of the people," "parliamentary control," "rights of man," and he would risk his head for them without a thought.

The ministers, trained only in obedience to their master and not in taking responsibilities, were anxious and vacillating at the evening session. Their only reply to the excited demands for Napoleon's abdication was a perplexed silence. The emperor's younger brother, Lucien Bonaparte, sprang to his feet and tried to save the throne. In time of need, he exclaimed, the only salvation lay in holding together. If France abandoned her emperor she would be dishonoring herself. Lafayette, carried away by his indignation, rushed up to the rostrum and thundered back:

"Do you dare to reproach us with failing in our obligations of honor, our duty toward Napoleon? Have you forgotten all that we have done for him? Have you forgotten that the bones of our children and brothers are strewn everywhere in witness to our loyalty—in the desert sands of Africa, on the banks of the Guadalquivir and the Tagus, along the Vistula and in the icy wastes around Moscow? During the past ten years and more, three millions of Frenchmen have lost their lives in the service of the man who now wants to enter into a struggle against the whole of Europe. We have done enough for him! Our duty now is to save our country."

Marmont's treachery had brought about the abdication at Fontainebleau, and Grouchy's hesitation the defeat at Waterloo; Lafayette's denunciation now brought about Napoleon's second and final renunciation of the throne. The tumultuous applause from the assembly made a retort impossible. All that Lucien Bonaparte could do was to gain a few hours by the proposal to hold a council of ministers that night, to be attended by delegations from the Upper and Lower houses.

As third vice-president of the Chamber, Lafayette could not be excluded from the meeting, and his presence made all compromise impossible. He knew Napoleon's quickly changing moods too well to abate his demands.

Benjamin Constant, the last bosom friend of Madame de Staël, in common with whom he had been exiled from the empire, had long been living at Weimar in the company of Schiller, Goethe, and Wieland, and had attacked the usurper as a "modern Genghis Khan." Weak as he was gifted, he fled at the first news of the landing at Fréjus, but turned back and became secretary to Napoleon, who used the well-known name as an advertisement of his conversion to democracy.

While the council was arguing the question of the abdication behind the lighted windows of the Tuileries, Napoleon was walking in the gardens with Benjamin Constant. A large crowd had gathered in front of the railings, and as often as the emperor's figure became visible the ever ready sympathy of the crowd made itself heard in the old cry of *"Vive l'Empéreur!"*

Napoleon pointed triumphantly to the street and said to Constant:

"Look at that! Those are not the people whom I have loaded with honors and wealth! What do they owe to me? I found them poor and left them poor. If I wished, if I would permit it, in an hour the rebellious Chamber would no longer exist. But no—the life of one man is not worth that price. I have not come back from Elba to inundate Paris with blood."

What a change of tone from Napoleon the conqueror!

Was it from calculation that he showed himself, provoking the cheers of the crowd in order to encourage his adherents? Who can say? In any case, Lafayette was unmoved by the demonstration. He would continue to demand the abdication even against the will of these grown-up children, who kneel in adoration before the men whom they have elevated into idols at the cost of their own suffering, just as the Fiji Islander prays to the wooden figure he has carved with his own hands.

Next morning the Chamber was raging with impatience when it learned that the abdication had not yet been signed. Lafayette sent Constant a note declaring that he would demand the deposition of the emperor. Then at last Napoleon made up his mind, signed his abdication, and immediately afterwards left the palace. He went to Malmaison, where he had spent his happiest hours with Josephine. He had given her this domain at the moment of their divorce; during her first occupation of it as ex-empress the Czar Alexander had been her guest there. At the time of the return from Elba she was dead, and her successor, the virtuous Marie Louise, had fled from Napoleon with his son and her lover. Only his adopted daughter, Hortense, who had become his brother's wife, walked through the park with him. She pressed upon the man who had enriched so many the diadem of brilliants she had received from him when she was crowned Queen of Holland.

IV. BETWEEN WATERLOO AND FOUCHÉ

NAPOLEON WAS FORGOTTEN in Paris before his carriage reached Malmaison. The cause of the war had been removed; the urgent thing now was to stop the advance of the Allied armies, to ward off the affliction of a second occupation of Paris; after that the nation could choose its new form of government. To secure this right for the people was Lafayette's weightiest care. Meanwhile, a provisional government, consisting of three members of the Lower House and two of the Upper, was set up by Parliament.

It was a simple task for the Duc d'Otranto to push aside the inconvenient zealot until the deal with the Bourbons was concluded. As minister of police he was familiar with every intrigue in progress and every interest concerned, and easily procured a majority for himself and his candidates. Lafayette was not the man to go canvassing for votes, and he found himself in a minority. He was entrusted by the provisional government with the pressing business of arranging an armistice. Two fellow commissioners, with Benjamin Constant as secretary, were to accompany him to the headquarters of the Allied monarchs. With Napoleon's abdication the common aim of the Allies had been gained, and a further advance was surely unnecessary. Lafayette probably himself preferred this important mission to a seat in the provisional government. Power he had never sought, and he would be much more drawn to the task of saving France from the ravages and the disgrace of invasion.

Fouché, the ex-Oratorian priest, even now that he was Duc d'Otranto, had no understanding of military affairs; but he knew human nature too well to believe seriously that the monarchs, and particularly their generals, would allow themselves to be persuaded to a right-about-turn within a few days' march of the enemy capital. Each of the Allies would want to be the first to enter Paris. It would be easier to swim up the rapids of Niagara than for the commission to force its way through the advancing troops to the headquarters of the monarchs.

Leaving Paris on June 25, 1815, a hundred times challenged, examined, and in danger of arrest, the two carriages rocked along the roads for five whole days. What did the officers of the Allied armies care for a scrap of paper drawn up by an unknown authority calling itself "provisional government"? Not until the 30th did Lafayette, the Comte Dupont, and the Duc de la Rochefoucauld-Liancourt reach the Allied headquarters at Hagenau.

The first disappointment for Lafayette was a refusal from the Czar to receive him. With an assurance of his undiminished personal esteem, Alexander informed Lafayette that the Allied monarchs had given a mutual undertaking not to negotiate with the enemy except in common, and he would therefore be breaking his word if he received the gentlemen. Taught by the experience of the first occupation, Metternich had resorted to the device of this mutual undertaking in order to prevent any fresh divagations on Alexander's part. The same pretext slammed the doors of the other monarchs and ministers in the face of the commissioners. When at last they succeeded in inducing some isolated representative of one or another of the Allied nations to negotiate with them, this concession proved to be nothing but a trick, as the errand devised by Fouché had been. The Allies' purpose was to secure time for their generals to reach Paris; meanwhile the negotiators were detained at headquarters with noncommittal discussions. Blücher's one concern was now to march into Paris before Wellington. After winning this race Blücher was nicknamed "Marshal Forward" in Germany; but he had been prompted by practical considerations as well as by military ambition, as proved by the two millions he at once extorted from the city. Marshal Forward was no less ardent a gamester than commander and took little of these two millions back to Germany; he lost most of the money in the capital he had conquered.

Strategically his haste would have cost him still more if Fouché had allowed himself to be persuaded to restore to Napoleon the command of the troops in and around Paris. The English under the Duke of Wellington were still two days' march from the city when Marshal Forward, with barely thirty thousand Prussians, arrived before the gates. The French troops of the line had poured into Paris after the defeat, and they alone were some forty thousand strong. In addition there were the National Guard and the garrison of the city. Napoleon's system of defeating his foes in detail would have been applied this time without any necessity for forced marching by night: Blücher had seen to that. He had effected his own isolation, and a French force of more than eighty thousand men would have annihilated the thirty thousand Prussians—if the Duc d'Otranto had not had an interest in the Bourbons. Napoleon sent courier after courier galloping from Malmaison to Paris, imploring permission to seize the opportunity. He swore to lay down the command again immediately and return to private life if he were but allowed to annihilate the Prussians, who had decided the issue against him at Waterloo and had now themselves walked into a trap! But the cold, glaucous eyes of the Duc d'Otranto were fixed on the compass of his own private interests. Blücher remained unmolested.

Meanwhile the negotiators at Hagenau wore themselves out in futile debates. With the tenacity of the shipwrecked sailor who at last has a glimpse of the coast, Lafayette clung to the plank of his old hopes—the sovereignty of the people, a constituent assembly, the unrestricted right of the nation to choose its own form of government. With Bonaparte beaten and the Bourbons fugitives, France had this time a genuine chance of freedom, if only the autocratic monarchs would desist from meddling in her affairs.

Hard words often passed. England's representative, Lord Stewart, demanded, as the first condition of peace, the surrender of Napoleon to the Allies. Lafayette indignantly retorted:

"I am astonished, my lord, that you should propose such a cowardly act to the French nation, and still more that you should put the proposal to one of the Olmütz prisoners."

But the enemy delegates were not interested in the tone or even in the subject of the discussions: their only concern was to keep them going. Scarcely had their crowned masters left Hagenau for Paris when Lord Stewart broke off the negotiations with the declaration that he had no authority to enter into binding obligations. Why, in that case, he had entered into discussions at all he did not explain; he hastened after Wellington, and left the French commissioners to return to Paris with an English escort.

When Lafayette's carriage reached the city, the capitulation had been signed some hours since, and the Duc d'Otranto had come to terms with the Bourbons. Yet that same evening the duke enacted the farce of holding a full council, at which he emphatically concurred in Lafayette's declaration that all negotiations with the enemy must be carried on with the knowledge of the popular assembly and that any personal agreement behind its back would be infamous.

Next morning the members found Parliament closed, with guards before the gates. The Chamber was declared dissolved by order of Louis XVIII, and Lafayette had the painful experience of seeing the way blocked for the representatives of the people by the National Guard which he had founded. He stated aloud that he was going home and would be glad to receive any of his colleagues as his guests. But what could a few members of Parliament do without any armed force behind them? The dream of a new France, free and democratic, was at an end.

As the park gate of La Grange closed behind the disappointed and duped Lafayette, the night of the darkest reaction fell over the whole of Europe. Narrowness, greed, and oppression ruled once more, ably brought into play by means of Prince Metternich's knowledge of human nature. If anyone spoke too loudly of "freedom of the press" or any such revolutionary idea, echo replied from every corner of Europe: "Guillotine!" The tragic word sufficed to reconcile the terrified citizen to every wrong. He had only the choice between putting his own head under the knife and foregoing every protest, however mild, against wrong and oppression; and he preferred to live.

Absurdly primitive as this dilemma sounds, the method has never failed through all history. With this sort of skeleton in the cupboard to disturb the sleep of the peaceful citizen, there is no wrong, no retrogression, nothing at all that cannot be carried through without opposition!

But the "veteran of liberty" was not sitting idly at La Grange. All young hearts with secret enthusiasms were turning toward him like sunflowers. At sixty the knight-errant of liberty became the conspirator, secretly whetting his dagger in the darkness, ready to gamble with the executioner for his head. No stake was too high, no venture too dangerous, so long as the game offered the old prizes.

V. THE OLD CONFLICT FLARES UP

THE BOURBONS did not succeed in muzzling their adversary for long. Lafayette's constituents, intimidated and watched like criminals, did not at first dare to vote for him when the vindictive régime of the second restoration commenced after Waterloo. But the growing pressure produced counter pressure, and the country house of the muzzled hero of liberty gradually became a place of pilgrimage. The youth of the nations, threatened everywhere with prison and gallows, crossed the frontiers and organized resistance; and all news of this came to La Grange as to a center of the movement.

By the end of 1817 things had gone so far that all the tricks and threats of the prefects were impotent to prevent Lafayette's return to Parliament. Elected by two constituencies at the end of 1818, he returned to the arena with undiminished ardor. Lady Morgan stated, after a visit to La Grange, that there was not a wrinkle on his forehead, and he soon showed in his public appearances that his temperament and his faith had remained equally youthful.

The news of Lafayette's reëlection was disturbing to the king. Paris society fought for seats at the opening of Parliament. Everyone wanted to see the hero of the Fédération facing Louis XVIII; it would be so exciting to hear him swearing fealty to the Bourbons!

Not only was the king alarmed, but the whole ultra-royalist majority clenched their fists when, on March 22, 1819, the ghost of the Revolution mounted the rostrum to defend the freedom of the press, after an interval of thirty years. The success of the bloodthirsty reaction in Spain, Portugal, Poland and Italy was humiliation for the émigrés, who in France still had to put up with attacks from the unsubdued Left.

As though his challenging defence of the insubordinate press were not enough, Lafayette took every opportunity outside Parliament to stir up the public against the existing régime. His reappearance brought unmeasured attacks from the reactionary papers. The editor of the *Ami du Roi* went so far that the public prosecutor was obliged to proceed against him for libel. But Lafayette smoothed the matter over. "Why not?" he asked, and he published his letter to that official in the much abused journals of the Left:

I have not asked any writer to speak well of me, nor disturbed anyone for having written evil. . . . I deprecate any prosecution.

In vain was he greeted with an outburst of wrath from the majority every time he rose to speak, in vain were insults and false accusations hurled at him. Lafayette was not the man to be intimidated when such matters as the restriction of the franchise were in question. The game pursued its normal course; the more the established rights of the people were whittled away the stronger became the forces of resistance. The tax qualification for the franchise was increased again and again. Even double votes were conferred on the electors whose interests were bound up with the régime through their rank and fortune, to entrench it against the growing opposition.

How could the foremost champion of civic equality remain a silent witness of this demolition of his work? Until the new elections in 1824, for six whole years, the "ultras"—the ultra-royalists—had to put up with Lafayette's attacks. He was now handling words as he had formerly handled the sword. He was no gifted orator, like Mirabeau or Vergniaud, but he was never short of a reply to any interruption. He knew only too well the secret of the scarecrow used to secure obedience; in his letters to his friends he accuses the Terror of having soiled with blood the ideals that had been so acclaimed, and of having presented the reaction with an arsenal of counter arguments. But nothing, not even the execution of the three women in his own family, guillotined one after another, could dim his judgment. His advocacy of the rights of the nation was interrupted by a royalist priest with a shout of:

"You want to have the guillotine again!"

"The guillotine," he promptly retorted, "is no more the Revolution than the massacre of St Bartholomew is the Catholic religion."

During the first two years of this unequal struggle the progressive minority used no weapon but the spoken and printed word. Lafayette's correspondence with his American friends contains only an irony without bitterness, and an unshakable confidence in gradual progress: even if the government did everything the émigrés asked of it, the new spring might be postponed, but not prevented. But, as so often in history, the violence of a hothead brought disaster to a whole nation. The young Duc de Berry, the elder son of Monsieur, and perhaps nearer to the throne than his father, who was already sixty-three, was stabbed in front of the opera house while assisting his wife into her carriage. The duchess was pregnant with her first child, the future Duc de Bordeaux. The deed was therefore utterly pointless and merely delivered the people over to the vengeance of the reactionary aristocracy.

The theater was quickly emptied; the dying man was taken to the royal box. While he lay there, bleeding to death, he begged the king, who had hurried to the spot, to pardon the murderer. With his last breath he implored his father and his crowned uncle not to avenge murder with murder, and he sank back comforted when Louis XVIII promised to fulfill his request—a promise he did not keep.

For the entourage of the former Comte d'Artois the father's grief was an unhoped-for pretext. Reactionary more from narrow pride than from vindictiveness, Monsieur allowed himself to be pushed by his adherents into demanding the dismissal of the so-called "moderate" ministry. Louis wept when he had to get rid of his favorite, but he could not refuse his unhappy brother's request, and could not, as the victim's uncle, ignore the charge that his government's forbearance had caused a fresh outbreak of terrorism, and had cost his nephew's life.

The incurable delusion that ideas can be got rid of by the use of force, that thought can be conquered by fisticuffs, opened the way for the accumulated vindictiveness of the "ultras." There was a shower of royal ordinances, written with the dripping dagger of the assassin, and giving a free hand to all the prefects and other representatives of the régime.

Never has a commonplace murder, which even the best administration cannot prevent, been used as argument against the established order; but against progress the mad deed of a

political fanatic is taken as sufficient justification for unlimited measures of suppression.

VI. THE PERIOD OF CONSPIRACIES

AFTER THE MURDER of the Duc de Berry, early in 1820, a new
period of oppression set in in France. All liberties were suppressed; the citizen was reduced once more to vassalage, and
the country ranged itself with the other absolutist, police-
ridden states of Europe. Light and shade are not more indis-
solubly connected than the abuse of power and the growth of
subterranean conspiracies, the last desperate resource of the
oppressed. If a nation is being throttled, it can no more be
particular in its choice of defence than a man grappling with
a thug. From Madrid to Warsaw, from Naples to Amsterdam,
and now throughout France as well, groups of political desperadoes were lurking in secret hiding places, ready to give
their lives if only they could destroy the executioners of their
friends and brothers and their country. Like two spiders' webs
closely involved together, the networks of the police spies and
of the conspirators stretched from end to end of the Continent.

And without any move on his own part, the first herald of
the rights of man became the patron saint of all exiles. The
Italian republican movement of the Carbonari spread to the
French youth, and it was natural that Lafayette, with his
record of nearly fifty years of steadfastness, should be regarded
as the head of all the liberal secret societies. Too poor to assist
the persecuted patriots with large sums, the lifelong enemy of
oppression joyfully seized every opportunity of giving his
personal support, at any rate, to the "inalienable rights of
man." Immediately after the assassination of the Duc de Berry,
when the reactionary Terror began, Lafayette hurled his profession of faith at the raging "ultras" in the Chamber:

The Revolution is the victory of right over privilege; it is the
emancipation and development of the human faculties, the restoration of the peoples; and that is so true that the friends of liberty
have always been, and still are, hated by the opponents of the Revolution in proportion to the efforts they have made to prevent it from
being soiled by crime and disfigured by excess.

It had always been Lafayette's habit, to his own injury and often also to that of his country, to meet the foe with open visor, and it was not his fault but that of his adversaries that at the age of sixty-five he became a conspirator. As the secret leader of the Carbonari and of the "society for the protection of the freedom of the press," he was unjustly accused of sending young men to their death while he himself remained in safety. How little Lafayette troubled about his own safety is shown by a saying of the rich banker Laffitte, who became later his most valuable assistant in the final struggle against the Bourbons. Lafayette took so little trouble to conceal his intercourse with political suspects, under the very eyes of the police, that Laffitte exclaimed:

"You are a statue in search of a pedestal! And you would let a scaffold serve for it."

Lafayette merely answered his friend with a smile, but in his family circle he once said openly:

"I have had a long life, I think I might worthily finish my career on the scaffold, as a sacrifice for Liberty."

This was no mere bravado; the conspirators were staking their lives. This was shown by the unsuccessful coup to which the execution of the four young sergeants of La Rochelle has given a melancholy fame. But plots of the Carbonari had been betrayed before this, at the cost of young lives. Lamartine says: *"Les idées végètent de sang humain"* ("Ideas are nourished on human blood"). Like the Minotaur, Liberty feeds on the bodies of human beings in the bloom of youth. Every step forward, every little addition to the common good, has cost blood.

The sixty-five-year-old leader, of whom every child in France knew, could not do the work of the young advance guard, and they took their secret to the grave; no promise could induce them to betray the honored veteran. The four young sergeants too, and an officer accomplice, went to death without speaking. But it was through no effort of Lafayette's that he escaped the executioner. Providence still had work for him to do, and itself intervened.

He had been chosen as head of the provisional government which was to conduct the business of state until a freely elected National Assembly could decide on the form of government; and he had to travel from La Grange to Alsace, half

across France. In various garrisons, officers and N.C.O.'s had
been won over to the plot. They were to take action as soon
as the new government was proclaimed at Belfort.

The journey led very close to the gallows. For all that,
Lafayette's only son sat at his side. It went without saying
that he should. But as the horses were starting his old valet
Bastien jumped onto the box unbidden. Lafayette stopped the
carriage, took the faithful servant aside and warned him of
the journey's dangers.

"I know where we are going," said the old man, "but do
not trouble about that. I am going on my own account. It
fits in with my opinions."

And he went back to the box.

The government had long known all about the conspiracy,
but it was waiting to catch all the participants together. The
Lafayettes would have walked into the trap if it had not been
the night of December 29–30 that had been selected for the
attempt at Belfort. Christmas Eve, so fateful a date in Lafayette's life, was, as we know, both his son's birthday and the
day of his wife's death. He had never got over his loss, and
this day belonged always to the dead. Everything in her death
room remained untouched; the entrance was walled up; but
on the anniversary of her death Lafayette would open a concealed door and shut himself in the room until the evening.
He could not disturb this hallowed tradition even for the
sake of his fatherland or of Liberty. For this reason he did not
start on the journey to Belfort until he had paid his tribute
to the dead; and this delay saved father and son, as though
her hand had stretched from the grave to ward off the danger from them.

At a few hours' distance from Belfort two students galloped
up to them with the news that everything had been betrayed.

The tardy warning would have been of little avail but for
the past of the "hero of two worlds," which provided a bodyguard for him in the shape of his friendship with all the great
statesmen of the New World. The government and the Court
would have been only too glad to put an end to the old rebel's
subversive activities. Leaving La Grange on Christmas Day,
and arriving at the country house of a friend, an opposition
member of Parliament, shortly before the time at which the

plot was to be carried out—how could father and son persuade anyone that they had driven through half of France simply to pay a visit? It was perfectly well known, of course, in Paris that Lafayette had been warned at the last moment, had left the Belfort road, and had spent a few days with his friend as a pretext. But without documents and evidence definitely convicting him of high treason, it was preferred to take no notice. Every gray hair on his head was protected by the respectful admiration of thousands, and not only in the New World. With the steady exacerbation of the struggle between the crown and the constantly growing number of its rebellious subjects, the old halo around Lafayette's name had acquired fresh radiance.

If his great fortune had returned to him with his fame, the four sergeants of La Rochelle would have escaped alive; the governor of the prison was ready to flee to America with the four victims placed in his charge, if he were assured a sufficient sum to make a fresh start. Unfortunately, only 60,000 francs in gold could be got together, of which Lafayette provided more than 40,000. The governor's salary was 20,000 francs a year, and the offer was not sufficiently tempting. He preferred to make a pretence of agreeing. Just as the last coin was being handed over to him, the police laid hands on the money and the intermediaries. General Dupont, who was to have gone over to the rebels with his whole garrison, was also executed. But none of the condemned would admit that Lafayette had had any part in the matter. Only the public prosecutor accused him and certain of his parliamentary associates of getting the young hotheads into trouble and then leaving them to their fate. As a protest against this insulting accusation, Lafayette demanded in Parliament the cancellation of his immunity, and published in the papers his letter to the public prosecutor in which he asked to be placed in the dock. Laffitte had spoken truly. But though everyone knew that it was only proof of Lafayette's undoubted complicity that was lacking, his adversaries were not willing to supply him with his pedestal, which would only damage themselves and raise the condemned man to the immortality he desired.

It cannot be said that Lafayette made it easy for the government to spare him. He lost no opportunity of stirring up further the accumulated wrath of the reactionary majority against himself. For a long time, in spite of all restrictions of the franchise, the number of the opposition members had been steadily increasing. Thus Manuel was reëlected in spite of all the efforts of the government. After Waterloo he had twice protested against the restoration of the Bourbons, and again in 1822 he had the boldness to declare in the House that it was only with repugnance that France had suffered the return of Louis XVIII. Regardless of the close ties of relationship between Ferdinand and the French dynasty, he characterized the bloodstained rule in Spain as "odious," and in spite of furious protests from the Right he courageously repeated the expression. On this he was excluded from the House as "unworthy" and his election declared void. He succeeded, however, unnoticed by the doorkeepers, in getting again to his seat at the next sitting. No threats from the president were of any effect, and a patrol of the National Guard had to be fetched to remove him by force.

The National Guard had been founded by Lafayette to protect the rights of the nation, and to see it performing policeman's work against the nation's representatives was too much. Sixty-six years old as he was, and deprived of all command for decades, Lafayette stood up from his seat as if in reminder of the past. He did not speak a word; he did not need to. The leader of the patrol hesitated; his men stopped. As though the walls of the chamber had opened and shown, behind the towering veteran, the picture of the Champ de Mars with the four hundred thousand cheering witnesses of the Fédération, the soldiers stood petrified. Their leader remembered the American battlefields and the Olmütz prison and stood there unable to proceed.

All the punishments threatened by the military code could not prevent open disobedience. With rage the majority of the house saw the armed forces, held in leash by a look from Lafayette, refuse orders.

Police had to be summoned in place of the citizen soldiers, to drag Manuel from the hall. The whole opposition, led by Lafayette, followed him. Some eighty members refused to attend the Parliamentary sittings any longer. The *Moniteur* and the other papers friendly to the government published the

order of the day which severely pilloried the disobedience of
the leader of the patrol and announced his punishment. In
reply, the *Constitutionnel* inserted a protest from Lafayette
against that undeserved aspersion on a "most praiseworthy"
deed. Instead of prosecuting him for his praise of military insubordination, amounting almost to an indirect incitement to
insurrection, the public prosecutor contented himself with
making the editor of the paper responsible for the contents
of the communication. Lafayette publicly challenged the
authorities to punish him for his utterances, and not the innocent instruments, but without result. Government and crown
avoided coming to grips with this fearless adversary.

In the long run these provocations would have been bound
to end in a trial of strength which would have brought the
"statue" to its bloodstained pedestal. At the new elections,
early in 1824, the government exerted its whole strength to
get its candidate into the Chamber in place of Lafayette. After
six years of uninterrupted struggle its inconvenient opponent
found himself again disarmed, and driven back from the public eye behind the gate of La Grange.

Louis XVIII and his ministers breathed more freely—and not
only they, but all the relations and friends of the indomitable
fighter. His admirers in America, ex-Presidents Adams and
Jefferson, had watched his dangerous activities with alarm,
and his loss of his Parliamentary mandate was not enough to
reassure them. They knew Lafayette too well and saw only one
way of keeping him out of danger—to remove him from the
arena!

After an inquiry in his own name, and Lafayette's acceptance, President Monroe, at the instance of Congress and in
the name of the whole American nation, addressed an invitation to the friend of Washington to come and see in its flower
the great state he had helped to found. The government of
the United States asked its guest to decide for himself the
European port at which he would prefer to embark, so that a
warship could be sent for him.

Disarmed in France, Lafayette could not resist the temptation of seeing with his own eyes the wonderful prosperity of
the only democratic state in the world and the happiness of
its free and equal citizens before old age made him too frail

for the journey. He took ship for America, for the fourth and last time, in an American merchant vessel, with his son, his secretary Levasseur and the faithful Bastien.

VII. ANTÆUS

EVERYBODY KNOWS the old myth of Antæus, son of Earth, who drew fresh strength from contact with his mother every time an adversary threw him to the ground. Lafayette, thrown down in the electoral contest by the maneuvers of the government, recovered his strength like Antæus. He had no suspicion of the great struggle which was awaiting him on his return to France. Providence, always indulgent to him, permitted him to pass a full year recruiting his forces, and restored the brightness of his aureole in anticipation of the duel he was to fight at seventy-three with a king of the same age.

On August 15, 1824, all the windows of the city of New York shook with the salvos fired from Fort Lafayette, as the fort saluted its "godfather" on his return to America. The Puritan Sunday was a day of absolute rest, and Lafayette remained until the next morning on Staten Island, as the guest of the Vice-President of the United States. Not until Monday did he cross the Hudson, escorted by an immense crowd of official and private craft of all sizes.

Behind the military cordon on the landing place there pressed forward a crowd of many hundreds of thousands, and flowers rained down on the old man. The soldiers had affixed to their tunics cards with the inscription "Welcome Lafayette!" The Mayor of New York greeted him in the name of the new and wonderful country, now arrived at maturity and bursting with confidence and energy, which was waiting to welcome the witness of its birth.

The first celebrations of the reunion lasted four days and four nights. At the banqueting tables, spread for a thousand guests, the old general, now only a few days from his sixty-seventh birthday, endured the swirling storm of speeches and public acclamation as once he had faced semistarvation snowed up in camp at Valley Forge. Everywhere he was accompanied by the invisible spirit of the old friend who had been as a father to him: General Washington, already a hero of myth, looked down with his wise and benevolent smile on this French-man, still full of the generous enthusiasms of youth, who had once helped him to create on this earth "a place of refuge for all the burdened and oppressed."

This forest fire of enthusiastic thanksgiving spread from town to town through a whole year, and to the most distant settlements in the Union. As "the nation's guest" Lafayette traveled in his coach throughout the territory of the States, followed everywhere by the acclamations of the people. Through three hundred and eighty days and nights they tire-lessly overwhelmed with honors of every sort the man who, half a century earlier, had shed his blood for their nation.

It was by a significant chance that the first half of this un-exampled triumphal procession took place under the Presi-dency of Monroe. The Monroe Doctrine drove a wedge between the Old World and the New, since there could be no community between America's free citizens and the enslaved states of European despotism. While Napoleon had been press-ing millions of men into military service and sacrificing whole armies every year to his ambition and greed, the seed of the War of Independence had yielded rich harvests. In Washing-ton's day the monarchs of the old hemisphere had sought to isolate their states from the center of infection of Freedom; now Monroe had sought to exclude from America the in-tolerant spirit of the police régime which was making of the whole continent of Europe a vast prison. Without the shedding of a drop of blood the territory of the United States had doubled in extent through the simple force of attraction of the principles of freedom. The great state of Louisiana had been freed from the war god, from Napoleon, without the expenditure of a single human life—bought for a sum of money.

There were, indeed, still colored men in slavery, and hostile Indian tribes; but the time was not far off when white men would pour out their blood in streams in the struggle for the extension of the "inalienable rights of man" to slaves who were being exploited and maltreated like beasts of burden. For the American citizen "independence" was no empty word; he was nobody's "subject." Great as was the difference between the life of the rich and the desperate struggle for existence of the poor, the human right to "fair play" in the competition for success, free from constitutional hindrances, had at least liberated even the poorest tramp from the crushing burden of hopelessness. The barriers of birth had been removed; everyone could find some consolation for privations in the equality of opportunity under which he might, perhaps, himself one day fill the highest office in the state.

This contrast with the hopeless state of the subjects of absolute governments in Europe brought home to all, even to the simple farmers living hard lives in the most distant log cabins, how much they owed to their benefactor Lafayette. Everybody knew, and could appreciate from his own experience, the privations Lafayette had endured at Valley Forge, snowbound in his canvas tent in the virgin forest. This rich French count had voluntarily abandoned the paradise of Versailles to endure these privations in winter quarters and had shed his young blood at Brandywine for the liberation of the American people; and he was idolized for it. There still lived up and down the country a few veterans of the War of Independence, but none of them had been a general at twenty and an intimate friend of George Washington! To the people of the United States Lafayette was not merely a guest: he seemed like a witness arisen from the grave to tell of the glorious past, almost a saint. The farmers came in from many miles around the still widely separated towns; women asked a saintly blessing on their children; there burst from twenty million hearts a tornado of gratitude which knew no cessation until Lafayette departed again from America.

He spent his sixty-seventh and sixty-eighth birthdays as the guest of the New World, and every morning, noonday and evening between these two signposts of his life was a link in a single unbroken chain of public receptions, welcomes and farewells, banquets, toasts, celebrations! Escorted from town to town, intercepted by waiting crowds at every posting house, the sixty-seven-year-old veteran of the fight for freedom covered almost the whole continent from north to south and east to west. Only occasionally was he able to take three or four days' rest, on the country estates of his best friends, and even during these rare breaks he had to shake hands and exchange a few friendly words with hundreds of admirers who flocked in from all around. Every house that gave him a night's shelter became a place of pilgrimage, and he could not refuse the homage of the good people who brought their children with them on horseback from hundreds of miles away, so that their far descendants should be able to say with pride that their forefathers had seen the great Lafayette face to face.

It was a strangely fitting dispensation of Providence that this frame, which it had chosen to be the bearer of a sublime idea, should be of steel rather than of flesh and bone! Lafayette was nearer seventy than sixty when he covered these many thousands of miles by coach, spending every evening as the center of a nightly changing company: few men in the prime of life would have been equal to the exactions of that triumphal progress.

On September 2, 1824, less than a month after landing, Lafayette received a letter from ex-President Jefferson. The old man would gladly have seen him once more, for the last time, but did not feel that he could expect him to make the endless coach journey south to Virginia, where Jefferson was resting on his estate:

I am afraid you will be killed with kindness. All the ceremonial receptions, it seems to me, will be more than your strength can stand. Where is the village in America that will not want to have you within its walls?

Jefferson underestimated the energy and enterprise of his friend, for all his increasing years! Was he to be deterred by the hardships of some weeks' journeying by coach from seeing again the state of Virginia, where he cornered Lord Cornwallis and forced him to capitulate—from revisiting the scene of his famous exploits? He was to visit not only the aged Jefferson but every inch of the country from the Canadian frontier to his first landing place, near the home of Major Huger, the father of his liberator at Olmütz. He crossed this immense territory in every direction, as though it were a simple prairie, as his memories led him, plucking every flower, no matter how remote or humble, that retained some trace of the fragrance of his youth. He laid the foundation stone of the monument to his brave comrade in arms Baron Kalb, and the names, completely unfamiliar to him, of a few aged men were enough to tempt him hundreds of miles away to little villages of log cabins, where he could press the wrinkled hands of old soldiers who had fought under his command.

He went to Mount Vernon to see his old friend's nephew and to take a belated farewell at least of the mortal remains of Washington and his wife. His hosts remained reverently waiting while he went with bared head into the tomb for silent communion with the dead. Alone by the sarcophagus, Lafayette in fancy resuscitated the dead man; nature's most precious gift, memory, brought the two together again. An hour passed before, with moistened eye, he came back out of the vault. Washington's heirs gave Lafayette, in memory of this last encounter, a miniature portrait of the general, with a lock of his hair which had been cut, when he lay on his bier, in order to be given to his friend.

It would be absurd to attempt here to enumerate all the swords of honor and other presents given to Lafayette in the course of his journeys, or even to give extracts from the countless speeches made. It is not in the details of this unparalleled triumphal tour but in its subsequent results that its historic importance lies. For the most rigid censorship could not prevent an undertone of the celebrations from awakening painful memories in the French readers of the accounts of them. The slightest allusion to the past was mercilessly suppressed and punished, but for diplomatic reasons it was impossible to suppress all mention of the official celebrations. And the official homage accorded on the other side of the Atlantic, in the miraculously flourishing and growing republic, was a slap in the face for the nation which was unable even to give a seat in its Chamber of Deputies to the man who brought it its freedom from tutelage!

The crowd has a short memory. Napoleon and ten years of Bourbon rule had driven the story of the dawn of the Revolution out of the heads of the younger generation. They had to learn from the mouth of a foreign statesman, from another nation, that they ought to be proud of this man, whose name was almost forgotten in his own land!

Seventy-four members of Congress introduced the Frenchman, in whose honor all the representatives of a great and powerful nation rose and bared their heads as he entered. In the name of twenty million Americans the Speaker, Henry Clay, addressed Lafayette:

The vain wish has sometimes been indulged that Providence would allow the patriot, after death, to return to his country, and to contemplate the intermediate changes which had taken place. . . . General, your present visit to the United States is the realization of the consoling object of that wish. You are in the midst of posterity! Only in one respect will you perceive no change—in the deep gratitude of the nation, the gratitude to you which every child in America bears in his heart.

Mere words? Mere rhetorical flourishes? No! If anyone mistrusted mere words he could find warrant for them in their very practical postscript, the unanimously voted Resolution of Congress:

Section 1. Resolved, by the Senate and Chamber of Representatives of the United States of America, assembled in Congress, that, in compensation for the important services and expenditures of Major General Lafayette during the War of Independence, the Minister of the Public Treasury is and remains authorized by these presents to pay him the sum of Two Hundred Thousand dollars.
Section 2. Resolved, further, that there be granted to the said Major General Lafayette, for the enjoyment of himself and his heirs, one complete and entire Township of Land,* which will be located by the President of the United States on any of the Public Lands which remain unsold.

Before these resolutions attained legal force, a rivalry had already started between the representatives of the different federal states, all eager to give their own state the honor of adding its own special tribute to the common gift.

Lafayette had already been traveling up and down the states for six months when this honor conferred upon him by Congress assured him an old age free from care. Every critical turn in his life had come toward the end of a year, and it would have been an inconsistency on the part of Destiny if she had not set his ceremonial reception and stay in the new capital, which had been named after Washington, at the accus-

*Twenty-four thousand acres.

tomed period of the year. The Congress celebration took place on December 12, 1824, and Lafayette spent the weeks up to the beginning of the new year in the capital, which had risen from the earth as at the waving of a magic wand. When he first reached America this soil was still covered by impenetrable forest; now there towered over its midst, as though built by fabled giants, the White House. Spreading from the streets and squares of this central site of authority, the invisible threads of the laws controlled the immense territories of the Union. For three weeks the city of Washington had its guest within its walls. On the night of the passing of the old year Lafayette sat with all the representatives of the authority of the state at their farewell banquet to him.

For the first time since the death of his faithful life's companion he had been unable to pass Christmas Eve alone in the room in which she died. But his grateful memory of her was not confined to that day. In none of his many letters to his children, grandchildren and great-grandchildren in La Grange did he omit a regretful reproach of the fate that had denied Mme de Lafayette the gratification of sharing in this triumphal progress.

Only once during these endless journeyings through the untamed wilderness of the New World did Lafayette run into danger. He had ventured for the first time to board the latest marvel of progress, a steamboat on the Ohio River. In the middle of the night a shock threw the sleepers out of their beds: the vessel had struck a rock and sank so rapidly that it was only with difficulty that the famous old man was saved by boat. All his luggage, all his decorations and presents received on the way were lost. The last of the sailors were up to their breasts in the water when they left the vessel. After that Lafayette wanted to go back once more to recover the most precious of his possessions, the snuffbox he had been given in memory of General Washington. His son Georges and his secretary Levasseur ventured onto the boat and succeeded in recovering the precious gift.

Lafayette remained to celebrate his sixty-eighth birthday, on September 6, 1825, on American soil. Next day the Mayor of New York addressed the last words of farewell to him in the name of all America. He could not say too much; nothing he could say could even be adequate, since from the youngest child at school to old ex-President Jefferson, now eighty-two years of age, from the most distant pioneer in the southern jungle to the Iroquois of the Great Lakes on the Canadian frontier, every heart beat more quickly when the name of Lafayette was spoken. The memory of the twenty-year-old hotspur who had landed for the first time in the "Land of Freedom" almost half a century before would remain imprinted forever, like the footprints of the gods on some rocky ridge, in the minds of the remotest generations to come, so long as America remained an inhabited continent.

Once more the guns of the fort named after him thundered their salute. What wonder if at the parting the old man could only call down God's blessing on this country and nation in a voice trembling with suppressed emotion? He was seized with the same melancholy presentiment which had been expressed long years before in Washington's farewell letter; and the realization of this was deeply affecting the old man of sixty-eight. Never again would he see these shores, though the roofs of New York would glisten, as they did that day, long after his eyes had closed and his bones had crumbled to dust.

Standing at the taffrail of the spruce little tender, christened *Mount Vernon*, that was taking him to his ship, Lafayette held himself as erect as his lameness permitted, to shout his last farewell to the crowd standing in respectful silence:

"God bless you, sir; and all who surround you! God bless the American people, each of their states and the federal government! Accept this patriotic farewell of an overflowing heart, which will remain full of gratitude until the moment when it ceases to beat!"

Like a sharp blade, the first narrow strip of water separated the little boat from the shore.

"Adieu! Adieu!" cried the old man once more in a choking voice.

Then fortunately the thunder of the guns and the shouting of hundreds of thousands of voices covered the little groan that was wrung from him, sharp like the breaking of a violin string. Slowly the *Mount Vernon* descended the Hudson toward the frigate which was to take Lafayette back to his country. She was named *Brandywine*—a last recognition of the

blood the old man had shed nearly fifty years earlier at Brandywine Creek for the liberation of America.

VIII. BACK TO THE ARENA

"BUT I WILL NOT REPINE; I have had my day." So General
Washington had written forty years before. And it might have
been the turn of his young friend of those days to let himself
now be carried uncomplainingly by the current of events until
it laid him with his fathers.

Yet the gray-haired veteran of Liberty was once more
whirled into the fighting line and once more assumed the
leadership of a rebellion. The new task was not of his asking.
The *Brandywine*, laden like a merchant ship, brought the
countless gifts which had been pressed upon Lafayette by every
state, almost every hamlet of the Union. One unassuming chest
had been quietly slipped on board among them, and the dock
laborers at Le Havre grunted beneath its weight as they
brought it ashore. It was filled with earth, which the old man
had brought with him in order that, even in his enslaved
fatherland, his mortal remains might rest beneath the soil of
the "sacred land of Liberty."

He was returning with the load of nearly seventy years of
life, but he would not have made provision for his grave if he
had not sincerely believed his long series of sacrifices and
struggles, tribulations and triumphs to be at an end. He went
straight back to his house at La Grange. The young Duc
de Broglie contentedly wrote:

> I found the general big and stout, ruddy and cheerful, realizing
> the dignity conferred by his age and position, and determined in
> future to employ himself and his fortune only in ways we can all
> approve.

This optimism proved premature. The young duke forgot
to take account of the events that had happened in France
during Lafayette's year's absence. Louis XVIII was dead, and
the former Comte d'Artois, Lafayette's fellow pupil at the
Versailles riding school, had been crowned King of France in
Rheims Cathedral, as Charles X. He had only just taken the

center of the stage as ruler when Lafayette landed at Le Havre in the limelight of the fame that had preceded him from America. For many years these two men had appeared alternately like the figures in the old barometers, as the political pressure changed. When the herald of progress and the rights of man emerged as commander of the National Guard, on the Champ de Mars, the Comte d'Artois was canvassing the kings of Europe for troops to use against his own country. When "Monsieur" reappeared, Lafayette retired to his manor of La Grange until low pressure in France and high pressure in America presaged a considerable tempest. Then the excessive pressure broke the spring, and the two figures of Progress and Reaction popped out together and collided.

Lafayette's twelve months' stay in the United States enriched the vocabulary of that country with a word: to "Lafayette" anyone is to load him gratefully with public honors. Now America had sent its hero back to his native land, to be received with hostility and distrust by the ruling powers and with hope by a nation longing for its lost liberties. And now a decision must come. Charles X had summoned up all the forces of the past. Anointed King of France from the fragments of the ever flowing sacred phial at Rheims, he left the exercise of power to the religious bodies and to the reactionary circle of his favorites.

The ceremonial reception of Lafayette at Le Havre took the authorities by surprise. Steps were promptly taken at Rouen to prevent a repetition of the "scandal." Crowds assembled beneath Lafayette's hotel window; cavalry charged them with drawn swords, and the cheers gave place to the screams of the wounded.

The contrast was too violent. The right of assembly was not confined to citizens of the New World. The "charter" which Czar Alexander had imposed on Louis XVIII had suppressed official tutelage in France—and already, under the new régime, the prefect decided at his own pleasure in whose honor French citizens might raise their voices.

And yet it seemed for a while as though young Broglie was right, at any rate so far as Lafayette's person, if not his new wealth, was concerned. The black pall of the Congress of Vienna still lay over the Continent. The accession of Charles X had brought France once more into the community of the clerical police states on the Metternich model. The repeated raising of the money qualification for the franchise reserved all influence on affairs of state more and more to the thin upper stratum of nobility, clergy and plutocrats. Of twenty-five millions of Frenchmen, only some twenty thousand were allowed to vote. If Lafayette had met with similar conditions on his journey through the twenty-four United States, he would not have hesitated for a moment to raise his voice in warning. In Europe he saw all nations fettered by the same chains. From all sides appeals came to him for help. Fugitives and the persecuted never knocked at his door in vain. A heavy post daily brought news of fresh abuses of power and fresh sufferings of the oppressed. The letters from Simon Bolivar, the liberator of South America, were the only bright spot in all this correspondence. The American national gift went bit by bit into the empty pockets of fugitive champions of Liberty.

Lafayette was inaccessible to the mistrust which might have spared him expense. His house and his purse stood open to every victim of oppression, and this frittering away of his time, his money, and his sympathy contributed perhaps not a little to the delay in the decisive fight against his old opponent. In Poland, Belgium, Italy, Spain, everywhere the sacred spark was glowing under the ashes. Death, too, sadly recalled old memories. The turn came of Princess d'Hénin, his faithful friend in evil days, and then of General Foy, the great orator of the opposition. The general had left a family unprovided for, but a single appeal from Lafayette to the gratitude of the people brought in a million francs.

In the same summer of 1826, and on the same day—by a curious freak of fate, the 4th of July, the birthday of American independence—there died two ex-Presidents of the United States, Adams and Jefferson, while the rockets hissed, the guns roared, and the bonfires blazed throughout their country in celebration of the anniversary.

There came a respite lasting for some years, as though the two antagonists, like exhausted duelers, were hesitating to renew the fight. The government provided provocation enough. All the concessions won in the sanguinary combats of the

Revolution were withdrawn. Every limitation of the royal despotism lapsed. The insatiable thirst for revenge of his aristocratic advisers and the ambition of the religious orders drove Charles X towards an open breach with the nation. The gathering of the political storm, however, did not bring the septuagenarian away from his peaceful existence, surrounded by his great-grandchildren. Were it not that a passionate interest in the Greek struggle for freedom was evident in all his letters, it might almost have seemed as though the old rebel had, as the young Duc de Broglie thought, become "reasonable"; so much so, indeed, that he even lodged a claim to a share of the milliard which was being raised by a special tax to indemnify the nobles for their losses in the Revolution.

This application of his, followed by his acceptance of the 350,000 francs conceded to him, has unjustly been described as "cupidity," on the part of this man who was accused by his relatives, not without reason, of having sacrificed his own property—"and not only his own"—for the common good and for the rights of the people. Was he to reduce his children's heritage still more, merely to augment the share of the traitors who had taken arms and recruited foreign enemies against their country? If he had been a member of the Chamber, he would certainly have left nothing undone to prevent the extortion of this milliard from the taxpayers; but the government had kept him out of Parliament.

Charles X himself did not refuse his old antagonist proper recognition. When émigrés who had returned with him made spiteful remarks in his presence on the part Lafayette had played in the Revolution, he declared with chivalrous fairness:

"There are only two men in France who have remained true to their convictions under all circumstances: M. de Lafayette is one and I am the other."

The "ultras" had no sympathy for that attitude. They could not forgive Lafayette for persisting in describing himself as "General Lafayette," in spite of the legal reinstitution of titles of nobility.

It was not until 1827, when both men had completed their seventieth year, that the consistency he had praised in Lafayette began to be inconvenient to Charles X. The redoubled ardor of the clerical reaction and the challenging arrogance of the nobles had so exasperated the disinherited middle class that, in spite of the restricted franchise and of the prefects' efforts the liberal opposition returned to Parliament in increased strength. Lafayette was among those swept back into the realm of politics by this tide, and he did not disappoint his electors. Now he faced his old antagonist once more in the arena, and the duel to the death could begin.

IX. THE FINAL STRUGGLE

THE CHALLENGE came from the king, who was cut off from reality even more completely than other monarchs, living, as it were, in the emanation of his own conceptions. His knowledge of public opinion was drawn entirely from the tendentious reports of his prefects and ministers; thus he felt so sure of the victory of the government candidates that shortly before the new elections he ordered the disbandment of the National Guard.

Lafayette justifiably took the greatest pride in having established this citizen guard. It had repulsed the first attack made by Europe. It had furnished Napoleon with famous marshals like Masséna and Ney, and Lazare Hoche, military genius and groom's son. This army, which elected its officers from its own ranks, instead of being subject to the whims of beardless boys, had been the source of the successful resistance of the Revolution. So it was not enough for Charles X that the election of officers had long been abolished, that its commanders were men he could rely on, and that the ranks were recruited from officials and inhabitants of the better-class districts of the city; his advisers urged him to get rid entirely of everything that recalled the shameful humbling of the royal power in the past. Even the "charter," though he had sworn to maintain it, was whittled away article by article. The bourgeoisie must learn to pay the utmost respect to their divinely ordained master and to give blind obedience to his decrees.

The growth of the opposition might have given pause to the crown, but for its invincible faith that force is the only medicine for discontent. Lafayette's reëlection at once produced an outburst of rage from the Right. Every time he spoke in Parliament he was exposed to the virulent hatred of the "ultras," who loaded him with abuse and vituperation. In their eyes he was responsible for all the privations they had suffered during the emigration. Lafayette met these venomous interruptions with the fire and readiness of his youth. He did not confine his efforts to Parliament, but used every opportunity of publicly warning the king's government. At the open grave of his friend Manuel, who had been forcibly expelled from Parliament, Lafayette sounded a trumpet call: "Our own part, fellow citizens, at the tomb of this faithful servant of the people must be to vow that we shall regard as the most sacred of our duties the defence of our inalienable rights!"

Every word was a challenge: the word "citizens" in a monarchy which recognized none but subjects, the veiled exhortation to insurrection from the mouth of the man who had declared revolt to be the "most sacred of duties" wherever oppression existed. An authoritarian government could not overlook such a challenge. The speaker himself was protected by his boundless popularity in America; accordingly the public prosecutor took proceedings against the journalists who had made a verbatim report of the funeral oration. But it was not Lafayette's way to allow the innocent to suffer on his account. He wrote to the courts challenging them to prosecute him, and published his letter. This left the government no choice but to place him in the dock or acquit the rest. The milder counsel prevailed.

But Charles X, like his unhappy brother before him, was told that the unrest throughout the country was merely the work of a few evil-disposed persons. The newly elected Chamber was therefore dissolved once more, and fresh elections ordered.

Of the twenty-five millions of Frenchmen only fifteen thousand were still entitled to vote. No means of pressure or corruption were neglected; but, for all that, there was a further growth in the opposition. The exasperated king had to dismiss the ministers who enjoyed his favor and nominated a "moderate" cabinet. Its members were too reactionary in the view of the progressives and too demagogic in the eyes of the "ultras," and therefore had to carry on a fight on two fronts, crippled from the beginning by the king's declaration:

"You know, gentlemen, that it was only the pressure of

circumstances that induced me to dismiss your predecessors. The course the late Cabinet was steering was mine."

Yet the Court nursed the hope that peace was now assured. *"Nous en avons pour vingt ans"* ("This will last for 20 years"), said the advocates of "moderate progress," grown modest in their expectations, and with the unshakable optimism that had led Lafayette long before to write to Washington that the Revolution would come about "little by little, without a great convulsion," he was now able, at seventy-one, to write reports full of a premature confidence.

To acquire popularity the king made a considerable tour of the country. The prefects had arranged addresses and receptions and had lined the pavements with loyal subjects, and Charles could fancy himself beloved. But for his disastrous circle of advisers, the septuagenarian king would not have embarked on any dangerous adventure. His own disposition was entirely conciliatory. This was evident from the interest he took in Lafayette. When he was riding through his old opponent's constituency he startled the prefect with the question:

"Is not this M. de Lafayette's constituency?"

Noticing the astonishment and confusion of his suite, he added deliberately:

"Oh, I know him well. We were born in the same year. We learned riding at the Versailles school together, and he sat with me in the assembly of notables. We had many a fight then. But he has rendered services to our family that I cannot forget."

With his dreams realized, himself anointed King of France and Navarre, the former Comte d'Artois had forgotten the wrath of the years of exile, and but for his advisers his essentially chivalrous character might have produced a magnanimous gesture.

Lafayette also undertook the long journey to Chavaniac, and he too had no desire to provoke antimonarchical demonstrations. He went only to pay a visit to the haunts of his childhood and to visit his son Georges, who was living there with his children and grandchildren. But the journey from La Grange to Auvergne was so prolonged by receptions and ceremonies, and by all sorts of unforeseen arrangements made in his honor, that he was still on the way on his seventy-second birthday, September 6, 1829. As though the French did not mean to be behind the Americans, the whole journey became an uninterrupted triumphal procession.

Lafayette left no opportunity unused to give voice to the universal discontent in the country. The progressive demolition of the "charter," and the obstinate fight of the "ultras" against the last remnants of Parliamentary control, were threatening to reëstablish despotism in its old vigor, and it is no exaggeration to say that in his speeches in the towns, where hundreds attentively listened to his every word, this septuagenarian was the herald of revolt. He said at Lyons:

I am among you at a moment which I should call critical if I had not seen throughout my journey that calm, almost contemptuous, firmness of a great people that knows its rights, feels its strength, and will be true to its duties; but under present conditions I am particularly glad to assure you of my devotion, to which you will never appeal in vain so long as I breathe.

There could be no doubt about the meaning and intention of this: it was an open declaration of war. In the absence of Parliament the crown was proceeding to rule by decree. Prorogation had robbed the representatives of the nation of the means of protesting, and had evaded the fresh elections prescribed by law which a dissolution would have made necessary. This exclusion by Charles X of his constitutional collaborators was a breach of his oath, since he had sworn to hold sacred the "charter" "granted" by his brother.

It was the Duc de Polignac, familiarly called "Jules" by the king, who had urged this scarcely veiled dictatorship. And it was to him that Charles, to his undoing, entrusted the formation of a new ministry.

X. THE EVIL GENIUS

THE PRINCELY HOUSE of the Polignacs had neglected no means of making their name hated by the people. Jules, fleeing with his brother, grew up in the poisoned atmosphere of the emigration. At twenty-nine he took part with his brother in the plot against the life of the First Consul, and spent ten of the best years of his manhood behind prison walls. When at last he emerged, thanks to Josephine's intercession, he was filled with a medieval, fanatical hatred for popular rule, parliamentarism and democracy.

Before the democratic members of the prorogued Parliament left Paris, they were invited by the indignant citizens to a great farewell banquet. Two hundred and twenty-one of the expelled representatives of the people utilized the opportunity for a collective protest. They declared the proceedings of the new government unlawful and the violation of the "charter" a breach of agreement which restored freedom of action to the French people. If the king did not keep to the obligations he had sworn, the nation, on its part, was released from the oath of fealty.

The thing that bound Charles X and the Prince de Polignac most closely together was their narrowness of outlook. In vain did even generals and high dignitaries give warning against the resort to obsolete methods of violence; the king was still the Comte d'Artois who in 1789 had advised the fateful coup d'état against the National Assembly. Unshakable in his belief in force as a panacea, he exclaimed, pointing to the spot where Louis XVI was executed:

"I will not draw back like my unfortunate brother; I have had only too much experience of the consequences of that."

His friend "Jules" was empowered to proclaim martial law and to mobilize troops against the "rabble." The public prosecutor was instructed to proceed against the 221 members who had set their names to the rebellious protest.

Lafayette, now seventy-three years old, remained at La Grange, quietly awaiting events. He had no qualms about his share in the signing of the protest, and he had no fears for the future of France. All the letters he addressed to friends and party colleagues breathe his firm conviction that the nation would be able to defend its rights if Polignac in his folly forced matters to extremities.

The peaceful manor house of La Grange was crowded with pictures, statues, swords of honor and gilded laurel wreaths. Admirers from all quarters made pilgrimages to the patriarch who for more than half a century had been the standard bearer of all democratic principles in Europe. The old man's

hand was on the pulse of the nation and was ready once again
to draw the sword if things actually came to a decision by
arms.

Even the absolute monarchs were tired of shedding blood
for the Bourbon crown. The wars and occupations of territory had made the ministers of foreign states better acquainted
with the character and claims of the French than were the
French émigrés, who after an absence of twenty-five years
had returned with their outlook as unchanged as though it
had been luggage in bond sealed for transit. Prince Metternich
wrote from Vienna to his Paris Ambassador, Count Apponyi:
"I should be much less concerned if the king and Prince
Polignac were more so."

But the history of the world would not be written in blood
and tears if the rulers could be persuaded that the ignorant
masses are ready to fight and, if they must, to die for such
illusory possessions as freedom and justice. The chosen favorites of fortune do not realize that it is just those who are
famished, who are never able to eat their fill, to whom their
"human rights" are a sort of Sunday clothes, their sole "real"
property. They forget how little the disinherited, struggling
in the slough of poverty, have to lose when they venture their
lives against rifles and artillery.

There are few such eloquent examples of this deeply rooted
error as the fatal course followed by Polignac. He packed
Parliament off home without calling for fresh elections because
he knew that if they were held the general discontent would
increase the strength of the opposition. Yet, in a lengthy secret
report, intended for the king alone, and unquestionably sincere, he wrote:

It is only the daily press that sustains the popular excitement,
giving it the semblance of a much more imposing character than it
can really have, and concealing the narrow limits within which the
movement is confined. Through it some people are deceived as to the
absence of all reason for the unrest.

So nothing but the agitation of an insignificant group of
intellectuals was ruffling the surface of the sea of contentment!
And yet the preliminary voting in the indirect election for a
new Chamber—a reliable gauge of opinion—showed such a

startling swing to the Left that the election had to be abandoned.

Prince "Jules" never explained this contradiction either to himself or to the king, but he devised a brilliant move to checkmate all agitators. Had not the "Corsican usurper" enslaved France in his day and compensated the nation by satisfying its vanity through his victories? So a formidable expedition was equipped against the desolate molehill of the Dey of Algiers, in order to divert public attention from the coup d'état at home. Only July 5, 1830, the banner of the Bourbons waved from the captured fortress of Algiers. The fastest ship in the fleet crossed the Mediterranean with the joyful news— and on July 26 the notorious "ordinances" appeared in the *Moniteur Officiel*.

If the text of these decrees is compared with their historical consequences, it is impossible not to feel amazed. Just as to this day no one knows the names of the men who first shouted "À la Bastille!" on July 14, 1789, so the authors of the July revolution of 1830 are unknown.

The main object of the decrees was the abolition of the freedom of the press. They hampered the publication of periodicals by requiring all sorts of guarantees. Cunning penal provisions made it possible for the government summarily to lodge in jail the author, printer and publisher of any article objected to. As for the Parliamentary control guaranteed by the "charter" and the king's oath, this was reduced virtually to nothing by further restrictions of the franchise, so that few but the large landowners and millionaires had any chance of winning a seat in Parliament.

Freedom of the press and franchise! The latter had long been taken from the mass of the people. As for the press, in the last debate on the budget Lafayette had denounced the trifling amount provided for education—fifty thousand francs a year for a nation of twenty-five million souls. How many among the poorer classes could go to school and learn even to read? Just as the Bastille, the prison for nobles, was stormed by ragged hordes from the faubourgs, so most of the thousands who were now to die for the "freedom of the press" were illiterates. Built into the base of the social edifice, the poorest bear the bulk of the common load, and every call to shake off the burden of despotism sweeps them irresistibly before the cannon's mouth.

Even Charles X had a vague feeling of the danger he was conjuring up. After signing the ordinances he said to his ministers:

"And now, gentlemen, we are bound together for life and death."

Only the "ultras" were whole-heartedly pleased. Now at last there was an end of compromises, they shouted enthusiastically, and the king was master again in his own house. A quiet boy-cott was started against those unreliable persons who ventured to express doubts, went about with long faces, or even re-signed their offices, as was done by two ministers of the re-actionary Cabinet. The least troubled of all the Court was the "responsible" Prime Minister, Prince de Polignac. He left St Cloud and went to Paris, as unconcerned as if the decisions of the *séance royale* were of no significance. Chateaubriand, who was a royalist, pertinently says that Polignac suffered from the suggestive influence of his own convictions, like a sleep-walker who fancies that he is on solid earth when he is poised on a tower of Notre Dame.

XI. ALL CLEAR FOR ACTION

THIS LACK of concern reassured the whole Court at St Cloud. Next morning the king and his son went hunting; only Mar-mont, Duc de Raguse, the same Marshal Marmont who had surrendered Paris and Napoleon to the Allies, wanted at least to know what was in the ordinances which it was his task to defend. But the only copy of the *Moniteur* was on the king's desk, and etiquette forbade its being touched. With no definite knowledge of the contents of the unpopular edicts confided to his protection, the marshal hastened to the capital, where state securities had already slumped heavily on the Bourse.

"They will rise again," remarked the dauphin indifferently, on his return from the hunt in the evening. Nobody wanted to be a bearer of ill news, and so the king went to bed with-out knowing that mounted police had charged the crowd, that the windows of Polignac's ministry had been smashed, and that the first blood had been shed in Paris.

Old Lafayette, too, was sitting unsuspectingly at La Grange when the first victims fell in Paris. With his ineradicable optimism he was writing to a friend abroad:

It is certain that August 3rd will see Parliament reopened by the king. In recent council meetings there has been great talk of a coup d'état, which is being discussed at Court, in the ministry, and among the government's supporters, as well as in their papers, as though it were a simple matter. Nevertheless . . .

With this "nevertheless" the letter breaks off; it ends with a postscript, dated Paris, July 28.

Rémusat, the author, who had married a granddaughter of Lafayette, had sent him a copy of the *Moniteur* by special messenger. One glance at the decrees was enough: Lafayette set out at once for the capital.

Marmont's troops were already stationed in the public squares, and the people of the faubourgs were out in the streets behind barricades of torn-up paving stones and lamp-posts when, late in the evening of July 27, the aged rebel arrived on the scene. Fearlessly, as fifty-five years earlier, he hurried to the defence of justice against despotism, careless of the dangers or the consequences of interference. The dissolution of the newly elected Chamber, which had not even been called together, had been a flouting of the law. Released from his oath of fealty by the perjury of the crown, he felt that his duty was solely to his compatriots who had placed their trust in him. To consider his personal safety would be treason to the brave men who were holding the barricades at the risk of their lives. His first care was to offer his name and his services to the revolution.

At four o'clock in the morning students were with him, seeking his advice. At dawn these ardent youths left the old man, to fight at the head of the people, and to sacrifice their lives. Blood was already flowing in all quarters of the great city when Lafayette at last succeeded in finding his fellow deputies in Audry de Puyravault's house. Here he also found his friend Laffitte, the rich banker, who had just arrived in Paris.

It was a strange company that he found there. It included men of rank and fame, General Sebastiani, the Duc de Choiseul, the Comte de Lobau, Marshal of France, General Comte Gérard, most of them members of the dissolved Chamber, with some representatives of the Upper House, all equally indignant at Polignac's trickery and Charles X's violation of his oath. All present were agreed that "something must be done." The editors of the opposition papers, themselves in a dangerous position whatever happened, took part as guests in the discussions.

On the morning of July 28 the bodies of the first victims of the revolt lay strewn around the barricades in the Place du Carrousel and on the borders of the Faubourg Saint-Antoine, where the Bastille formerly towered over the roofs of the houses. The watchword was *"À bas les Bourbons!"* and this battle cry was echoed everywhere in the faubourgs. Barricades shot up out of the ground like mushrooms; the women threw down boiling water and heavy pieces of furniture on the troops who were killing their husbands and sons below.

These events in the streets of Paris were no concern of the representatives of the people who "happened to be in the capital"! Their discussions in a friend's house had nothing to do with the shooting outside. They indignantly rejected the repeated requests for leadership that came from the various groups of fighters. When unauthorized persons posted up placards with the false news that Charles X had fled and that a provisional government had been formed under Comte Gérard, the Duc de Choiseul and Lafayette, the duke called all present to testify against the calumny—of which he was to boast proudly twenty-four hours later.

To take sides before the issue was decided did not suit the cautious temperament of this "chance" assemblage. Lafayette's impatience for them to assume the leadership of the revolt threatened to compromise dangerously all those present; in the end the meeting broke up, agreeing to continue its discussions in Laffitte's house in the Place Vendôme. Prince Polignac issued warrants for the arrest of Lafayette and Gérard, and on the same morning Marmont proclaimed a state of siege.

The energy of the troops was sapped not only by a tropical heat such as they had never before experienced, but by demoralizing doubts as to the reason why they were called on to decimate their compatriots. The name and the presence of the famous veteran Lafayette would have been worth a couple of army corps to the people in their furious but planless defence. As soon as he was recognized in the street, the septuagenarian was implored to take over the leadership of their rightful resistance to tyranny, but his companions protested indignantly:

"Do you want to get the general shot?"

Lafayette returned home late at night—on foot, as the paving of all the streets had been torn up. At important crossroads veritable little forts had been constructed, and, as the old founder of the National Guard passed, he proudly inspected these improvised defences, which, although built by simple artisans, could not, he said, have been much improved upon by Vauban himself. The old man's tall figure, still upright, was recognized at many corners as he strode along. *"Vive le Général Lafayette!"* whispered the sentinels of the revolutionaries into his ear, in order not to compromise him if the rising were defeated. An opposition newspaper, *La Tribune*, has preserved for posterity an impressive picture of this night round through the armed city:

Between 1 and 2 A.M. a weary old man, stumbling along with the support of a friend on each side, appeared in front of the barricade in the Rue Cadet, which controls the way to the Faubourg Montmartre.

"Halt!" cried the sentinel: "corporal, come and see these people."

The corporal was a simple workman, shouldering a gun. "Forward to the guardroom," he said. "You will have to tell us what your business is, limping about so late."

The group marched to the guardroom, and there each of the strangers was scrutinized. A man getting on in years, of dignified appearance, for whom two or three barricades had had to be breached, and accompanied by three others, who seemed to be at his orders, like aides-de-camp—all this looked very suspicious to the commandant of the National Guard, who questioned the old man with vehemence. The latter replied:

"Captain, I am moved to the bottom of my heart by the spectacle I see here . . . I am one of your old comrades."

The commandant hesitated.

"It is General Lafayette!" cried a workman.

They all embraced him; then the commandant restored discipline, summoned the whole of the guard, and drew them up before the general, who formally inspected them in regular army fashion.

As candid as the grown-up children who were risking their lives in their thousands in the streets of Paris, the honest, self-sacrificing old man sat among the intriguing politicians, who were out to secure their own advantage in the event of a popular victory but in the meantime were taking no risks. "No precipitancy! No departure from legality!" Their anxiety to justify their own conduct by recording such principles in the minutes effectively checked any action by the meeting, even when the corpses were already piling up in the streets and every house in the principal thoroughfares had become a hospital.

A separate clique had gathered round Laffitte. Alongside Sebastiani, one of Napoleon's generals, were young Guizot, who owed his election to Lafayette's support, and the gifted young journalist Thiers, on the staff of the *National*. They intended to set on the throne the Duke of Orleans, the "liberal" son of Philippe Égalité, if the reigning dynasty were dispossessed.

Louis-Philippe, whom long ago Danton had selected for the throne, who had been an officer of the Revolution at the battle of Valmy and had been compelled to earn his living for a time as a teacher of geography at a Swiss school, posed discreetly as a democrat. He did not let his friends forget that in his youth he had fought under the tricolor, while at Court he was equally concerned to assert his position as a prince of the blood. When the disturbances broke out he prudently disappeared. Even his nearest relatives were not supposed to know his whereabouts. He too was waiting—like the careful paladins —for the outcome of the street fighting.

Since the time when Marshal Marmont, Duke of Ragusa, had delivered over France to the Allies without a blow, a new verb, "to raguse," had become current in the faubourgs. The troops were more afraid of the reproaches hurled at them by the people than the defenders of the barricades were of the fire of the soldiers. Long before Lafayette had come to a decision the rumor was already rife that he had openly taken the popular side and recalled the National Guard to the colors. He had arrived in Paris late on July 27; about midday on the

29th he appeared at Laffitte's residence, and addressed these words to the scared assembly:

It has been made clear to me that it is the desire of a large number of citizens that I should accept, not as a member of Parliament, but as an individual, the command of the National Guard. An old name of 1789 may be of some value in the present grave situation. We have been attacked by arms and must defend ourselves by arms——

That was as far as he got; for at that moment an officer rushed in with the news that the garrison of the Louvre had fled or been killed and that the palace had been occupied by the populace.

This was no mere rumor and no meaningless local success; the evacuation of this building, crowded with treasures of art, was a serious decision, at which Marshal Marmont could not arrive light-heartedly. The gossip about the unreliability of the troops gained more credence, and in these circumstances the members of Parliament who "happened to be in Paris" no longer objected to one of their number taking the plunge at his own risk.

The patriarch in the middle of the hall was himself electrified by the good news and continued in a ringing voice:

The people await my answer. Do you think that, in the presence of the dangers which threaten us, it would be worthy of my past life and my present situation to remain inactive? No! my attitude at seventy-three will be what it was at thirty-two. I realize that it is necessary for the Chamber, as such, to show reserve; but for myself, citizens, duty commands me to devote myself to the common cause.

Who does not recognize the "statue in search of its pedestal"? He would not long let his path to the scaffold be barred against him. With the fearless impetuosity of the young man of twenty, who threw himself in front of the English bullets at Brandywine Creek, the man of seventy-three demanded his share of the danger.

His example had fired the Orleanists: in any case they were loath to hand over all the power to the old republican. Lafayette unsuspectingly surrendered the civil authority to a committee—happy in any solution that freed him from following the fight as a mere spectator. In the square outside the house the crowd was shouting with growing impatience: *"Vive Lafayette!"* "Down with the Bourbons!" The tumult drew this decision from the frightened assembly:

In view of the excitement outside, it is essential that General Lafayette should show himself to the citizens, and should accept the command of the National Guard.

He stood on the balcony of the Hôtel Laffitte, as formerly in the Champ de Mars at the Fédération, surrounded by the intoxicating music of his popularity. Tears were on his furrowed cheeks as the old man staggered back happily into the hall. The Orleanists seized the opportunity to nominate General Gérard as commander-in-chief of the troops who passed over to the popular side. This deprived the old dreamer of a substantial slice of power, and nothing need now keep him from risking his head as an "individual."

General Gérard, an honest soldier, unversed in politics, declared himself happy "at being allowed to serve under Lafayette," and the two generals left the hall together. They thus missed a spectacle which might have taught them a good deal. Two regiments of the king's troops refused to fight any longer against their brothers, and fired into the air in front of the house. In a second the assembly dispersed. "Treachery! Treachery! They are coming to arrest us!" cried the deputies; some fled into the garden and hid behind bushes, some ran up to the garrets, until the misunderstanding was explained. Laffitte, who had a sprained ankle, was unable to leave the president's chair, and he and his nephew received a deputation of officers who, in the name of the two regiments, asked to be allowed to withdraw, retaining their arms. A little confused and disordered, the runaways trickled back to the hall.

XII. TRIUMPH

MEANWHILE LAFAYETTE took his way towards his former residence, the old Hôtel de Ville, into which he had moved forty-one years earlier in similar circumstances, as creator and commander of the National Guard, the first organized body of armed citizens.

It was with difficulty that he made his way through the

crowd. As he passed along, a shower of tricolor ribbons, cockades, and bows rained down on him from the windows. The three colors which he had first combined together in the Hôtel de Ville, the City Hall of Paris, had now traveled round the world. They had waved from Moscow to the Pyramids, from Schönbrunn to the Escurial, had floated over all the palaces and forts of Europe. There was no sea that they had not crossed, no country that had not greeted them with the thunder of guns. With pride Lafayette had "his" flag hoisted on the Hôtel de Ville. For the third time the banner of the Bourbons yielded to the people's flag. After all the vicissitudes of half a century of struggle, the barometer of civilization stood once more at "Progress," and crowned reaction had to leave the stage. Those who have not forgotten the meeting, at the German inn, between the prisoner from Olmütz and the royal prince with his suite, may imagine Lafayette's pride as, back at his starting point, he once more breathed the ether of his first triumph.

"Do not trouble, I know my way in this building," he said, smiling at the attentions of the inevitable courtiers of success. But the mere hoisting of the tricolor over the Hôtel de Ville would not defeat Marmont. At the Tuileries, where he had established his headquarters, and where Prince Polignac was in residence, the lily banner still floated, and reinforcements from all the neighboring garrisons were being hurried to Paris. The king had plenty of soldiers to replace the casualties, which amounted to less than a thousand killed and wounded. The losses of the populace were more than twice as heavy. But the hatred of the traitor Marmont gave strength to the defenders of the barricades, while all the fighting spirit was shamed out of the soldiers and officers by the shouts of the people:

"Shoot us down so that Marmont can pay his debts!"

Everyone knew that the expenses of living like a prince had degraded the Duc de Raguse to a venal tool. The marshal himself suffered from the contempt against which all his palaces and wealth were no protection. When Polignac urged him to make more use of his artillery, Marmont exclaimed bitterly:

"Am I to raze Paris to the ground?"

And again and again he hesitated to use case shot against the populace.

Courier after courier galloped to St Cloud with the entreaty that the ordinances might be withdrawn and a Parliamentary government established. But the phantoms in the palace considered it to be "impossible" for the king to retreat before the will of the armed mob, and Prince Polignac hastened on horseback to anticipate Marmont's ambassadors and avert the disgrace of a capitulation.

When the first news of the fraternization of the troops with the people was brought to Marmont, an officer rushed breathlessly with the news into the minister's room. He returned to the marshal in despair:

"We are lost! The minister does not understand the French language. When I told him that the troops were fraternizing with the rebels, he replied: 'Then you must fire on the troops as well.'"

Marmont's supreme aim now was to prevent the contagion spreading to the troops who were still loyal, and he ordered the concentration of all his forces in the courtyard of the Tuileries until the arrival of reinforcements. He himself regarded the king as greatly at fault in violating the laws he had sworn to respect and hoped to persuade Charles to give way; meanwhile he did all he could to gain time. More and more uniforms of the forbidden National Guard were appearing in the streets. The best thing he could do was to keep the two camps apart.

But the ghosts of the past played him a trick. The dead arose and put to flight the Swiss mercenaries, the most reliable of all! These professional soldiers, mainly from the German-speaking cantons, asked no questions about the rights or wrongs of the conflict. They were just plying their trade—selling courage. They had been posted at the windows, and from there were firing on the mob and repelling all attacks on the palace. By mistake, the order to the troops to assemble in the courtyard was transmitted to the commandant of the Swiss guard as well, and they left the windows.

A half-grown lad noticed the disappearance of the red-jackets, and climbed up a rain pipe to get a look at the king's apartments. The silhouette of this boy against the pale evening sky called up memories of the frightful butchery of 1792, when, hunted from story to story and from room to room, the hated red-jackets were slaughtered like wild beasts, struck down with pikes, knives and life preservers.

"The people! The people are in the Tuileries!" shouted, panic-stricken, the first Swiss who saw the boy, and in a moment Marmont's best troops took to flight; it was only with difficulty that he halted them at the Arc de Triomphe. To bring them back into the city was impossible. The sight of the leaderless Swiss running away provoked a general *sauve qui peut*. The victor of so many battles was compelled to evacuate Paris and retreat in humiliation towards St Cloud, yielding to the half-armed mob. Before nightfall the tricolor of insurrection was flying over the royal palace. The duel between the two septuagenarians was at an end.

In the stifling atmosphere of the crowded rooms of the Hôtel de Ville, Lafayette was sitting as the sole master of Paris. With Marmont's withdrawal all power was in his hands; the victorious people listened to him alone. Ragged and barefooted rebels, who a couple of days later would sink back into their poverty, brought him treasures from the royal palace, including a money box belonging to the Duchesse d'Angoulême, full of gold coin. No crime was to sully the people's victory. Travelers, pressed for time, begged him for passports; from all points of the city he was called upon for orders or for decisions on doubtful questions, and the old man was so besieged that he could hardly get free to draft his first proclamations. He was governing Paris! All confusion flowed to him, like the blood to the heart, and all order returned from him through the city's arteries. He remained at his post until late at night—long after the palace at St Cloud had fallen into the silence that guarded the sacrosanct slumbers of the king who, without being aware of it, had already ceased to be king.

Early in the morning the first negotiators came from St Cloud. As though they came from another century, these high ambassadors oscillated between Paris and the Court, always some hours behind the time that had struck in Paris. Benjamin Constant summed up in a sentence the hopelessness of their attempt at salvage:

"It would really be too convenient if a king could shoot down his people and then be free simply to declare that nothing had happened."

The fate of Charles X and his dynasty was already sealed. The crushing defeat of his old opponent had placed the future of France in Lafayette's hands. One word, and the crowd would enthusiastically have hailed him president of the new republic or king of a new constitutional monarchy.

But the sower who through all his life had paced with open hand over the plowed field had not learned at seventy-three to close his fingers and grasp. Instead of seating himself in the president's chair or stooping for the crown, Lafayette was concerned only for the realization of his old ideal. It was not for an individual, not even for Paris, but for the whole nation freely to choose the form of the future state. A France with a strictly democratic Constitution, and with a strong and well-armed citizens' guard to uphold the laws, was the object for which he had fought throughout his life, just as the Comte d'Artois had fought for despotism by the Grace of God.

Over the chasm between these two extremes the energetic pioneers of private interests threw a bridge for the Duke of Orleans. Not merely for hours, but for two full days, Lafayette remained in the Hôtel de Ville as the candidate of Fate and of the Parisians. The victors of those murderous days were expecting the old republican to take the step that would fulfil their dreams of Liberty, which were also his own. A settlement was urgently needed; the fever of the life-and-death struggle had given place to the uncertainty of waiting. All the shops and factories were closed, no one was earning anything; the streets were still ripped up, and transport was impossible. Every hour that passed increased the readiness of the middle class to put up with any solution at all that enabled transport and business to start again. It was as though the congealed blood of the fallen were choking the whole economic circulation of Paris. The dead must be put away and the roads reopened to life.

XIII. THE GAMBLE FOR THE THRONE

THE ADHERENTS of Louis-Philippe harnessed this impatience to their candidate's car. For the moment he was merely to take over the regency under the title of Lieutenant-Général du Royaume until the majority of the Duc de Bordeaux. Born after the murder of his father, the Duc de Berry, this child was still an unknown quantity. Charles X abdicated, and made his son abdicate, in order at least to keep the crown for his grandson.

But Louis-Philippe, Duke of Orleans, did not disappoint his supporters, who had chosen him as their favorite in the race for the throne. Not that he was in a hurry. As long as shots were being fired he was not to be found. His father's fate had taught him that it is possible to be the darling of the people and be called "Égalité" and yet end under the guillotine. His service as a general of the Revolution at Valmy compelled him to show special caution in face of the legitimate dynasty. He remembered Danton, who had once chosen him as a candidate for the throne and had paid with his head for his royalist plans. Hidden in a remote hunting box, he awaited the issue of the murderous struggle and left it to his supporters to risk their heads for his crown.

But on the morning of July 30, after Marmont's retreat and Lafayette's occupation of the Hôtel de Ville, the duke's candidature could no longer be deferred. The augurs at Laffitte's house clearly realized the danger of a republic under Lafayette's presidency. The outcome of the adventure could not be foreseen. It might lead to a new European crusade against France. The alternative was to rush public opinion at the psychological moment. Two days more, and the respectable middle class would prefer even the rule of the Shah of Persia to the continuance of an uncertainty that was bringing them to ruin.

To put an end to Lafayette's autocracy, the "deputies in Paris" moved from Laffitte's house to Parliament, so transferring the official seat of the "will of the people" from the Hôtel de Ville to the Chamber. At the same time, young Thiers, the talented editor of the opposition *Constitutionnel*, was commissioned to fetch the Duke of Orleans back to Paris at all costs. The man who forty years later was to make peace with Bismarck and become first President of the Republic, won his spurs on this occasion.

The duke's wife and sister would not betray the cautious candidate's hiding place, but Thiers was able to persuade them to send a message to the prince. At dead of night and in disguise, without the knowledge even of his partisans, Louis-Philippe slunk into the strictly guarded city and reached his Paris house, which was soon to have a solid reason for its name of Palais Royal.

Never have two more unequal parties confided their lot to more dissimilar leaders than the student partisans of Liberty who rallied round Lafayette in the Hôtel de Ville and the politicians at Laffitte's house, who, with the single exception of the rich banker himself, attached the heavily laden gondola of their ambitions to the balloon of the duke's fortunes. Hidden in his palace, the duke secretly received the party leaders. Their favorable reports of the fighting convinced him of the necessity of emerging from obscurity, though in such a way that if the situation should change he would be able to sacrifice his supporters and exculpate himself at Court.

The Prince de Mortemart, whom Charles X had originally selected to succeed Prince "Jules," was the ex-king's ambassador in the negotiations with the rump Parliament and Lafayette's committee; he did his utmost to save the crown for his master's grandson. The placards in favor of the House of Orleans, and the duke's presence in Paris, did not inspire confidence. When the king's representative was asked to visit the Palais Royal on the morning of July 31, he refused at first to go; it was only because a regency until the majority of the legitimate heir was the last chance left that Mortemart ultimately allowed himself to be persuaded to see the Duke of Orleans.

What a sight! The first prince of the blood was stretched on a straw mattress, as though there were no better bed in his palace, and he showed all the external signs of brutal treatment. In a voice trembling with indignation he told his visitor:

"If you see the king before I do, tell him that I have been brought to Paris by force, but that I shall let myself be cut into pieces rather than let the crown be placed on my head."

Converted from his mistrust, with tears of repentance in his eyes, the Prince de Mortemart declared after this interview that the duke had shown himself worthy of the name of Bourbon. The one thing that he kept from even the most trusty of his companions was a roll of paper he had put into

his cravat, in order to convey to the king, without hindrance
and without endangering the duke, this written undertaking:

. . . But if, amid these frightful disorders, it should happen that
there was imposed upon me a title to which I have never aspired, let
Your Majesty be persuaded that I shall receive any sort of power
only temporarily and in the sole interest of our house; I hereby offer
this formal pledge to Your Majesty.

Politicians of the type of Guizot and Thiers could devote a
grimace of appreciation to the ambiguous phrase "in the
interest of our house"; and yet a few hours sufficed to make
even this cautious declaration appear so precipitate that the
Duke of Orleans demanded the return of the document, and
the good Mortemart had to tie his cravat afresh.

Forty years had passed over the "revolutionary services" of
the candidate; the Convention, the Directory, the great
shadow of Napoleon, and fifteen years of reaction, had covered
the figure of "General Égalité." Those who looked back only
knew that the return of the royal family had cost France two
invasions. And on the top of that the three days of bloodshed! Had two thousand Parisians fallen and five thousand
been maimed in order to exchange the older branch for the
younger one, Charles X for Louis-Philippe?

"No more Bourbons! We've done with the Bourbons!" was
the incessant growl in the faubourgs and around Lafayette in
the Hôtel de Ville.

But the whole art of the politician faced with opposition is
to turn it about and harness it to his own wagon. A republic
was a reminder of the Terror, of the Committee of Public
Safety, of inflation, of the guillotine. Lafayette, ran the murmur from shop to shop, meant a new republic, and a new republic meant a new war. Let every man who did not want to
deliver France again into the hands of a plundering soldiery,
let all who wanted to protect their country from fresh anarchy
hasten to present the wavering masses and the foreign diplomats with a *fait accompli!* The Duke of Orleans was a democrat by conviction; he had been a schoolmaster and knew what
earning a living means; and at the same time he was a royal
prince, legitimized as a monarch in the eyes of the outside

world; would he not provide every guarantee? Lafayette must be taken by surprise before he was able to arm the masses and involve the nation in fateful adventures.

While opinion in Paris was being manipulated by the duke's paladins, Louis-Philippe had merely the task of driving Charles X and his family to flee from the country, when he would be rehabilitated in the eyes of the European monarchs and able to ascend the abandoned throne. In his letters he assured the king that he would take over the conduct of business of state merely as administrator for the heir apparent in his minority; but at the same time he was saying impatiently to his confidants: *"Il faut qu'ils partent enfin!"* ("It is high time they went!") A hotch-potch of an "army" of loafers, equipped with sporting guns and pikes, mixed with National Guards and a few detachments of troops, was thrown together and set in movement towards St Cloud.

Once more memories of the past formed the advance guard of this carnival procession. At the first news of the approach of the Parisians, the Duchesse de Berry, wringing her hands, awakened the king from his sleep. She was trembling for her children; and the number of courtiers who had vanished, leaving the palace half empty, showed the king how far, without taking a step, he had left the throne behind him. For the moment the Court merely withdrew to Rambouillet; but this first retreat decided the issue.

XIV. WHEN TWO FALL OUT—

THE VERY FIRST PROCLAMATION which Louis-Philippe of Orleans addressed to the Parisians in his own name—on July 31, 1830—was a little masterpiece of easy-going impudence, devised by the practiced cunning of the future "citizen king" and dished up in appropriate language by young Thiers's clever pen:

I have not hesitated to come and share your dangers, to place myself in the midst of this heroic population, and to make every effort to save you from civil war and anarchy. On re-entering the city of Paris I wore with pride those glorious colours which you have re-adopted, and which I myself had long worn.

The two Chambers will meet at once; they will see about the means of ensuring the rule of law and the upholding of the rights of the nation.

The Charter will henceforth be a reality.

The signature "Louis-Philippe d'Orléans" did not anticipate events, and modestly left it to the readers to determine the degree of their gratitude for the "sharing" of their dangers. Nevertheless, the proclamation had the worst conceivable reception at the Hôtel de Ville. The university students around Lafayette and the heroes of the three days of sanguinary struggle protested indignantly against these rushing tactics. Either the nation should be consulted and a new constituent assembly elected to determine the future form of government, or Lafayette should proclaim a republic and at once assume the presidency, to prevent the possibility of another Bourbon slipping in through the back door after all. Bonaparte's coup d'état had shown the people how little a man who has once seized power need be bound by his promises.

Without Lafayette's assistance all the contriving of the Orleanists would be in vain. Laffitte accepted the task of explaining to the duke that he would have to fetch his crown from the lion's den—the Hôtel de Ville. No one but Lafayette had sufficient influence with the masses to impose a new king on them. The sacred oil had become discredited, but confidence in the veteran of Liberty was greater than ever; whoever was to wear the crown must receive it from Lafayette's hands.

To overcome the conscientious scruples of the credulous old gentleman was the simplest part of the task. The passage through the crowded streets with Laffitte, Thiers, Guizot, Constant and the rest was a more dangerous matter. The whole population was still armed, and no fresh organ of executive government had yet been appointed. The voice of the septuagenarian idol of the people was the only governing power in existence.

Eyewitnesses declared that the Duke of Orleans was as white as a sheet. The nearer he came to the Hôtel de Ville, the more unfriendly, even threatening, was the attitude of the crowd, and he certainly breathed more freely when at last he was re-

ceived by Lafayette in the Hôtel de Ville, at the bottom of the
staircase. He recovered his color—and his cunning with it. As
he came up to Lafayette he said:

"You see before you an old National Guardsman of '89 come
to call on his old general."

Who could have found a better compliment with which to
present himself to Lafayette? The old gentleman pressed a tricolor into the duke's hand, led him up to the balcony, and
there embraced him and kissed him on the forehead. At the
sight of the duke busily waving that flag and embraced by its
deviser, the easily moved, easily deluded crowd broke into
shouts of:

"Vive Lafayette! Vive le duc d'Orléans!"

Chateaubriand wrote later, with more wit than justice, that
Lafayette had struck the crown from the head of Louis XVI
in order, as a convinced republican, to kiss it onto—Louis-
Philippe's. This is unjust, because Lafayette risked his own head
to save Louis's head and crown. As for the implied reproach
to Lafayette's republicanism, Napoleon III was to prove that
it would have been premature to proclaim a republic in 1830.

This overhasty championship of the Duke of Orleans was a
bitter disappointment for the students and the fighters for
the July revolution. They placed implicit trust in Lafayette;
not the slightest doubt was felt of the personal integrity of
the old republican; but he had allowed himself to be won over
with fine phrases instead of using his power at least to extract
written guarantees for the nation.

The moment this was said, Lafayette declared his readiness
to make good the omission. He worked out with the students
a minimum program of democratic reforms which he would
get the duke to sign. On the following day he called at the
Palais Royal with this document in his pocket.

He was charmed by the refreshing informality of his reception, so reassuring in its contrast with the past pomp and ceremony of Versailles. The duke had himself spent some years in
America and spoke with enthusiasm of the republican form of
state. He anxiously asked Lafayette whether he thought that
France was ripe for a similar democratic advance. In face of
this noble candor, Lafayette found it impossible to present his

document. The youngest lieutenant would have regarded such mistrust as insulting. Men of honor do not demand signatures from one another! The word of a prince of the blood has more weight than a scrap of paper.

In no spirit of mistrust, simply in order to calm his followers and to avoid all possibility of misunderstanding, Lafayette summed up his demands in this definite form:

"My ideal, and it seems to me realizable today, is a throne resting on republican institutions."

"C'est tout à fait mon idée" ("That is exactly my idea"), replied the duke, cordially gripping Lafayette's hand.

The old gentleman went away as happily as if he were taking back to his young friends at the Hôtel de Ville the signature and seal of the future ruler on the document.

Had he allowed himself to be duped? Had he allowed the blood of the dead and wounded to be sacrificed for empty promises? Later, when the students, bitterly disappointed, asked him why he had not proclaimed a republic, and himself, as its first president, watched over its establishment on a firm democratic foundation, he put his hand affectionately on the shoulder of one of the young men and spoke the words we have placed at the beginning of this book as the motto of his whole career:

My long life has taught me that in important personal questions the best thing is to decide against one's own interest.

An armless man is not more entirely at the mercy of a horde bristling with weapons than the man who is guided by this principle in a society organized from top to bottom on the basis of personal advantage. Lafayette imagined himself to be living already in the world it had been his lifelong dream to build. At seventy-three years of age he had been carried once more up to a pinnacle, but he rejected crown and presidency alike, noble and trusting like the little savage of long ago who had come away from his native forests. Alongside this spotless integrity, what was the worth of the eighteen years' reign of the "citizen king?" With all his cunning and unkingly mentality, Louis-Philippe was unable to hold even to the end of his own life the crown he had cadged.

XV. —THERE'S A THIRD SMILING

THE FUNERAL PROCESSION of the fallen dynasty moved with painful slowness through the west of France. In vain did the three commissaries of the new ruler press for a decision: the old king held on hour by hour, imagining that the whole country would rise against the infamous usurper. He tried to gain time for his loyal subjects to rally round their anointed lord. But the doors and windows of the great châteaux were closed and shuttered wherever he passed. Families that had taken the most eager advantage of his liberality and had been the loudest in protest against making any concession to modern ideas, seemed to have died out in the short week since his fall. No one among them was ready to risk the displeasure of the new dynasty. Only the simple villagers and small townsfolk, whose fellow subjects the old man in his blindness had had shot down, thronged the pavements with bared heads, downcast and crestfallen. They knew how heavy-handed is misfortune and greeted its victim with respectful consideration.

Charles X dragged out his journey from Rambouillet to Cherbourg until August 15; there two ships were waiting to convey his small company to exile in England. It was hard for this old man of seventy-three to leave his country now for the third time and for all time. More kingly than his successor, who on a foggy night in 1848 was to slink over the frontier in disguise, Charles retreated only a step at a time, endeavoring up to the last, with touching simplicity, to preserve the outward appearance of his lost power. In a village inn he found a round table laid for his family party, and for two hours he wandered in a neighboring wood while the local carpenter made an oblong table-top. The Kings of France must always sit at the head of the table! Dethroned, driven out, ignominiously hustled, he still clung to the traditional dignity of a crown which was already being worn by another.

Duobus litigantibus, tertius gaudet—when two fall out, there's a third smiling! The struggle between the two septuagenarians, who had been fighting one another all their lives, had thrown up Louis-Philippe d'Orléans as the lucky third party. Untouched by moral scruples, he faithlessly drove the head of his house out of the country. Meanwhile he abused the trustfulness of Lafayette until he felt sufficiently secure on the throne to shake off that troublesome creditor. His promises had only been made to delude him.

The "citizen king" had not been brought up behind the gilded gates of a park, like other monarchs, in ignorance of the world: he had learned in his youth that vanity and greed are excellent limed twigs for catching men. He had long forgotten the days when, as a general at the battle of Valmy, he had seen an army of ragged and barefooted citizen soldiers die for the happiness of coming generations. All he remembered was the privations he had endured from the disease called Poverty; and from the throne he carried on a thriving business in such remedies as wealth, office and power. *"Enrichissez-vous"* ("Make your fortune") became the motto of his eighteen years' reign, until the moral decay so busily promoted brought destruction to a state worm-eaten by cupidity.

Louis-Philippe was an amazingly energetic commercial traveler on his own account; he spared neither vows nor promises as means of ingratiation, and so started a frenzied competition for the goods in his showcase. The noisiest champions of divine right, those who had done most to launch Charles X on his fatal adventure, suddenly discovered their passion for democracy, and surpassed one another in doing homage to the new ideal.

Suddenly they were exposed by a man whose bold and downright words deserve to be carved in granite in places where men prostrate themselves before some idol whose power rests on their own abjectness. On August 8, 1830, a week before the final departure of Charles X, the members of the two Chambers met to determine the precise wording of the oath which was to be publicly read out and sworn to as "sacred and inviolable" by the new king. As always in such cases, the sitting was a mere ceremony. The text of the pact to be concluded between the people and the crown had been agreed point by point with Louis-Philippe. It was only for form's sake that the official reading before the two Chambers preceded the coronation assembly.

Contrary to all expectation, after the reading by the president a member of the Upper House, a peer of France, the Vicomte de Chateaubriand, rose to speak. This famous writer was a convinced advocate of divine right, a glorifier of the Catholic Church and unshakably loyal to the house of Bourbon and to the person of Charles X, who had honored him with his friendship. He began his speech with words that aroused inexpressible astonishment:

Never was a fight more just or more heroic than that of the people of Paris. They did not rise against the law, but for the law. So long as the social pact was respected, they remained peaceful; uncomplainingly they bore insults, provocations, threats. . . . Only when a palace Terror, organized by eunuchs, set out to take the place of the Republican Terror and of the iron yoke of the Empire, did the people arm themselves with their intelligence and their courage; and it was found that these shopkeepers were able to breathe the fumes of powder without complaining.

The turncoats listened with relief to this special pleading in justification of their faithlessness: here was the Vicomte himself denouncing the attempted absolutist coup d'état. But this was only preliminary. In the breathless silence the next sentences exploded like a bomb:

I have troubled the Throne and the Upper House sufficiently with my warnings, uselessly as Cassandra herself; they have been ignored. Now I stand amid the wreckage of the disaster I so often predicted. After all I have done and said and written on behalf of the Bourbons, I should be the basest of wretches if I abandoned them now, when for the third and last time they are travelling into exile. That craven rôle I leave to those great-hearted monarchists who never sacrificed an obol or an office to their loyalty, those champions of the Altar and the Throne who in the past treated me as a renegade, an apostate, and a revolutionary. All you loyal libellers, the renegade now summons you: come and stammer one word, one single word with him for the unfortunate master who overwhelmed you with his gifts and whom you have destroyed.

You who provoked coups d'état, where are you? Your silence of today is worthy of your effusiveness of yesterday. It is only natural that all these cavaliers, whose plans for grandiose activities have ended in the ignominious expulsion of the descendants of Henri Quatre, should now be crouching in terror under the shelter of the tricolour. It may protect their persons, but will not cover up their cowardice.

On August 10, only two days after this farewell harangue from Chateaubriand, the two chambers again sat together to consummate the ceremonial act of the "election" of the new king. The throne stood ready, under a gilded canopy, to receive Louis-Philippe when the deal had been concluded. The duke and his two sons sat on three modest folding chairs in front of its lowest steps while the president read out the text of the contract. Only after the duke, bareheaded, with one hand on his heart and the other raised to swear, had vowed before God that he would keep all the prescribed conditions were the folding chairs removed; the duke than ascended the steps of his throne as King Louis-Philippe I. The same dignitaries who had knelt in Rheims Cathedral to hand to Charles X the scepter, sword, orb and other insignia, now presented the new ruler with these consecrated symbols of power. Not one of them was troubled by the contempt Chateaubriand had poured over them; not one dreamed of resigning his office.

Old Lafayette himself was at first all contentment. Never since the world began had it been made so abundantly clear to a sovereign that he owed his crown to the nation's trust and was only the people's nominee for the execution of the laws.

Only gradually did the divergences of interest become apparent. For Louis-Philippe the humiliating way in which he had obtained the throne was one more reason for showing the legitimate sovereigns of Europe how little account he took of the obligations of the contract which had been imposed on him. In the reactionary Europe of Metternich the "citizen king" behaved like a parvenu in feudal society. No one dealt so hardly with political refugees as he did; he cruelly handed back the Spanish fighters for freedom to their executioners across the frontier and set his police to spy on the Polish, Belgian and Italian revolutionaries and hunt them out of the country.

Only the honeymoon of king and nation was unmixed joy.

The organization of the National Guard was revived throughout the kingdom, and it was placed under the chief command of its aged founder, General Lafayette. The king seized every opportunity to push the honored veteran of Liberty into the foreground. In his youth Lafayette had himself sounded warnings against putting the whole of the citizen army of the kingdom under one leader. Now, at seventy-three, he had given sufficient proofs of his respect for the civil power to feel worthy of this expression of unlimited confidence. Once more he marched the National Guard of Paris past the king on the Champ de Mars.

Was it not to be expected that his heart should beat faster at this resurrection of his life's work? He would not have been human if his wrinkled cheeks had not flushed when he communicated to his soldiers in the orders for the day the words addressed to him by the monarch:

As an eyewitness of the Fédération of 1790, on this same Champ de Mars, I am able to compare past and present, and I am delighted to inform you, my dear General, that what I have just seen is far superior to the spectacle of the past which I thought so fine and which our enemies found so formidable.

The old man was rejuvenated by the demands his task made on him and by his renewed prominence. Once more Paris echoed his name, and his portrait looked down on him from every wall. A hastily compiled account of his life found six hundred thousand purchasers in France in a few weeks, and the cheap lithographs which showed him wounded at Brandywine Creek, or in the Champ de Mars at the Fédération, or in prison at Olmütz, adorned the walls of the poorest hovels in the remotest villages.

No wonder that he surrendered himself unsuspectingly to this happiness of his declining years. It had never been his way, indeed, to peep distrustfully behind the scenes. But he had not forgotten the ideals of his youth, and now that his name had again acquired weight he hastened to put his popularity to good use. He introduced into Parliament a bill for the emancipation of the colored slaves in all the French colonies. He proposed the erection of a memorial to the executed sergeants of

La Rochelle and devoted all his eloquence to securing the abolition of the death penalty.

He had always been ready to face danger and was not afraid now of the murmurs of the masses, who at once saw through his purpose in this last proposal. He wanted to use the abolition of the death penalty to save Prince Polignac and his three colleagues in the ministry. But the widows and orphans, the sisters and mothers of the two thousand dead and the five thousand disabled of Paris demanded justice! The man who had so light-heartedly taken upon himself this heavy responsibility must pay for it with his life.

Lafayette regarded it as his knightly duty to protect his personal antagonist; and he had strong arguments to advance. The execution of the guilty would not recall the dead to life. And the heads of the four ministers would be regarded by the reactionary ministers of all Europe as damning evidence against the July revolution. No one knew better than the prisoner of Olmütz the peculiar system of accounting followed by reactionary governments. The corpses of the obscure victims who fall fighting for the right are held of no account; the death of a single person of high rank is avenged on a whole nation.

King Louis-Philippe too knew that he would be cast out of the society of legitimate monarchs if his crown were soiled by the blood of a prince. He was thus compelled to humor Lafayette until the trial was over, since even the bitterest opponent of the old Liberty crank had to admit that only Lafayette's halo and the authority it gave him could save the lives of the accused ministers. In October rioters furiously attacked Vincennes in an endeavor to fetch out the prisoners from their cells and execute them. When they were repulsed by Lafayette's National Guard, the would-be lynchers tried to penetrate into the Palais Royal, in order to demand the heads of the murderers of the people from Louis-Philippe. Both at Vincennes and at the Palais Royal there would have been disaster but for Lafayette's fearlessness and his ability to calm the popular fury.

Lafayette did not make it easy for the king to endure his presence in public life. An unkind fate started conflagrations in all parts of Europe, each one greeted excitedly by Lafayette:

the Belgians' fight for independence, the attempted rising against the murderous rule in Spain, the recrudescence of the Polish war of liberation, the underground conspiracies against Austria in northern Italy. Everywhere the leaders were liable to be caught in the nets spread by Metternich. An army of spies, *agents provocateurs*, jailers and executioners pursued the fugitives; only the supreme head of the National Guard of France, official personage though he was, opened his purse to them and offered them the shelter of La Grange.

Suppressing his annoyance, Louis-Philippe ordered his police to turn a blind eye to this. Only in one case did the king find it impossible not to disavow the incorrigible old man. Lafayette, convinced of the king's undiminished love of liberty, had promised sanctuary on French soil to General Mina, the leader of the Spanish rebels. In the enormous correspondence Lafayette carried on with all the oppressed peoples of the whole world, this one letter to General Mina contains the only reference to any item of the millions that had been pouring out of Lafayette's pockets for sixty years—ever since his purchase of the *Victoire*—like the water out of the cistern of the Danaïdes. Louis-Philippe had promised not to permit any gathering of the rebels on the French side of the frontier, and Lafayette wrote to the general that he could not ask the king to break his word; he was therefore sending with the letter a considerable sum "collected," to meet the cost of flight to another country.

While he had to disappoint Lafayette in a matter of this importance, the king kept the old man content by showing readiness to meet his desires in home affairs. Thus in many of the French prisons the cell doors were at last unlocked and the political victims of the Restoration were given their freedom. The day came when a lackey threw open the doors of the audience chamber of the Palais Royal and announced with a low bow:

"Messieurs les condamnés politiques!"

It was a scene which anyone, not only a "childish old man," might witness with joy and pride. Was it not a rare satisfaction to bring the liberated men back to human society, not through a secret back door, but through the royal palace, to be received as free men by the very power that had cast them out?

The moment the critical period of the trial was over, the king put an end to this "child's play."

XVI. THE LAST ACT

WITH AN UNWEARYING ENERGY which would have been admirable even in a younger man, Lafayette organized the transfer of the accused ministers from Vincennes to the Luxembourg palace in Paris, where for the five days of the proceedings he set up his headquarters, and his camp bed into the bargain. Again he made his way through the sea of humanity with the fearlessness which most surely makes its impression on the crowd. In his addresses and orders of the day he appealed with such warmth and persuasiveness to the humanity and loyalty of his soldiers that after the verdict the ministers were able to reach the fortress of Ham with whole skins.

They had been condemned to imprisonment for life. With the clanging to of the doors of their cells, the gateway to freedom sprang open for Louis-Philippe. It must be admitted that he lost no time. The Chamber of Peers gave its verdict on December 21, 1830. Three days were allowed after this for expressions of thanks to the National Guard, the regiments of the line, and above all, to Lafayette; then, on the 24th, always the critical date in Lafayette's life, the government brought before Parliament a bill to place all the National Guards of France under the minister of the interior. Lafayette was offered in compensation the title of Commandant d'Honneur, an emollient which aggravated rather than healed the wound. On that very day he resigned his command of the Paris Guard as well, and took leave of his comrades in a last order of the day. Friends tried to dissuade him, but he wrote:

"No, no, I am aware of my position; it is time that I retired. I know I am a nightmare to the Palais Royal."

There was no lack of protests designed to put all the blame on Lafayette's touchiness. It was "with great distress" that Louis-Philippe announced the general's decision. Every line of the king's proclamation to the National Guard hypocritically expressed regret at the failure of every effort to overcome the old man's obstinacy.

Laffitte was the next to be got rid of. Few men are magnanimous enough to forgive those who have done them favors, and no man had less of magnanimity than Louis-Philippe.

There is no need to recount the bitter disillusionments suffered in the last three years of his life by the old man whose own uprightness made him so easy to deceive. When the democratic newspapers, forced into opposition, referred to the *"programme de l'Hôtel de Ville,"* agreed upon with Lafayette, the king declared once for all that he had no knowledge of any such agreement. With his hopes betrayed, Lafayette, at seventy-four years of age, took up the fight anew. At every retrograde step taken by the government he rose to make his protest. With a fire which younger man might envy, he fought the government proposal to restrict the franchise to those who paid at least two hundred francs a year in taxes. Still more fiercely did he fight against the inheritance of peerages, which would have replaced an assembly of the most distinguished men in the country by a company of nobles owing their inclusion to the accident of birth. Nothing, in his eyes, justified placing such presents in the cradles of new-born babes. The speeches Lafayette made at seventy-five and seventy-six years of age in Parliament or at the funerals of his friends recall the young man of twenty in America in their outspokenness. Latour-Maubourg, his companion in the years of imprisonment, Benjamin Constant—one by one those who had watched and worked with him in the past were falling. With a soldier's intrepidity he would shout a last farewell over the grave of the dead comrade and then return at once to the battlefield. All the honors showered on him from near and far were powerless to assuage the bitterness of his last disappointments.

Louis-Philippe leaned on the rising middle class where his predecessors had leaned on the nobility and clergy. In the place of the peasant serf there was now coming the industrial worker, to be similarly exploited. In 1831 the starving homeworkers of the Lyons silk-weaving industry revolted against their intolerable conditions of existence; the "citizen king" had the rebels shot down by Marshal Soult. The horrible details of this repression by massacre pursued the old herald of "the inalienable rights of man," now the involuntary accomplice of the triumph of a third privileged class.

Fettered to their rock like Prometheus by the reigning power, and exposed in their helplessness to the beak of the vulture Cupidity, the poorer classes were nevertheless stirring. They appealed to Lafayette for help; his figure acted like a magnet on their scattered defenders. A terrible epidemic of cholera in Paris drove the most threatened section of the population in flight before it. With the destroying angel of the pestilence in their rear, the people were no longer to be intimidated by bullets or shrapnel, and the funeral of General Lamarque, the most eloquent orator of the Left in Parliament, became the occasion for action: he should be taken to the Panthéon and there buried.

Lafayette followed the bier on foot, as a pallbearer, as far as the Pont d'Austerlitz. There the way was blocked, and a wild fight broke out between the guardians of public order and the crowd as it tried to press forward. Nothing was more welcome to Louis-Philippe than this opportunity of playing the strong man. The ruthless use of arms—against the very masses who had raised him to the throne—would sever relationships between him and his embarrassing associates.

Lafayette had to abandon his friend's funeral procession lest he should be run down by the fleeing crowd or cut down by the attacking troops. He entered the first hackney coach he came to. But the students recognized him and enthusiastically cheered him, unharnessed the horses and hauled the carriage to his home amid a constantly growing crowd, swelled by streams of people pouring out from their refuge in the side streets.

Here was more than enough food for the suspicions of a government anxious to discredit Lafayette. Nor was the suspicion entirely unfounded: this man of seventy-five was still cheerfully ready to throw himself into the fight. One of the students said jestingly on the way that if the general were thrown into the Seine it would be difficult for the government to clear itself of suspicion of being responsible for the murder.

"Mais ce n'est pas une si mauvaise idée" ("Now, that's not such a bad idea"), said Lafayette encouragingly. He was quite

prepared to give the few years he still had to live, in order to hasten the fall of the power whose installation was a load on his conscience.

But the crowd did not want his corpse, they wanted the challenge of his name, the magnetic attraction of his legendary figure. At the general's house the students begged him to take the leadership of the revolt.

"My friends, a chair—put a chair for me somewhere, and I am at your service," exclaimed the indomitable old man. So in the valley of Roncesvalles the dying Roland had sounded once his desperate call on the bursting horn.

Still more astonishing than this flaming up of the fighting spirit in the aged veteran was the terror aroused by his reëmergence. Louis-Philippe, surrounded by his paladins in the Palais Royal, hurried, white-faced, up to everyone who came in, to ask with quivering lips whether Lafayette had been persuaded to lead the rising. The King of France, supreme commander of the whole of the country's fighting forces, with all the parvenus and profiteers in his camp, trembled before the old patriarch, so often deceived and so assiduously derided, whose coöperation might give the public unrest the force of an avalanche.

For two days fresh outbursts continued to shake the faubourgs of Paris; and, easy as it was for the regular troops to scatter the leaderless and scattered groups, so long as shots were heard and there was a possibility that old Lafayette might issue a proclamation which would provide a standard and a rallying point for disaffection, the "citizen king" felt his throne rocking under him. Only when the rising had been suppressed without the dangerous old fighter having seized the opportunity it offered did the government breathe freely again.

There was no need for sanguinary strife: it was enough for Lafayette to preside at a banquet, to attract the uneasy attention of the sovereigns of the remotest countries. If he proposed a toast, his every word was examined under a magnifying glass, as though a few words from the ancient lips of the powerless veteran were sufficient to conjure up tempests in Europe. When a company of liberal German students, dining in Paris, were inspired by a speech of Lafayette's to give a cheer for Liberty, Prince Metternich wrote anxiously to his ambassador:

The German banquet presided over by the "hero of two worlds" is a noteworthy symptom. The existence in Paris of the central point of all revolutions needs no further demonstration. Propaganda has never avowed its plans and hopes more impudently.

This banquet took place in June, 1833, less than a year before Lafayette's death. The orator who shouted the dreaded word "Liberty" into the graveyard silence of Europe was seventy-six years old, but so long as he still breathed Metternich was ill at ease.

A last, peaceful summer at La Grange, a last Christmas Eve spent in meditation in the room in which his wife had died, were the farewell gifts of life before the year of his death, 1834, opened. As old forest trees with their branches entwined in the confusion of the primeval thicket fall only when all the supporting and protecting growths around them have been cleared away, so death seemed unable to reach Lafayette until it found him isolated one day, at the graveside of a friend.

General Dubourg had fallen in a political duel, and therefore in the front line, so that his old comrade in arms could not deny him the last honors. Although he was halfway through his seventy-seventh year, Lafayette was not to be dissuaded from following the bier on foot, bareheaded, to the grave, where he pronounced over his dead comrade's remains a farewell address which was to be his own farewell to life. Stricken by the treacherous damp cold of that January day, the tough old frame struggled for over four months with the scytheman, who seldom cuts a richer harvest at one stroke. On May 19, 1834, a friend wrote to Talleyrand, who was then ambassador in London:

Monsieur de Lafayette s'en va mourant, aujourd'hui, demain, ou après au plus tard (Lafayette is dying; it may be today or tomorrow, or the day after at latest).

Next day, May 20, the tireless fighter had finished his fight. In his last moments the dying man's waxen hands fumbled for something; his son guessed his wish, and placed between his seeking fingers his wife's portrait, which Lafayette had worn round his neck on a gold chain. The old man's chilling fingers lifted the locket to his lips, and his last breath passed over the portrait of his life's faithful companion, who had waited so long in her grave for their reunion.

For the king and the government it was an unexpected stroke of good fortune that they were not obliged to bury this stubborn adversary in the Panthéon. Even the obituary notice published in the *Moniteur*, the government organ, so annoyed Princess Metternich that she could not refrain from writing to protest against this panegyric, in an official journal, of an incorrigible rebel. It would have cost a sanguinary struggle to prevent the Parisians from burying Lafayette in the Panthéon. But it had been his dying wish to be placed alongside his wife.

It was no ordinary graveyard that received him. He was buried in a secluded garden, surrounded by high walls, and with no public entrance—a garden with a poignant history. Toward the end of the Terror an empty plot in the Rue Picpus had been selected for the mass burial of the daily "batches" of forty to fifty corpses. On her return from Olmütz Mme de Lafayette had quietly bought this piece of land, which was the last resting place of her mother, her grandmother, and her sister. With the assistance of many other mourners she had its high walls built round it, and a Convent of Sisters of the Perpetual Adoration blocked up the only entrance. Only the guest who is admitted by the pious sisters into their garden is able to see the crowded memorial tablets on the inner side of the walls and to learn that the turf over which he walks covers the old lime pit dug in order to destroy every trace of the hundreds of beheaded corpses.

In this inaccessible hiding place Lafayette's earthly remains were buried, not far from the spot where once stood the Bastille, which he had had razed to the ground. Over the high walls come the sounds of the poor and overpopulated streets surrounding them, where the struggle for daily bread never ceases. It is a worthy resting place for the protector of all the burdened and oppressed.

What was the significance of the prescribed military honors compared with the deep sigh of relief which was

Louis-Philippe's involuntary farewell obeisance to his dead opponent?

Polish fighters for Liberty carried the corpse on their shoulders in its triple casing of wood, lead and brass. The pallbearers were marshals covered with decorations, and Marshal the Comte de Lobau led the escort of three thousand National Guards. Ministers, dignitaries and officers in full-dress uniform followed; there were mountains of flowers. All this was to be expected: what was unusual was the great military force which Louis-Philippe mobilized against the dead body, triply encoffined, of the seventy-seven-year-old friend of humanity. The garrison of Paris was not enough. The National Guard was brought out—unarmed; for "the maintenance of order" neighboring garrisons had been sent for, hotfoot; the whole route from the dead man's home to the Rue Picpus was lined by a triple chain of soldiers. They had come with their rifles loaded with ball cartridge and with a full round of ammunition; and loaded guns were placed at the four corners of the walled graveyard, their gunners standing by the threateningly open muzzles with fuses lighted, ready to pour death and destruction into the crowd.

When has a ruling power, believing in nothing but the might of its firearms, ever bowed more deeply before the force of ideas?

INDEX

WITHDRAWN

Emory & Henry College Kelly Library